F.V.

 St. Louis Community College

Forest Park
Florissant Valley
Meramec

Instructional Resources
St. Louis, Missouri

Hearing Things

Leigh Eric Schmidt

HEARING THINGS

Religion, Illusion, and the American Enlightenment

Harvard University Press

Cambridge, Massachusetts, and London, England · 2000

Excerpt from "The Most of It" is quoted from *The Poetry of Robert Frost*, edited by Edward Connery Lathem, copyright 1942 by Robert Frost; © 1970 by Lesley Frost Ballantine; © 1969 by Henry Holt and Company, LLC. Reprinted by permission of Henry Holt and Co., LLC.

Library of Congress Cataloging-in-Publication Data

Schmidt, Leigh Eric.
  Hearing things : religion, illusion, and the American enlightenment / Leigh Eric Schmidt.
    p. cm.
  Includes index.
  ISBN 0-674-00303-9 (alk. paper)
    1. Listening—Religious aspects—Christianity—History of doctrines—18th century. 2. Piety—History—18th century. 3. Enlightenment—United States. 4. United States—Church history—18th century. 5. Listening—Religious aspects—Christianity—History of doctrines—19th century. 6. Piety—History—19th century. 7. United States—Church history—19th century. I. Title.

BV4647.L56 S34 2000
277.3′07—dc21   00-038930

To my family
Marie, Zachary, and Ella
and to one of my teachers
Edwin Scott Gaustad

Preface

Along the way a friend of mine, half in jest, described this project back to me as a book about "religious wackos." That mirrored reflection was troubling because it seemed to reverse so much of what I was trying to say. What I really wanted to offer was an excavation of my friend's assumption—the ready equation of "hearing things" with deviance, illusion, and insanity. As humorist Lily Tomlin has remarked, "Why is it when we talk to God we are said to be praying, and when God talks to us we're said to be schizophrenic?"

So, no, this is not a book about "religious wackos," but instead one that reveals the devotional ordinariness of hearing voices, the everyday reverberation of spoken scriptures, and the expectedness of a conversational intimacy with Jesus (as well as angels and demons) in pietistic Christian circles. In no way do I intend to minimize the torments, fragmentations, and dangers that have recurrently haunted such hearing, but I do try to render historically contingent the formation of modern ears, to denaturalize the auditory world of those for whom divine voices became so shifty, so amusing, and so aberrant. Without indulging in that favored postmodern sport of Enlightenment trashing, I scrutinize with due suspicion the performances that supported the emergence of a natural history of religion. I hope to make apparent the artificial, multiplicitous voices that strangely bolstered reason's imagined univocality.

At the same time, this book is not an express defense of devotional practitioners and mystical writers—a nostalgic retrieval of a soundscape supposedly lost to modernity. At best, it evens up the terms of debate, showing how the habits of listening among Christian contemplatives and experimental philosophers were equally enmeshed in history, culture, language, and the body. Though I find the devotional cultures of Christianity engrossing, I owe too much to the *philosophes* to make this a straightforward brief against the knowledges they produced; for starters, I owe them a vocation, since the freedom to study religion on historical and cultural terms would be unthinkable without their critique of revealed religion. Born from such tensional sympathies, *Hearing Things* is inescapably entwined with both the playful illusions of learning and the animated practices of Christian piety. Even as I remain concerned about the snarled fates of the Enlightenment and Christianity, I take my interpretive measure in these pages from religious and cultural history.

What I offer, by way of the ear, is an excursion into the sensuousness of Christian experience and its denials. Christian devotion has always been deeply bound up with the refusal and deflection of the senses, whether plugging the ears, averting the eyes, or avoiding the touch, constantly negotiating the temptations of the body through the body. The celebration of the sensuous has been of equal longevity—from the quivering harmonies of angels to the aromatics of sanctity to the tastes of the Eucharist. The senses, their management and augmentation, became a crucial proving ground in the making of modernity, and the spiritual sensorium of Christianity was caught up in those perceptual projects, hearing especially. The new sensory disciplines, refinements, and pleasures cultivated during the Enlightenment and its aftermath were steeped in their own forms of sensuality and repression. Practices of listening revealed those conflicts with particular intensity: What were people allowed to hear? What ecstasies permitted, what voices denied, what sounds entertained, what diseases invented, what angels invoked or silenced?

Hearing Things began as a book about constructions of trust and deception, the real and the fake in American religion. It is still about those issues, but appropriately it has come to wear other masks as well. One of those guises I have refashioned from an earlier book, *Holy Fairs,* which explored a related question: namely, what happened to Christian practices in their encounter with various Enlightenment and bourgeois reformers who hoped to subdue and civilize the ecstasies of popular devotion? This time I have sought to make sense of that conflict by seeing the dilemma of Christian spiritualities in light of the encyclopedic culture of natural philosophy. Carried within that expanding range of knowledges was an anatomical knife that isolated each of the senses for close inspection and that eventually made possible the materialist disassemblage of the very body of Christian experience. Some may think I have been marked all too deeply by that sensationalist anatomy in my perverse sequestration of hearing, but I take this singular emphasis to be a useful way of getting inside a learned culture which was committed to breaking the senses apart and bringing order to them.

As with any project of such duration, the book did at times seem like an unreasonable, even wacko, undertaking. For helping me work my way through various tangles, I thank my colleagues and friends in the Department of Religion at Princeton University, as well as those in the Center for the Study of Religion. I am particularly grateful for the license that the Center provided me to organize a conference on Religion and the Senses in May 1999, and am even more grateful to all those who participated in it. The students who helped me create a graduate seminar on the same topic—Tom Bremer, Brian Johnson, Anthony Marsh, Mandy Terc, Eric Thomas, and Tisa Wenger—also added substantially to the refinement of my own thinking. I offer special notes of thanks to Leora Batnitzky, Ava Chamberlain, Lisa Gordis, David Hall, Kevin Herlihy, Paula Kane, Elizabeth Kronzek, David Morgan, Sally Promey, Jana Riess, Ann Taves, Peter Thuesen, and Bradford Verter for contributing reflections as well as sources.

I was aided in my research by a grant from the Lilly Endowment, administered through James Hudnut-Beumler and Daniel Sack, directors of the Material History of American Religion project. My compatriots in that group were wonderful sounding boards, and so, too, were my colleagues in the Visual Culture of American Religions project. I especially value the exchanges I have had with two historians of science, Penelope Gouk and Emily Thompson, both of whom have indulged my fondness for their field of acoustics. Their scholarship and their collegiality have helped me to hear things that I otherwise would have missed. I also benefited from the feedback I received in presenting pieces of this research at the University of Pennsylvania, the University of Chicago, Harvard University, the annual meeting of the American Academy of Religion, the Winterthur Museum, and Trinity College, University of Dublin.

I profited as well from the advice of Grant Wacker and his anonymous readers, who examined an earlier version of the first section of Chapter 4, which then appeared in *Church History* in 1998 under the title "From Demon Possession to Magic Show: Ventriloquism, Religion, and the Enlightenment." Also, much of the last section of Chapter 3 on Elihu Vedder appears in David Morgan and Sally Promey, eds., *The Visual Culture of American Religions* (University of California Press). I appreciate the permissions to make use of revised versions of those essays here. My warmest thanks to Carroll Odhner at the Swedenborg Library and Julia Walworth at the University of London Library for helping me navigate their fine collections, and also to Maeve Callan and Adam Becker for assisting me with their Latin expertise. Harvard University Press editors Peg Fulton and Maria Ascher have been wonderful, and I thank them for their guidance and vigilance.

My family has again been a shaping presence for my work. My parents, Roger and Ann Schmidt, and my in-laws, Charlie and Nan Griffith, continue to enliven me with their loving and discerning spirits. My spouse, Marie Griffith, has been a source of inspiration all her own, a heartening partner through the anxious twistings of academic coupledom as well as a graciously candid critic. Zachary was born in the early stages of writing this book, and Ella was born as the project went to press. With a thankfulness for those gifts that cannot be balanced, the book is dedicated to Marie, Zachary, and Ella.

And, with like asymmetry, it is dedicated to one of my teachers—Edwin Scott Gaustad, who introduced me to American religious history, especially the Great Awakening and the Enlightenment. It is the learning made possible through listening that allowed the ear to rival the eye in Aristotle's evaluation of the senses. Later in this book I will register my suspicion of such sensory hierarchies, but here I want to recognize the wisdom of that particular appraisal.

Contents

Illustrations

Take just the human ear, for example. A whole book could be written about the remarkable and unheard of aspects of it.

—Emanuel Swedenborg

I think that I will do nothing for a long time but listen,
And accrue what I hear into myself . . . and let sounds
   contribute toward me.

—Walt Whitman

If man had only eyes, hands, and the senses of taste and smell, he would have no religion, for all these senses are organs of critique and skepticism. The only sense which, losing itself in the labyrinth of the ear, strays into the spirit or spook realm of the past and future, the only fearful, mystical, and pious sense, is that of hearing.

—Ludwig Feuerbach

Introduction

Joe Nickell is a magician who tracks superstition. Working as a researcher for *The Skeptical Inquirer*, a glossy magazine published in Buffalo, New York, and committed to unmasking pious frauds, Nickell has seen it all: tongue-speaking, healing, weeping icons, Marian apparitions, stigmata, transmuted rosaries. With a buoyant confidence in scientific investigation, Nickell keeps alive the Enlightenment dream of exposing the illusions, impostures, and credulities of religion; and with a magician's eye for sleight-of-hand, he also sees himself as valiantly carrying on the "Houdini tradition" of debunking spiritual charlatanry. The motto for those in his business, he says with good humor, is: "There are no haunted houses, only haunted people." Writing extensively on religious phantasms of all sorts, this self-described freethinker keeps a running inventory on "fantasy-prone personalities." "All the mystics are fantasy-prone people," he told me in a phone conversation. He has even devised a standardized test to help him determine if a subject should be sorted into this psychological category. By definition, people who hear divine voices are among the fantasizers.

Going to Conyers, Georgia, was a natural trek for Nickell—a place where visionary Nancy Fowler is in recurrent communication with the Virgin Mary and where pilgrims flock in droves. Though already saddled with a busy round of investigations, Nickell knew Conyers would make a good stop. The sacred statuary at this improvised American shrine had, for some devotees, reportedly come to life, and all of Nickell's skepticism flared at the idea that people experienced the statues as animated, that these figures contained such power that some of the pious could feel them pulsating. So, when he visited Conyers, Nickell hid a stethoscope under his coat and discreetly listened to the statues. Nothing. "Obviously statues don't have heartbeats," he told me, again with easygoing affability, and fortunately he had the critical apparatus to prove it.[1]

Nickell's desire to listen to the statues, to hear their silence, is a reenactment of an Enlightenment acoustics of demystification. The stethoscope,

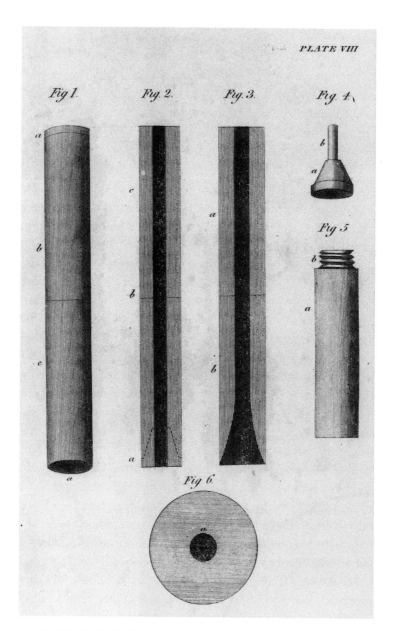

PLATE VIII

1. Wood-Cylinder Stethoscope
In inventing the stethoscope, made out of a wood cylinder, the French physician
R. T. H. Laënnec applied his acoustic knowledge to the diagnosis of diseases of the
chest. By the middle of the nineteenth century, the stethoscope had come to stand
as a model instrument for the rigorously trained ear. From R. T. H. Laënnec, *A
Treatise on the Diseases of the Chest, in Which They Are Described According to Their An-
atomical Characters and Their Diagnosis Established on a New Principle by Means of
Acoustick Instruments*, trans. John Forbes (London, 1821; Philadelphia: Webster,
1823), plate VIII. Courtesy of the Princeton University Library, Rare Books and
Special Collections.

dreamed in the late seventeenth century by Robert Hooke and realized in the early nineteenth century by René Laënnec, was one of those technologies of mediated sound and penetrative discernment that embodied reasonable ways of hearing, the trained ear with its carefully acquired perceptions. The instrument required a listener with well cultivated powers of "selective attention," the habits of both concentration and disregard that made one a learned auditor. Eventually enshrined as a symbol of medical authority, the stethoscope came to epitomize the values of professional distance and detached knowledge.[2]

Within this modern acoustic framework, Nickell's stethoscopic listening stands as a mock sacrament of enlightened empiricism—an effort to establish a deanimated silence through a ritual that makes the absence manifest. His performances, closely allied to his knowledge of natural magic, connect him not only to Houdini but more substantially to a much longer train of skeptical magicians, many of whom took pleasure in the oracular illusions supposedly perpetrated upon the credulous. Concocting a wealth of speaking statues, acoustic temples, and ventriloquial deceptions, they showcased the hollowness of heavenly voices and the treachery of priestly artifice. As with Nickell's latter-day reproduction, Enlightenment fantasies of disenchantment were constituted through play, imagination, and amusement, through technologies and practices of realized emptiness.

The Enlightenment changed the senses. Like any cultural regimen of perception, it dulled and sharpened simultaneously. The honing was perhaps most apparent: it took, after all, a well-trained ear to know what to listen for through the stethoscope, to diagnose pulmonary or respiratory disease from the subtly different sounds heard through this resonant device. In the advancing Baconian, Lockean, and Common-Sense enterprises, the external senses were to be constantly improved, corrected, and extended; the "good management" of them, the steady cultivation of their precision and delicacy, was a crucial part of establishing and preserving the right habits of mind. Hearing shared keenly in that reeducation of perception. If not quite equal to vision's grand enhancements through the microscope and the telescope, the ear nonetheless evoked its own fantasies of augmentation and refinement. Natural philosophers played with sound, imagined the mechanized reproduction of voices, the creation of artificial ears, the invention of talking automata, and the vast extension of hearing through speaking tubes and trumpets. The desires for "the improvement of the ear" often reached dreamy heights, evident in the early nineteenth-century

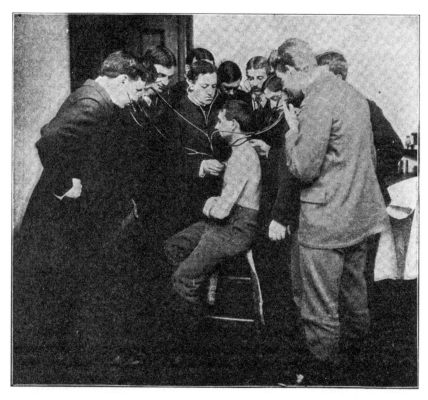

2. A Multiple Stethoscope in Use
It was anything but accidental that skeptic Joe Nickell turned to the stethoscope to
establish the deanimation of the sacred statuary in Conyers, Georgia. Learning
how to listen through the stethoscope had long been celebrated as a quintessential
embodiment of the modern education of the senses, both an exemplar of disciplined perception and an enactment of abstracted medical knowledge. Here
twelve students learn simultaneously the sounds to which they should pay attention as reliable signs and those that they should disregard as meaningless. From
Richard C. Cabot, *Physical Diagnosis*, 4th ed. (New York: Wood, 1910), 144. Courtesy
of the Firestone Library, Princeton University.

story told of one man who, it was claimed, had learned to hear so precisely
that he was able to detect the sound of a flea treading on his nightcap: "If
we can suppose the ear to be alive to such delicate vibrations, certainly
there is nothing in the way of sound too difficult for it to achieve."[3]

Natural philosophers dreamed as well of the exquisite purification of listening—the end of the credulous acceptance of all the *hearsay* about the

miraculous, the marvelous, the revelatory. This, then, is the dulling: the quieting of all those heavenly and demonic voices by which "superstition" had for so long impeded the advancement of knowledge. Shamefully, the disease had often infected the learned themselves: witness Socrates, who followed the voice of a guiding spirit or *daemon;* or Augustine, whose conversion was sparked when he took a child's singsong utterance as a divine command to open the Bible and read it; or even Edward Herbert, deistic progenitor, who heard a clear heavenly prompt to publish his streamlined credo. To spare themselves such embarrassments and to tame the endless effusions of religious enthusiasm, enlightened literati—whether Christian Baconians or freethinking anticlericalists—cultivated a markedly new acoustics.

Antiquarian John Beaumont, an early eighteenth-century student of mystical wonders, dramatically conjured up the spiritual world that had been thrown open for learned conquest. "I shall here give Instances of what perception Men have had of *Genii,* or Spirits by the *Sense of Hearing,* . . . many having heard strange Voices or Noises, who have never seen any thing," Beaumont noted in opening his devoted exploration of the mysterious sounds of angels, demons, and apparitions. A self-professed Christian contemplative, Beaumont was in a good position to describe (and defend) this acoustic labyrinth of the spirit. He had canvassed pagan and Christian history from Socrates to Luther for cases; he had scoured the contemporary scene, including remarkable accounts from New England; and, best of all, he had some truly "extraordinary Visitations" to report himself. The spirits had first surprised him outside his window and then appeared repeatedly for two months, eventually by the hundreds. "They called to me, sung, play'd on Musick, rung Bells, sometimes crowed like Cocks, &c. and I have great Reason to believe these to be all good Spirits, for I found nothing in them tending to ill; their drift in coming, as far as I could perceive, being only to compose my Mind, and to bring it to its highest Purity."

Beaumont's celestial concert, with its barnyard trills, is the counterpoint to Nickell's stethoscope. Possessing his own empiricist exactitude about the sensory patterns of his experience ("I had perception of [the spirits] by four of my Senses"—through sight, sound, the smell of "a dark smoak," and the elusive tactility of spirit hands; he lacked only a taste), Beaumont cultivated an especially fine-tuned ear for the voices, sounds, and noises of the divine world.[4] One of God's many listeners, he heard a cosmos charged with portentous words, knockings, whistlings, groanings, clappings, callings, and ringings. Beaumont was well aware how his contemplative, oracular piety sounded to the growing ranks of rationalists and skeptics, to all those learned men who had come to see such experiences as instances of superstition, delusion, and imposture. In the natural philosophy of the seventeenth and eighteenth centuries, "the LAND of SPIRITS" became "a kinde of AMERICA," a vast region for scientific colonization whose inhabitants often did not fare well under such close inspection.[5] Beaumont, like his renowned contemporary Emanuel Swedenborg, shared in that experimental inquiry only to hold out against any demystification: nothing was more real than these angelic visitants and their beckonings. It is "no uncommon thing," he concluded, "for Men to have their Spiritual and Corporeal Senses wrought on in this extraordinary manner."[6]

This book takes as its subject that pitched battle over modern hearing. It addresses the unresolvable struggles of enchantment and disenchantment as they have been imprinted on a very specific part of the human body, the ear. The problems that the Enlightenment posed for pietist Christianity are often thought of as theological abstractions—to take a prime example, the nature of God in the face of mechanization. The divine could not possibly speak or call or intercede in a world of such predictable laws, such mathematical order, such perfect rationality. Immediate revelation—what the American deist Ethan Allen mocked as a "heavenly dictating voice"—was made an abomination to devotees of nature's Great Architect. As the revolutionary pamphleteer Tom Paine concluded with characteristic bluntness, "I totally disbelieve that the Almighty ever did communicate anything to man, by any mode of speech, in any language, or by any kind of vision." The very idea of a God who speaks and listens, a proposition integral to Christian devotionalism, became a "monstrous belief" to men like Paine, and the voice of reason was offered as a mechanically reliable replacement for these divine attributes. In the seventeenth and eighteenth centuries, divine absence, far more than presence, had to be constructed, and philosophical argument alone was insufficient material: the rules and practices of auditory experience had to be reshaped as a condition of heaven's silence.[7]

The detachment of God's voice from the world (or, at least, the careful containment of its more eruptive presences) demanded a range of performances and embodied regimens. As part of a polite reeducation of the senses, the reorganization of hearing flowed through wide intellectual sluices, proceeding as much from the temperate Christian Enlightenment of Scots Thomas Reid and Dugald Stewart as it did from the radical deists. This retraining of the ear intersected with grander disciplines of minds, bodies, and senses in the service of civic virtue, genteel refinement, natural philosophy, and political order. In these didactic traditions, so integral to the formation of American pedagogy, a well-regulated mind was the internalized analogue of a watchmaker universe, and among the many things that such mental organization required were proper habits of listening.[8] Historian of science Steven Shapin sees a "disciplining of experience" at the heart of the new natural philosophy of the seventeenth and eighteenth centuries—a series of demonstrations, instruments, and social maps designed to make sensory impressions reliable, to distinguish learned reports from vulgar tales, to establish genteel measures of trustworthiness, and hence to secure the progress of knowledge. Associated in complex ways with learning, the passions, credulity, ecstasy, and Christian proclamation, hearing possessed an ambiguous, unstable power that made its careful management especially urgent. Marked as a spiritual, emotional, and superstitious sense, the ear posed a potential danger to the clearsightedness of reason. The etymology of "mysticism," after all, is rooted in a closing of the eyes (Greek *myein*).[9]

This account opens with an attempt to identify the larger narratives that have shaped the history of hearing in the modern West. Two, in particular, are addressed. First, the sovereign nobility of vision, ostensibly redoubled by the Enlightenment, has made the modern story almost always one of profound hearing loss in which an objectifying ocularcentrism triumphs over the conversational intimacies of orality. That assumption of the eye's modern hegemony has deprived the ear of its own history since the Enlightenment, and it has made for a relative neglect of the learned fascination with acoustics—an interest that very much complemented the famed curiosity about optics. The identification of visuality as supremely modern and Western has also been sustained (most noticeably in the work of Marshall McLuhan) through the othering of the auditory as "primitive" or even "African." The equation of modernity with its gaze has often upheld some of the most basic cultural oppositions of us and them.

The second grand narrative is the tying of modern hearing loss to an inexorable disenchantment—to what historian and literary critic Walter Ong has called "the devocalization of the universe." Agreeing with Ong that the question of secularization is effectively explored as a problematic in the cultural history of the senses, I nonetheless find little that is irreversible about the disenchantment of voices and hearing at the hands of print and visuality. The stories I favor are not hard-and-fast oppositions—say, between elite and popular, instrumental and magical, ocular and aural, or secular and sacred—but instead half-planned poachings, mediations, and transmutations. Front and center are cultural minglers: natural philosophers fascinated by magical exhibition or vocal mimicry, genteel Christians drawn to medical psychology or acoustic inquiry, and Swedenborgian mystics immersed in anatomy or harmonial mathematics. As Henry David Thoreau once remarked, "The fact is I am a mystic—a transcendentalist—and a natural philosopher to boot." However intent deistic skeptics were in their practices of demystification and their performances of suspicion, the path of the Enlightenment proved treacherous, littered with blockages, switchbacks, and outright reversals. In refusing the story line of devocalization, narratives about modernity and the senses find reemplotment through facing the cragged, contradictory presences of religion.[10]

After this sweep through these two modern mythologies of the senses, the history gets a lot grittier. In the second chapter, I listen to thunderous claps and trumpet blasts, calls to preach the gospel, whispers of prayer, reverberations of scripture, and revival noises in an attempt to establish a baseline of aural perceptions and habits among devout Protestants. I take the evangelicals to be the Enlightenment's most vociferous rebuttal, and none more so than the early Methodists who gave ancient strands of Christian devotionalism a democratized vigor. It is the very ordinariness of divine companionship, the ritualized familiarity of a conversational relationship with Jesus, the intense and recurrent presences of this auditory world, that Chapter 2 foregrounds. To hear the mystic auditions deeply embedded in Christian piety, one hardly needs to turn to the medieval flights of Hildegard of Bingen, Julian of Norwich, or Richard Rolle, however soaring. The voices are historically closer to us than that, and more common.

In Chapters 3 and 4 I consider how the Enlightenment reshaped experiences of voices and sounds, how the widening authority of natural philosophy provided new contexts and meanings for hearing. I start by exploring the use of pagan oracles and acoustic technologies in Enlightenment imaginings of religion as a product of priestly imposture and popular credulity. I emphasize how during the early Enlightenment a lasting critique of immediate inspiration was forged through combining a revised history and politics of the oracles with the mechanization of sound made available through the newly codified domain of acoustics. In effectively detaching the voice from the body through such instruments as speaking tubes and talking machines, the literati were able to raise the suspicion that any disembodied voice stemmed from mastered techniques of illusion, not the immaterial presence of demons, angels, spirits, or God. In the fourth chapter, I tease out the shifting meanings of ventriloquism at the end of the Enlightenment, how that reimagined art was made to serve the philosophical ends of turning spiritual voices into a rational entertainment and a perceptual fallacy. Attention to these necromantic subtleties moved from the realm of demon possession to magic show, from divine agency to fragmented selves and medical pathology. Religious experiences that revolved around hearing things were increasingly nullified as hallucinations, anatomically located in the diseases of ear and the brain, and, at the extreme, institutionally confined to asylums.

The auditory projects of the Enlightenment ranged across wide domains of knowledge, and I have grasped hold of the acoustic amusements of the *philosophes* as an especially compact entry into those encyclopedic efforts. Such rational recreations furthered one of the most basic designs of the learned—namely, the ambition to reeducate the senses and to awaken critical inquiry, especially among the young.[11] Occult sounds were not only explained, but also imagined, staged, and performed. Natural philosophy was sportive, and these exhibitions provide helpful inlets into the production of new habits of listening and reasoning. They serve here as the condensing vehicles by which to explore the psychology, history, epistemology, politics, anatomy, and technology of modern perception.

These recreations are also useful for suggesting another branch in the complicated genealogy of the critical study of religion. The literati's stance of interpretive suspicion toward the fraudulence of popular religion was recurrently grounded in instruments and demonstrations refurbished from Renaissance natural magic—ones that made illusion and artifice commonplace preoccupations. The gradual separation of natural magic from its formerly close association with celestial and demonic magic and the consequent transformation of its artificial contrivances into rational recreations ended up providing useful technologies for inventing a natural history of religion. Through the magic lantern and the acoustic tube, through the ventriloquist and the phantasmagorist, the *philosophes* lifted the masks of religious power and chased away the projections of spiritual presence. In other words, the postures of suspicion, so basic to much of the modern study of religion, have a cultural history in which the literati learned their discriminating techniques through performance, exhibition, and play-acting.

After these Enlightenment excursions, I hearken in the final chapter to the ongoing presences of the oracular, the angelic, and the tongue-speaking in antebellum American religion. The early republic resounded with prophets and trance-speakers, with inspired guides to scripture and fortunetellers, and I pull together a "gifted" group of harmonialists, mediums, and mystics to explore that bustle of voices, especially concentrating on visionary Emanuel Swedenborg and his American progeny. Unlike the Methodists, who soared to numerical preeminence, the Swedenborgians (formally known as the Church of the New Jerusalem, or, simply, the New Church) garnered only a small American following, counting a mere 1,450 members in 1850; but their influence, along with that of their seer, was diffuse. They formed an important, representative capsule of a wider religious culture of immediate revelation, Spiritualism, Hermeticism, harmonialism, and Whitmanesque inspiration. No group on the American scene had a more complicated sensorium or a more developed understanding of the spiritual senses. No movement conceived a more thoroughgoing answer to the literati's fascination with the deceptiveness of voices and the artificiality of language than did Swedenborgians, with their imaginings of the perfect transparency of angelic speech. In turn, few groups felt the problem of religious authority quite so acutely: the potential presence of message-bearing angels, including the ghostly shade of Swedenborg himself, proved an ungovernable proposition.

One thing the Swedenborgian case underlines is the importance of paying close attention to the ongoing shifts in the canon of mystical writers: for example, among early Methodists, the memoirs of two seemingly minor Catholic ascetics, Jean Baptiste de Saint Jure and Gregory Lopez, made the grade, while the writings of John of the Cross and Teresa of Avila were not on the map. The seventeenth-century contemplative Jeanne Marie Guyon and the eighteenth-century devotionalist William Law cropped up all over the place in early nineteenth-century America, while most of the mystics who were in the canon a century later—thanks to the work of writers such as Evelyn Underhill, W. R. Inge, and Rufus Jones—made no showing. Thus it was, within these shifting currents, that Emerson could appoint Swedenborg as the representative mystic of the ages, and, later, William James, who grew up in the shadow of his father's substantial Swedenborgian associations, could herald the mid-nineteenth-century

New Churchman Thomas Lake Harris as "our best known American mystic." (In turn, Swedenborg could just as quickly fade from view with the Anglo-American reinvention of Christian mysticism at the beginning of the twentieth century, only to reappear as a favored seer, the "Buddha of the North," among prominent mid-century phenomenologists of religion.) So the term "mystic," sometimes employed to evoke timeless or perennial forms of religious experience, is used here in an expressly historical way, sensitive to specific subcultural contexts and cognizant of the continuing shifts in who was utilized by whom to constitute the category of mystical writers. John Fletcher's self-described "evangelical mysticism" meets up in these pages with the resurgent popularity of Thomas à Kempis' *Imitatio Christi*, both of which then enjoy the company of Swedenborg's angels.[12]

With the Swedenborgians, as with Mormons, Adventists, Shakers, and Methodists, one thing was clear: God was hardly falling silent. Instead, with the crumbling of established authorities, God had more prophets, tongues, and oracles than ever before; thus, the modern predicament actually became as much one of God's loquacity as God's hush. All was not lost for the Enlightenment, though: the very fragmentation and privatization of religious authority constituted a considerable victory; a significant number of American Christians continued to absorb the mental habits and disciplines of the Scottish Common-Sense philosophy well into the nineteenth century; and evangelicals, Spiritualists, and Swedenborgians all scrambled to put themselves on respectable scientific footing. So people talked with angels, had tongues of fire descend upon them, and listened to ancient harmonies, but they did so with distinctly modern accents. Such oracular ways of hearing, however commonplace, remained embattled—within sympathetic religious circles as well as with the bearers of modern acoustics whose knowledge of the unsound mind and its illusions became ever more inescapable.

I think of this as a story with an American mooring, but one that regularly lifts anchor to crisscross the Atlantic. The English movement of Methodism became in little more than a half century the largest crusade in North America, and the Wesleyan exchange was decidedly transatlantic, especially in the shape of its devotional culture. The Swedenborgian and Romantic religious connections were likewise cosmopolitan from birth. The mediating points of the Enlightenment were similarly multifarious. American novelist Charles Brockden Brown, for example, traded heavily on the European Enlightenment in his masterwork on religious voices, *Wieland*.

Benjamin Franklin kept up on the study of acoustics, concerned himself with speaking machines, and contributed famously to the eighteenth-century inquiry into the natural causes of thunder and lightning. Likewise, Benjamin Rush lectured on the new anatomies of the ear, studied hearing with a precise care worthy of his Edinburgh mentors, and propelled the American study of mental diseases through an emulation of European models. Leaders of the Scottish Enlightenment—Thomas Reid, Dugald Stewart, and (on the late edges) David Brewster—became so well known in the antebellum United States as to be virtually adopted citizens. Because of the extent of these exchanges, I am tempted to claim this as more than an American narrative—a sensuous account of religion and modernity, a peculiar narrative of the ear's pious wonders and its wondering inquirers. More modestly, I imagine it as an effort to take the religious culture of the American Enlightenment seriously, right alongside the ballyhoo of evangelical awakenings.[13]

It is often a bad omen when an author feels compelled to announce at the outset what his or her book is *not*. Still, certain expectations about what falls within hearing's range warrant acknowledgment, and it is important to recognize the books that I might have written but have ultimately resisted. This is not, for example, a study of orality, literacy, and the print revolution—important and well-studied topics, to be sure, but ones I take on only obliquely.[14] It is not a study of speech, whether Puritan fluency, political eloquence, or pulpit performance, nor is it an exploration of architectural acoustics—issues very well handled elsewhere.[15] It is not a study of music and hymnody; these enter the story only incidentally in connection with the devotional flights as well as acoustic inquiries that music inspired.[16] The musical ear deserves more study on the order of James H. Johnson's fine cultural history *Listening in Paris,* but I have settled here for brief forays into the religious ecstasies of heavenly music rather than an exploration of Enlightenment and Romantic aesthetics. While I have learned much along the way from those who have written on these banner questions, this is a cultural history that attends instead to the formation of devout ears and to those voices of reason who fashioned, with only limited success, modern replacements. Like historian Alain Corbin, who has studied the "auditory landscape" of nineteenth-century France through its bells, I have tried to re-create the religious conflicts of modernity through close attention to the postures and practices of hearing things.[17]

In giving such concerted attention to listening, there is one historical echo that I imagine could prove particularly misleading and that I wish to forswear at the outset: namely, the apparent reiteration of Protestantism's bias toward logocentrism. As Martin Luther famously declared, "God no longer requires the feet or the hands or any other member; He requires only the ears. . . . The ears alone are the organs of a Christian." Given such foundational preoccupations, Protestants have long been presented as exclusive privilegists of the auditory, iconoclastic Hebraicists in an increasingly ocularcentric world.[18] But Protestantism's visuality—from emphases on the visible gospel of the sacraments to the use of popular prints to spread its teachings to a proliferation of devotional souvenirs—has now been well established, so aurality can hardly be taken as coextensive with Protestant sensibilities. The presentation of hearing as "the sense of faith, the sense which receives instruction and accepts the divine word," is, after all, as much a Catholic as it is a Protestant understanding.[19] While Luther, Calvin, and their varied descendants intensely valorized hearing, the singular anatomy of Protestantism, its common reduction to the ear, comes now with a lengthy proviso. Any schema that continues to posit predictable ratios between the eye and the ear in any given tradition (whether Protestant, Catholic, Jewish, or Muslim) needs to be laid aside.

Despite my sometimes perilous reach across the loosely bounded expanse of modernity, I remain keenly aware of the comparative limits of my own hearing. This became all the more evident after an American Muslim shared with me the metaphysics of the medieval Sufi exegete Ibn al-'Arabi. There I read a passage that powerfully captures the dialectic of divine speaking and human listening so fundamental to Judaism, Christianity, and Islam, a rendering that could stand as an epitome of the religious sides of this work: "The first thing we knew from God and which became connected to us from Him was His speech and our listening. . . . Therefore, all the messengers came with Speech, such as the Koran, the Torah, the Gospels, the Psalms, and the Scriptures. There is nothing but speech and listening. There can be nothing else. Were it not for Speech, we would not know what the Desirer desires from us. . . . We move about in listening."[20] This gift of Ibn al-'Arabi's exegesis is a humbling reminder of the very provinciality of studying Christianity and the Enlightenment apart from larger conversations on the American religious scene. Still, the history of the senses, like the history of the body, has to be written tradition by tradition, era by era; and cross-cultural conversations have to be built with the same patient attentiveness to particularity. Cognizant of the dangers of comparative shortcuts that bypass difference, I hope, nonetheless, that this book can serve as one offering in an ever-widening exchange of voices and ears.

Hearing Loss

The voices of the past are especially lost to us. The world of unrecorded sounds is irreclaimable, so the disjunctions that separate our ears from what people heard in the past are doubly profound. I can see evangelist George Whitefield's crossed eyes in a portrait; I can still see some of the pulpits from which he preached; I can pore over his sermons; I can read his journals. But I can never lend him my ears or eavesdrop on his prayers. Almost all of history is eerily silent, and so, to evoke these stilled and faded voices, the historian must act as a kind of necromancer. The historian's ventriloquy, like that of the Witch of Endor, allows the living to hear the dead. And that is the inevitable direction of travel: historians bring the past into the present, a conversation that then necessarily rings with contemporary questions.

With the sense of hearing, the presence of the contemporary at the historian's table has created not only resonance but also an excess of clarity about the past. This is especially evident in two sprawling discourses about hearing's modern diminution, twin narrative structures of loss and absence that have taken on the aura of the universal. The first involves the eye's clear eclipse of the ear, the decline of listening in the face of the ascendant power of vision in modern culture. The second concerns the dwindling of hearing as a spiritual sense and the lost presence of divine speech—that is, the peculiar acoustics of modern forms of alienation, disillusionment, and secularism. Recognizing how the sense of hearing has been framed within the metanarratives of modernity is a prerequisite for a more intricate historical narrative. It allows for acknowledgment of the universalized philosophical and religious inscriptions with which modern ears have been marked. The prisoners in Plato's cave, it is easily forgotten, were troubled not only by flickering images but also by echoes. What historians hear reflected back to them often proves to be little more than the sounds of their own tongues, but this particular treachery of knowledge is a reality to face, not efface.

More Than Meets the Eye

The hearing impairments of modernity are often presented as so extensive and profound that one is sometimes tempted to scramble for a hearing-aid or perhaps the early modern equivalent, an ear-trumpet. As much of the writing on the modern sensorium has argued or presumed, vision is the dominant sense of modernity, the other senses being comparably repressed (such as smell) or vestigial (such as hearing's former centrality in oral cultures). In the very long view, the shift from orality to literacy—according, most famously, to Walter Ong and Marshall McLuhan—gradually transformed people from engaged speakers and listeners into silent scanners of written words, isolated readers in the linear world of texts. The print revolution of the early modern period sharply accelerated this bending toward visuality, this hearing loss, as books, newspapers, tracts, broadsides, charts, and Bibles flooded the cultural marketplace. Words became printed objects more than breathed speech, things to be seen rather than voices to be heard.

With its clear-eyed pursuit of detached observation, imperial sweep, and visual instrumentation, the Enlightenment was the keystone in the arch of the eye's ascendancy. "The ocular obsession of Enlightenment thought," as historian of the senses Constance Classen has recently labeled it, served to clinch the gaze's domination of the modern sensorium. So the favored story goes. From this critical perspective, the consumer society of spectacle, with its mediated and cinematic pleasures, becomes little more than the froth on the Enlightenment's visual wave, the bedazzled eyes of the shopper and the spectator only redoubling vision's power. With Chance the gardener, in the film *Being There*, we moderns like to watch. In a culture of science, spectacle, surveillance, sexism, shopping, and simulacra (to conflate the views of many cultural critics into one), voyeurism is often the least of the eye's transgressions.[1]

That ocularcentrism is peculiarly modern may seem at first glance surprising, especially given the deep-rootedness of such visuality in classical orderings of the senses. For both knowledge and delight, the sense of sight was, according to Aristotle, "above all others"; it was the most developed sense, the clearest and most discerning, the one most able to bring "to light many differences between things." Hearing was a close second, superior for its conduciveness to learning; taste and touch, associated with animality, had the "least honor"; and smell fell as a mediator in the middle. Despite

Christian reservations about the dangers of the eye and its seductions, this hierarchic view of the senses was widely replicated in theological terms from Augustine onward, including Aquinas' repetition of sight's crowning perfection in the *Summa theologica* (followed still by hearing and smell, then by taste and touch). In commentary on the senses, this has been one of the most deep-seated philosophical formulas—to follow the ancients in establishing a hierarchy of perception, a system of nobility. Though hearing has had its apologists, from Lactantius in the fourth century to Charles de Bovelles in the sixteenth to Walter Ong in the twentieth, sight has commonly stood at the apex for more than two millennia. Even after the time-worn suppositions have largely passed that made such rankings seem so sensible—ordered relationships of honor and nobility are not how one would think modern citizens would imagine the senses—the Aristotelian forms of appraisal have continued, often with a vengeance.[2]

If the supreme nobility of sight is thus deeply ingrained in Western religious and philosophical traditions, many nonetheless argue that this privileging of visuality reached its apogee only during the Enlightenment and its aftermath. Modernity is seen as distinctively ocularcentric, even hypervisual; it is marked, as philosopher Jacques Ellul puts it, by "the unconditional victory of the visual and images." Historian Martin Jay, in his monumental account of modern ocularcentrism, has surveyed the dominance of the eyes and the ambivalences that power has generated, especially since the ascent of what he calls Cartesian perspectivalism. It is evident, Jay concludes, "that the dawn of the modern era was accompanied by the vigorous privileging of vision. From the curious, observant scientist to the exhibitionist, self-displaying courtier, from the private reader of printed books to the painter of perspective landscapes, from the map-making colonizer of foreign lands to the quantifying businessman guided by instrumental rationality, modern men and women opened their eyes and beheld a world unveiled to their eager gaze." While acknowledging some Enlightenment dissenters from the visual paradigm, Jay nonetheless builds on and replicates the hierarchy of the senses in which sight is the noblest and most powerful. Whether in Francis Bacon's aphorism, "I admit nothing but on the faith of the eyes," or in Thomas Reid's, "Of all the faculties called the five senses, sight is without doubt the noblest," Jay lifts up vision as "the dominant sense in the modern world." He also presents the technologies of vision—from the microscope to the panopticon—as the quintessential instruments of the modern "scopic regime." Sight, "the most comprehensive of all our senses," as John Locke concluded in his *Essay Concerning Human Understanding*, reigns with unquestioned supremacy over the Enlightenment enterprise.[3]

The counterpart to the history of increasing ocularcentrism has been the history of diminished hearing. As an aspect of cultural history, this account of the senses was pioneered by the *Annales* school, especially Lucien Febvre and Robert Mandrou. In an evocative section entitled "Smells, Tastes, and Sounds" in *The Problem of Unbelief in the Sixteenth Century*, Febvre commented of Rabelais and his contemporaries: "They were open-air men, seeing nature but also feeling, sniffing, touching, breathing her through all their senses." Smell and hearing for pre-Cartesians, Febvre argued, "were exercised much more and were more highly developed (or less atrophied) than ours." "The sixteenth century did not see first," he concluded; "it heard and smelled, it sniffed the air and caught sound" (*pace* the considerable evidence that Aristotelian privileges were still widely accorded to sight). Only in the seventeenth century was this experiential hierarchy reordered, Febvre hypothesized; only then was "*vision* unleashed in the world of science as it was in the world of physical sensations, and the world of beauty as well." Mandrou followed Febvre in detailing a history of hearing loss in his inventory of the senses in early modern France: sight, "dominant today, stood in third position," he calculated, "a long way behind hearing and touch. The eye, which organizes, classifies and orders, was not the favorite organ of a period which preferred to listen." The quotidian evidences for such claims were slim—a touch of poetry here, a smuggling of Luther there—but the conclusions were certainly enticing, especially since they meshed so well with wider cultural criticism of the modern emergence of a society of cold observation and spectacular consumption.[4]

If there was a thinness to these early attempts to incorporate perceptual modalities into the history of *mentalités*, subsequent efforts in French historiography to offer a historical anthropology of the senses have been richer and more nuanced. This is especially evident in the work of Alain Corbin, who, in *The Foul and the Fragrant*, *Village Bells*, and *Time, Desire, and Horror*, has plotted "the organization and balance of the senses" in the late eighteenth and nineteenth centuries, notably the shifting thresholds of the tolerable and the intolerable, the sensory gauges of the pure and the polluted. Smell, in particular, became the dangerous (and hence alluring) sense of the period, used repeatedly to imagine social difference—that is, to distinguish the refined and the reasonable from the uncivilized, the erotic, the diseased, the animal, and the unclean. Thresholds around sound were similarly reworked, Corbin has argued, and the construction of the category of noise also reverberated off the cavernous walls of the social imagination. By analyzing fragrances and odors as well as tolling bells, Corbin has broken out of the vision-dominated story line and has brilliantly connected the pursuit of these sensory modes to social representations. With an evocative subtlety, Corbin shows the limits of the eye's modern ascendancy by tracking the powerful emanations of sound and odor, both of which were so ambiguously intertwined with fear, desire, memory, and difference.[5]

The history of the senses has hardly been left to the French alone. On the North American side, Father Walter Ong—historian, literary critic, cultural commentator, and Jesuit—has been the most sustained interpreter of hearing's modern diminution, again offering a historical account that is intended simultaneously as a critique of modern visuality and its disenchantments. Ong's view is ironically panoramic as he moves from ancient "oral-aural" cultures through literacy and print to the visualism of modern science to the "secondary orality" of the electronic media (this last ascendancy still fails to reverse the prevailing epistemic regime of detached observation and silent reading). With a deeply Pauline conviction guiding him—faith comes through hearing—Ong offers his own metaphysics of sound, his own homily on the immediate face-to-face encounters of speakers and listeners in oral cultures, on the human and divine presences in spoken words. For Ong, the ear, or what T. S. Eliot called "the auditory imagination," stands as the other to modernity's fractioning eye, the embodiment of the bardic and the inspired, the now muted vehicle of both community and God's revelation. To understand the richness of oral traditions is, at some level, restorationist: it is, for Ong, a way to reconnect to the auditory modes that underpin scripture itself and that make possible Christian redemption.[6]

Ong's development of the sensorium as a domain for religious and cultural history, more than his metaphysics or his sweeping history from orality to literacy to visuality, remains a generative contribution. Like Jay's focus on ocularcentrism, Ong's picture of "visualist man" as the presiding power over modernity left the auditory without much of a history after the Enlightenment—after the Lockean assimilation of "the entire sensorium to sight," after the early modern "watershed dividing residually oral culture from typographical culture," after the learned quest for "total written control over the spoken word," after "the devocalization of the universe" through the visual objectification of the physical world. How could listening get a hearing in the face of such a lofty mythology about the eye's dominion? Ong, one of the ear's great apologists, ironically helped sever it from the history of the Enlightenment and the modern aftermath.[7]

Dismay in the 1950s and 1960s about shifting patterns in communications, about human senses vastly extended and overwhelmed by technological change, gave Ong's grand historical narrative a propitious timing. But it was Ong's mentor, Marshall McLuhan, who made it chic. As technological guide and probing analyst, McLuhan was the epigrammatic therapist to those who felt the "collective sanity" of contemporary society was fraying under the influence of the new media. In offering up a comprehensive myth of Western history timed to the revolutions in media, McLuhan saw modernity as built on the inexorable rise of a Newtonian sight, a "cool visual detachment" again made concrete via the vast extension of typography in the early modern world. Even as successive waves of media innovations—the telegraph, telephone, phonograph, radio, and television—were unraveling this print culture, the visuality at the heart of the Gutenberg revolution remained in McLuhan's account a defining matrix for the making of modern knowledge.[8]

Crucial to McLuhan's construction of his mythology of modern Western visuality were common rhetorical strategies of alterity. The other to this Western technology and epistemology was for McLuhan the "ear culture" of tribal, nonliterate peoples in which spoken words had "magical resonance." With an unreflective colonialist lens, McLuhan made Africa his imaginary for constructing through black-and-white contrast a sense of who modern Europeans and North Americans were at their epistemic core. "The African" lived in "the magical world of the ear," while modern Western "typographic man" lived in "the neutral visual world" of the eye. The one was a world of vision, objectification, and progress; the other a world of sound, magic, and timelessness. The animated intensity of the auditory was something that the lettered had been forced to set aside but that oral peoples all experienced—tribal worlds which were characterized by an "overwhelming tyranny of the ear over the eye."[9] If McLuhan, as a Catholic convert, shared in Ong's antimodern yearning for the living presences of Christianity's revivified Word, he was also far more fearful than his Jesuit companion about the return of the repressed (evident in his imagining of the "tribal drum of radio" and his condescension toward Romantic "irrationalists" like Mircea Eliade). At best ambivalent about the revival of a "primitive" aurality through the new electronic media, McLuhan wanted to engineer a new synthesis, an orderly transformation in this momentous sensory struggle: "There can be no greater contradiction or clash in human cultures than that between those representing the eye and the ear," he exhorted with typical excess. He wanted to move people through the entrancing effects of the new media and to awaken them from the hypnotic modern drugs of television and advertising. He hoped to stay "the return to the Africa within."[10]

McLuhan's cultural juxtapositions make all too apparent how the discourse of modern Western visuality has often rested on a larger racialized frame of comparison: "the inability of oral and intuitive oriental culture," as McLuhan phrased it in *Understanding Media*, "to meet with the rational, visual European patterns of experience." Given such a grand story of modern ocularcentrism, a history of modern aurality is hardly possible, especially a history of religious modes of hearing, since in this myth the very origin of modern culture is grounded on the exclusion of the "primitive" or "ancient" ecstasies of listening. The otherness, blackness, or primalness of the auditory keeps it from a having a history within modern Western culture (at least, on McLuhan's terms, in between the Gutenberg revolution and the twentieth-century proliferation of electronic media). Accounts of bardic songs, narratives of oracular voices, encounters with oral scriptures, and stories of mystical auditions are plots that work for "other" cultures—societies that are all ears—not modern ones that are all eyes. "With them the binding power of the oral tradition is so strong," anthropologist Edmund Carpenter wrote of Eskimo perception, "as to make the eye subservient to the ear. . . . In our society, to be real, a thing must be visible. . . . We trust the eye, not the ear." In a word, we look, they listen. If McLuhan's badinage and Carpenter's ethnographic adaptations now seem exotic themselves, this discursive polarity nonetheless lingers. In necessarily subtler form, the story line continues to structure descriptions of "a Western sensory model" of visuality in contrast to the complex orality of "premodern" cultures—that is, to divide the world between us and them.[11]

These, then, are two of the larger twentieth-century motifs around which the story of modern vision and hearing has been plotted: (1) a hierarchy of the senses, with sight vastly ennobled and hearing sharply diminished; and (2) a marked dichotomy between eye and ear cultures that has commonly drawn on racialized constructions of Western rationality and ecstatic primitivism. What such narratives demand is not a carnivalesque reversal—not a dethroning of the eye and a raising up of the ear; that would only perpetuate the hierarchic, oppositional convention. As Ong's own theology of listening suggests, to romanticize hearing at the expense of vision is an all too common counter-Enlightenment move already; it hardly needs reamplification. Instead, as in the work of Alain Corbin, the multisensory complexity of the social, religious, aesthetic, and erotic imaginations of the culture of the Enlightenment and its successors warrants further attention.[12] The modern sensorium remains more intricate and uneven, its perceptual disciplines and experiential modes more diffuse and heterogeneous, than the discourses of Western visuality and ocular-centrism allow. This is true of the religious dimensions of the sensorium, but it is also true of its Enlightenment valences, even that notorious source of scopic dominion, seventeenth- and eighteenth-century natural philosophy.

The learned from Bacon and Mersenne onward were intent on advancing not only optics, but also acoustics—a field of inquiry that was broadly extended in the seventeenth and eighteenth centuries. Bringing together physics, anatomy, and music, the newly demarcated science of sound throve as part of the expanding experimental philosophy. Bacon, for example, was as intent on listening as on viewing, any self-profession about singular reliance on the eye to the contrary. In the *New-Atlantis* (1627), his blueprint for a model college to advance learning, Bacon envisioned "perspective-houses" for the study of light, color, and vision, but he also had "sound-houses" and "perfume-houses" without any noticeable difference in endowments.[13] Following both classical and Renaissance arguments about the considerable effects of music on body and soul, he presented hearing as the most powerful sense in its operation upon human "manners." What "men" listened to had the power "to make them warlike" or "to make them soft and effeminate" or "to make them gentle and inclined to pity." Such hidden powers in sound required penetration, and Bacon lifted up "visibles" and "audibles" together as central to his experimental program. "The sight of the eye," he concluded, "is like a crystal, or glass, or water; so is the ear a sinuous cave." Bacon never shied away from that labyrinthine complexity, and it is the sinuous cave of the ear, more than the crystalline glass of the eye, that stands as the better similitude for the modern sensorium's twistings.[14]

"The enquiry about sounds is worthy of philosophers," Robert Boyle wrote in a letter in 1665, and his appraisal ended up widely shared among the learned. In 1684, when natural philosopher and churchman Narcissus Marsh outlined for both the Royal Society in London and its inchoate equivalent in Dublin a program of research on acoustics, he started with a revealing "comparison 'twixt the Senses of *Seeing* and *Hearing* as to their improvements":

> I mean, by shewing, that this lat[t]er of *Hearing,* is capable of all those improvements which the Sense of *Seeing* has received from Art; besides many more advantages, that the *Ear* may enjoy, by the help of our Doctrine, above the *Eye;* all which moreover will be of as great benefit to mankind, as any thing that *Opticks* have yet discovered, if not of greater; which, with some other preeminencies that it has upon another Score, will happily render *Acousticks* the nobler Science of the two.

Marsh dwelled especially on the technological potential in acoustic instrumentation, particularly *"Microphones* or . . . *Magnifying Ear Instruments"* for rendering "the most minute Sound in nature distinctly *Audible,* by *Magnifying* it to an unconceivable loudness." Otacousticks, implements that could act as reliable hearing-aids for those in old age, Marsh thought were even more important than eye-spectacles, "forasmuch as the Hearing of what's spoken is of more daily use and concern to such men, th[a]n to be able to *Read Books* or to *View Pictures."* A notably auditory hierarchy, Marsh's—one that suggests clearly how the ear could rival the eye for experimental attention.[15]

The learned inquiry into acoustics only accelerated in the eighteenth and early nineteenth centuries. A summary sense of the perceived revolution in the science of sound and its prominent place in the Enlightenment can be garnered from the *Edinburgh Encyclopaedia* (1832), an eighteen-volume landmark that had both British and American incarnations. Surveying "the exquisite refinements in modern mathematics" and "the spirit of experimental philosophy, which has diffused itself over Europe since the time of Bacon," the encyclopedia lifted up the achievements in acoustics as one of the great fruits of these modern inquiries:

> By the labours of these philosophers, Acoustics has been brought to a state of great perfection. The science now presents a very different aspect from what it exhibited in the time of the ancients. The properties by which bodies act in producing sound, are now known; and their mode of operation has, in general, been successfully investi-

gated;—the laws which sound obeys in its transmission to the organ of hearing, have been reduced to the common principles of mechanics;—the essential differences between various sounds have been detected; and their mode of action upon the ear pretty well understood: thus affording us a more complete knowledge concerning sound, and the sense of hearing, than we possess with respect to any other of our senses or their objects.

The fact that the *Edinburgh Encyclopaedia* was compiled by the eminent Scottish natural philosopher David Brewster, who was renowned for his work in optics and hence never one to slight the eye, makes this estimation all the more telling. Light was hardly an unrivaled emblem of mastery and progress.[16]

In at least one crucial way, the expanding inquiry into acoustics did demonstrate the ocular biases of knowledge-making in the experimental philosophy, for it was one of the central ambitions of early modern students of acoustics to visualize sound. The very invisibility of sonorous vibrations was recognized as an impediment to understanding them, so the goal was to render them "more sensible to the eye by a little artifice"—namely, through observing the vibratory patterns reproduced in water, sand, or flames of light. Already in the early 1670s Robert Hooke conducted acoustic experiments in which patterns of vibrations were displayed through the use of flour, and by the end of the eighteenth century E. F. F. Chladni had performed widely recognized demonstrations of sound's motion through the changing patterns of sand on brass plates. Arising with the Enlightenment was a new visual culture of sound, a spectacle of the auditory, that became all the more marked on the lecture circuit in the nineteenth century, with popular demonstrations that featured a whole panoply of devices for showing off acoustic principles. Also, with the growing anatomical attentiveness of the seventeenth and eighteenth centuries, the ear itself was increasingly visualized through dissection as the body was broken down graphically into ever more precise parts. The new experimental philosophy sought at a number of levels to make sound intelligible by rendering it manifest to the eye.[17]

It would be wrong to turn this visualizing impulse simply into further evidence for the singular power of vision—that the ear was made intelligible only on the eye's terms. Visualizing sound was indicative also of the sensorial play of natural philosophers, the concern with the movement between and among the senses. For example, since sound vibrations could be felt as well as seen, tactility was crucial to acoustic study. The touch of vibrations provided, indeed, a peculiar corporeality to the notion of "sound bites." As Galileo observed in his dialogues on music, sound produces "a Titillation upon the Cartilage of the *Timpanum*"; certain tones seem "at one and the same Time to kiss and bite." Also with an expanding set of auditory technologies—from the speaking trumpet in the 1670s to the stethoscope in the 1810s—sound was given a new material culture, a hands-on tangibility that the phrase "hearing things" is intended to evoke alongside its psychological and illusory connotations.[18]

The philosophical exchange among the senses was evident in another endeavor of the late seventeenth and eighteenth centuries: that is, the effort to remake the spectrum of colors into a scale of music, a mathematical system of correspondences between light and tone. Hence, the play between sound and sight worked also in the other direction—as in Newton's speculations on vibration theory in which he suggested that "vision is very conformable to the sense of hearing which is made by like vibrations." The model drawn from acoustic vibrations became such a forceful analogy for how sensation worked that some Enlightenment theorists, such as David Hartley and John Elliot, were ready to incorporate all of sensory experience into an acoustic paradigm. "Since the discovery of the analogy between colours and sounds," Elliot explained in his *Philosophical Observations on the Senses of Vision and Hearing* in 1780, "the various kinds of tastes and smells have been considered as so many different tones or notes of these sensations." Under this model, even the very fragrances of a garden were joined to musical experience. As Benjamin Rush, one of Hartley's American disciples, explained, "The rose and the pink resemble tenor; and the jonquil, the minionet and wall flower are striking analogies of the softness and delicacy of treble tones."[19]

The crucial counterpoint to the growing visualization of knowledge among Enlightenment natural philosophers was the inductive concern with the senses as a whole. The very sensationalism of the Lockean epistemology ultimately made each of the senses the source of intense study, vigilance, commentary, and pleasure. Take, for example, Edmund Burke's "erotic empiricism," in which all the senses were explored for their powers to produce the sublime and the beautiful. Or take Etienne Bonnot de Condillac's intent examination of all modes of sensation as sources of knowledge, with primacy accorded to touch, part of what historian Elisabeth de Fontenay identifies as "a carnival of the senses" in the French Enlightenment. Or even take Thomas Reid's *Inquiry into the Human Mind,* the flagship of Common-Sense thought, a tome that grew out of a series of discourses presented before the Aberdeen Philosophical Society and dedicated to the discrete analysis of the senses. While there is little room for mistaking Reid as anything but a privilegist of the eye, he accorded such honor only after giving distinct scrutiny to smell, taste, hearing, and touch as well. In the nuances that the literati discovered through all their sensory comparisons, inspections, meditations, and delights, sight often ended up toppled from its lofty perch. This was evident, for example, in David Hartley's observation in 1749 that "the ear is of much more importance to us, considered as spiritual beings, than the eye."[20]

Benjamin Rush, sharing in Hartley's view of the harmonies of Christianity and vibrational mechanisms, directly echoed this estimation of the ear's spiritual supremacy in his lectures on the senses to his students in Philadelphia. This did not make Rush, though, the patron of any one sense: sometimes touch was on top, at other points vision or hearing, and all of them were the source of intense pleasure and unbridled possibility. "Our bodies may be compared to a violin: the senses are its strings," and the fleshly concert that results is one of "nearly constant pleasure," Rush told his pupils. What mattered most to this American *philosophe* was the cultivation and relishing of all the senses, the perfecting of their exercise through education: "The more acute and extensive we render the senses in their capacity of receiving impressions, the more we shall be able to encrease our knowledge." As he told his medical students, "In a sick room, we should endeavour to be all touch, all taste, all smell, all eye, and all ear, in order that we may be *all* mind; for our minds, as I shall say presently, are the products of impressions upon our senses." Enlightenment understandings of the senses were inevitably much more fluid and sophisticated than any emphasis on vision's hegemony suggests.[21]

None of this insistence on sensuous complexity is intended to make the Enlightenment ways of knowing seem innocent—that is, to put aside the substance of critical concerns over the objectifying gaze of manly autonomy or the watchful eye of state surveillance through an emphasis on a free play of sensual pleasures. Many of the counter-Enlightenment concerns about the detached imperiousness of the philosophical observer or the omnipresent, interiorized eye of modernity's various wardens have their counterpart in similarly sinister modes of listening. Jeremy Bentham, for example, imagined a vast system of eavesdropping through speaking tubes as a crucial part of the panopticon, and Benjamin Rush illustrated how the sense of hearing works by alluding to the Ear of Dionysius, part of a legendary prison of antiquity in which "spiral windings" were supposedly used to hear "the smallest whisper" uttered by the inmates.[22] In their cultivation of acoustics and their training of the ear, the literati also imagined a mastery of eavesdropping, an invasive mode of hearing that found embodiment in the desire to turn the new technologies of the auditory into tools of surveillance. *Walls have ears*—the saying was given new meaning during the Enlightenment.

One thing that all these acoustic ambitions make plain is that printing had plenty of company in the technological transformation of listening in the early modern world. Walter Ong imagined a long-term disincarnation of the voice—the body that makes the words—and connected that loss of presence, including the participatory encounter with divine speech, to the spread of typographic models of knowledge. Certainly, developments in communications had profound effects on the way the literati thought about the auditory qualities of revealed words. Illustrative is deist Tom Paine's sharp depreciation of speaking compared to printing: "A man's voice can be heard but a few yards of distance; and his person can be but in one place. . . . But the art of printing changes all the cases, and opens a scene as vast as the world. It gives to man a sort of divine attribute. . . . He can be everywhere and at the same instant." Paine actually made this technological observation about simultaneity in the context of deriding Christ's "pretended mission," since Jesus had relied exclusively on verbalized expressions in delivering his message: God's *real* son, Paine suggested snidely, would have arrived with a command of printing. Finding all of Christian revelation a bundle of "hearsay upon hearsay," Paine gave such unreliable voices all the less credit in comparison to the promethean medium of print. On top of these word-of-mouth vulnerabilities, the mastered art of printing, Paine reasoned, only multiplied the instabilities of the scripture as a text: "That books says (Genesis 1:27), '*So God created man in His own image*'; but the printer can make it say, *So man created God in his own image*." To Paine, print was subversive of a speaking God, calling into question the value of an oral gospel and pointing up the contingencies of its textualization.[23]

Paine's use of printing to discredit the auditory qualities of Christian revelation was embedded in a larger mechanistic critique of the oracular voice. By the time Paine's *Age of Reason* appeared in the 1790s, natural philosophers had long been trying to detach the voice from the presence of the speaker through a series of artificial mediations. Speaking trumpets, acoustic tubes, ventriloquism, voice-producing statues, and talking machines all suggested the disembodiment of the human voice, the transmission of sound from an absent, hidden, detached, or simulated speaker. Printing, in other words, had performative accompaniments in the disincarnation of spoken words, counterparts that have very much continued to thrive—from the mediated voices of radio to computer simulations. (Today "electronic impersonators" not only reproduce but even generate a person's voice, turning particular pieces of speech into a "voice font" completely independent of the speaking body.)[24] The growing fascination among natural philosophers with the ventriloquizing of human voices, with the machineries of reproduction and illusion, also fed their critique of the suspicious immateriality of heavenly voices. God's voice, too, seemed increasingly hard to place: Was not that voice an illusory presence as well? The sinuous cave of the ear beckoned philosophers into complex entanglements with the auditory, with hearing and voices, and those imbrications need to become a fuller part of historical narratives about modernity. There is so much more to the Enlightenment than meets the eye.

Absences and Presences

The discourse of modern visuality has a corollary. It is not just that we moderns are hard of hearing, that for us seeing (and only seeing) is believing. The problem is, at bottom, a spiritual impairment; as in the biblical cadence, we have ears but do not hear. Historian Michel de Certeau put this as beautifully as anyone:

> Before the "modern" period, that is, until the sixteenth or seventeenth century, this writing (Holy Scripture) speaks. The sacred text is a voice. . . . The modern age is formed by discovering little by little that this Spoken Word is no longer heard, that it has been altered by textual corruptions and the avatars of history. One can no longer hear it. . . . The voice that today we consider altered or extinguished is above all that great cosmological Spoken Word that we notice no longer reaches us: it does not cross the centuries separating us from it. There is a disappearance of the places established by a spoken word, a loss of

identities that people believed they received from a spoken word. A work of mourning.

To de Certeau, a Jesuit who wrote eloquently on glossolalia and mystical language, the modern disenchantment of the universe was fundamentally a predicament of listening, a fracturing of words and revealer, a loss of God's living voice.[25]

In this perception, de Certeau has had plenty of distinguished company. Poet John Hollander, nicely twisting a phrase from Dryden, called this acoustic disconnection "the untuning of the sky." Philosopher Jacques Ellul long sounded analogous themes, decrying "the present humiliation of the word" and connecting the modern "rupture with God" to the wreckage of hearing. Avant-garde composer R. Murray Schafer, whose *Tuning of the World* served as an ecological primer for reviving the art of listening amid the "sound sewer" of modernity, assumed an underlying loss of mysticism, clairaudience, and devotional silence. Amid his anguish over a polluted "soundscape," Schafer ended on a deeply contemplative note, invoking Meister Eckhart: "Still the noise in the mind: that is the first task—then everything else will follow in time." Even Alain Corbin's recent history, *Village Bells,* is emplotted under a similar shadow of ruin—the slow desacralization of church bells and the "loss of meaning" entailed in this diminished listening. The story of modern hearing loss, it seems, can hardly be told any other way: it is always, finally, a story of religious absence.[26]

No doubt those absences are real, often painfully so for those who invoke them. One recent work in the philosophy of religion, Nicholas Wolterstorff's *Divine Discourse,* begins with the assumption that since the enshrinement of Locke's epistemology of religious belief, truly modern people have been scarcely entitled to make the claim that God speaks to them. "What we really want to know," Wolterstorff writes, "is whether we—intelligent, educated, citizens of the modern West—are ever entitled to believe that God speaks." In a Lockean framework in which reason is the ever vigilant judge over religious experiences of immediate inspiration, God's silence is both assumed and desired. Amid the order of rationality, sensory discipline, and miraculous cessation, making the case for a speaking God, as Wolterstorff's own philosophical agility suggests, is an arduous task. The patina of the unrepeatable has grown all too thick on the biblical world of prophecy and tongues of fire: "Thou shalt be as my mouth," God beckons Jeremiah.[27]

The issue would be largely settled if everyone were playing by the Lockean rules. The story that de Certeau, Ong, Hollander, Schafer, and Corbin tell would be the right story. Within Enlightenment habits of listening, the spaces left open for the presence of divine voices (or the preservative magic of sounding bells) appear all too narrow, no matter how much one wriggles. But the salvation or, at least, complication is that other rules, disciplines, and communities remain in profusion. In analyzing the account of a colleague at an East Coast university who, in February 1987, was disconcerted to hear God imparting a message to her, Wolterstorff comments wryly: "Perhaps I should add that though Virginia is, and was at the time, a Christian, she neither is nor was what anyone would classify as an *Evangelical*. It's worth saying that, because Evangelicals have the reputation of believing that God speaks to them rather more often, and rather more trivially, than most of us think God would bother with; hence we quite easily dismiss their claims that God is on speaking terms with them."[28]

Contained within Wolterstorff's droll aside is a serious problem. To go on perpetuating these stories of hearing loss is to fail to take measure of the religious complexity of modernity itself. The considerable efforts of Enlightenment philosophers to contain the power of spiritual gifts, scriptural presences, angelic voices, prayerful exchanges, and mystical auditions have clearly been of very mixed results. Whether the learned find people "entitled" to their understandings of divine speech has often been beside the point. Various communities—evangelicals and Pentecostals not least among them—have played by different rules, though those precepts remain internally complicated and inherently conflictual (which voices are authentic experiences and which ones dangerous illusions? how are those determinations made?). Within a broadened perspective, Lockean ways of assessing divine speech look far more local and contingent than their pretense to universality suggests. And so do the endlessly reiterated narratives about modern absences, ruptures, and silences. Those tales, too, have turned out to be quite limited and particular stories—sometimes little more than intellectuals mistaking their social world for the world as a whole. This much is now clear: modernity has turned out to be not so modern after all.

Ong's meditations on presence and absence are themselves testimony to how disenchantment has been braided with enchantment. Though structured as a lamentation, his work has also served as a witness to the vibrancy of auditory pieties amid modernity, to the flourishing of counter-Enlightenment, antivisualist spiritualities of hallowed listening. Ong's praise of sound rolls forth like a litany, a liturgy of adoration for the breathing words of God: "Sight isolates, sound incorporates. Whereas sight situates the observer outside what he views, at a distance, sound pours into the hearer. . . . By contrast with vision, the dissecting sense, sound is thus a unifying sense. . . . The auditory ideal, by contrast, is a harmony, a putting together." It is misguided to read Ong primarily as a historian or literary critic; he needs to be listened to as a Christian contemplative who has tuned his ear for a revelatory exchange of presences, a participatory encounter with a God who "'speaks' his Son" (to use his own expressly Christological formulation). Hardly an isolated call, Ong's sanctification of hearing was built on the wide-ranging reverence for the spoken word and the dialogic relationship among twentieth-century Christian and Jewish thinkers, from Eugen Rosenstock-Huessy and Franz Rosenzweig to Martin Buber and Jacques Ellul. Taken together, this broad philosophical, theological, and devotional confluence cuts against the very assumption that the Enlightenment's anatomizing eye successfully dispelled the wonder of divine speech and auditory presence. The primacy of the living voice over the dead letter—that has been the refrain of Ong and a much larger chorus: "Ye heard the voice of the words, but saw no similitude; only ye heard a voice" (Deuteronomy 4:12).[29]

In addition to such twentieth-century currents, the complex hearing of early modern natural philosophers needs to be acknowledged. Edward Herbert's case is suggestive. A seventeenth-century harbinger of English deism who was in combat with both skepticism and sectarianism, Lord Herbert of Cherbury was one of those who narrowed the scope of revelation and presented oracular voices as at best superfluous and at worst mere priestcraft. Yet in deciding whether or not to publish his *De veritate* (1624), with its trimmed-down religion of deistic commonalities, he beseeched the "eternal God, . . . Giver of all inward illuminations," for "some sign from heaven." He had no sooner made this prayer, he reported in his autobiography, when "a loud though yet gentle noise came from the heavens, for it was like nothing on earth, which did so comfort and cheer me, that I took my petition as granted." He thought there was no chance of his being "superstitiously deceived herein"; the sky was serene and cloudless, and he could even pinpoint the place whence the noise came. And this sound lingered as a disturbance: a Massachusetts Unitarian in the 1820s, who recognized Herbert as an ally in the battle against "popular superstitions," had to subject Herbert's own story to rationalistic explanation in an effort to bridge the rift between this heavenly "voice" and "the principles of mental philosophy."[30]

A complicated voice of reason, Herbert's, and so was David Brewster's, whose career spilled out of the Enlightenment into the 1830s and 1840s. As an arch-debunker of acoustic illusions, Brewster occupies an important place in this story, a figure who harvested the autumnal fruits of the Scottish Enlightenment and widely disseminated them. An evangelical Presbyterian ally who merged his Baconianism with Christian orthodoxy, he remained torn in his daily life about the very spectral world that he dismissed as a batch of superstitions. In the fine phrase of his daughter, who also served as his memoirist, he was "afraid of ghosts, though he did not believe in them." He lived in an old house with "the strangest and most unaccountable noises," and even once thought he saw the apparition of an Episcopal clergyman. Yet all along Brewster continued to dwell "upon the difficulties of evidence in everything connected to the supernatural." His writings forwarded naturalistic explanations for any hearsay about unusual voices and spectral visions he came across. For Brewster, science largely took the place of Christian devotion (he started his career as a tongue-tied Presbyterian minister, before becoming a fluent natural philosopher). "While the calm deductions of reason regulate the ardour of Christian zeal," he observed, "the warmth of holy enthusiasm gives a fixed brightness to the glimmering lights of knowledge." Still, despite his transposed enthusiasm, Brewster lived suspended, in-between, wishful about wonders though endlessly distrustful of them. Those who denied the presence of voices and the mystery of sounds often continued to pursue them in spite of their incredulity.[31]

Such complexities should not obscure those epistemological strands within the Enlightenment that were naturalistic and depersonalizing and that displayed little tolerance for the intimate voices of Christian piety. Time and again the *philosophes,* particularly the more skeptical and anticlerical, privileged absence and sought to reveal the emptiness at the heart of revealed religion (or superstition, capaciously defined). The vacancy within Enlightenment theories of religion is most fully displayed in the imposture thesis—"the most popular of all seventeenth and eighteenth century accounts of religion," as historian Peter Harrison has observed, and one in which religion's origin and perpetuation were presented as rooted in a series of political deceptions propagated by power-grabbing priests. With this theory, the literati attempted to legitimate their own cultural authority by delegitimating traditional religious authorities. Priestly practices of all sorts were characterized as tricks of mystification, as empty signs without transcendent referents. This hermeneutics of suspicion still echoes in the Foucauldian view that all devolves into the mask of power, that what matters interpretively is the politics of knowledges and practices. "I put for a generall inclination of all mankind," Thomas Hobbes wrote famously in *Leviathan*, "a perpetuall and restlesse desire of Power after power, that ceaseth only in Death."[32]

Narratives of suspicion in religious studies have inherited more than a touch of this politics of absence, this explanatory predilection to take away the voices of things, to deanimate the universe through an explication of the cultural strategies by which the "sacred" is produced. In contemporary scholarship, those who would explore the meanings of presence, alongside power and its fabrications of presence, appear bedraggled. Historian of religion David Chidester, for example, confesses forthrightly at the outset of his *Word and Light:* "I have become less interested in the meaning of symbols than in their power—the power to legitimate, the power to mobilize, the power to focus the concerns of competing interest groups." In the face of such questions, "the poetics of seeing and hearing" appear to him but "a luxury item," a self-indulgent leisure, and he stifles his book on Augustinian pieties at its very birth by embracing the ascendant questions of domination. While sharing in the prevailing inquiry into the interlocked repertories of power and knowledge, I nonetheless assume that understanding only goes halfway until the presences of the religious imagination are faced: the surprise of voices experienced as beyond the self, the shock of sounds that overwhelm the subject. Without forsaking the suspicious— those who continue to chase the absences at the heart of all signification—this account makes the pursuit of absence itself a historical phenomenon. The naturalistic inquiry into pious illusions of divine presence, an important piece of the bedrock of the critical study of religion, has its own peculiar politics and cultural history.[33]

The grounds that I have used for thinking about the presences in voices are not metaphysical or theological. Instead, this interpretation rests on the historical recognition of perception as commonly entailing an active exchange, a participatory encounter. With roots in the phenomenology of Maurice Merleau-Ponty, among others, the animated aspects of vision have been recaptured in the last two decades. Art historians especially have rediscovered the iconic image, how it creates a charged reciprocity between viewer and viewed, how it returns the onlooker's gaze, how vision is less a matter of spectator and object than a fused commingling. As art historian James Elkins writes in *The Object Stares Back*, "Seeing alters the thing that is seen and transforms the seer. Seeing is metamorphosis, not mechanism. . . . Seeing is being seen." Looking is rarely "just looking," Elkins insists; whatever the observer's pretensions may be, vision is hardly passive or disinterested, but a nest of entanglements involving desire, pain, violence, longing, and presence. "And so looking has force: it tears, it is sharp, it is an acid. In the end, it corrodes the object and observer until they are lost in the field of vision."[34]

The case for hearing may seem more difficult, since it has long been dogged by classical views of its relative passivity and hence, often, its femaleness.[35] Philosopher Hans Jonas remarked, in confirming the greater nobility of sight, that sound "intrudes upon a passive subject," and hearers, with nothing for their ears that correspond to eyelids, remain "at the mercy" of a percussive agency outside themselves. Yet, when these gendered judgments about autonomy and action are critically engaged rather than presumed, hearing's capacity for a similarly spirited exchange becomes recognizable—a dialogic movement between speaker and listener, a sympathetic vibration between sounding bodies. It takes, indeed, a very short excursion into the auditory to know how closely listening is knotted with feeling, desire, responsiveness, and touch, with the stirring and soothing of passions—whether joy, love, grief, courage, or heavenly yearning. It is precisely hearing's potential for participatory dynamism that has long made it so threatening to those philosophical models in which the eye is celebrated for its freedom, disengagement, and perspective at the ear's expense. As John Dewey, one of those critics who liked to turn this sensorial relationship upside down, remarked in *The Public and Its Problems* (1927), "Vision is a spectator; hearing is a participator."[36]

In Christian practice, prayer is one exemplar of this blurred exchange among ears, voices, and sounding bodies: the words of the speaker are conditioned by a listener and by the possibility of an answer, and full interpretation of such an encounter requires a recognition of this in-betweenness, this intersubjectivity of a listening speaker and a speaking listener. Merleau-Ponty highlighted such "reversibility," "reflexivity," or "circularity" in bodily perception, and prayer regularly presents this sort of doubling or entwining in which "one no longer knows who speaks and who lis-tens." God's "calling" of a preacher, in evangelical parlance, presents another model: a beckoning voice that requires a reply, a hearkening. It is a response very much akin to the devout relationship to iconic images, one that is "predicated on the assumption of presence," an experience of both acting and being acted upon.[37] The very obediences of devout hearing, long celebrated in Christian piety and routinely renounced through Nietzschean suspicion, must be understood in this dialogic context—a sub-mission that is, at the same time, an expansive reimagining of the subject.

Religious ways of knowing that emphasize the aliveness of sounds, the power of scriptures to speak, the capacity of music to heal or to inspire ec-stasy, the voices out there that become doubled voices within, and the sym-pathetic vibrations that connect one body to another are immersed in ines-capable relationships of exchange. Such animated forms of hearing are not mere vestiges or survivals, are not "archaic" or "primitive," but reveal still crucial elements of the tangled reciprocities of modern perception and signification. As philosopher David Michael Levin observes, "When I listen to myself, to my words, to the sound of my voice, I can hear others: I hear others 'inside' myself. Living others, dead others; others near and others far. . . . I can hear my ancestors." Religious affirmations of presence, whether in hearing and being heard or in seeing and being seen, need to be taken seriously on their own terms, but, at the same time, the acknowledg-ment of that intersubjective framing is not intended to free such experi-ences from the contextual densities of culture and power. A poetics does not exclude a politics, and vice versa.[38]

In order to pursue a religious and cultural history of hearing, it is neces-sary to broaden attention beyond preaching, communications media, and musical performance to the whole of the devotional soundscape. Just as the study of visual culture has spilled well beyond the borders of "high art," the historical and anthropological study of the rest of the senses re-quires moving through a wide expanse of lived experience and everyday objects: in the case of the auditory, it includes attentiveness to noises, joyful and awful; to thunderous sounds of Judgment; to sobbing, sighing, groan-ing, and laughing; to necromantic voices like the Witch of Endor's; to the blare of festival and the silence of contemplation; to cosmic harmonies and choral ones; to incantations and blessings; to psalms, bells, and trumpets. The very corporeality of hearing needs to be materialized, snatched out of an airy evanescence through the rituals, disciplines, performances, mechanisms, and commodities that make up the sounding body as well as the attentive ear.

At the same time, the tones that cannot be heard externally must also be recalled, the fleshless voices audible only to what Augustine imagined as the "interior ear," part of his cultivation of what he and other Christian devotionalists imagined as the spiritual senses. "What do I love when I love my God?" Augustine asked famously in his *Confessions*. "It is true that I love a light of a certain kind, a voice, a perfume, a food, an embrace; but they are of the kind that I love in my inner self, when my soul is bathed in light that is not bound by space; when it listens to sound that never dies away."[39] In going down this path, a history of the auditory becomes also a history of spiritual perception. With a respectful patience for the arcane, the historian follows the devout to those bodily thresholds where the senses themselves seem to lose their very sensuousness, where the dangers and limitations of the sensual are transfigured. The spiritual senses of Christian mysticism, for all their Augustinian remoteness, still figure prominently as part of a religious history of the post-Enlightenment world.

By now, it should be apparent that the plot for this history cannot be borrowed from the conventional modern story lines: it is neither an elegy for divine presence nor a chronicle of vision's dominion. What is conceived instead is a cultural history which allows the ear an unromanticized place alongside the eye and which realizes that hearing (as much as seeing) was implicated in the various enterprises of the Enlightenment, including its ventures in demystification. Imagined, too, is a religious history that aids contemplation of the modern braidings of presence and absence, voice and illusion, trust and distrust, identity and fragmentation. In the novel *Pierre*, Herman Melville, multiplying theological conundrums for the "enthusiast youth" of his title, observed: "Silence is the only Voice of our God," and only "impostor philosophers" would claim to "get a Voice out of Silence." If Melville found the prospect of hearing an answering voice an absurdity, never was there any shortage of expectant listeners. As Robert Frost wrote in his poem "The Most of It,"

> He thought he kept the universe alone;
> For all the voice in answer he could wake
> Was but the mocking echo of his own
> From some tree-hidden cliff across the lake.

Some morning from the boulder-broken beach
He would cry out on life, that what it wants
Is not its own love back in copy speech,
But counter-love, original response.[40]

Between silence and voice, mocking echo and original response, this history makes its way.

Sound Christians

2 New Englander Ebenezer Newell, a young man adrift in the new republic, was unsure what to do with his life. His options eventually seemed to come down to two: he could teach school or, as a Methodist convert within the citadel of Congregationalism, he could go and preach the gospel to suspicious, often hostile auditories. For all his thankfulness for his deliverance from sin and Calvinism, it was a hard decision to become a Methodist preacher, work that commonly entailed endless travel, little money, familial rupture, delayed marriage (or none at all), the jeering violence of ruffians, the exacting scrutiny of the saints, and often enough an early death.[1] An austere calling, to be sure, and Newell, like so many of his contemporaries who grappled with the same decision, went back and forth.

After struggling for many months, even trying for a while to run away from the dilemma by journeying to Canada, Newell found resolution in a dream turned vision. Waking up, awed and meditative, he seemed to hear a voice. Its charge plain and clear, he did not bother to distinguish whether it was an internal or external impression: *"Go preach the Gospel and I will deliver thee from every thing that would harm or mar the blessed work of thy ministry, and cause thy labors to be blessed in winning souls to Christ!"* In a moment of submission and betrothal that he cast in feminized terms, he exulted, "My passive soul, like Mary, said, Lord I am thine and all the world is thine; thou knowest my obligations and my duty; I give myself to thee without reserve, I will go! I will go! . . . for my Savior and my God will be with me, and all shall be well!" Language threatened to fail Newell at this point, words proving insufficient "to convey any adequate idea of this portion of my experience." He moved on quickly, almost thrown off by the auditory immediacy of his own story or perhaps by his confessed vulnerability, simply concluding: "From this time I had no doubt concerning my duty to go and preach the Gospel."[2]

A little to the south, in New Jersey, also in the first decade of the nineteenth century, another Methodist convert, Jarena Lee, a black "servant
maid," struggled to sort out her own call to preach the gospel. Born in the
year that the American Revolution ended and separated from her family at
the age of seven, Lee journeyed uneasily to a sanctified faith, torn between
heavenly whispers of salvation and demonic temptations to suicide. Spiritual drama likewise marked her "Call to Preach the Gospel," of which she
related:

> Between four and five years after my sanctification, on a certain time,
> an impressive silence fell upon me, and I stood as if some one was
> about to speak to me, yet I had no such thought in my heart. But to
> my utter surprise there seemed to sound a voice which I thought I dis-
> tinctly heard, and most certainly understood, which said to me, "Go
> preach the Gospel!" I immediately replied aloud, "No one will believe
> me." Again I listened, and again the same voice seemed to say,
> "Preach the Gospel; I will put words in your mouth, and will turn
> your enemies to become your friends."

Though Lee wondered whether Satan might have counterfeited these
words in order to deceive her, she found her extraordinary call validated
subsequently in dream and vision. Even so, unlike Newell's ability to act
immediately on his sense of divine calling, Lee's ministry was deferred,
first because of the initial opposition of Richard Allen, the leading figure
among African Methodists, to a woman preaching, and then because of her
marriage. Finally, eight years later she could tarry against the Lord's bidding no longer, rising up as if, she said, by "supernatural impulse" to exhort
and itinerate.[3]

Divine calls, like those of Newell and Lee, were both extraordinary and
quite ordinary: they were innovative when placed in the longer view of
Protestant understandings of ministerial calls and calling, yet unexcep-
tional when heard within the vernacular of popular evangelical piety and
broader strands of Christian devotionalism. These beckoning voices—God
speaking with transformative directness to (or within) the pilgrim
soul—are an invitation to consider the auditory intensity of early modern
spirituality. Entry into the evangelical ministry took on a markedly experiential timbre over the course of the eighteenth and early nineteenth centuries, and these divine calls serve as an inlet into a piety of intimate voices
that was, by turns, relished and reviled. While the political economy be-

hind such religious experiences—the swirl of market fluidity and democratic revolution—is a critical matrix, equally important is the devotional world of evangelical Christianity, the integuments of spiritual formation. What were the resources within Christian piety that allowed for such keen discernments of voice among these hardscrabble farmers, shoemakers, slaves, maids, schoolteachers, and tanners? In a word, how did the devout hear? What were their ears like?

People heard things within multilayered devotional frameworks, whether the things heard were the oracular words of scripture, the inner whisperings of Christ, or the voices of angels and demons. They lived with the ever ringing echo of Jesus' admonition, "He that hath ears to hear, let him hear" (Matthew 11:15), as well as Paul's affirmation, "Faith cometh by hearing" (Romans 10:17). Contemplative devotional traditions, embodied especially in the *Imitatio Christi* of Thomas à Kempis, pulsed through one renewal movement after another in seventeenth- and eighteenth-century Christianity, Protestant and Catholic alike. The eminent Methodist devotional writer John Fletcher spoke of "evangelical mysticism," and the phrase is an apt one for the wider popularization of devotional exercises in the period.[4] Deeply etched disciplines of self-denial, prayer, and meditation, along with mystical understandings of the spiritual senses, were crucial for forming pious ways of hearing.

In eighteenth-century Britain and North America, the devout—Quakers, Baptists, Moravians, Methodists, evangelical Congregationalists and Presbyterians, among them—heard with an acuteness that was often overwhelming. To gain a feel for the portentous and encircling sounds of that world, this chapter moves widely from divine calls to scriptural words, from ascetic silences to spiritual senses, from demonic taunts to the Last Judgment, from the unnerving noises of revival meetings to heavenly music. Though preaching remained absolutely central to Christian experience and worship, the "spiritual hearing" of early modern Protestantism (again to invoke Fletcher) entailed far more than attentive listening to sermons. The gyrating voice of a preacher often paled in comparison to the prayerful soundings in the interiors of listeners—a prompting to turn to a given scriptural verse, a voice of instruction in a dream, or a fragment of the Savior's speech. Many of the most influential words in evangelical circles were not spoken between people and were not necessarily even heard aloud, but were listened to within, a hearkening.[5]

Extraordinary Calls

To Old Lights, those New Englanders who opposed the insurgency of the evangelical movement, much was wrong with the revivals of the 1740s: the extemporaneous harangues of firebrand preachers, the scenes of unbridled fervor, the brash assurance of salvation, the fanning of separatism. But the crowning problem—"that which I take to be the Foundation of all the rest," said opposer Timothy Walker in 1743—is "Some Men's pretending to an *immediate Call* and *special Mission* to preach the Gospel." These "bold Pretenders" had hardly been *"regularly called"* to that office, yet they undertook that "solemn Calling" all the same, solely on the basis of "extraordinary Communications," the "secret Whispers of the HOLY GHOST." The practice of itinerancy was clearly among the most overt challenges to the standing order that the revivals fostered, but to Walker the deeper issue was the underlying experiential claims that authorized such wayfaring preaching. Perhaps indeed the most troubling issue, especially for established ministers, was the sudden eclipse of "a proper Call" by "an *immediate Call.*"[6] Contained within the evangelical movement was a larger and lasting revision of the doctrines of call and calling, an experiential reimagining of these keywords in the Protestant lexicon. A special call from God could now dissolve the obligations of a particular calling, could thrust a person dramatically on a whole new course in life—in effect, setting the Christian's call to preach at odds with the durability of social vocation.

Though repeatedly latched onto as part of a Weberian analysis of the Protestant consecration of work and rational disciplines—part of the supposed modernity-making temper of Puritanism—the doctrine of calling was, to a large degree, socially conservative. Puritan William Perkins defined a calling as "a certain kind of life ordained and imposed on man by God for the common good," and others made similarly clear that vocation was a construct of political and economic order, offering endless variations on 1 Corinthians 7:20: "Let every man abide in the same calling wherein he was called."[7] Hence, Charles Chauncy in his infamous tract *Enthusiasm Described and Caution'd Against* (1742) counseled all those would-be preachers and exhorters who thought they had *"immediate calls"* from God not "to leave their callings," but "to *abide in their callings.*"[8] Chauncy invoked what any solid Protestant would have in the face of such disorderly characters: the injunction to abide in a given occupation. Someone could not be a tailor one day and a minister the next, or by turns a maid and a preacher. Within a hierarchic, deferential, patriarchal social world, callings did not work with such free intermittence, and immediate divine calls were not to override this deeper, divinely sanctioned ordering of society, with its established offices, settled professions, and gendered categories. The common adjectives used to describe a calling—"lawful," "regular," "proper"—were indicative of the constancy and submission associated with its very conception. Such diction was handy even for John Wesley, who, poised awkwardly between Anglican hierarchy and evangelical leveling, used it to try to rein in his own preachers from usurping priestly prerogatives: "I earnestly advise you, abide in your place; keep your own station."[9]

As in their understandings of more worldly vocations, magisterial Protestants tried to shore up a stabilizing view of the pastorate. In his *Institutes of the Christian Religion,* Calvin treated the minister's call as primarily a question of "the public order of the Church" and passed over the "secret call" as a matter of internal scrutiny between the minister and God. Of primary concern to him was "an ecclesiastical call"—that is, how the call of ministers worked as an aspect of church government, discipline, and order.[10] "No man ought to take upon him the office of a minister of the Word without a lawful calling," so advised the Westminster Assembly.[11] The aim was to define the minister's call as a careful judicial process—one that explicitly barred "restless and turbulent persons" (in Calvin's phrase) from thrusting themselves into the preacher's office based on special gifts or irregular credentials. Most crucial for Reformed usage of the ministerial call was "an outer public and constitutional procedure"—the system of examination and installation—that, duly conducted, was essential for the true ministry.[12] Hence, in Puritan ministerial manuals (such as Cotton Mather's *Manuductio ad Ministerium*) the focus was on formal preparation, training, education, and congregational office, and the serious devotion required for pastoral readiness was situated within this larger discipline. The call was primarily ecclesial, not (at least by later evangelical standards) experiential and immediate. Though the Puritan ministry was clearly deeply pietistic in practice and self-understanding, the minister's call itself remained carefully institutionalized within the frameworks of what historian David D. Hall has labeled "Reformed sacerdotalism."[13]

The radical sectaries of the seventeenth century, who compelled many of the efforts to stabilize the doctrines of calling and the practices of Protestant ordination, had already made plain the fragility of such ecclesial propositions. Among shoemaker George Fox's fundamental insights—or "openings from the Lord"—was that "being bred at Oxford or Cambridge was not enough to fit and qualify men to be ministers of Christ," and such formal attainments were replaced in Quaker piety by an infusion of immediate presences, voices, dreams, and promptings. Having forsaken all the priests and even the "separate preachers," Fox related, "Oh then, I heard a voice which said, 'There is one, even Christ Jesus, that can speak to thy condition.'" Fox's *Journal* reads not only as a testimonial about divine vision and inner light, but also as a play of inward voices, sudden words, and scriptural echoes: "And as I was walking by the steeplehouse side, in the town of Mansfield, the Lord said unto me, 'That which people do trample upon must be thy food.'"[14]

Fox's colonial American heirs spoke in the same accents of immediacy. John Woolman, cultivating a studied indifference to his worldly occupations as shopkeeper and tailor, led a traveling ministry based on divine promptings, or, in the Quaker vernacular, "drawings." Given to momentous dreams, Woolman also received a vision of divine light accompanied by "words spoken to my inward ear which filled my whole inward man." The words, repeated twice, were "Certain Evidence of Divine Truth." At another point he "heard a soft, melodious voice, more pure and harmonious than any voice I had heard with my ears before," and "believed beyond doubting that it was the voice of an holy angel."[15] A series of spiritual leadings, openings, and dreams superseded a settled vocation for Woolman (and for any number of other Quaker missionaries), and thus did Quakers and other sectaries break the ministerial calling open through a leveling experientialism. As satirist Thomas Brown mocked a Quaker prayer, "Give us our true *Primitive Pastors, Lay-Elders, Reverend Tanners, Religious Basket-makers, Upright Cobblers, Conscientious Millers,* and more *Conscientious Taylors, Reform'd Weavers, and Inspir'd Broom-men.*"[16] Evangelical radicalism reminded just about all its opponents of seventeenth-century upstarts like the Quakers and Baptists, and the spiritist wellsprings of the itinerant emphasis on immediate calls and extraordinary missions were apparent. It was not far from the call story of a Baptist separatist like John Bunyan, tinker's son, to those of later itinerants.[17]

The experiential reimagining of the ministerial call was clearest in the Methodist movement. To justify his itinerants and lay preachers, Wesley drew a distinction between the offices of preacher and priest; the latter had a regular, ordinary call—a sacramental office with episcopal ordination and university education behind it, but the commission of his preachers was "extraordinary," in line with the summoning of the prophets. Early Reformed apologists had drawn a similar distinction, but limited the extraordinary calls of apostles, prophets, and evangelists to the biblical world, which left the current church with the ordinary offices of pastors and teachers (based on Ephesians 4:11). As Calvin said, the extraordinary offices have "no place in well-constituted Churches."[18] Wesley and company took the common distinction and inverted the traditional conclusion. His preachers were *"extraordinary messengers"* with a special evangelistic mission of preaching the gospel distinct from the ordinary priestly office; like Paul, they were ones "on whom the Holy Ghost" had come "in an extraordinary manner."[19]

The distinction of an extraordinary call became dear to Methodist apologists. Adam Clarke, in his influential preacher's manual, recognized that Methodist itinerants had no "ordinary" call by Anglican or Reformed standards. "You are an extraordinary messenger, or no minister at all; and you have either an extraordinary call, or you have no call whatsoever," he concluded. The word "extraordinary" became a Methodist mantra of sorts; in Clarke's phrasing, Methodist preachers "all testified that they had an extraordinary call, to do an extraordinary work, by extraordinary assistance." Likewise, in Wesley's conflicted views of preaching by women, this was the cornerstone of any defense. As he wrote one of the Methodist female preachers in 1771, "I think the strength of the cause rests there—on your having an *extraordinary* call. So I am persuaded has every one of our lay preachers."[20]

Wesley and Clarke hardly systematized this blessing, and the working out of this extraordinary call was given the same sort of latitude in practical theology as the experiences of new birth and perfection. The spiritual impressions that accompanied a call to preach, one Methodist noted, vary "greatly in clearness and intensity in different individuals, and in the same individual at different times."[21] That very flexibility, though, was necessarily joined to prescription: "My Call to Preach" became a commonplace of evangelical autobiography, part of a public testimonial, a recognized vernacular of self-authorization, open to young men especially, but sometimes usable by women as well to help override the assumed Pauline injunctions.[22] Itinerant William Swayze reported that it was "no uncommon thing for our brethren to question the preachers on this subject," and that it was "viewed as a crime of the greatest magnitude, for a man to intrude himself into the ministry without a Divine call."[23] A convincing story of a call experience—one deemed "agreeable to the call of the Apostles," as preacher Billy Hibbard put it—emerged as a formative concern.[24] Though Methodists still had to deal with the inevitable tensions between individual experience and church order, they had widened considerably the authority of these extraordinary calls and the auditory piety that went with them.

The sensational Lorenzo Dow, as wild and successful as Methodist evangelists came, reported his "Call to Preach" in his autobiography, and it was exemplary of the vivid narrative conventions that emerged in popular Methodism. One day, early in 1793, retired in solitude for prayer, Dow related, "these words were suddenly impressed on my mind; 'Go ye into all the world and preach the gospel to every creature.'" What followed was a series of still more dramatic episodes of divine commissioning, including a genuinely Pauline moment in which Dow, while riding along on horseback one day, was "seized with an unusual weakness, and my eye-sight entirely failed me." Even then, incredibly, Dow continued to struggle with his call (as with conversion experiences, calls often remained long and tortuous affairs, punctuated with doubt and temptation, their vocal directness notwithstanding). Dow, like many others, found resolution in a dream—in this case, one in which John Wesley himself came back from the grave to look him square in the face and tell him, "God has called you to preach the gospel; you have been a long time between hope and fear, but there is a dispensation of the gospel committed to you. Woe unto you if you preach not the gospel." The dream left Dow shaken, and, within the month, despite parental opposition and no official license, he set out to preach. God had called him directly in prayer, and the sainted Wesley, acting as angelic mediator and ordaining authority, confirmed the summons. This was no demonic temptation, as the youthful and barely lettered Dow had initially feared, but an extraordinary call.[25]

The ascent of such dramatic call stories was hardly unbroken, even for the early Methodists. Some thought that the drama of the call had become too prescriptive and tried to tack back, in their spiritual narratives, to a more decided emphasis on preparation. Joshua Marsden, who published his memoir of international itinerancy in New York in 1813, resented the Methodist reputation for an illiterate ministry. Describing instead a path of intense study, he knew many of the devout would wonder why he stressed "mere human preparation": "Was not you thrust out, and compelled to go and call sinners to repentance?" he imagined being rebuked, as if he had heard the challenge too many times already. "I do not know that the parallel will hold good betwixt a minister of the gospel now-a-days, and Moses or Jeremiah," he replied. Those Methodists who talked about divine calls, he thought, had "not sufficiently qualified their observations." Such God-directed compulsion "is rarely the case, and ought never to be laid down as a standard, lest many should be discouraged who have not this compelling call." He now regretted his own youthful indiscretion in plunging into preaching without more formal education, and was ready to see the Methodists move toward professional legitimacy for their ministry. In the 1810s Marsden's view remained a minority opinion among populist evangelicals. Most preferred the diction of extraordinary calls to such sobering preparation, and, as Marsden discovered to his chagrin, the laity remained all too ready to demand an account of such a legitimating experience from their preachers.[26]

Notwithstanding the internal debates within evangelical circles about the very validity of such experiences, the question lingers: What made these extraordinary calls a vital possibility in the first place? For those who hearkened, this was fundamentally an issue of divine agency, not of any social determination, individual freedom, or private judgment. In Christian piety, even for the most Arminian, it was always far more a matter of being chosen than choosing. It is not a question about *agency* that the historian usually asks: How is it that God broke into these very mundane and common lives as a beckoning voice? These are remarkable claims: I heard a mysterious voice repeating a scripture, or I seemed to hear an internal yet perceptible whisper from Jesus, or a luminous angel descended before me and announced, or John Wesley came to me in a dream and confirmed God's commission. "It is notorious," one English critic lamented as early as 1747, "that the Methodist writings abound with intimations of divine communications, prophetic whispers, and special guidances."[27]

It would be easy to pass over these infamous assertions en route to the safer terrain of social explanation, but Christian spiritual traditions were what most deeply formed these experiences—discursive assumptions and devotional practices that permeated the varied contexts in which such voices were heard. While ever marked by the particularities of gender, race, social standing, and age, these extraordinary calls were joined to an overarching teleology within evangelical devotion that worked toward divine intimacy, toward a palpable relationship with Jesus. As Methodist Mary Fletcher described a visionary moment in 1763, "There seemed but one yard distance between my Saviour and me—when he spake, with a voice clear and distinct, these words: 'I will send thee to a people that are not a people, and I will go with thee. Bring them unto me.'"[28] Behind this intimacy—Jesus so close she could touch him, so audible she could hear him plainly—was a metaphysics of the senses, and this metaphysics, along with the bodily education that was its accompaniment, formed the basis for any other cultural work that such revelatory presences performed. So it is helpful to take a step back and ask: What allowed people in moments of retreat, revival, or sleep to hear things? How had the bodily senses been prepared to become spiritual senses?

God's Oracles

As Jesse J. Goben, a Baptist farmer raised eight miles south of Man's Lick, Kentucky, struggled with whether he was fit to preach the gospel, he prayed that the Lord would make a direct manifestation "to me as he did to Moses," preferably an audible commission in a dream or a vision. With no sign forthcoming and the torment mounting, Goben instead took up his Bible "with the prayerful desire that the Lord would cause it to fall open in some place, and direct my eyes to some portion that would give me relief. It fell open at the second chapter Proverbs, and it appeared to me that the Spirit of life from God entered into the words, and he appropriated it to me and for me, just as much as if he had spoken to me from heaven." The long scriptural passage that Goben alighted upon began with the condition, "My son, if thou wilt receive my words," and ended with a pledge of knowledge and understanding of God for the faithful supplicant. Goben was elated with this bibliomantic result: "When I had finished reading . . . I turned to my wife and said, 'Did you hear that?' She said, 'Yes.' I then read it over again to her, for it was the most life-giving, soul-cheering, heart-rejoicing reading that I had ever read; for now God had spoken to me, even apparently mouth to mouth, as he did to Moses, calling me his son, and telling me that he gave wisdom." The next Sunday, Brother Goben told his story of deliverance and confirmation, told how God's words had come alive and been personally applied to him, and the little church fellowship immediately licensed him "to go and preach wherever God in his providence cast my lot."[29]

Brother Goben's story suggests how the charged words of scripture were reiterable and animated, how they brought a divine voice within earshot in the daily life of evangelicals. Nathan Cole, a New England farmer reborn in the revivals of the 1740s, loved his Bible so much that at one point he nuzzled it. "I felt just as the Apostles felt the truth of the word when they writ it," he said, "every leaf, line and letter smiled in my face; I got the bible up under my Chin and hugged it." Few texts are caressed or cuddled in contemporary culture; in a demolitionist's dream, they are broken part, their cracks exploited, their fault lines shaken, their fissures widened. So it is of first importance to acknowledge this strange world of textual intimacy, the sacramental presence and living voice of this holy book. As Jonathan Edwards related of his Bible reading at one point, he could never get very far in the text because "almost every sentence seemed to be full of wonders." In one of the most commonly used tropes for the scriptures, endlessly repeated from the apostle Paul (Romans 3:2), these writings were God's oracles, a revelatory voice in waiting. God kept speaking because God had already spoken.[30]

Scriptural words were reverberant; they echoed in the interiors of those who knew them with such tender familiarity. Whether in moments of prayer or meditation, conversion or calling, God's voice was commonly experienced as a sudden and overwhelming impression of a Bible verse or fragments of verses. One Methodist, describing how the Lord's Spirit overpowered him during his experience of sanctification, related, "I felt such a weight of glory that I fell with my face to the floor, and the Lord said by his Spirit, 'You are now sanctified, seek to grow in the fruit of the Spirit.'" The voice of the Lord's Spirit was but a gloss on Galatians 5:22–23, a partial and percussive reiteration of scriptural verses this convert knew were central to fathoming the blessing of spiritual perfection.[31] A female Methodist preacher, Fanny Newell, had scriptures dart into her mind continually, strengthening and prodding her: "This day many passages of Scripture flow through my mind with power and solemnity," she noted in a routine passage that would have held true for any ardent pilgrim. The divine intimacy of evangelical piety was formed in a scriptural echo chamber.[32]

God's oracles were often oracular in a still more literal sense. As Goben's use of the Bible suggests, people employed the scriptures to divine their futures, their salvation, or their calling. The scriptures were fortune-tellers. Most evangelicals would have cringed at such a blunt characterization, but bibliomancy was a common Christian practice with ancient roots; the obsessive scripturalism of Protestants only enhanced its popularity. Adam Clarke, for one, condemned "divination by the Bible"—"dipping into the Bible, taking passages of scripture at hazard, and drawing indications thence on the present and future state of the soul"—but he was hard-pressed to deny its prevalence. (Wesley himself used the Bible this way; at one point, a scriptural lot convinced him that his martyrdom was imminent.) Clarke even noted how such practices had been formalized in the use of "Scripture cards," a deck of biblical texts from which people drew "for the purpose of showing the success of journeys, enterprises, etc."—"trifles" that he feared were all too popular in Methodist circles.[33] Such worries over the excesses of scriptural divination only call attention to the usualness of such biblical practices. Where a Bible fell open was regularly charged with oracular power. After a day of youthful "wantonness," John Woolman saw a Bible on a window ledge near his bed. Drawn to it, he opened it up and "first cast my eye on the text, 'We lie down in our shame, and our confusion covers us.'" "Meeting with so unexpected a reproof," he then went to bed "under remorse of conscience," the words having become instantly a breathing prophecy of judgment.[34]

A particularly dramatic example of how God's words were a living oracle comes in the call story of Billy Hibbard, another New England Methodist convert in the aftermath of the Revolution. Deeply impressed that God was calling him to preach, yet wary of deception, Hibbard, the son of a shoemaker, wanted a surer sign. So he knelt and prayed that "I might open the Bible on some text, clearly expressing the duty of one called of God to preach. But if not, that I might open on a text, expressing danger of running before I was sent." Shutting his eyes, secretly hoping for disconfirmation, he opened his Bible and his finger settled on Ezekiel 3:17–18: "Son of Man, I have made thee a watchman unto the House of Israel: therefore, hear the word at my mouth and give them warning for me." The passage went on to forecast very dire results indeed for the watchman who failed to give warning to the wicked. Hibbard's excuses seemed to be fast running out, but, wriggling, he resolved, in effect, to go for two out of three. This time he decided to enlist his wife to find his biblical fortune, and, though she found her husband's zeal on this occasion almost amusing, she solemnly obliged, closing her eyes and landing her finger on Luke 9:60: "Jesus said unto him, let the dead bury their dead; but go thou and preach the kingdom of God." That was the end of Hibbard's resistance: "I yielded and gave myself up; poor, and weak, and simple as I was."[35] God's oracles had worked their magic one more time: he would preach now and worry about a license later. Hibbard, like other evangelicals, was immersed in the echoing effects of God's words: the Lord had spoken, so the Lord still speaks.

Spiritual Disciplines, Spiritual Senses

Caught up in the revivals of 1800, Kentuckian Jacob Young was so spiritually overwrought that he said he desired "a hermit's life." Trying to ascertain a divine call to preach, Young retired to a grove with two other young men who felt inklings of the same commissioning. Going out early in the morning "without eating or drinking," they spent "the day in fasting, weeping, and praying," each in isolated devotions, each waiting alone to be "filled with the Holy Ghost," and each rewarded that afternoon with at least temporary clarity in the circuitous pilgrimage toward the ministry.[36] Their ascetic retreat was hardly unusual. Another evangelical pilgrim and fellow Kentuckian, James B. Finley, as part of his reclusive devotions, "would crawl, feet foremost, into a hollow log, and there read, and weep, and pray." Prayer, meditation, and retreat were the constants in evangelical stories of conversion, calling, and holiness, and the voices that they heard need to be understood within the rubrics of those spiritual disciplines.[37]

The spiritual hearing that these practices cultivated was based on a prior form of withdrawal—an ascetic commitment to a regimen of perceptual purity. In the Christian tradition, the senses were the inlets to body and soul and as such had to be regulated carefully. As historian Elizabeth Sears has noted of early Christian apologists, a recurrent question was: "What should a Christian allow himself to hear, see, smell, taste, and touch?"[38] For the always vulnerable Christian body, the senses were the weak points, the permeable places of contact, danger, and profanation. What one looked at, what one ate, what one listened to, what one felt, what one smelled were the bodily indices of the soul's condition. (That understanding was formally recognized in the Catholic rite of extreme unction, in which the organs of sense—the eyes, the ears, the nose, the mouth, the hands—were each anointed in turn and forgiveness sought for all the sins committed though them.) Like their Catholic counterparts, Protestant commentators remained concerned with the moral and spiritual import of what the five senses took in. In a classic and widely repeated image, these were the "*five gates,* by which the world doth besiege us, the Devill doth tempt us, and the flesh ensnare us." The devotional key for Christians was the "heavenly Exercise" of the senses: "Let *eye, eare, touch, tast, smell,* let every *Sence,* / Employ it selfe to praise *his* providence."[39]

How to keep the ears pure was a venerable Christian concern. In John Bunyan's *Pilgrim's Progress*—a Puritan spiritual guide that had only increased in popularity among the evangelicals—a repeated gesture of the pious wayfarers was to "put their fingers in their ears" to avoid contamination and distraction. "Such be the *eares,* they are planted in the high-rode-street, and exposed to a world of incursions," one seventeenth-century writer of pious resolutions observed. "I heare many things I would not heare."[40] Keeping the ears clean necessarily led back to the mouth. The ears could be protected from lies, blasphemies, obscenities, curses, and vulgarities only by a wholesale disciplining of what by all accounts was an extremely unruly member, the tongue (following James 3:8).[41] One of the basic rules for Methodist preachers and their people was this regimen around talking and listening. "Let your motto be, 'Holiness to the Lord.' Avoid all lightness, jesting, and foolish talking."[42] For the Methodist convert and black preacher Boston King, "the horrible sin of Swearing and Cursing" led his list of preawakening transgressions; after a burning apocalyptic dream scared him onto the path of righteousness, the first things he renounced were "swearing and bad company."[43] The devout believed that they had to stop listening—to tavern banter, bawdy songs, lewd jests—before they could start listening for God. As Ebenezer Newell noted of his restraint when he painfully found himself among some noisy carousers in a tavern, "I was silent; I neither drank, joked, or talked."[44]

Renunciation was preparation for retreat, for prayer and meditation. Lorenzo Dow's call to preach was initiated in prayer, "whilst kneeling before God." It was then that the biblical words "Go ye into all the world and preach the gospel to every creature" came to him as a personal commission. Those words were in turn part of a larger interior dialogue, some of which Dow recorded: "I instantly spoke out, 'Lord, I am a child, I cannot go; I cannot preach.' These words followed in my mind, 'Arise and go, for I have sent you.' I said, 'Send by whom thou wilt send, only not by me, for I am an ignorant, illiterate youth; not qualified for the important task':—The reply was—'What God hath cleansed, call not thou common.'" For all the Pauline drama of Dow's experience of divine calling, there was something quite prosaic about this particular exchange. Christian prayer was an intimate and familiar conversation. "There is no better means to awake us," noted a seventeenth-century manual on prayer, than "to set ourselves *a-talking to God*" and "to *hear God speaking to us.*" Through meditation and prayerful retreat, Dow entered a familiar soundscape within the Christian tradition.[45]

The venerable contours of this prayerful dialogue can perhaps be best gauged by turning to the *Imitatio Christi* of Thomas à Kempis, a perennial that enjoyed resurgent popularity in the late eighteenth and early nineteenth centuries in large measure because of its extensive pietist and evangelical appropriation. Whitefield heralded the book as "my great delight" in his widely disseminated *Journals;* Woolman counted on it as a keystone in his own pious reading and lifted up its author as the truest of Christians; the Catholic mystic Jeanne Marie Guyon, whose spiritual autobiography and guide to prayer also exercised substantial influence among early evangelicals, gave primacy to the *Imitatio* as a devotional book. John Wesley's esteem for the manual as a pattern for the Christian life ran so high that he became the volume's consummate publicist and editor. (There were at least twenty-four British Methodist editions of his varied versions before his death in 1791, and his American missionaries were peddling these London editions by the early 1770s.) Making the book a catalyst for his own teachings on Christian perfection, Wesley urged its regular reading in all his societies and even encouraged memorization of especially earnest portions. For everyday pilgrims, the book appeared to be the model behind their own models—Wesley, Whitefield, Woolman, Guyon.[46]

Though New Englanders had contemplated publishing the *Imitatio* in 1667 (before reneging because of supposed Catholic vestiges), the book's first American incarnation did not come until 1749, in Germantown, Pennsylvania, and only two more editions appeared before the Revolution.[47] After the war the *Christian's Pattern*, as it was commonly called, rode the rise of the Methodists and the wider revivals to new heights of popularity. The American Methodist publishing concern made it the very first book off its newborn press in August 1789, and then issued it again and again, usually in handy pocket-size. There were five editions from Philadelphia alone between 1789 and 1794; between 1800 and 1815, there were at least fifteen more, including American incarnations of German and French versions; another twelve editions were off the presses in the following fifteen years, up to 1830. The text clearly had a wide reach: humble itinerants such as Billy Hibbard and Jacob Gruber reported employing and promoting it.[48] Few, if any, devotional works were more popular in the American republic between 1790 and 1830. It exceeded Richard Baxter's *Saints Everlasting Rest,* William Law's *Serious Call to a Devout and Holy Life,* John Wesley's *Plain Account of Christian Perfection,* and any work by a New England Puritan. It even held its own with Bunyan's *Pilgrim's Progress.* Through this one book,

the *Christian's Pattern* of Thomas à Kempis, the Protestant devotionalism
of the early republic retained (or regained) a late medieval Catholic tenor.[49]
"O that God would write in your hearts the rules of self-denial and love laid
down by Thomas à Kempis!" John Wesley had prayed, and there is every indication that his prayer was answered among his American brethren.[50]

It is little wonder that the *Imitatio* spoke so compellingly to evangelicals,
that its evocation of "the mysteries of the inward kingdom of God" resonated deeply with those who, as Wesley put it, "have read the same things
in their own souls."[51] Thomas à Kempis began where the evangelicals began: with an incessant emphasis on holiness, self-denial, and closeted retreat for devotion. "Keep all thy senses under discipline, and give not thyself over to trifling mirth"; "Leave desire, and thou shalt find rest"; "It is
vanity to follow the desires of the flesh"; "Withdraw thyself from superfluous talk and useless visits, as also from hearkening after news and ru-
mours."[52] Opening up from the purgative renunciations of its first book,
this gnomic text moved into a detailed exploration of the inward life of
prayer in Books II and III. It then closed in the fourth book with meditations on the Eucharist and the gifts of Communion (a section made congenial, with a little maneuvering, to Protestant sacramentalism). Breathing
humility, the book assured that these spiritual attainments were open to all:
"God speaks unto us sundry ways, without respect of persons"—a devotional leveling that dovetailed with evangelical convictions. Wesley liked to
paint many of his ordinary converts as enjoying "a close, uninterrupted
communion" with God, a life of "continual prayer," every bit the equal of
mystic saints and hermits: "He with whom we have to do is no respecter of
persons."[53]

In the third book, especially, the *Christian's Pattern* took up prayer as conversation, and it is from there that most can be gleaned about the mystical
locutions of this spirituality. Prayer is founded on a *"familiar friendship with
Jesus,"* a closed-eye dialogue in which the devout listened for *"the inward
speech of Christ"*:

I will hear what the Lord God will speak in me. Blessed is the soul that
heareth the Lord speaking *in her,* and receiveth from his mouth the
word of comfort. Blessed are those ears that receive the whispers of
the divine voice, and listen not to the whisperings of the world.
Blessed indeed are those ears that hearken not to the voice which
soundeth outwardly, but unto the truth which teacheth inwardly. . . .

Consider these things my soul, and shut up the door of thy sensual desires, that thou mayst hear what the Lord God speaketh in thee.[54]

The *Christian's Pattern* exemplified that very conversation as Christ answered the narrator at length, the book relating a string of such contemplative encounters and serving as a model for further exchanges and for the very formation of such devout ears: "Blessed indeed are those ears."

Given the immediacy with which Thomas à Kempis reported these inner conversations, the book was bold and potentially combustible, especially in the religious atmosphere of the new republic. "SPEAK, Lord, for thy servant heareth. . . . Let thy speech distill as dew," prays the Christian pilgrim. And, again and again, in the *Imitatio* the Lord speaks, comforts, beckons, admonishes with an intimate directness: "I am thy peace, thy life, and thy salvation"; "Son, I am the Lord, that giveth strength in the day of tribulation. Come unto me when it is not well with thee." The saint's subjectivity was formed through this internal exchange with a voice that was within but also beyond the self. Prayer had a dissociative quality, a splitting, this other voice being heard on top of the petitioner's own, the voice of reverberant biblical words. Yet, since in this practice of prayer there was a presumed coherence to these divided voices, a telos to the dialogic exchange, these pilgrims often discovered closure in ecstasy, union, and holiness.[55]

The practices of speaking and listening within prayer broached what devotionalist John Fletcher, following Christian writers from Origen to Augustine to Bonaventure to Edwards, termed "the spiritual senses," particularly in this case "spiritual hearing." Fletcher, as a renowned advocate of "evangelical mysticism," was among the most popular expositors of "experimental religion" on both sides of the Atlantic in the second half of the eighteenth century. His *Six Letters on the Spiritual Manifestation of the Son of God* was crucial, along with Edwards' *Religious Affections,* for presenting the doctrine of the spiritual senses to evangelical audiences. Cautious about enthusiasm, Fletcher used the contemplative idea of the spiritual senses, in some ways, as a check: "The things of the Spirit of God cannot be discovered but by spiritual, internal senses. . . . They are the only medium by which an intercourse between Christ and our souls can be opened and maintained." New ways of seeing and hearing, of experiencing, were disclosed to regenerate souls, but these refined perceptions of divine things did not ordinarily come from "our bodily external senses." Be vigilant, in other words, with those who claim to have seen or heard too much with their "bodily organs." Later in the *Letters* Fletcher was less definite, however: he confessed that God's manifestations might still be to the external senses. However extraordinary, such biblical wonders had not ceased with the apostles; they remained "more frequent than many imagine." He wanted nonetheless to direct primary attention to the spiritual senses, including the "spiritual ear."[56]

Such theological language helped capture (and construct) a suprarational world of experience—one dramatically unveiled to those whose internal senses were opened up by the Holy Spirit. "The exercise of these senses is peculiar to those who are born of God," Fletcher avowed, and it was a point that Methodist-turned-Shaker visionary Rebecca Cox Jackson echoed in her own descriptions of the soul's unsealed gates: a whole new realm of perception and a whole new set of senses were made available to the newborn soul. The spiritual senses were finally more a mystic's incitement than an enthusiast's constraint; they served as a way of authorizing, framing, and invoking these divine voices, a way of encountering such revelatory presences. "When St. Paul was caught up into the third heaven, did he not 'hear words unspeakable'?" Fletcher asked. "And, far from thinking spiritual hearing absurd, or impossible, did he not question, whether he was not then out of the body?" Natural philosophers, those who would "turn everything into body or matter throughout the universe," might scoff at such spiritual propositions, Fletcher admitted: "Being chiefly conversant with bodies, . . . they regard the soul and metaphysics as mere romances" (an oddly relevant observation on contemporary scholarship). The spiritual senses were, to Fletcher, a traditional Christian path around what he saw as the materialist precipice of philosophers and enthusiasts alike. How could one have "an experimental knowledge of the invisible God," how could spirit be known to flesh, without senses that perceived what was hidden to the bodily senses? Spiritual hearing legitimated the voices that the faithful heard, even as it made them all the more arcane, pushing them into the interstices between body and soul. This was, Fletcher had to admit, a "mysterious subject."[57]

Perhaps it is easier, with the discipline of prayer and the language of the spiritual senses in mind, to understand why evangelicals, in their narratives, spoke with some equivocation about the nature of the voices they heard. "There seemed to sound a voice," Jarena Lee had noted of her call experience; and she speculated later that perhaps all her attentiveness to the things of the Spirit had made her sense of hearing somehow "more acute," readier to receive such "uncommon impressions." One of Boston King's experiences underlined the elusive yet realistic quality of these voices: "Engaged in prayer and meditation, I thought I heard a voice saying to me, 'Peace be unto thee!' I stopped, and looked round about, to see if anyone was near me. But finding myself alone, I went forward a little way, when the same words were again powerfully applied to my heart." Billy Hibbard, aiming perhaps to cut through such ambiguities, said that he heard a word from the Lord within his mind "as plain as it could have been spoken to my outward ears."[58] What was the medium of these divine impressions? The question was clearly perplexing to believers themselves. How were they hearing what they were hearing?

The ear was a model for the subtleties of divine-human encounter in prayer and meditation. The acquiescence of listeners opened up a way of imagining how it was that God acted upon them; their yielding made clear the lines of divine power and human submission. As the contemplative Jeanne Marie Guyon explained in her *Short and Easy Method of Prayer,* "Hearing is a sense formed to receive sounds, and is rather passive than active, admitting, but not communicating sensation; and if we would hear, we must lend the ear for that purpose; so Christ the eternal Word, without whose divine inspeaking the soul is dead, dark and barren, when he would speak within us, requires the most silent attention to his all-quickening and efficacious voice." A classical shadow still hovered over the ear in which its associated passivity and femaleness made it the appropriate organ for God's action upon the soul. In a traditional patristic gloss, the Virgin Mary had actually conceived Jesus through the ear, and this implanting of the angelic words of annunciation starkly suggested the symbolic power that hearing possessed for elaborating God's incarnational presence in the world, for revealing the axial Christian exchange between body and soul, fleshly obedience and divine revelation.[59]

These evangelicals lived in the penumbra of the Incarnation, and the voices they heard took shape in this liminal space where the spirit and the flesh were under constant negotiation. The words were so real, so discernible, so resonant, yet somehow beyond the external ears, beyond "outward hearing," their very elusiveness a way of embodying the disembodied, a way of imagining how an immaterial, immutable God might be disclosed within the evanescent body. As itinerant James Horton noted of an ecstatic moment in the midst of prayer and meditation, "A bright sheet of glory fell on me, and these words seemed to be spoken to me, 'Be a child of mine and I will be a father unto thee, and thou shalt see where thou art to dwell.' Whether in the body or out of the body, the Lord knows." Guyon explained these moments of ecstatic exchange with her Savior as part of "a facility of speaking without words." Of one prayerful moment of encounter, she remarked, "When I say, that I spoke thus to him I must explain myself. It all passed almost in silence, for I could not speak. My heart had a language which was carried on without the sounds of words." No words, no sounds, and yet only words and sounds: in her stilled interior, Jesus "never ceases to speak." Invisible yet resonating in the flesh, fleeting yet charged with presence, sounds and words were the apt media of such in-between experiences. Marked by the incongruity of a transcendent immanence, these noises were silent yet heard, external yet internal, transient yet deathless, in the body yet beyond the body. "Marvel not," John Fletcher had said, "if we find it impossible to tell you all the particulars of a Divine manifestation."[60]

"The Startled Ear of Night": Voices of Temptation, Sounds of Judgment, and Songs of Heaven

Born a slave in St. Mary's County, Maryland, in the 1790s and catechized as a Roman Catholic, Thomas Henry "embraced religion" in 1819 in a pietist German family and then joined the Methodists. He soon wondered whether he was called to the ministry. "Then my troubles began," he said, "and before this my troubles were with God and myself; then the devil introduced himself in the subject, and this made three. I thought, as it were, that I heard the voice of a man saying to me, 'you want to be a Methodist preacher, I see; you cannot be a preacher; you have not reached the requirements in education; the people will laugh at you; you have no language.'" Discouraged by this demonic voice that stoked his self-doubt, he kept meditating on his call for six more months, asking God for guidance.

Then, one day, lying in the basement of a house, seeking shelter from a storm, Henry lapsed into "deep meditation" on what the Lord had in mind for him: "There was a wonderful peal of thunder, and a great blaze of lightning ran around the room where I was lying. There was a short interval between the thunder and the lightning, and in this interval I heard a voice that was too distinct to be mistaken. I was perfectly awake; and the voice said this: 'I must work the work of Him that sent me, while it is called day.' I sprang upon my feet and exclaimed: 'Yes, Lord! yes!' I had no more doubt."[61] While Henry's story underlines again the devotional matrix for hearing this divine voice of both resolve and resolution, his narrative also highlights two of the more foreboding dimensions of this auditory piety: the sinister voice of the devil and the awesome power of thunder and lightning for the pious imagination. Ominous sounds—thunder, trumpets, bells, rattling chains—were crucial to the configuring of pious ears. In a world of demonic menace and terrifying judgment, the devout listened fearfully and yet also expectantly for the heavenly strains that signaled the final defeat of those terrors.

Henry handled the devil's intrusion of his mocking voice adroitly enough, but others had a harder time. In the throes of conviction in October 1772, Benjamin Abbott, for example, faced one demonic assault after another. "As I was passing through a piece of woods the devil suddenly suggested to my mind, that as I was one of the reprobates and there was no mercy for me, I had better hang myself and know the worst of it." Then as he was looking for an appropriate place to do this, he thought he heard another voice, "This torment is nothing to hell." Terrified, he hurried home, only to get into bed and then feel that he was "rolling, bed and all, into the flames" and that "huge devils stood ready" to receive him. Likewise, in a moment of visionary and audile terror, Jarena Lee saw "the awful gulf of hell" open beneath her and thought she heard "the howling of the damned" and "the rattling of those chains" that held them there. The near-inevitable presence of the grim murmurs of damnation regularly made the interior conversations of the devout torn, splintered, and even tortured.[62]

Satan's suggestions often directly disrupted the spiritual disciplines of the saints, adding another layer of complexity to their dialogic prayers. One day, retiring as usual to "a sequestered spot for reading, meditation and prayer," Fanny Newell initially discovered much elation in her devotions. Many passages of scripture sweetly floated through her mind, and she found herself bursting into song to praise her Redeemer. Within this exultant piety, though, despair hovered as the intimate companion of joy. "In the midst of these ecstacies," Newell related, "suddenly and unexpectedly I was stopped by a voice, that seemed to utter the following words: 'What! are *you* praising God? even that God who cannot look upon sin with the least shadow of allowance—the demons themselves might as well praise him.'"[63] The same sort of hesitancy the devout displayed in describing the voices of God, Jesus, and angels extended to the voice of the devil.

What was the medium of this *seeming* voice? Where were these words coming from? How did they suddenly materialize in prayer and meditation? Could these impressions be trusted? Satan's capacity for dissimulation, especially his ability to disguise himself as an angel of light, made the faithful all the more uncertain how to talk about what they were hearing—indeed, compounding that indeterminacy with the question of *who* they were hearing. The devil was the first deconstructionist, and his powers of masquerade and mimicry regularly made Christian experience a bottomless pit of suspicion.

Less obscure and more dramatic was the demonic voice of possession. Though cases of possession were ostensibly rarer by 1800 and were certainly incapable of precipitating a massive social crisis the way they had in Salem in the 1690s, popular Christianity remained the haunt of demons—ones still ready to take possession of people and to utilize their vocal organs. This meant that the devil's voice often had a quite tangible reality for the devout, one more clearly embodied than God's or Christ's. Methodist Andrew Manship, for example, told how itinerant Solomon Sharp encountered a possessed woman at a revival at the turn of the nineteenth century. Convulsed of body, she taunted Sharp in an altered voice, what Manship called "a sepulchral tone": "You are a pretty preacher of the Gospel!" she said as he drew near. Sharp, sensing that it was the devil himself that uttered this contemptuous expression through the mouth of this woman and believing that he had the power to cast out demons, proceeded to exorcise this one. "I command you to come out of her," he ordered, and the evil one did—an event that earned Sharp a powerful local reputation, as well as the nickname *"the devil-driver."*[64]

The evangelist was not always so successful. Preacher William Swayze, for example, reported on a man who, in the midst of revival meetings, would be overcome by a demon and then "commence swearing and damning in the most spiteful and Satanic manner." "He said it was not himself that swore," Swayze continued, "but the wicked spirit that was in him." Praying for the man did little good, and the paroxysms repeated themselves at other services, especially when "evident operations of the Holy Spirit" appeared to descend on the congregation. Swayze was left on this occasion only to wonder at this prodigy of the devil—his apparent ability to make someone his unwilling mouthpiece.[65]

That the devil had a popularly recognizable voice, right into the early nineteenth century, is evident as well from a bit of evangelical theater.

Tired of one ruffian's spleen, a young Methodist took matters into his own hands and impersonated the devil to terrify the persecutor. Costuming was crucial—including "a false face" and "a cloven foot"—but essential, too, were sound effects, notably "a clanking chain" and vocal mimicry. As this sham devil cornered the perpetrator, he roared out in "a grum tone of voice, in guttural sounds": "You must go with me," upon which, itinerant Dan Young reported gleefully, the rowdy disintegrated, wishing helplessly that he "was a Methodist!" This bit of theater may well have been less effective than Young imagined, but what the story made clear was the tacit cultural knowledge not only of the devil's visible appearance, but also of his unearthly tones. From cases of possession as well as popular tales of demonic encounters, the devout (and even their enemies) had definite expectations about the guttural sound of the devil's voice.[66]

Just as frightening as Satan's tormenting presence was God's wrath-filled Last Judgment. The evangelical movement was charged with eschatological urgency: Repent now, or face that final scene with truly terrifying unreadiness. As a prospective event that everyone knew would be inaugurated by a trumpet blast, the Last Judgment was conjured up especially by sounds. In the words of a typical camp-meeting hymn,

> Now hark! the trumpet rends the skies!
> See slumbering millions wake and rise!
> What joy, what terror and surprise,
> The last great day is come![67]

Trumpets were very much the favored sign: they were often used at camp meetings to call people to devotion or to awaken them in the mornings. As one woman noted of a massive camp meeting near Philadelphia in 1806, seven people were employed "to blow trumpets to sound round the camp every morning and evening, when reports were made of the number brought to God"—a dramatic ritual, indeed, of eschatological anticipation.[68] Lorenzo Dow, before preaching a sermon on the Last Judgment, was reputed to have sent a boy up into a tree with a trumpet in order to have him blow on the instrument at just the right moment.[69] At other times the heralded sign was not of Dow's own engineering: during one revival on Long Island when a trumpet happened to sound from a passing sloop, it combined with the rumble of a storm to create, Dow said, "the most awful representation of the day of *Judgment* of any thing I ever beheld." At such moments the Last Judgment was not so much prospective as present.[70]

The sounding of trumpets was not the only alarm that resonated in devout ears. On a stormy night when itinerant Andrew Manship was awakened by a loud bell, he "sprang from the bed hastily" and felt certain "this is the end of the world." Though he thought that he would "soon see the Judge descending upon his great white throne," he also felt ready for Jesus and shouted "Hallelujah, God appears on earth to reign." A random bell, rung suddenly in the night, created a scene worthy of Edgar Allen Poe's tintinnabulation of bells:

> What a tale of terror, now their turbulency tells!
> In the startled ear of night
> How they scream out their affright!

Manship's own startled ear of night triggered a mental rehearsal of the Last Judgment and sent him through a whole gamut of emotions, from fear to joy and then to disappointment.[71]

In a setting of such auditory expectancy, even the vocal trickery of the irreligious might become a portentous sign. Itinerant Dan Young told the story of an impious youth who crept up on a house early in the morning, hiding himself behind a large stump and crying out, "Awake thou that sleepest, and arise from the dead, and Christ shall give thee light." The couple inside the house, suddenly roused from sleep and unable to see anyone outside, quickly "came to the conclusion that it was a supernatural voice" and heeded the urgent message of awakening. In this evangelical world in which the surprise of Judgment was a given—Christ will come as a thief in the night—even the slippery voice of deception might become, in spite of itself, an agent of warning and salvation.[72]

Thunder was a consummate sound of Judgment, and, like the trumpet blast, it made for an old refrain. Increase Mather had devoted two chapters to thunder and lightning in his work on remarkable providences, and his son Cotton was similarly enthralled, giving considerable space to this awesome noise in his *Magnalia Christi Americana*. The sudden rise of a thunderstorm during worship sent the younger Mather off on "an *extemporaneous contemplation*" on "the voice of God in the thunder," assuring his hearers that God is "now speaking," reminding people of his glory, power, and commandments.[73] Evangelicals from Edwards to Asbury only augmented the importance of these deep-seated aural cues. "The fierce forked lightning and tremendous thunder," Billy Hibbard observed starkly of one storm-swept meeting, "reminded us of the day of judgment." The very

The following was written by the Rev. JOHN WESLEY, of London, in 1774; and a copy of it was sent to the King of England, which has ever since put a stop to the play, called "The Day of Judgment," which was about that time performing in the London Theatres.

BY COMMAND OF THE KING OF KINGS,[a]
And at the desire of all those who love His appearing.[b]

SEARCH THE SCRIPTURES.
John v. 59.

a) Rev. xix. 16.—1 Tim. vi. 15.
b) 2 Tim. iv. 3.—Tit. ii. 13.

At the Theatre of the UNIVERSE,[c] on the Eve of Time,[d] will be performed,

THE GREAT ASSIZE, or
DAY OF JUDGMENT.[e]
THE SCENERY,

c) Rev. 20, 11.—Matth. 24, 26.
d) Rev. 10, 6. 7.—Dan. 12, 13.

e) Heb. 9, 27.— Ps. 9, 7. 8.— Rev. 6, 17.
2 Cor. 5, 10. — Zeph. 1, 14 to 17.

WHICH is now actually preparing, will not only surpass every thing that has yet been seen, but will infinitely exceed the utmost stretch of human conception. f) There will be a just representation of all the inhabitants of the world, in their various and proper colours; and their customs and manners will be so exactly and minutely delineated, that the most secret thought will be discovered. g) "For God will bring every work into judgment, with every secret thing, whether it be good, or whether it be evil." Ecc. xii. 14.
This Theatre will be laid out after a new plan, and will consist of PIT and GALLERY, only; and, contrary to all others, the Gallery is fitted up for the reception of people of high (or heavenly) birth; h) and the Pit for those of low (or earthly) rank. i) N. B. The Gallery is very spacious, k) and the Pit without bottom. l)
To prevent inconvenience, there are separate doors for admitting the company; and they are so different, that none can mistake that are not wilfully blind. The door which oppens into the Gallery is very narrow, and the steps up to it are somewhat difficult; for which reason there are seldom many people about it. m) But the door that gives entrance into the Pit, is very wide and commodious, which causes such numbers to flock to it, that it is generally crowded. n) N. B. The straight door leads toward the right hand, and the broad one to the left. o)
It will be in vain for one with a tinselled coat, and borrowed language, to personate one of High Birth, in order to get admittance into the Upper Places, p) for there is One of wonderful and deep penetration, who will search and examine every individual; q) and all who cannot pronounce Shibboleth, r) in the language of Canaan, s) or has not received a White Stone and a new name, t) or cannot prove a clear title to a certain portion of the Land of Promise, u) must be turned in at the left hand door. w)

f) 1 Cor. 2, 9.—Isa. 64, 4.—Ps. 31, 19.
g) Matth. 12, 36. — 1 Cor. 4, 5. — Rom. 2, 12, 16.
h) John 3, 3, 5.—1 Pet. 1, 23.—Rom. 8, 14.
i) James 3, 14, 15.—Hos. 8, 6, 7. 8.—Gal. 5, 19 to 21.
k) Luke 14, 22.—John 14, 2.
l) Rev. 9, 12.—19, 20.

m) Matth. 7, 14.
n) — 7, 13.
o) — 25, 33.
p) — 7, 21 to 23.
q) Ps. 44, 20, 21.—Jer. 17, 10.—Zeph. 1, 12.—2 Tim. 2, 19.—John 10, 14.
r) Judges 12, 6.
s) Isa. 19, 11.—Zeph. 3, 9.
t) Rev. 2, 17. u) Heb. 11, 8. 9.—Gal. 3, 9, 29.—2 Cor. 18, 5.
w) Ps. 9, 17.—Heb. 5, 17 to 19.

THE PRINCIPAL PERFORMERS

Are described in 1 Thes. 4, 16. 2 Thes. 1, 7. 8. 9. Math. 24, 30, 31.—25, 31. 32. Dan. 7, 9, 10. Judg. 14, 4. Rev. 20, 12 to 15. &c. But as there are some people much better acquainted with the contents of a Play Bill than the Word of God, it may not be amiss to transcribe a verse or two for their perusal. "The Lord Jesus will be revealed from Heaven with his mighty angels in flaming fire, taking vengeance on them that obey not the gospel, but to be glorified in his saints. A fiery stream issued and came forth from before him. A thousand thousands ministered unto him, and ten thousand times ten thousand stood before him: The Judgment was set, and the Books were opened, and whosoever was not found written in the Book of Life, was cast into the Lake of Fire."

Act First of this Grand and Solemn Piece,

Will be opened by an Arch-Angel with the Trump of God. x) "For the trumpet shall sound and the dead shall be raised." 1 Cor. 15, 52.
ACT SECOND—will be a PROCESSION OF SAINTS, in white, y) with Golden Harps, accompanied with shouts of joy and songs of praise. z)
ACT THIRD—WILL BE AN ASSEMBLAGE OF THE UNREGENERATE. a)
The Music will consist chiefly of Cries, b) accompanied with Weeping, Wailing, Lamentation and Woe. c)

x) 1 Thes. 4, 16.—Matth. 24, 31.
y) Rev. 7, 14.—19, 14.
z) — 14, 2. 3.—15, 2 & 4.
a) 1 Cor. 6, 9. 10.—Math. 13, 41.
b) Luke 23, 3.—Rev. 6, 16.
c) Luke 13, 28.—Math. 13, 49. 50.—Rev. 1, 7.—Ezekiel 7, 10.

To conclude with an Oration by the Son of God.

It is written in the 25th chapter of Matthew, from the 34th verse to the end of the chapter; but for the sake of those who seldom read the Scriptures, I shall here transcribe two verses:— Then shall the King say unto them on his right hand, 'Come ye blessed of my Father, inherit the Kingdom prepared for you from the foundation of the world.' Then shall he say unto them on his left hand, 'Depart from me, ye cursed, into everlasting fire, prepared for the Devil and his angels.'

AFTER WHICH THE CURTAIN WILL DROP!

Then! O to tell!	
John 5, 28. 29. Some raised on high, and others doom'd to hell!	Luke 9, 14. 27. While those who trampled under foot his grace,
Rev. 5, 6. 9. These praise the Lamb, and sing redeeming love,	Math. 25, 30. Are banish'd now forever from his face.
Luke 16, 22. 23. Lodg'd in his bosom, all his goodness prove :	Luke 16, 29. Divided thus, a gulph is fixed 'between,
	Math. 25, 46. And [everlasting] closes up the scene.

Thus will I do unto thee, O Israel; and because I will do thus unto thee, prepare to meet thy God. Amos 4, 12.

[d] James 4, 2.—1, 15. 16. 17.—Col. 3, 5. 6.

Tickets for the PIT at the easy purchase of following the pomps and vanities of the fashionable world, and the desires and amusements of the flesh: d) to be had at every flesh-pleasing assembly. "If ye live after the flesh, ye shall die." Rom. 8, 13.
Tickets for the GALLERY, at no less rain than being converted, e) forsaking all, f) denying self, taking up the cross, g) and following Christ in the regeneration : h) To be had nowhere but in the Word of God, and where that word appoints. "He that hath ears to hear, let him hear, and be not deceived; God is not mocked; for whatsoever a man soweth, that shall he also reap." Matth. 11, 15. Gal. 6, 7.
N. B. No money will be taken at the door; i) nor will any tickets give admittance into the Gallery, but those sealed by the Holy Ghost, k) with Immanuel's signet: l) Watch therefore; be ye also ready, for in such an hour, as ye think not, the Son of Man cometh. Matth. 24, 42. 44.

e) Matth. 18, 3.—Acts 3, 19.
f) Matth. 19, 21.—Luke 14, 26. 33.
g) — 9, 23 to 26.—Matth. 16, 24.
h) Matth. 19, 28. 29.—Galater 5, 24. 25.—Eph. 5, 1. 2.
i) Acts 8, 20 to 23.—Zeph. 1, 18.
k) 2 Cor. 1, 22.—1, 30.—Eph. 1, 13.
l) Rev. 7, 3.—14, 1.—Exod. 9, 4.

sounds of thunder were a form of divine speech, and the prayerful were well prepared to decipher its urgent messages about the soul's salvation.[74]

One itinerant after another turned to thunder evangelism. Benjamin Abbott's efforts in this line can stand as a representative of what just about any revivalist worth his salt instinctively did amid a summer thunderstorm. As Abbott started preaching to a crowded auditory, "the Lord out of heaven began also":

> The tremendous claps of thunder exceeded any thing I ever had heard, and the streams of lightning flashed through the house in a most awful manner! . . . I lost no time, but set before them the awful coming of Christ, in all his splendour, with all the armies of heaven, to judge the world and to take vengeance on the ungodly! It may be, cried I, that he will descend in the next clap of thunder! The people screamed, screeched, and fell all through the house.

There was almost an erotics of thunder for the evangelist, as the terror of his audience turned, for him, into an undisguised thrill. "My soul was happy beyond description," Hibbard noted of his beseeching alarmed sinners amid an awful thunderstorm. The ears of the devout had been schooled in fear and expectancy, in dread and hope. The imminence of the Last Judgment and its alarming noise put their sense of hearing on edge, made it terribly acute, ready to hear God in the ringing of a bell or a peal of thunder.[75]

Tuning the ears to eschatology was not only about the ominous, but also about the joyous. The Judgment was but a threshold beyond which rang, for the regenerate, the songs of the New Jerusalem. Heaven was the place where the Christian's senses were perfected, glorified, and trans-

3. Day of Judgment
The auditory world of eschatological expectancy is made apparent in this Wesleyan broadside. Amid thunder and lightning, the solemn scene of Judgment opens with the blast of the angels' trumpets; the centrality of this sound is made manifest visually through the placement and elongation of the instruments. The next act is the procession of the saints to the New Jerusalem "with Golden Harps, accompanied with shouts of joy and songs of praise," and the third act is the wailing assemblage of the damned, whose "Music will consist chiefly of cries." From a broadside entitled "By Command of the King of Kings," Harrisburg, Pennsylvania, ca. 1800. Courtesy of the Library of Congress.

formed, where the pilgrim's quest after the purity and exquisiteness of perception was fulfilled. The ear would possess such delicacy in heaven, Jonathan Edwards dreamed, that the saints would be able to have the most delightful and intimate conversations "at a thousand miles' distance" (an image that suggested how Christian eschatology was happily fused with Baconian ambitions). And the saints would sing and sing and sing, with a joy scarcely imaginable. As Edwards effused over these heavenly perfections, "When I would form in my mind an idea of a society in the highest degree happy, I think of them as expressing their love, their joy, and the inward concord and harmony and spiritual beauty of their souls by sweetly singing to each other." Just as with the apocalyptic din, inklings of these empyrean sounds were available to the devout this side of eternity. The harmonies of angels and saints, ringing out their praises of God in heaven, were ritually anticipated in the hymns and choruses of pilgrims below.[76]

This heavenly music was also anticipated in meditative retreat. The popular devotionalist William Law, whose *Serious Call to a Devout and Holy Life* (1728) was critical for the formation of the daily routines of evangelical holiness, joined the private singing of psalms to the heavenly chorus. In a venerable devotional technique, Law envisioned contemplative pilgrims dwelling on the seraphic choirs in such detail "till your imagination has carried you above the clouds; till it has placed you amongst those heavenly beings." The earthbound saint became, in a moment of prayerful transport, one among these celestial singers: "your voice is added to theirs," "angels join with you, and you with them." In so thoroughly imagining their participation in these heavenly realms of angelic choirs, people were often opened to other calls as well. As a friend told Zilpha Elaw after a period of entranced song in the company of heaven, "Ah, Zilpha! angels gave it me to sing; and I was told that you must be a preacher."[77]

Psalms and hymns in worship and meditation trained Christian ears to another order of sound, made them expectant to hear that eternal music. This heavenly music was not merely a trope, not a geometric or harmonial abstraction (as the music of the spheres often became in the new astronomy), but a highly tangible part of the evangelical imagination. "We have had several instances of music heard before or at the death of those that die in the Lord," John Wesley observed in 1753. "May we conceive that this is, literally, the music of angels? Can that be heard by the ears of flesh and blood?" Poised yet again on the borders of body and spirit, Wesley faced the compelling mysteries of Christian acoustics and concluded that this music was not simply inward but "the effect of an angel affecting the auditory nerves, as an apparition does the optic nerve or retina." The heavenly music of the saints could be heard in this world, a vibratory incursion of the angels into the fleshly ears of the sanctified, a sounding from that Holy City beyond the Judgment. "A few days since," Lorenzo Dow reported in one elaboration of Wesley's views, "there was heavenly melodious music heard, from whence could not be ascertained: and at the same time a young woman died happy."[78] The distance between this world and the next narrowed in the ears of the devout. Heaven was so close that on a good day they could hear it.

Angels sang, the saints intoned praises around God's throne in glory, and every once in a while a devout believer, in moments of prayer, meditation, ecstasy, revival, or death, heard those sounds. At times the faithful, like Zilpha Elaw's friend, were even enabled to join in. Fanny Newell gave rich expression to this mystical possibility in describing an experience during June 1809, part of her quest for the sanctified experience of perfect love:

> I was dead to all below; yet my mind was active and sensible—led on with ravishing delight to those joys that beggar all language. . . . I thought that I came into the celestial city and saw God and his throne; and as I came into the place, I saw countless armies of shining spirits, who were praising God and giving glory to the Lamb. . . . They sang in loud strains. At first I could not sing with them or learn their song. . . . I longed to join them in singing one of those heavenly anthems; and one of them said to me, You shall, and immediately I struck in and sang as I never did before or since.[79]

Newell, like Thomas Henry, lived in a world of demonic temptation and threatening judgment, and her ears were well trained in fear and foreboding. But the devil never had the last word, nor was the Last Judgment in itself the real ending, and thus did shouts of praise and songs of heaven ultimately drown out those ominous sounds.

The Noises of Revival

James Finley, the fellow who liked to cram himself into a hollow log for his secret devotions, was still seeking direction from the Holy Spirit. He had spent most of the previous day ensconced in the log (in the snow no less), reading his Bible and praying. At dawn the next morning he arose and immediately headed for his barn to pray. He never made it:

> Just as I passed the corner of the house on my way, suddenly God poured upon me the Holy Spirit in such a manner, and in such a measure, that I fell, my whole length, in the snow, and shouted, and praised God so loud, that I was heard over the neighborhood. As soon I was able to rise, I returned to the house, and my wife having risen, I caught her in my arms, and ran round the house, shouting, "Salvation! salvation!" . . . While thus exercised, I felt as though some one had spoken to me, "Go preach my Gospel." I instantly replied, "Yes, Lord, if thou wilt go with me."

Evangelical piety was nothing if not demonstrative and loud. During revivals, at prayer meetings, alone in devotions, people shouted, clapped, groaned, and cried. Finley's exuberant, noisy response, heard all over the neighborhood, was but a personal echoing of the clamor of revival, something he had already abundantly witnessed and clearly internalized. At the Cane Ridge meeting in 1801, Finley had listened in awe to the shrieking and shouting: "The noise was like the roar of Niagara." Perhaps it is not surprising that amid all the pious hubbub, these evangelicals, as Finley did, were enabled to hear God's voice, whether a whispered blessing or a divine call.[80]

Evangelicals were noisy—to their opponents appallingly so. That consummate antirevival diatribe, Charles Chauncy's *Seasonable Thoughts on the State of Religion in New-England* (1743), needs to be listened to as much as read. The revivals offended his ear: "the *Groaning, crying out, falling down and screaming*"; the *"terrible speaking"* of itinerants; the clapping, stomping, singing, roaring, and *"hearty loud Laughter."* It was the shouting that turned into screams and screeches that especially disgusted. These outcries "often begin with a single Person, a *Child*, or *Woman*, or *Lad*, whose *Shrieks* set others a *Shrieking*; so the Shrieks catch from one to another, 'till the whole Congregation is alarmed, and such an awful Scene, many Times, open'd, as no Imagination can paint to the Life." The same shudder of disgust was evident in Frances Trollope's listening at a camp meeting nearly a century later. "How am I to describe the sounds that proceeded from this strange mass of human beings?" she asked. "I know no words which can convey an idea of it. Hysterical sobbings, convulsive groans, shrieks and screams the most appalling, burst forth on all sides. I felt sick with horror." The visceral

pain that Chauncy and Trollope experienced in listening suggests a resonance with philosopher Jacques Ellul's phenomenological observation on
sound's potentially disorienting effects: "The noise assails and haunts me. I
cannot close anything, as I would my eyes, to shut it out. . . . Sounds produce incoherence."[81]

The sounds of revival rattled those who could not contain them. For
opposers overwhelmed by the din of revival, hearing was a potent indicator
of social order or chaos, evident in the long-standing prominence of musical analogy for political economy. The ear, indeed, was a crucial guide to
social harmony, discord, and concord: Condillac, in his *Traité des sensations*,
actually divided the sense of hearing into two parts, the perception of "harmonious sounds" and that of "noises," the latter constituting "a state of
confusion," an incoherent commingling. Noise was the category for
sounds that the trained ear could not discriminate or appreciate, the
sounds that caused it pain instead of pleasure, that disrupted hearing's delicate harmonial balance. Noise very much acted as a social category as
much as an aesthetic one. The evangelicals were not only defined by their
noises; they *were* noise.[82]

The other offends the senses. Historians and anthropologists have
pointed out the density of "olfactory distinctions" that govern racial
and class hierarchies, the supposed stench of the poor, the immigrant,
or the slave that provokes a visceral revulsion. As George Orwell famously
remarked, the "real secret of class distinctions in the West" was "summed
up in four frightful words": "*The lower classes smell.*"[83] Noise, too, defines
alterity: the other is loud, discordant. To patriarchy's defenders, feminists
are "shrill" or "screeching"; the very tone of their voices repels and is
constitutive of difference. And the same applies to Victorian middle-class stereotypes about the loudness of new immigrants and the threatening cacophony of the cities. So, too, religious others have been defined
by their intolerable noise. Chauncy reached back to the Quakers as embodiments of the loud, the roaring, and the groaning (without a hint of
their concomitant emphasis on silence). Religious sectaries, in many ways,
were constituted in the imaginations of their opponents by their dangerous sounds, by their "Drumming, Trumpeting, Laughing, Whistling,
Hissing," by their "Gulpings, Hiccupings, Foamings," as one critic described the French Prophets. "I believe these People only meet to make a
Noise," Thomas Brown concluded succinctly of the Quakers. Sound was a
measure of order—and truth. Loud faith was bad faith; it was demonstra-

bly "a public nuisance" and an imposture. As Tom Paine concluded in an essay attacking church bells, "Religion does not unite itself to show and noise. True religion is without either." If religion had any hope of being useful in Paine's dream of the modern state, it would have to be very, very quiet.[84]

Whereas their opponents marked them out as disgusting because of their uncontrolled sounds—their noise pollution—evangelicals drew people in through the power and allure of their boisterous gatherings. To critics, the people had *"itching Ears,"* scratched by the extemporaneous harangues of exhorters and the contagious shrieking of converts; but to those pulled in by the clamor, as was James Finley, the varied noises of revival were captivating.[85] The sounds of rebirth gripped people; they rang out into the night and through the streets and in the woods and barns. One convert reported being heard at his devotional exercises three-quarters of a mile away; another noted how the noises of one revival were "heard at the distance of three miles." It was common for observers to detail how the shouts of the saved and the cries of the distressed were "heard afar off." (Since there was generally less ambient noise in the air in 1800 than there is now, the reach of this camp-meeting din would have been all the more extensive and extraordinary.)[86] Though these sounds of awakening were left, of course, "unrecorded," some of their gripping intensity can be registered if the familiar images of them are not only viewed but also "heard." Listen, for example, to the well-known watercolor of J. Maze Burbank of a camp meeting in the 1830s, the crumpled heaps of people praying and weeping, the wide-open arms of praise and exhortation, the clatter of the crowds and horses, the wailing throes of the repentant. Images, art historian W. J. T. Mitchell reminds us, are mixed media, and the sounds they attempt to record are an integral part of pictures. They are an especially crucial aspect of revival depictions such as Burbank's, in which the visual serves to evoke an aural and interior drama.[87]

These revival sounds, so far-reaching and invasive, also followed people. Itinerant Andrew Manship carried his revival ecstasies into bed, shouting out for joy in his sleep and disturbing the rest of a fellow preacher. One pil-

🖼 4. *Religious Camp Meeting,* by J. Maze Burbank
Burbank's famed depiction of a camp meeting, painted around 1839, offers a visual record of the noises of revival—the shouts, sobs, groans, harangues, and whispers of evangelical piety. Courtesy of the Old Dartmouth Historical Society, New Bedford Whaling Museum.

grim, who left a camp meeting early, arrived home only to find that the call to salvation was not so easy to escape. He heard an audible voice, apparently coming from the barn: "go back, and seek religion this night"; and, necessarily, he did. Even on a deathbed, the hollers of "Glory, glory!" from revival meetings were commonly repeated, the sounds of rebirth echoing at the end of earthly life, the roared affirmations of heavenly triumph. As one saint exclaimed as she expired, "The chariot is coming—are you all ready? . . . Now! Now! Here it comes. Glory! Glory! Glory! Shout! Shout! . . . Are you all shouting?"[88] Thus did the murmurs, sighs, moans, groans, cries, shouts, and calls of revival reverberate; they stayed with people, the echo of the transitory. "These sounds waiting for a language," "these 'obscene' citations of bodies," as historian Michel de Certeau described such noises, resounded from the gut of evangelical experience, a wrenching exchange between sorrow and hope, death and rebirth, pain and bliss. The very excesses of their sounds, more than their preached words or their printed texts, made evangelicals different, but those extremes also enfleshed what they felt as the staggering otherness of God, an overpowering presence made sensible through these unverbalizable "sounds of the body."[89]

Out of the sensory intensity of revivals came a readiness to hear. In the crowded fervor of prayer meetings, mourners' benches, and altar calls, amid the sobs and the groans, devout ears were formed and prepared. Fanny Newell described one such scene in which a preacher and the saints prayed intensively over her at the end of a meeting. "If you will kneel down with us, we will all try to pray for you," the preacher offered. As Newell got down on her knees, "these words came to me as though some one had spoken to me, and I know not but they were spoken by someone present: 'Renounce the world, the flesh and devil, / You shall have *pardon, peace,* and *Heaven.*'" In the confused din of the praying throng, even Newell herself was uncertain whether the voice was not simply one of her companions in travail with her. It hardly mattered. On her knees from sunset to midnight, surrounded by others praying, with her external eyes largely shut in inward meditation, she was "lost" to the world, caught up in an interior combat between demons and Christ. Finally, in a sounding vision, she was offered mercy from the Savior himself: "Give me thine heart," Jesus said to her. "I have taken thy sins away." Then, immediately, she "felt something in my heart like a burning fire"; it was "a refiner's fire," Jesus assured her. As the people around her came back into focus, she arose and lustily shouted her praises to God.[90] Chauncy had long ago registered his opinion that all the outward tumult of Spirit-filled worship was deeply intermeshed with an interior openness to "hearing Voices."[91] Newell's experience, like Finley's, testified loudly to those synergies.

"Take Heed, Therefore, How Ye Hear": Making the Ear Compliant

To liberal-minded opponents like Chauncy, the vocal immediacy of evangelical piety was not in harmony with the Puritan fathers and genuine Reformed devotion; it smacked of the Quakers and the French Prophets. "The *Spirituality* of Christians does not lie in *secret Whispers,* or *audible Voices*," Chauncy pronounced confidently.[92] If stalwart evangelicals lacked such blanket clarity, they had similar misgivings. Ever wary of the dangers of enthusiasm and the claims of immediate revelation, many evangelical ministers would have been ready to concur with the Anglican rector Benjamin Bayly, who in 1708, maddened by inspired sectaries, dismissed "this way of Revelation, *by Calls and Voices,*" as "the lowest and most dubious of all." "It becomes Men of Learning and Piety, methinks, . . . not to ground their Belief upon so idle a thing as a *hollow Voice,* or *little Noise,* coming from behind a Wall, or no Body can tell whence." Even as Bayly wanted to protect the unique persuasiveness of the divine voice that spoke to the biblical prophets, he did all he could to delegitimate these slippery, disembodied soundings among his contemporaries. "The common and vulgar Interpretation of these *Calls and Voices,*" wholly failing the tests of rational judgment as well as miraculous confirmation, was "a very insufficient Ground" upon which to build the faith.[93]

Chauncy and Bayly were representative of the weight of the Reformed and Anglican traditions. Much of magisterial Protestantism served, indeed, as a system of restraints on spiritist experiences and sectarian propulsions. It was a system that worked on multiple levels and included: the postbiblical cessation of miracles and extraordinary spiritual gifts (such as prophecy and tongue-speaking), the consummate interpretive authority of ministers, the disciplining power of church courts and state establishments, the complete sufficiency of scripture (ruling out any new and divergent revelations), the formation of Christian knowledge through catechesis and doctrinal examination, and the primacy of sanctification (or holy living) over any enthusiast fancies.[94] Eighteenth-century evangelical leaders, especially of Reformed and Anglican derivations, inherited most of those restraining assumptions and practices, even as the movement they promoted ultimately cracked open all of them. While the Enlightenment posed a massive challenge to the revelatory voices and devout hearing of popular piety, the faithful necessarily worked all along on their own ways of delimiting what the ear was allowed to hear.

Checks internal to evangelicalism often did as much as the raillery of opponents to set limits on the mystical flights of Christian experience. Jonathan Edwards' *Treatise Concerning Religious Affections* (1746) was an exemplar of such caution. In Edwards, more than in a Methodist like Fletcher, the cultivation of the "spiritual senses" was a direct counter to the auditory expressiveness of popular piety. In a virtuoso balancing act, Edwards defended most of the revival phenomena, including even such "bodily effects" as groaning and crying out, as potential accompaniments of genuine "spiritual affections," while at the same time he insistently drew the devotional focus away from these manifestations. Edwards looked for the opening up of a new "divine sense" in the regenerate soul, one deeply drawn to the beauties and practices of holiness. This "spiritual supernatural sense," Edwards insisted in a turn of phrase that set him at odds with the prevailing philosophical sensorium from Aristotle to Locke, was "infinitely more noble" than any of the bodily senses, even the long-enshrined eye. As a divinely wrought state, such sanctified perception was expressly not the product of mere rational improvement and sensory management. Edwards' preferred figure for this new sense was not spiritual hearing but "spiritual taste," a discriminating knowledge, a delicate aesthetic that allowed for a piety of both honeyed sweetness and sharp distinctions. For the literati, from Shaftesbury and Voltaire to Hume and Reid, taste emerged as a definitive aesthetic and cultural measure, the very embodiment of the power of discrimination. Edwards' elaboration of "spiritual taste" fit well within this learned celebration of a differentiating stringency, even as he worked against the grain of the Enlightenment in his fundamental understanding of Christian perception.[95]

Edwards' tasteful discernment was evident in the way he handled what many converts took to be one of the best signs of saving grace—namely, scriptural words "brought suddenly and wonderfully to mind" as if spoken to them personally. In uncompromising terms, Edwards set aside these reverberant biblical voices as being spiritually unimportant and epistemologically indeterminate. "There is no higher sort of power required in men, to make the sounds which express the words of a text of Scripture, than to make the sounds which express the words of an idle story or song," Edwards concluded. Also, the wiles of Satan, Edwards reminded, included the power to "bring sounds or letters" into people's minds, so such impressions and voices, he made plain, were unredeemably slippery. They were subject to the intertwined treacheries of the imagination and the devil. "Here is the devil's grand lurking place, the very nest of foul and delusive spirits," Edwards said of the imagination and all the counterfeits it generated.[96]

Edwards was quite specific about these fake voices, often representing in his *Treatise* the very words that misguided laypeople attributed to divine impressions. He imagined, for example, a convert announcing his deliverance based on "some voice or words coming as if they were spoke to him, such as those, 'Son, be of good cheer, thy sins be forgiven thee,' or, 'Fear not, it is the Father's good pleasure to give you the Kingdom,' which he takes to be immediately spoken by God to him." In another instance he pictured a man at prayer having "those words which God spake to Jacob, Gen. 46, suddenly and extraordinarily brought to his mind, as if they were spoken to him; 'Fear not to go down into Egypt . . . and I will go with thee.'" Edwards then painstakingly showed what was wrong with this man's application of Jacob's story to the immediate circumstances of his own life, how this surprising impression failed the test of genuine spiritual understanding because it made up "a new meaning" for the biblical passage rather than hewing closely to what was *in* the text already. Edwards was prepared with Chauncy to consign such revival experiences—the "inward whispers," "immediate suggestions," "pleasant voices"—to the realm of delusion. The true saint, grounded in the full sufficiency of the scriptures, "won't want any new speaking of God to him, what he hath spoke already will be enough with him." Edwards lost this battle badly at the level of popular evangelical piety, but his admonitions suggest how the varied Protestant chastisements of spiritist voices in the seventeenth century still throve in the apologetics of a Reformed revival.[97]

Much of the Calvinist anxiety over the vagaries of these voices circled back to the issue of the minister's authority. In the *Institutes,* Calvin noted that God does not dwell "among us by a visible presence, so as to make an audible declaration of his will to us," but instead "for this purpose he uses the ministry of men whom he employs as his delegates . . . that he may himself do his work by their lips; just as an artificer makes use of an instrument in the performance of his work." The duly called minister was in that sense a divine mouthpiece, the veritable temple of God's oracles. In this Reformed understanding of the proclaimed word, the holy scriptures came alive in preaching. To *"Preach Scripturally,"* demonstrating every sermonic point with well-chosen biblical texts, was, as Cotton Mather noted in his ministerial manual, crucial for those "who would *Speak as the Oracles of God.*"[98]

Preaching, so intimately entwined with the reiteration of scriptural words, made the Reformed minister the exalted medium of God's voice. "God does not chuse to speak immediately from heaven himselfe, nor to speak by Angels," the Reverend William Adams of Dedham, Massachusetts, explained typically, "but he raises up instruments of the sons of men whom he fits and qualifies . . . and by them he finds and speaks his mind to other men." Such views were intended to secure the status of the Reformed clergy through what historian Harry S. Stout has called a "monopoly" on divine discourse.[99] Superhuman ventriloquy: the question for early modern Protestants was not whether, but in whom and through whom God was allowed to become a living voice.

Ministers were always quick to realize that the routine deferences of their auditories—the bodily habits of silent attention, the *"well-composed Countenances,* and *becoming Gestures"* of reverent concentration—were a constitutive part of their own standing. In his "Directions [on] How to Hear Sermons," George Whitefield, for example, took up the text "Take heed, therefore, how ye hear" (Luke 8:18), advising people to hang upon the words of their ministers as they would have on the words of Jesus himself: that is, they must listen dutifully to "those whom the Holy Ghost has made overseers over you." The classical Protestant disciplines of the ear were designed especially to safeguard the ministerial enfleshment of God's oracles and to uphold the interpretive dominion of God's ambassadors. "Receive every Gospel-Sermon as by Christ, *preached,*" related Daniel Burgess in his standard set of eighteenth-century rules on the pious etiquette of listening to ministers. A politics of hearing was always the paired complement to the politics of speaking in these churchly settings; being a good hearer (by Anglican and Reformed standards) involved the whole body in a series of *"reverent Postures"* of humility that signified deference to God and, necessarily, to his ministers as well. "Fill the Time of your Hearing," Cotton Mather advised, "with Repeated, with Numberless, *Acts of Compliance.*" The rambunctious impressions of biblical words, the immediate calls, and

the sudden promptings posed an unnerving threat to this hierarchic conception of clerical authority, to the uniquely hallowed resonances of the
minister's voice, and to the very prostration entailed in the proper hearing
of preached words.[100]

The debates internal to Protestantism about the regimens of pious hearing, about who was and was not a sound Christian, looked increasingly pa-
rochial from outside these bounds. To the literati, the ecclesial paradigm of
submissive listening sounded ever more tyrannical, a species of priestcraft,
while the evangelical vernacular of sudden impressions, heavenly voices,
and extraordinary calls sounded ever more ridiculous. In stepping back just
a little from the world of Protestant preachers and evangelical awakenings,
it quickly becomes evident that these ways of hearing, for all their vigor,
were also under severe scrutiny in this age of reason. The very audacity of
pietistic ways of hearing only gave added gravity to the Enlightenment
campaign to discipline the senses, silence the oracular, tone down hearsay,
and retrain the ear. The devout were all too aware of these critical suspicions, though the tendency has been to act as if the revivals washed away
the American Enlightenment. The knowledges of the Enlightenment were
encyclopedic—a cultural web of learning, progress, gentility, experimental
exhibition, anticlericalism, autonomy, and mastery that became the coin of
the civic realm. Evangelicals might baptize many of the Enlightenment's
powers and ambitions, but they would never completely submerge them.

In 1801 James Finley, in witnessing the Cane Ridge revival, said he was
tempted "to philosophize," to reduce the whole to "mere sympathetic excitement—a kind of religious enthusiasm, inspired by songs and eloquent
harangues." Finley knew better than to philosophize this way about auditory manipulation, but he was also well aware of other explanatory frameworks and how they were deployed. Likewise, in the late 1790s Billy Hibbard was alarmed at the popularity of Paine's *Age of Reason,* an explosive
bestseller, on two of his local New England circuits; he found that many
were ready with the deists "to ridicule all religion, and make it a phantasm." Pious fears were often justified: deism was far from spectral; skeptical ideas circulated widely in what has been called, alternately, the provin-
cial Enlightenment or the village Enlightenment. Still, in the 1820s a young
Methodist convert, Stephen Bradley, had the discomfort of rooming with
"a Deist" in New York—one who argued with him regularly that "there
was no supernatural power that ever operated on the mind of man, and
that we perish or are annihilated at death." Underneath all the stock images

of the vanquished skeptic were blustering, face-to-face exchanges from which evangelical combatants hardly emerged unscathed. Alexis de Tocqueville, it is helpful to recall, was taken not only by the "almost wild spiritualism" of the early republic, but also by the "almost insurmountable distaste for whatever is supernatural"—an "instinctive incredulity" that was founded on "a very lofty and often exaggerated opinion of human understanding." Natural philosophy and rational autonomy became increasingly important cultural measures, not least of the oracular pieties and devout obediences within Protestant circles.[101]

It would be wrong, though, to turn too quickly to Enlightenment regimens and away from these sound Christians. Extraordinary calls and sudden leadings continued to flourish in popular Protestant piety, and evangelical ways of hearing hardly lost their resonance; if anything, they radiated ever more widely in modernity's wake. Evangelist Amanda Berry Smith, part of a surging revival movement in postbellum America that emphasized holiness or entire sanctification, spoke of her extraordinary call to preaching and mission in a Wesleyan language untempered by Reformed or Enlightenment disciplines. In a moment of prayerful vision, in which the letters G and O appeared to her, Smith reported that then "a voice distinctly said to me 'Go preach.' The voice was so audible that it frightened me." In another moment of calling in 1869, the Lord told her to go to Salem and "gave me these words: 'Go, and I will go with you'"—"the very words he gave to Moses, so many years ago," she observed of this echoing biblical voice. Inevitably worried about Satan's deceptions and wanting to be sure this was the Lord's voice, Smith prayed for confirmation, "to hear Thee speak to me, and tell me where to go." And the voice came again, "'Salem,' and I said, 'Lord, that is enough, I will go.'" For Smith, and the vibrant evangelical subculture of which she was a part, talk of extraordinary calls remained common, as did the devotional world of prayer, meditation, and revival.[102]

Pentecostal preachers spoke in similar accents, only redoubled now with experiences of healing and tongue-speaking. In his autobiography, entitled *The Call* (1971), Oral Roberts told of his youth during which his father left the Methodists to become a minister in the Pentecostal Holiness Church. Amid the tent revivals in Ada, Oklahoma, that the family frequented, Roberts himself was healed of tuberculosis. It was just prior to that moment of restoration that God "called me to take His healing power to my generation. His words rang clear to me: 'Son, I am going to heal you and you are to take the message of my healing power to your generation.'" And then, with the warm hands of the praying evangelist pressed upon his head, healing came. Within two months Oral Roberts, with no formal training and the apostles as his professed model, was out preaching revival himself.[103] Perhaps this divine call was extraordinary, yet the surprise of God's voice was familiar, even expected, given the enveloping devotional culture of these sound Christians. Still, for Roberts, as for many others, that very intimacy with divine speech proved a two-edged sword, imperiling his standing in the wider society and ultimately turning him from evangelist to laughingstock. If Roberts managed to supply his own floodlight by transforming God into a vengeful hospital fundraiser, the learned had built the stage for the discrediting of such listeners long before.

Oracles of Reason

New Englander William Frederick Pinchbeck, who described himself as "a mechanic and a philosopher," liked a good show. In 1798, he had made decent money touring the country with a Pig of Knowledge which he had trained in such a way that the pig seemed able to tell time, do arithmetic, and identify concealed cards. With a name aptly evocative of the counterfeit—"pinchbeck" was a common form of imitation gold used to make cheap jewelry—this entrepreneurial philosopher even claimed to have exhibited the Learned Pig "before the President of the United States with unbounded applause." So it was with a blend of professional rivalry and scientific curiosity that Pinchbeck set out in late 1804 to see a new attraction on the American circuit of entertainments, "a certain Philosophical Machine lately arrived from France, which engrosses universal attention": the Acoustic Temple. The mechanism, its principles of construction, its powers of illusion, its disembodied female voice, and its technological sophistication, with hidden tubes and large trumpets for the transmission of sound, captivated Pinchbeck, so much so that he studied the temple long and hard in preparation for building his own for display at the Washington Museum in Boston.[1]

The "wonderful and incomprehensible exhibition" was marketed in part as an occult mystery, with all the forbidden allure of Hermetic magic: "In a temple, representing those where the Egyptians delivered their oracles, is a small altar, and a crystal (as described by Dr. Dee, &c.) for consulting spirits." Pinchbeck was a knowledgeable magician—too knowledgeable for his soul's good, in the estimation of his neighbors. Of course, some of these same people, Pinchbeck noted ruefully, had feared that the Learned Pig was bewitched and should be put to death; many had seen a ghost that haunted the local churchyard; and still more believed in the devil and the pacts that magicians struck with evil spirits. For these folks, the specter of John Dee, the Elizabethan magus, might give the Acoustic Temple and the

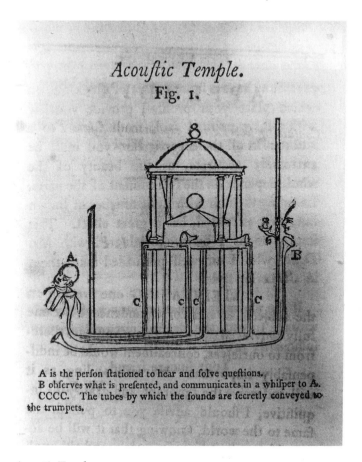

Acoustic Temple.
Fig. 1.

A is the perfon ftationed to hear and folve queftions.
B obferves what is prefented, and communicates in a whifper to A.
CCCC. The tubes by which the founds are fecretly conveyed to
the trumpets.

5. *Acoustic Temple*

A rational amusement designed to expose the imposture of the ancient oracles, the Acoustic Temple made the rounds of museums and stages in the early republic. Its chief technologies for mediating the voice were acoustic tubes and speaking trumpets. From William Frederick Pinchbeck, *The Expositor; Or, Many Mysteries Unravelled* (Boston: n.p., 1805), 81. Courtesy of the American Antiquarian Society.

Astonishing Invisible Lady who spoke out of it a magical and even dangerous aura, but Pinchbeck only scoffed at such gullibility. If anything, it was Dee the mathematician, not Dee the necromancer, who appealed to him. "Where superstition waves her bloody banners," this would-be Voltaire exhorted, "Philosophy and the arts must hide their heads."[2]

And that is how the Acoustic Temple was really marketed—as a performance that evoked the magical in order to dispel that very enchantment. Certainly Pinchbeck, who wrote two tracts on this and similar amusements, wanted people to garner that sort of lesson from the Acoustic Temple, the original as well as his facsimile. Anyone who witnessed this reproduced Egyptian oracle, he confidently asserted, would "easily conceive how the Pagan priests by making use of tubes deceived the people, and by thus imposing on their credulity, induced them to believe that these idols or oracles returned answers to their questions." As a spectacle that allowed the inquiring eye to correct the deceived ear, the illusion was designed "to open the eyes of those who still foster an absurd belief in *ghosts, witches, conjurations, demoniacs, &c.*" as well as to "enable the attentive observer to form a just idea of the artifices" that charlatans have used to impose on "the *credulous* and *superstitious,* in this and former ages." The Acoustic Temple beckoned natural philosophers and "amateurs of Science"—everyone dedicated to the advance of learning and invention—to a performance of the Enlightenment, a vanquishing of superstition and priestcraft. As one 1805 broadside proclaimed, "Attend, and never after give credit to the improbable tales of Witchcraft and Supernatural Agency." The amused questioner of this Egyptian oracle would come away satisfied that oracular voices were illusions and that the ingenious mechanisms of the Enlightenment exposed them as such.[3]

Pinchbeck's dream of progress centered on the enlightening power of illusionist exposure. His mission, he related after debunking the story of an apparition as just one more chimera, was to "convince the world that in order to support wisdom, and banish folly, whenever any uncommon sounds are heard, or any unnatural visions seen, it is indispensably necessary to search into the secret causes of such sounds and visions." In one of his pamphlets he had his imagined interlocutor testify to the conversionist effects of such "philosophical experiments":

> Your conceptions respecting the manner in which responses were delivered from the ancient oracles, has been my opinion ever since you favoured me with the principles of the Acoustick Temple. But your manner of exposing the deceptions of these designing men and heathen priests, (who misled not only the ignorant, but even the learned, the statesman, and the warrior) appears to be so reasonable and grounded on such evident demonstrations, that were I as superstitious as the worshippers of the Grand Lama, I should on reading such

a production, abjure my tenets and become a proselyte to principles founded on such a solid basis.[4]

His dream (and in fairness to Pinchbeck, it should be noted that this was not his word: he liked dreams about as much as he liked ghostly voices)—his dream of illusionist Enlightenment would be easy to dismiss as a sideshow, right along with the Acoustic Temple, if it were not finally so revealing of the delights, ambitions, and fantasies of the new natural philosophy.

With the cultural historian replacing the showman as operator, the Acoustic Temple can be made to speak anew. The historical wizardry of puzzling out the device's significance requires entering an intellectual maze of religion, politics, science, and technology—a labyrinth every bit as complicated as the hidden tubes that made the whole contrivance work. First, why an Acoustic *Temple*? Why would a display that reproduced pagan oracles, a millennium and a half after their passing, have cachet with the "numerous crowds" who came to see it? Why would the exposure of the oracles as priestly frauds still matter? Second, why an *Acoustic* Temple? What significance did these early modern auditory technologies—the speaking trumpets, acoustic tubes, and talking machines—have? As one Massachusetts writer explained in puffing this newfangled device, "I passed several days in reflecting on this impenetrable deception. I applied myself to the study of Acoustics, and perused all the writers on this wonderful Science, that I could procure, and soon had the inexpressible satisfaction of discovering what a second examination convinced me was correct, the principles and construction of the curiosity in question." What sort of knowledge would be gained about sound and voices by studying the newly extended science of acoustics so attentively? What were people trained to hear (and not hear), to discern (and not discern), to experience (and not experience)? How was the ear educated, entertained, enlightened?[5]

Rational amusements, such as the Acoustic Temple and ventriloquism, serve as performative distillations for exploring much wider Enlightenment frameworks of knowledge about sound, voices, and hearing. These theatrical ventures in practical acoustics, trading on the artifices of natural magic, exemplify the reeducation of the ear and the management of auditory illusions that the learned pursued. The story begins with the oracles, since from the end of the seventeenth century natural philosophers showed a peculiar penchant for unmasking the divination techniques of antiquity, whether Greek, Roman, or Egyptian. What the literati crafted through exposing the pagan oracles was a secular history freed from the incursive presence of supernatural voices, demonic and otherwise, as well as a republican politics of imposture that proved highly flexible in attacking religious tyrannies of all kinds. An expanding knowledge of acoustics, especially auditory technologies such as the speaking trumpet, proved instrumental in the formation of this new history, providing the learned with the mechanisms by which a distrust of disembodied voices could be manufactured. In this chapter the story closes (and it is only a provisional ending) by probing the condition of those "modern" souls who took this oracular silencing to heart and who then found the devocalized universe a disturbingly quiet place. The American artist Elihu Vedder, who both internalized and visualized God's silence, is taken as an exemplar. Vedder was among the casualties of modernity—a self frayed by the loss of a stable religious identity and the absence of a communicative deity.

Working the Oracle: A History and Politics of Imposture

Dreams, processions, vaporous caverns, animal sacrifices, spirits, speaking statues, talking trees, visions, miraculous water, shrines, cures, and prophecies—was it any wonder that the pagan oracles demanded notice, whether the offerings of devotees, the fearful denigrations of early Christian apologists, or, later, the scandalized outrage of the *philosophes?* At Dodona the devout listened for whisperings in a grove of oaks, sacred to Zeus, through which they hoped to discern divine answers on matters of healing, commerce, or love. In Book VI of Virgil's *Aeneid* the Sibyl of Cumae was pictured in an ecstatic frenzy of bodily quaking and prophetic inspiration—images that still very much haunted early modern ideas of what counted as religious enthusiasm. At Delphi, the Pythia, mounting a tripod, became possessed, spoke in altered tones, and embodied the veritable voice of Apollo. As the Stoic Lucan described the "madness and ecstasy" of the Delphic priestess, "She moans and utters loud, inarticulate cries. Then her wailing rises in the huge temple." After she receives and delivers the oracular pronouncement, "Apollo closes her throat and cuts short any further words. Oracles! Guardians of destinies! Secrets of the universe! Apollo, master of truth!"[6]

As bearers of such complex religious powers, the oracles entered the Christian imagination ambivalently. They were signs of demonic danger, to be sure, but they were also tests of the force of Christian redemption.

For the early church fathers—Origen, Eusebius, Jerome, Augustine, on down the line—the silencing of the oracles was a hallmark of the signal turning point in the new sacred history, the advent of Christ, the reversal of the devil's thralldom over humanity since the Fall. So, despite their dismissal as idolatrous shams, the oracles proved useful, even compelling, for Christian apologists. They were emblematic of history's fundamental hinge: their swinging closed was the sign of the new opening in God's time; their silencing became part of the very axis of redemption. This mapping of Christian history was long dear to Protestants and Catholics alike. As Jonathan Edwards observed in his *History of the Work of Redemption,*

> The famous heathen oracles in their temples where princes and others for many past ages had been wont to inquire and to receive answers with an audible voice from their gods, which were indeed answers from the devil, I say, those oracles were now silenced and struck dumb, and gave no more answers. And particularly the oracle at Delphos, which was the most famous heathen oracle in the whole world, which both Greeks and Romans used to consult, began to cease to give any answers even from the birth of Christ. . . . Thus did the kingdom of Christ prevail against the kingdom of Satan.

Well into the eighteenth century, the demonized oracles were revered for the shape they gave to Christian history, for the mapping of a universal narrative of redemptive time.[7]

Pagan divination proved useful too because some early Christian writers, building on prior Jewish appropriations, managed to make a few of the oracles augurs of their own eclipse. The Sibyls, for example, were creatively Christianized as gentile prophets of the Messiah, earlier texts interpolated and reinvented in order to strengthen the Christian cause against paganism. These recast Sibylline prophecies, with their hymns to Christ and revelations of Judgment, became widely enough accepted that Augustine numbered the Sibyls among those who belonged to the City of God, and eventually Michelangelo even enshrined them with the Hebrew prophets on the ceiling of the Sistine Chapel. These inspired prophetesses proved an enduringly rich source for Christian apocalypticism, nurturing centuries of eschatological commentary, from Lactantius to Joachim of Fiore. "I will speak the following with my whole person in ecstasy / For I do not know what I say, but God bids me utter each thing"—so was the heady opening to one Sibylline book. The prophetic images tumbled out with blazing urgency:

For all the stars of luminaries will fall from heaven
and no longer will well-winged birds fly on the air
nor will there be walking on earth, for all wild beasts will perish.
There will be no voices of men, or beasts, or birds.
The world, in disorder, will hear no useful sound.

The "wondrous words" of these prophecies still inspired some eighteenth-century exegetes, who continued to lay them alongside John's book of Revelation to help calculate the events of the millennium, the full circle of God's drama. One English Protestant commentary from 1713, for example, insisted that the Sibyls had actually predicted the Reformation and had offered detailed clues for discerning the millennial import of current political events.[8]

With their commanding history in antiquity and with their second life in the Christian tradition, the oracles presented a doubly tempting target for seventeenth- and eighteenth-century philosophers. First, with all the tales of supernatural signs and voices, these divination practices stood as the very embodiment of enthusiasm, superstition, and priestly artifice, a primeval fount of all that was still wrong with religion. And second, because of the hallowed place the oracles had come to hold in Christian renderings of sacred history, they were a prime location for testing new critical, historical methods, for trying the chronicles of demon possession and miraculous expulsion by the standards of natural history. To explain the oracles through mechanistic means and to rework the way they were remembered would assist the unfolding of the Enlightenment: at a minimum, it would perform the necessary work of exposing popular superstitions and magical beliefs; for the more radical, it would do even more—it would unhinge the Christian narrative of an overarching, redemptive history.

Those double aims made the investigation of the oracles part of the much larger Enlightenment endeavor of establishing "religion" as an abstracted object for historical and philosophical study. Seventeenth- and eighteenth-century theorists turned the question of the origins of religion into one of overriding importance and ended up offering a panoply of naturalistic answers for why people seemed so incurably "superstitious": the primacy of fear and the excess of hope in human experience, the apotheosis of dead heroes and kings (or Euhemerism), and the ignorance of natural forces that were consequently anthropomorphized or fetishized. The oracles were made to speak to most of these theories, but especially to one of the dearest of Enlightenment hypotheses: namely, that religion originated in and was sustained by the impostures of priests, who for political and economic gain concocted deceptions to stupefy the simple and the vulgar.

The "imposture thesis," as historian Frank Manuel has labeled it, posited two classes of people, priests and dupes, those in the know about these tricks and those who were hoodwinked by them. Guile was the dominant characteristic of priests, and credulity the chief attribute of lowly commoners. This anthropology had its corollary in "the twofold philosophy," which maintained that the religion of an initiated elite had always been clearly marked off from the vulgar beliefs of *hoi polloi*. Studying the oracles of antiquity helped establish a social and religious map of the philosopher's own world; the accrued knowledge was one way of inventing the divisions between learned and popular religion, between the enlightened and the rest of humanity—primitives, women, children, and the unlettered. Such propositions drew numerous scholars and provocateurs to the feet of the oracles in the age of Enlightenment—people ranging from Pierre Bayle and Bernard Fontenelle at the end of the seventeenth century to Eusèbe Salverte and Edward Daniel Clarke at the beginning of the nineteenth century.[9]

To take up the supposed charlatanry of the ancient seers, natural philosophers hardly had to create their blasts *ex nihilo*. The ambivalence within Christian apologetics provided an opening wedge. The early Christian attacks on the oracles worked from an inescapable supernaturalist framework in which the reality of evil spirits was assumed, but the attacks also contained the pervading scriptural rhetoric of idolatry in which the pagan forms were treated as hollow fabrications. The 1797 edition of the *Encyclopaedia Britannica*, for example, cited Theodoret's fifth-century *Ecclesiastical History*, a text frequently quoted by enlightened exposers. In that devout history the Alexandrian Bishop Theophilus is heralded as deliverer, but on terms quite serviceable for the *philosophes:*

He not only overthrew the idolatrous temples from their very foundations, but also disclosed the frauds of the priests to those whom they had deceived. These impostors had provided hollow statues, made of bronze and wood, with the back fitted against the wall, whence they secured an entrance into them. Having secreted themselves within the statues, they issued whatever commands they pleased, and the hearers, deceived by the fraud, obeyed them.

The literati dropped the Christian supernaturalism that ran through such pious histories—for Theodoret, these sham shrines were still "the temples of the demons." Or, to borrow the felicitous phrasing of literary theorist Kenneth Gross on the animus behind iconoclasm, the oracles remained for Christians "a peculiar composite of idol and demon," "a thing at once dead and uncannily alive." In the place of such doubleness, the *philosophes* dwelled entirely on the side of priestly cunning, on the fabrication of the sacred by those desirous of power.[10]

These traditional Christian perceptions of the chicanery of the oracles coalesced with Protestant fears of popish idolatry, and Reformation cleavages fueled interest in the purported wiles of pagan priests as Protestants routinely transferred the techniques of the "cousening oracles" over to their Catholic opponents. These Protestant presuppositions were so thoroughly absorbed in early skeptical writings that it is difficult to mark where the Protestant's polemic ends and the rationalist's begins. Reginald Scot, one of the great heralds of a naturalistic understanding of demonism and witchcraft at the end of the sixteenth century, simply worked back and forth between exposing the knavery of the ancient oracles and their latter-day analogues in the "the popish church." Two generations later Thomas Ady, who sought to extend Scot's views on witchcraft, made the same moves, dwelling by turns on the "deluding Impostures" of the priests of Apollo and "the secret Impostures of the Popish Religion." Similarly, in his inquiry into pagan religions, Edward Herbert borrowed images from the Protestant reformer Heinrich Bullinger according to which ancient priests were "wicked, vain, covetous wretches." The management of the oracles to control the people was a window on those priestly manipulations that continued to prevent the reign of pure religion—in Herbert's case, not Protestantism so much as his universal religion of deistic commonalities.[11]

Since the early deists hoped to transcend the religious warfare of Protestants and Catholics, to find common ground in a streamlined religion of nature, they hardly wanted to rely simply on Christian apologetics and Protestant polemics for their sources. A more appealing move was to turn to ancient satirists of the oracles and to revive skeptical observations on religion from classical materials.[12] No other ancient text was more often invoked to establish the nature of religious imposture than Lucian's second-century tale *Alexander; Or, The False Prophet,* which described how a slick conjurer managed to set up an oracular shrine with a freshly minted snake-god, Glycon. The charlatan's tricks included an ingeniously crafted puppet by which he delivered "Vocal Oracles" and passed off his own words as "the Voice of the God himself," a mechanical contrivance that Lucian painstakingly dissected. All of this worked for Alexander because of his ability to play on the "Terrours," "vain Hopes, and superfluous Desires" of "the sniveling and unthinking Mob," those "fat Heads" who allowed themselves to be fooled because of their wretched need to believe. Here were several of the literati's fonder propositions about bad faith dramatized in an appealing satire: the psychology of desperation and wishfulness, the economy of social bifurcation, and the politics of priestly theater.[13]

Freethinker Charles Blount, author of *The Oracles of Reason* (1693), summoned Lucian's satire to the aid of the deist movement. "This is the History of an Impostor," Blount announced at the opening of his translation, and from there he was off for a sardonic romp in the world of Alexander's "Legerdemains, Stratagems and Impostures." The point for Blount was to assume illusion, to give no credit to "meer Toys," to presume reason can provide a naturalistic explanation for oracular displays, even when such critical suspicion does not provide immediate penetration of the illusion. Lucian's tale likewise so captured the imagination of David Hume that he summarized it in his essay on miracles as an example of why testimonies about religious wonders were untrustworthy, so fraught as they inevitably were with the credulity of the vulgar. Since Lucian was one of those respected in the "mart of learning," not one of the "ignorant and stupid," Hume happily credited the reliability of Lucian's jaundiced tale of exposure, and thought it "much to be wished" that "every ALEXANDER" would meet "with a LUCIAN, ready to expose and detect his impostures." If deists and skeptics had their way, that is exactly what each new prophet (from George Fox, James Nayler, and Sabbatai Zevi to Ann Lee, Richard Brothers, Joanna Southcott, and Joseph Smith) would encounter—a stock image of the prophet as impostor. For the learned, Lucian's text was archetypal: one knew how to detect modern impostors by knowing this satire of Alexander of Abonuteichus and the oracle he had so brazenly set up.[14]

The modern brief against the oracles was in large part a pastiche of repositioned classical, patristic, and Protestant materials, but the argument began to take on its own original form with historical reevaluations of the Sibylline prophecies. Just as seventeenth-century scholarship redated the writings of Hermes Trismegistus and announced their primeval Egyptian pretenses a fraud, so too did the learned go after the primordial attributions of the Sibylline revelations—their supposed anticipations of Jesus and their confirmations of apocalyptic conflagration. It was the "common Opinion of the Modern Criticks," one defender lamented in 1715, that "the *Sibylline* Oracles, quoted by the most primitive Christians, were . . . forged by some among themselves, a little before the middle of the Second Century; and from such a forged Copy were alledg'd by those Primitive Writers for their Religion." That argument was especially associated with the seventeenth-century Protestant scholar David Blondel, though it quickly became common intellectual property among critics. Blondel and his allies thought that they were doing Christianity a service by cleansing it of these Sibylline counterfeits: that such fraudulent texts had for too long encouraged "the extravagant Imagination of the *Millenaries*," that acceptance of their inspiration validated the enthusiasm of disorderly women, and that, at bottom, truth could not be served by forgery. Disposing of the Sibyls was seen as a judicious historical correction, but this knowledge also served as another way of delegitimating Christian sectaries.[15]

The historical critique proved potent. By the end of the eighteenth century, attempts to vindicate the Sibylline prophecies had collapsed into silence. As the 1797 edition of the *Encyclopaedia Britannica* summarized the new state of knowledge, the Sibylline verses "are universally reckoned spurious; and it is evident that they were composed by some of the followers of Christianity, who wished to convince the heathens of their error, by assisting the cause of truth with the arms of pious artifice." This sort of critical scholarship had a corrosive effect on Christian historical narratives: the early church was pictured as afloat in fabricated apocalypses, fake epistles, and counterfeit oracles, many of which the church fathers had knowingly embraced. That kind of historical detection meshed well with wider Enlightenment perceptions of religious imposture: things passed off as truths were self-serving lies that required unmasking. In all, it was an astonishingly effective silencing of these oracular texts—ones that had for centuries stimulated the Christian imagination. Few bothered to read these Sibylline prophecies with devotional seriousness after the new scholarship removed them from the realm of religious vision and firmly consigned them to the category of political imposture.[16]

The attack soon widened well beyond the Sibyls to take on all the oracles. The most celebrated and enduring work in this bombardment was Bernardle Le Bovier de Fontenelle's *History of the Oracles, and the Cheats of the Pagan Priests*, first published in French in 1686, then translated into English in 1688, and appearing frequently thereafter over the next century and a half. Fontenelle's fashionable work was based on the sprawling scholarship of a Dutch Anabaptist physician of Socinian sympathies, Antonius van Dale, whose *De oraculis* (1683) provided the bedrock upon which Fontenelle played. Together van Dale and Fontenelle showed their allegiance to the republic of letters, to the overarching philosophical community committed to the new learning and to illumining superstition. As impresario of that cosmopolitan exchange, savant Pierre Bayle sensed the important place of this latest turn in the world of erudition, opening the very first issue of his journal *Nouvelles de la république des lettres* with a careful summary of van Dale's treatise on the oracles. The influence of the new history on the *philosophes* proved decisive—so much so that Voltaire could remark, in the entry on the oracles in his *Philosophical Dictionary*, that "there is no man of education and respectability who now calls it in question."[17]

Among the grander effects of the new learning was to undermine the Christian view of history that took the demise of the oracles as the greatest victory that "the Christian Religion obtain'd over the Heathen," "an Event so remarkable, that it was almost one continu'd Miracle, during the first Ages of the Church." In place of this long-hallowed conviction that "the Silence of Oracles" resulted from "the sole Power of our Saviour's Divinity," Fontenelle and van Dale advanced a series of secular explanations for their cessation.[18] Patristic accounts of oracles struck dumb by the sign of the Cross, the prayers (or mere presence) of Christians, the invocation of Christ's name, and the reading of the gospels were replaced by legal, political, and cultural explanations (for example, the effects of the repressive edicts of Christian emperors and the discrediting powers of pagan philosophers). For the universal Christian chronology that saw the advent of Christ as the decisive watershed for precipitating the decline of the oracles, a more convoluted narrative was substituted in which some oracles fell into ruin long before the Incarnation and many others flourished long after the Savior's death. "There is not the least difference," Fontenelle concluded, between those oracles "that were delivered after the Birth of *Jesus,* and those that were pronounced before it." In a word, Christ was no longer the hub of the new story—a natural history full of priestly intrigue and political contingency, now (de)centered on "the Contrivances and Deceits of Men."[19]

The old sacred history was intended to give shape not only to the past, but also to the present, in its ongoing relevance for Christian missions and colonial encounters. The revised history challenged an underlying assumption in this story of oracular cessation—namely, that Christ was still very much replaying this original victory, continuing to demonstrate his glory through the triumphant displacement of heathen idols. One Jesuit missionary in the East Indies, in a reply to Fontenelle from the field, wrote to attest that Christians need not worry: the ancient wonder of divine suppression was still being performed in his confrontations with indigenous oracles. The demons in the heathen idols were falling silent in the face of the same ancient signs—namely, the proclamation of the gospel and the invocation of Christ's name. This was a significant colonial buttress with global relevance: one early chronicler of the Spanish extirpation of indigenous religious practices in Peru noted, for example, the "astonishment among the Indians" at the "silence of their oracles," that the arrival of the Spanish had "left their oracles without the power of speech." Not that the new critical history was any kinder to "heathen" practices—unless there was some gain in being pitied as a dupe rather than attacked as an idolater. One defender of Fontenelle's history, in direct contrast to the Jesuit's report, surveyed the religions of China and the Indies to show the relevance of the revisionist analysis, the global prevalence of imposture and credulity.[20]

Beyond historical revision of the grandest sort, the most immediate aim of Fontenelle's work was to circumscribe the power of demons—in antiquity and his own day. This was his leading proposition: "I advance boldly to prove that *Oracles,* of what nature soever, were not deliver'd by *Daemons.*" In dismissing demons as the source of the oracular voices, Fontenelle shifted responsibility entirely to the artifices of priests—that is, to human design, not supernatural powers. It was a marked revision. How much so was evident in the frontispiece to Jesuit Jean Baltus' reply to Fontenelle: there the demons still proceeded into and out of the mouths of pagan prophetesses, priests, and statues. The image strongly marked the mouth as the orifice of demonic ingress and suggested the dangerous vocality of possession; it is the trampling female character, representing the church, who bears the silencing power of the Cross. For Fontenelle, by contrast, the issue was not the insurgent vocality of the divine world, but the priestly manipulation of sounds, noises, voices, blessings, and words.[21]

The debate about the fraud of pagan oracles readily slipped into a conflict over the authority of scripture—that is, to recall the Pauline construction, "God's oracles." Though Fontenelle, a delicate negotiator of the church's ire, was highly diplomatic on this point, others were far less cautious in extending the critique of oracular inspiration to the biblical testimony. In *The Oracles of Reason*, Charles Blount pushed the contest along, making no bones about his low opinion of both pagan divination and scripture in comparison to reason. On critical examination, the oracles of God began to sound a lot like their pagan counterparts. Blount mocked the account of Eve and the serpent, for example, in which the latter is "indued with the faculty of speaking like the Trees in *Dodona's* Grove"; he had only contempt for those who say that "under the shape of this Serpent was hid the Devil, or an Evil Spirit, who using the Mouth and Organs of this Animal, spoke to the Woman as it were with an human voice." Reason, the "sovereign Rule and Touchstone," made such scriptural accounts as suspect as pagan divinations and pointed to the all sufficiency of natural religion. The oracles proved a peculiarly powerful tool for deists—one they used to shift the locus of authority from inspired words (necessarily artificial) to nature, reason, and mathematics (exquisitely pure).[22]

Charles Blount's juggling of the oracles became paradigmatic for later deists—a means of taking away the numinous power of revealed religion and conferring that aura upon reason itself. Ethan Allen, in offering an American compendium of Enlightenment critiques of superstition in 1784, marveled at people's belief in dreams, divinations, and demons as well as the excessive Christian attachment to the oracular words of the Bible. What title did he choose to give his learned manifesto? *Reason the Only Oracle of Man*. The deist lecturer John Stewart, who included the new American republic in his cosmopolitan itinerancy, also invoked the "true Oracle" of "natural Reason" against the "metaphysical phantasms" of the devout, "those supernatural, or rather unnatural oracles of inspired intercourse." At the outset of his *Opus Maximum*, Stewart even rendered his foil tangible by picturing a priest sneaking into the base of a statue and then setting that oracular contrivance at the farthest remove from the light of reason and the attainment of manly autonomy. Thomas Jefferson embraced the same devices. When, at God's prompting, a Methodist preacher wrote him an ardent, eleven-page letter seeking his conversion, Jefferson replied calmly that reason was "the umpire of truth," the arbiter that stood above the preacher's "special communication" from heaven: "It is the only oracle which god has given us to determine between what really comes from him, and the phantasms of a disordered or deluded imagination." Reason alone was mystified, a solitary oracle of the sovereign mind.[23]

What especially troubled Allen, Jefferson, and other deists was religious enthusiasm, and that was one of the most common subtexts in the learned invocation of the ancient oracles. "All our notions of the immediate inter-

J. A. Seidel sculp.

position of divine illuminations, inspiration or infusion of ideas or revelations, into our minds, is mere enthusiasm and deception," Allen concluded and went on to lift up the Shakers as an indigenous exemplar of "ghostly" communications run riot. The enlightened sought a handle on latter-day enthusiasts, all those diverse bearers of immediate inspiration, through conjuring up those ancient female ecstatics, the Sibyls and the Pythia. When Anthony Ashley Cooper, the Third Earl of Shaftesbury, looked for an analogy by which to make sense of the "prophetick Extasys" of the French Prophets in his *Letter Concerning Enthusiasm,* he turned to those pagan priestesses. The outcries of one "Vision-struck" enthusiast "brought into my mind," he noted, "the Latin Poet's Description of the *Sibyl,* whose Agonys were so perfectly like these." A bitter critic of the revivals in the colonies in the 1740s easily made the same comparison: the new evangelicals, with all their "Contorsions of the Body and vocal Energy," "swell and shake like *Virgil's* enthusiastick Sibyl." The literati, in calling to mind these pagan ecstasies, hoped to expose the "delusive Voices" of latter-day enthusiasts, those of overwrought women especially.[24]

Thinking with the oracles helped the learned to imagine the limits of revelation and enthusiasm, but such habits of mind were of still greater assistance in tightening the reins on priestcraft. "The Frauds of Priests," even more than "the Dreams and Visions of Enthusiasts," came to define the ancient oracles. To display all the tools by which superstitious terrors were excited—the subterranean vaults, the hidden confederates, the acoustic devices, the smoke and mirrors, the benumbing vapors, the faked thunder—was an overriding ambition for van Dale, Fontenelle, and those who followed them. "What Frauds may be acted with Glasses, Speaking Trumpets, Ventriloquies, Echoes, Phospherus, Magick Lanthorns, &c.?" John Trenchard asked in his *Natural History of Superstition* (1709). Knowing these technologies of power and deception—the instruments of natural magic as well as their illusionist offspring in the experimental philoso-

6. Christianity's Triumph over the Pagan Oracles

The long-standing Christian history of the oracles viewed them as inspired by demons that Christ then vanquished. Note how the demons come out of the mouths of the pagan prophets and statues, and how it is the light of the Cross that silences them. From Jean Baltus, *Réponse à l'histoire des oracles, de Mr. de Fontenelle, de l'Académie Françoise* (Strasbourg, 1707; Strasbourg: Doulssecker, 1709), frontispiece. Courtesy of the Firestone Library, Princeton University.

phy—became one means for creating a natural history of religion, for imagining how clerics had managed to exploit so thoroughly the credulities of the people.[25]

Of all priestly treacheries, the manipulation of words, blessings, and voices held special alarm—that is, how priests took "odd, unintelligible, and ill-favoured Words" and imbued them with terror and mystery. "Men are never weary of being deluded with Sounds," Trenchard and collaborator Thomas Gordon concluded in the *Independent Whig*, "and a pious Word, artfully prostituted, and devoutly pronounced, will at any Time lure them into the grossest Impostures." The republican lesson about priestcraft demanded a special vigilance against the knavish abuses of the ear, the sacerdotal exploitation of listeners through magical prayers, liturgical blessings, enthusiastic harangues, and clanging bells. For this admonition about the peculiar acoustics of clerical imposture and the auditory manipulation of popular credulity, the speaking trees of Dodona made a fine didactic example: "The oracles were delivered by the priests, who, by artfully concealing themselves behind the oaks, gave occasion to the superstitious multitude to believe that the trees were endowed with the power of prophecy." In this republican philosophy of language, pious words had to be cheapened, the artificiality of their signification exposed, in order to subdue the abusive powers of priests.[26]

For Whig writers like Trenchard and Gordon, the political implications of such exposures for ecclesiastical power were clear, and others saw the same handwriting on the wall. From knowledge of "the vile ambiguity and chicane of the oracles," a Scottish writer concluded in 1755, "we receive the most sensible conviction that there can be nothing more detestable than such a *religious* establishment." The attack on pagan priestcraft easily flowed into anticlerical suspicions of ministerial hirelings closer at hand, as well as the corrupting alliances of church and state. Tom Paine wrote orac-

7. The Priestcraft of the Oracles

Oracular scenes that showed how priests exploited the mechanical artifices of natural magic took on great polemical importance for the literati of the early Enlightenment. In this multilevel scene of intrigue, murder, and spurious revelation, speaking trumpets are among the devices used to disorient the devotee, hurling voices and ominous sounds at him. From Antonius van Dale, *De oraculis veterum ethnicorum dissertationes duae* (Amsterdam, 1683; Amsterdam: Boom, 1700), plate VI. Courtesy of the Firestone Library, Princeton University.

ular manipulation into his philosophy of history in the *Rights of Man* (1791–1792): the first sort of government inimical to natural rights was that founded on "superstition," "a government of priestcraft." "When a set of artful men pretended, through the medium of oracles, to hold intercourse with the Deity, as familiarly as they now march up the back-stairs in European courts," Paine blasted, "the world was completely under the government of superstition." The American deist Joel Barlow agreed on the terrible dangers posed in "governing men by oracles," a phrase that condensed the religious ills not only of antiquity but of any established church: the loss of liberty, "vigorous manhood," rational inquisitiveness, tolerance, and compassion. As long as power was consolidated under such religious auspices, as long as a priest was able to pass off his voice as the voice of God, governments felt "no necessity to establish any mode for consulting the people." The revised history of the priestcraft of the oracles proved quite serviceable within a republican politics ever on guard against civil and ecclesiastical tyranny.[27]

Much of this political knowledge easily crossed into Christian versions of republicanism, but the marks of the Enlightenment were still apparent as the oracles now revealed far less about God's grand history of redemption than about the Whiggish ascent of religious and civil liberty. The Christian republican Elias Smith, for example, formulated his own history of oracular decline in 1809: people, when "ignorant of their rights, and liberty," consulted the oracles and were "duped by priests"; only with the proclamation of "genuine *Liberty, civil* and *religious*" (which Smith equated with the joined purity of the primitive gospel and republican government), did the oracles lose their credit. Whether in the deist Paine or the evangelical Smith, the unmasked oracles were a token of republican freedoms; their exposure augured a society rid of the corrupting powers of religious establishments and the dark conspiracies used to maintain those tyrannies.

8. *Histoire des Oracles*

In a paradigmatic performance of the Enlightenment, the distanced observer is shown the artifice of the revealed words of an ancient oracle. The lamp of a confederate, shining into the cut-away base of the statue, inadvertently exposes the machinery behind the speaking statue, the acoustic tube that mediates the voice of a priest. From Bernard Le Bovier de Fontenelle, *Oeuvres diverses,* 3 vols. (The Hague: Neaulme, 1728–1729), vol. 1, opposite p. 240. Courtesy of the Princeton University Library, Rare Books and Special Collections.

The history of the oracles had been refracted through a republican lens, and it was no longer a story about God's sovereignty—now it was about the people's. It had become, in other words, another modern narrative of emancipation..[28]

The Acoustic Temple, that "Philosophical Machine lately arrived from France," was Fontenelle's quarrel with the oracles turned into a republican show. Its successful display was indicative of the spread of a critical, diverting engagement with the natural history of demonology, enthusiasm, and priestcraft. That diffusion very much continued throughout the first half of the nineteenth century, as numerous authors further disseminated knowledge of the natural magic of pagan priests. In *Des Sciences occultes* (1829), savant Eusèbe Salverte offered this learning in its radical form, sweeping Christianity into his popular exposé of ancient prodigies—a work that managed nonetheless to be toned down enough in translation to go through three American editions with Harper and Brothers between 1847 and 1862. With his *Letters on Natural Magic*, the Scottish inquirer David Brewster achieved his greatest literary success, pumping out nineteen editions (including eight American ones) between 1832 and 1855. A Presbyterian of avowed orthodoxy and an undoubted scion of the Enlightenment, Brewster had strong appeal in the American marketplace, and his technological expositions of the arts of mystification, especially the spectral and acoustic illusions manufactured by pagan priests, became standards. In his turn, P. T. Barnum, anti-Calvinist debunker of Congregationalist tyrannies, made the oracles a main exhibit of supernatural humbug in his own moralizing history of impostures.[29]

Barnum's appropriation of this history points again to the transit of the oracles into an amusement, and it is worth returning to that diversion. The account of Cambridge antiquarian Edward Daniel Clarke in his *Travels in Various Countries of Europe, Asia and Africa* (1811–1823) is especially suggestive on this performative transformation of knowledge. His travelogues, at once genteel, Protestant, and enlightened, gained an audience on both sides of the Atlantic; within his rambles, the revised history of the oracles found its culmination as a leisured touring of antiquities.[30] Whereas Fontenelle and van Dale had to rely on reinterpreting classical authorities, Clarke was able to appeal to the archaeological record as the spread of colonial empires multiplied the possibilities for both scholarly travel and amateur plunder. A contemporary of Lord Elgin, Clarke was himself a prominent collector of marble statuary.

At Telmessus, Clarke visited an "Oracular Cave" where he thought he uncovered a concealed recess designed as the hiding place for a soothsayer, "so that when persons entered the vault to consult the oracle, a voice, apparently supernatural, might answer where no person was visible." At another site, his pleasure was even greater when the expedition stumbled upon "one of the most curious *tell-tale* remains yet discovered among the vestiges of Pagan priestcraft: it was nothing less than one of the *Oracular Shrines of Argos* alluded to by *Pausanias,* laid open to inspection, like the toy a child has broken in order that he may see the contrivance whereby it was made to speak." The analogy was evocative: The superstitions of the vulgar came to seem ever more infantile to the learned, but who in this case were the children who would turn this "curious relique" into a mechanical toy split open for their own amusement?[31]

The scene that followed remade the learned travelers into children at play. Having sighted "a secret subterraneous passage" underneath "the *fictile* superstructure" of the altar, Clarke imagined a priest creeping along this tunnel, hiding behind "some colossal statue," and impersonating the voice of the gods before prostrate votaries. Then the fantasies of Enlightenment knowledge turned into performance, into playacting: "We amused ourselves for a few minutes by endeavouring to mimic the sort of solemn farce acted upon these occasions: and as we delivered a mock oracle, *ore rotundo,* from the cavernous throne of the altar, a reverberation, caused by the sides of the rock, afforded a tolerable specimen of the '*will of the Gods,*' as it was formerly made known to the credulous votaries of this now-forgotten shrine." The Enlightenment's script predetermined the lesson that Clarke drew from this scene of archaeological discovery and mimetic play. "Surely it will never again become a question among learned men," he (fore)closed the interpretation of this shrine, "whether the answers in them were given by the inspiration of evil spirits, or whether they proceeded from the imposture of priests." Clarke's "modern curiosity" amid these Grecian ruins was revealing mostly for what it could not imagine or hear. Combining Anglican suspicion with learned exhibition, Clarke staged a performance that enacted the vacancy of the oracular, a re-creation that revealed the emptiness of the enthusiast's inspiration. For Clarke, the Enlightenment knowledge of the oracles was experienced as a fantastic delight in the hollowness of the signs.[32]

It is not hard to see why this late seventeenth-century knowledge of pagan priestcraft remained so alluring a century and half later, why indeed the works of those brokering these ideas—such as Clarke, Brewster, and Salverte—proved appealing in the antebellum United States. In a culture captivated by the instabilities of social identity, the impostures of con men, and the sophistic dangers of demagoguery, the oracles offered an inventory of charlatanry, a catalogue of theatrical deceptions, a guidebook to the stratagems of designing men, whether priests, politicians, merchants, or prophets. The oracles taught the need for suspicion, for "scrutinizing observation," in a world filled with "men who trade in the credulity of their fellow-creatures," those who out of their own self-interest manipulated the hopes and fears of the people. Likewise, in a culture suffused with both republicanism and Protestantism and marked by incessant consternation over Catholics, Masons, and (by the 1830s) Mormons, the oracles provided a primer on the dangers of priestcraft—on subterranean passageways, contrived ceremonies, secret-laden temples, and money-mongering religious institutions, on all the devices that kept the credulous in thrall. Moreover, in a culture swept by prophets, clairvoyants, trance-speakers, and evangelists, the not-so-new learning on the oracles provided a space of disengagement from all those voices, a habit of suspicion, a mechanical mode of explanation, a naturalistic means of tuning out the proliferating delusion of inspired voices. In a very noisy religious world, it was one way of not listening, a form of soundproofing.[33]

But this knowledge of the oracles was always unstable, always beckoning as much as forbidding. The prerogatives of priestcraft, the mastery of natural magic, and the theater of the temple were terribly alluring—especially on masculine terms. What were the results of oracular manipulation but power, wealth, and knowledge? Salverte and Brewster credited the ancient priests with a storehouse of scientific learning, viewing them as an esteemed intellectual elite who guarded their temple secrets and obtained "unbounded influence" through technological control. Those superior men who had this insider knowledge had autonomy; those capable of this instrumental inventiveness, however abused, had dominion. The rest were dupes—the weak, the servile, the ignorant, the dependent, the female. The "initiated," Salverte related enviously, "had all the hidden treasures of science laid open to them." It was hard to dream about all the machinery of priestcraft without yearning to become a master of such technologies, without imagining a transfer of power from ancient magician to modern philosopher, scientist, and entrepreneur. Certainly, William Frederick

Pinchbeck knew these desires intimately as he built his own Acoustic Temple for display in Boston and dwelled on his mastery of sound.[34]

By the 1860s and 1870s, "to work the oracle" was a proverbial expression for behind-the-scenes maneuvering, for pulling strings with the aim of self-advancement. The supposed mechanisms for producing religious power had, in other words, become a reverie for the strategies of the wide-awake go-getter in the modern marketplace. With their *daemons* quieted, their place in the history of redemption dissolved, and their politics exposed, the oracles were ready to lend an aura of ingenuity to the techniques of science and commerce. That the most prominent Oracle in contemporary culture is a giant of the computer industry suggests how the history set in motion in the early Enlightenment still resounds. Working the oracle as an engine for e-business: now, *that* is one fine piece of modern magic, as worthy of the Astonishing Invisible Lady as it is of the invisible hand.

Acoustics and the Mechanization of the Oracular Voice: Animated Statues, Speaking Trumpets, and Invisible Ladies

"The nature of sounds," Francis Bacon observed in his *Sylva Sylvarum; Or, A Natural History* (1627), has in some measure been explored, "as far as concerneth music. But the nature of sounds in general hath been superficially observed. It is one of the subtilest pieces of nature." Bacon proceeded to work his way through dozens of experiments that could be conducted on sound—on the harmony, production, amplification, dampening, motion, duration, medium, imitation, and reflection of sounds. Though Bacon exaggerated the ancients' inattentiveness to these questions, he nonetheless stood at the front edge of a wave of experimental philosophers who strove to subject "one of the most hidden portions of nature" to "exact inquisition." Sound, "incorporeal and immmateriate," would be made intelligible, controllable, and mechanical. Two centuries later the first edition of the *Encyclopaedia Americana* (1829–1833) ratified the conspicuous success of that particular Baconian "inquisition of nature": "The science of acoustics, like other physical sciences, has been in a constant state of advancement since the revival of learning."[35]

As a province of experimental learning and as an aspect of physics distinguishable from music theory, acoustics, or the science of sound, was virtually invented in the seventeenth century. Bacon's inquiries into the acoustic art were most fruitfully followed up by the French monk and natural philosopher Marin Mersenne, who, by the 1630s, had explored a wide range of acoustic problems and had broadly disseminated his demonstrations. By the 1680s and 1690s, the new science had been largely demarcated through a series of reports and experiments at the Royal Society in London and the Académie des Sciences in Paris. In 1701 the French natural philosopher Joseph Saveur belatedly arrogated to himself responsibility for naming the field as a distinct domain of knowledge—"a science superior to music that I have called *acoustics* and that takes for its object sound in general." The dominant theoretical and experimental questions in this enlarged enterprise included establishing the velocity of sound, determining the effects of different media (such as air, water, or a vacuum) on the propagation of sound, explaining echoes, mathematizing the phenomena of vibrations (especially in strings), debating whether sound is diffused in waves or rays, discerning the range of frequencies that the human ear is capable of hearing, fully anatomizing the ear and the voice, and continuing the mathematical study of musical harmony. Even this very partial list suggests the multilayered quality of the early modern inquiry into the nature of sound.[36]

Such questions held the attention of a galaxy of seventeenth-century natural philosophers—Galileo, Mersenne, Huygens, Newton, Hooke, and Boyle, among numerous others who joined this swelling enterprise. Most Enlightenment savants, from Fontenelle to Franklin, continued to follow developments in acoustics with supportive interest, even when not directly absorbed in its experiments, and many, such as Diderot and d'Alembert, offered full-scale treatments of sound and music. As the Newtonian theorist Matthew Young concluded in 1784, "The phaenomena of sound are so interesting and amusing, and, at the same time, so surprising, that we cannot wonder they have been found amongst the principal objects that have engaged the attention of philosophers." In all this attentiveness, the investigators' underlying dream, as Marin Mersenne had cast it early on, was to become masters of sound in the same way the "masters of optics," through invention and experiment, were rendering light comprehensible and were extending the empire of the eye.[37]

In addition to pursuing a physics and a physiology of sound, acoustics was a technological field, an applied discipline. Among the principal aims of inquiry was the invention and perfection of acoustic instruments to rival those so esteemed in optics—mechanisms that would measure sound, or that, through augmenting it, would make the inaudible audible. One of the simplest of these implements was the ear-trumpet, or, more grandly, the otacousticon, a conical device for the hard-of-hearing that Bacon had already noted as a sort of "ear-spectacle" and that garnered renewed attention from the Royal Society in the late 1660s. Even such an ordinary apparatus might inspire utopian caprice: "There may be a Possibility," Robert Hooke daydreamed, "that by Otocousticons many Sounds very far distant (I had almost said as far off as some Planets) may be made sensible." Two of Hooke's other technological ambitions had similar long-term resonance. One was to devise a machine, using teeth on revolving brass wheels, to reproduce *"Musical and other Sounds,"* including "the sound of the Voice in speaking," and the other was an instrument akin to the stethoscope: "There may also be a Possibility of discovering the Internal Motions and Actions of Bodies by the sound they make, . . . that one may discover the Works perform'd in the several Offices and Shops of a Man's Body, and thereby discover what Instrument or Engine is out of order." Hooke's "phantastick" conjectures imagined for hearing what the telescope and the microscope had attained for seeing: the dramatic extension of human perception.[38]

The grandest dream was expanding the reach of communications. Through his collection of experiments in *Sylva Sylvarum,* Bacon pushed a hopeful agenda for extending the transmission of voices: "It would be tried, how, and with what proportion of disadvantage, the voice will be carried in an horn, which is a line arched; or in a trumpet, which is a line retorted; or in some pipe that were sinuous." Into the early nineteenth century the main technologies for such enhanced voices remained speaking trumpets, sounding boards, and acoustic tubes, but these limitations were only a goad to would-be inventors, ever more electrified by the Baconian prospect: "The enthusiast in the impressiveness of sounds," an American amateur in acoustics declared in 1839, "might wish for a channel for their instant conveyance over the earth, that he too, by one general force, might move men's minds and hearts. The dreams of the ardent sometimes foretoken realities."[39]

So far, so good. After all, these are the sorts of trajectories, discoveries, inventions, and ambitions that have long been acclaimed by insider histories of acoustics, the modern advancement of scientific learning that culminated in the great technological achievements of the second half of the nineteenth century and only redounded in the twentieth. Two dominant emphases are discernible in this paradigmatic modern story of progress. One is internal to the history of science: how natural philosophers attained increasing exactitude in their mathematic understandings of the mechanics of sound—for example, reliably measuring its velocity and its propagation in different media. The other is pragmatic: how the Baconian model of inductive experimentation led slowly but surely to technological innovation, to useful instruments for measuring or amplifying sound. Both emphases have warrant, but to give the story over to such modern teleologies leaves at least one critical piece out of the puzzle: the long shadow that Renaissance occultism and natural magic cast over natural philosophy. Historians of science from Frances Yates and Paolo Rossi to Thomas Hankins, Robert Silverman, and Penelope Gouk have explored these early modern borderlands, and, within that historiography, it has become increasingly clear how critical the pursuits of natural magic were to the emergence of modern acoustic technologies.[40]

Bacon's research program in *Sylva Sylvarum,* indebted at various points to Giambattista Della Porta's *Magiae naturalis* (1558), is indicative of the interplay between such magical traditions and the acoustic art. For example, in studying the "similitude" between natural sounds (such as running water or snarling dogs) and human articulations, the endpoint of such knowledge for Bacon was the possibility of making, whether "for curiosity or strangeness' sake," a "puppet or other dead body . . . pronounce a word." To animate the inanimate, to make a puppet or statue speak, traded heavily on Hermetic ambitions, even as Bacon kept that aspiration within the safer confines of the artifices of natural magic. At another point, in a passage anticipating the ventriloquist experiments of the next century, Bacon wondered about those who "could counterfeit the distance of voices . . . in such sort, as when they stand fast by you, you would think the speech came from afar off, in a fearful manner." He authorized further inquiry into this vocal artifice in order to understand the necromantic impostures of those who simulate the voices of ghosts and spirits. Also, in his imagined sound-houses in the *New-Atlantis,* part of the experimental show was a series of vocal illusions and imitations. Such artifices, Bacon assured, were mastered for didactic purposes: namely, for disciplining the "deceits of the senses" and for improving the reliability of observation.[41]

Interest in the illusionist effects of natural magic long remained a common thread in acoustic study. Take, for example, the *Encyclopaedia Britannica* of 1797, which in both Edinburgh and Philadelphia renditions concluded its lengthy summation of acoustics with a sampling of *"Entertaining Experiments and Contrivances."* These included detailed directions on how to make a "Conversive Statue," an "Oracular Head," and "Communicative Busts," all illusions created through the application of what natural philosophy had learned from natural magic. "The practice of Acoustics," the *Edinburgh Encyclopedia* seemed to explain tamely in 1832, "is confined to instruments for the production of sound;—for the transmission of sound to greater distances;—for concentrating sound after its transmission;—and for measuring the relations of sounds." Then, though, the entry devoted two out of nine subsections to explaining ventriloquism and "the Invisible Girl," another name for the illusions of the Acoustic Temple. Two more subsections were devoted to speaking trumpets and acoustic tubes, both of which Pinchbeck had used in constructing his mock oracle. Historians Thomas Hankins and Robert Silverman have effectively assessed the significance of such magical devices in the formation of acoustic instrumentation, the complex interweavings of natural magic and experimental demonstrations. But how did these contrivances—oracular heads, speaking statues, and invisible ladies—influence modern imaginings of religion? Since, after all, these exhibitions traded on the mysteries of the oracles, it is important to ask how these technologies affected the way natural philosophers fantasized about those who claimed to hear revelatory or demonic voices.[42]

Most of the inquiry into acoustics was theologically benign, readily assuming consonance between Christian cosmology and the new experimental philosophy. Leading seventeenth-century thinkers—from Mersenne to Newton—still thought of the universe in terms tuned to a Pythagorean music of the spheres, believing that the study of sound would yield an underlying divine symmetry, a celestial mathematics of harmony demonstrative of God's cosmic order.[43] Mersenne, in his experiments on sound's velocity and propagation over vast distances, even suggested that such study afforded insight into how the angel's trumpet blast on the Day of Judgment would reverberate throughout the earth. The seventeenth-century Jesuit Athanasius Kircher found a more immediate use for one of his newly minted acoustic devices, employing amplifying trumpets to call people to devotions at a shrine from several miles away. One of Bacon's chief examples for the study of room acoustics was determining the best placement of pulpits for projecting the preacher's voice, and the same concern was evident in churchman Narcissus Marsh's formative essay on acoustics in 1684. Early modern acoustic experiments were regularly yoked to pious pur-

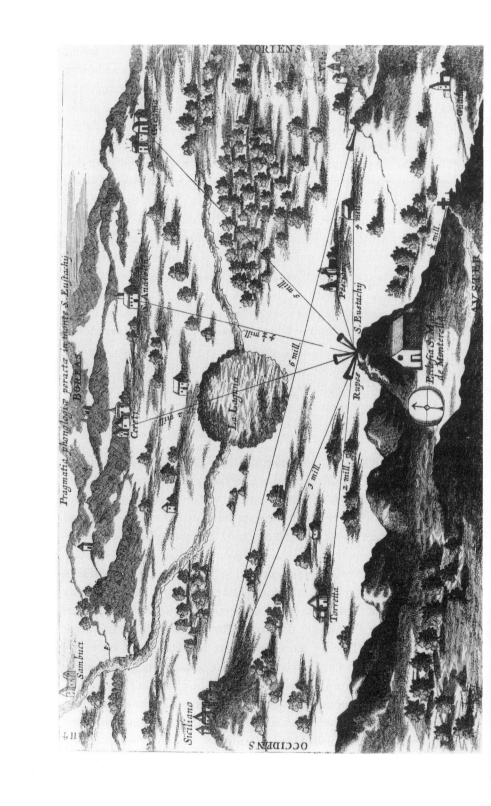

poses; indeed, they often found their very inspiration in Christian devotion and eschatology.[44]

For all this harmony between Christianity and the flourishing inquiry into acoustics, the religious issues soon proved more complicated, especially in the overlapping domains of natural magic, auditory technologies, and Enlightenment entertainment. The recurring desire to invent a speaking statue revealed those intricacies most clearly. In the cosmology of magi such as Heinrich Cornelius Agrippa and John Dee, the dream of creating an oracular statue was embedded in an enchanted world in which such auditory marvels were intertwined with astrology, angel magic, kabbalah, numerology, crystal-gazing, healing, and alchemy. In one of the most alluring passages in the writings ascribed to Hermes Trismegistus, so crucial to the Renaissance revival of magic, the teacher heralds the gnostic power of the initiated to realize a genuinely oracular statue, "statues living and conscious, filled with the breath of life, and doing many mighty works; statues which have foreknowledge, and predict future events by the drawing of lots, and by prophetic inspiration, and by dreams, and in many other ways."[45] Behind the mechanical arts of natural magic pulsed the forbidden desire of statues that were animated with real spiritual presences.

These Hermetic aspirations were given powerful expression in one of the great works of Renaissance magic, Heinrich Cornelius Agrippa's *De occulta philosophia libri tres* (1533), which was published in translation in London in 1651:

> No man is ignorant that supercelestiall Angels or spirits may be gained by us through good works, a pure minde, secret prayers, devout humiliation, and the like. . . . Let no man therefore doubt that in like manner . . . the Gods of the world may be raised by us, or at least the minist[e]ring spirits. . . . So we read that the antient Priests made statues, and images, foretelling things to come, and infused into them

9. Calling the Faithful through Speaking Trumpets
Seventeenth-century acoustic knowledge joined seamlessly with Christian understandings of a transcendent harmonial order, and technological innovations were often harnessed to pious designs. In this case, the seventeenth-century Jesuit Athanasius Kircher experimented with mammoth speaking trumpets to beckon devotees from the surrounding countryside to a hilltop shrine. From Athanasius Kircher, *Phonurgia nova* (Kempten, Germany: Rudolph Dreherr, 1673), opposite p. 114. Courtesy of the Scheide Music Library, Princeton University.

the spirits of the stars, which were not kept there by constraint in some certain matters, but rejoycing in them, *viz.* as acknowledging such kinds of matter to be suitable to them, they do alwaies, and willingly abide in them, and speak, and do wonderful things by them; no otherwise th[a]n evill spirits are wont to do, when they possess mens bodies.

In Hermetic magic, this was one of the most compelling and controversial dreams—to bring down the spirits into material form and to allow them to speak. If widely decried as demonic magic, ancient divinations nonetheless lived on in early modern occultism, where they were still revered as part of the mystical discovery of "the highest secrets of the Divine Essence."[46]

While Renaissance natural magic long remained intertwined with the conjuration of angels, astrology, alchemy, sympathetic cures, and scriptural hieroglyphs, many of its practitioners emphasized ever more expansively their mastery of artificial contrivances. Della Porta's *Natural Magick,* for example, included a chapter on "Whether material Statues may speak by any Artificial way," in which he dismissed claims that such a feat can be accomplished by "Magick Arts" and offered instead details of "leaden Pipes exceeding long" through which voices could be transmitted (and hence statues made to talk).[47] Likewise, the Catholic magus Athanasius Kircher filled his *Musurgia universalis* (1650) and *Phonurgia nova* (1673) with mechanized sounds and speaking figures: hidden tubes and cones allowed for the creation of one vocal illusion after another, including the supposed reproduction of the speaking statues of the Egyptians. In citing Kircher as its authority on such devices as "The Communicative Busts" and "The Oracular Head," the *Encyclopaedia Britannica* delighted in his use of such contrivances to "utter feigned and ludicrous consultations, with a view to show the fallacy and imposture of the ancient oracles." Among those rational amusements designed to stimulate an interest in "mechanical philosophy," "FATHER KIRCHER'S ORACLE" remained a standard well into the nineteenth

10. Speaking Busts
Athanasius Kircher, renowned for his counterfeiting of an oracular statue, served as an important bridge between Renaissance natural magic and Enlightenment rational recreations. Filling his works with various mechanical devices for creating acoustic illusions, Kircher provided an especially imposing setting for his speaking statues. From Athanasius Kircher, *Phonurgia nova* (Kempten, Germany: Rudolph Dreherr, 1673), 162. Courtesy of the Scheide Music Library, Princeton University.

H. Gravelot delin.   Vivares Sculp.

11. Automata

The Enlightenment mechanization of sound found material expression in ever
more elaborate automata. Among the most famous were Jacques de Vaucanson's
musicians, but still more renowned was his animated duck with its artificial quacking and fully functioning digestive system. From Jacques de Vaucanson, *An Account
of the Mechanism of an Automaton*, trans. J. T. Desaguliers (London: Parker, 1742),
frontispiece. Shelfmark 1600-927. Courtesy of the British Library.

century. The presences of Hermetic statues slipped into the artifices of natural magic, and these, in turn, slid into the Enlightenment command of
oracular illusions.[48]

That series of slippages in acoustic knowledge underpinned Fontenelle's
treatment of the oracles as he explored "animated *Statues*" as the archetype
of ancient priestly deceptions. Circumspectly leaving open the possibility
that God in all his power might have "sometimes permitted the *Daemons* to
animate *Idols*," Fontenelle still concluded: "But generally speaking, there
has never been any such thing," and thus the main question became the
artifices by which the priests acted. As he asked mockingly, why is it that
the demons "did never animate a Statue, in some common Road, where
four high Ways met, exposed on all sides to the view of the World?"
Leaving barely a trace of Hermetic danger, Fontenelle's polemic helped
turn the mechanized speaking statues of natural magic to the didactic purposes of Enlightenment anticlericalism. Better, Johann Beckmann noted in
his *History of Inventions and Discoveries*, that "the vulgar" should learn of
such subterfuge through these rational entertainments than be prey to "a
continual deception from priests."[49]

As natural philosophers pursued the artifices of oracular statues, they
were interested not only in how such illusions were manufactured, but also
in how voices could be mechanically reproduced. The enterprise of dupli-
cation—the effort to disjoin spoken words from the human mouth through
technological facsimile—was both extensive and enduring. Jacques de
Vaucanson, for example, became famed for his automata in the 1730s, including a flute player with an artificial tongue, as well as a fully operational
duck that quacked, ate, and even defecated. These wonderful machines of
automated sound highly impressed the literati (Vaucanson's quacking duck
proved such a sensation that Edgar Allen Poe still made mention of it in his
essay on automata in 1836). Equally celebrated was Wolfgang von
Kempelen, who worked diligently in the 1770s and 1780s to build a machine
that could reproduce human speech. A halting success, his speaking machine managed to squeeze out a handful of words and phrases, including
the tongue-twister *Mississippi*.[50]

In imitating von Kempelen, Charles Wheatstone of King's College, London, made an experimental exhibition out of an "improved" speaking machine in the 1830s. He regularly opened his public demonstrations with a
historical account of the pagan oracles and the artifices of speaking statues.
The mechanical achievement of the natural philosopher seized the spot-
light against a backdrop of priestly manipulation and popular superstition.

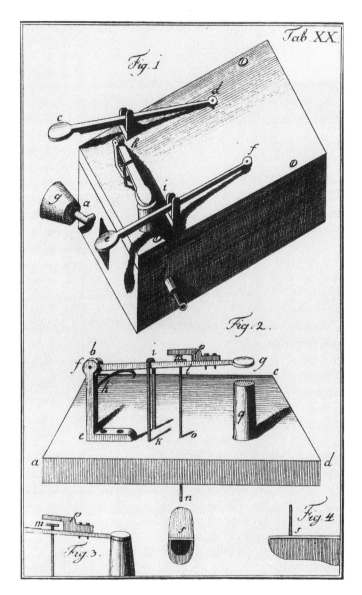

12. Speaking Machine

The reproduction of the human voice was hotly pursued among the learned. Wolfgang von Kempelen's experiments with vocal mechanics included the creation of an artificial glottis, mouth, tongue, and lungs—all part of his ambition to perfect a speaking machine and hence to effect a technological separation of the voice from the body. Among the earliest words mastered by his talking machine were "anatomy" and "pantomime." From Wolfgang von Kempelen, *Mechanismus der menschlichen Sprache nebst der Beschreibung seiner sprechenden Maschine* (Vienna: Degen, 1791), plate XX. Courtesy of the Firestone Library, Princeton University.

As a boy, Alexander Graham Bell still "devoured" von Kempelen's research, witnessed Wheatstone's creation first-hand, and launched his technological mastery of the disincarnated voice by building his own "automaton speaking machine," which he equipped with a wooden tongue and rubber cheeks. The emancipatory power of modern acoustic technologies, including science's success with the telephone, was yet imagined in light of the dark, despotic history of oracular religion.[51]

The play between the illusions of oracular voices and the mastery of talking machines remained in evidence in another famous contrivance of the nineteenth century, Thomas Edison's phonograph. When *Scientific American* introduced its readers to the new invention in 1877, it marveled at the deceptions made possible through "mechanical speech"—how the talking machine was able to copy voices, how it even contained the necromantic potential of giving apparent life to the voice of the dead. What the phonograph possessed, the reviewer observed in an especially revealing phrase, was the power to create *"the illusion of real presence."* The simulation of the speaking statue became the reproduced voice of the talking machine—an artificial, mediated voice, part of an ever-widening culture of counterfeit sounds where real presences were all part of a technological mirage. Edison's phonograph still evoked wonder, sometimes even of a Spiritualist turn, but the illusionist qualities of the new machine clearly made the Wizard of Menlo Park a devotee far more of Brewster's natural magic than of Agrippa's Hermeticism.[52]

Less obvious than the speaking statue and the talking machine as a technology of oracular absence was the speaking trumpet, more fancifully dubbed the "Tuba Stentoro-Phonica"; but it ended up holding a prominent place in the debate over the oracles and in their subsequent exhibition. The invention of the stentorophonicon is generally credited to the Englishman Samuel Morland in 1670, though Athanasius Kircher claimed that he had already invented something very much like it more than twenty years earlier and issued a substantial treatise in his own defense. At a minimum, Morland's work brought the instrument to international notice: it received considerable publicity through the Royal Society's cosmopolitan networks. Following up his experiments with a short treatise entitled *Tuba Stentoro-Phonica, an Instrument of Excellent Use, as well at Sea, as at Land* (1672), Morland heralded the manifold uses of the new instrument in extending the human voice two or three miles. It held particular potential for communication between ships; another possibility even included use as a burglar alarm (should "Thieves and Robbers attaque a House that is

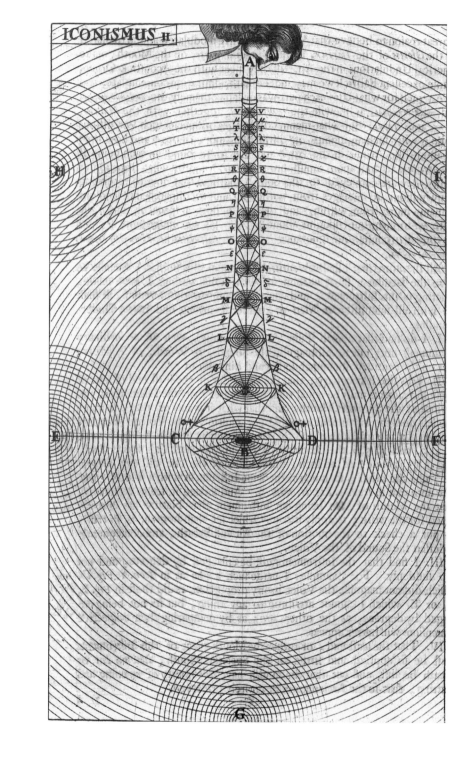

lonely, and far from Neighbours, by such an I[n]strument as this, may all the Dwellers round about, within the compass of a Mile or more, be immediately informed"). The crucial theoretical question was explaining in mechanistic terms why these massive trumpet-shaped devices (up to twenty-one feet in length!) were so effective in amplifying sound, why the voice in passing through them "is prodigiously magnified and augmented," while the pivotal practical issue was how to maximize their reach by improving their design. Morland even imagined enlarging one to the point that "it might render a Voice audible at least eight or ten Miles."[53]

Fontenelle was drawn to this technology for its strategic uses against priestcraft. "How many Machines were at work in those dark places?" Fontenelle asked insistently of the oracular shrines. One temple, he said, had "the resemblance of a *Theatre;* and the voice of Men, and the sound of Trumpets was multiply'ed by the echoes of the Rocks. Do not you believe then, that they knew how to make even these Echoes of great use to 'em?" The learned were committed to establishing the mechanics of "rebounding Echoes" and also to rationalizing architectural acoustics, so this observation already imprinted Fontenelle's work with two of the current marks of the natural philosophy of sound. "Perhaps too," he continued, "that sort of Trumpet which multiplies the sound, was not then altogether unknown: it may be Sir, *Samuel Moreland,* has but revived this secret, which the *Pagan Priests* knew before him; tho' they chose rather to get profit by concealing it, than honour by publishing it," a sin that seemed especially damning in that supremely literary culture of enlightened savants. In these "dark *Sanctuaries,*" this was one of "the machines of the *Priests,*" the only technology Fontenelle named so directly: Morland's Tuba Stentoro-Phonica. In the nimble hands of the *philosophes,* the speaking trumpet edged into an ironic materialization of any and all revelatory voices, even suggesting a subversive play on God's oracles: "The voice which I heard was as it were a trumpet talking with me" (Revelation 4:1).[54]

13. Acoustic Experiment with a Speaking Trumpet
Samuel Morland's experiments with the amplifying powers of speaking trumpets paid off especially in improving communication between ships at sea. The instruments were soon found to have another use unforeseen by Morland—that is, as a mechanical explanation of the vocal impostures of priests. From Samuel Morland, *Tuba Stentoro-Phonica, an Instrument of Excellent Use, as Well at Sea, as at Land* (London: W. Godbid, 1672), opposite p. 9. Courtesy of the Henry E. Huntington Library.

This move of imagining the ancient priests with "their speaking Trumpets" left Jesuit Jean Baltus, Fontenelle's leading critic, incredulous. "What might not I say," he bantered, "to give a little Life to the Subject I am upon, on occasion of all those Machines, you so liberally allow to the Idolatrous Priests in their acting these Comedies? . . . What appears the most pleasantly fancy'd of all are the Trumpets you put into their Mouths, to raise their Voice, and magnify the Sound of it in a manner proper to create fear, of which you with so much probability suspect they might likely have found the Secret before Sir *Samuel Morland* who is reputed the Inventer of them." Baltus found the retrofitting of the ancient priests with speaking trumpets "to counterfeit the Voice of the Gods" a chimerical explanation, Fontenelle's own wishful illusion of knowledge's power. About that, Baltus was especially perceptive. Such mechanistic explanations of imposture were convenient detours around the phenomena of oracular voices and animated objects. Fontenelle's use of "Sir *Samuel Morland*'s Trumpets" was a learned technique of evasion.[55]

Few of the literati thought Baltus had much of an argument. (His insistence on the power of demons made him easy to lampoon; Voltaire scoffed that "the devil could not have chosen a more tiresome and wretched advocate." And his refusal to accept the literati's partitioned anthropology of popular credulity made him all the more bothersome. "I do maintain on the contrary," he said, "that the People are not more easily deceiv'd . . . than the most learned and intelligent Persons.") The problem for Baltus was that he was jousting not only with the philosophy of mechanization, but also with a recreation of the Enlightenment. Samuel Morland's trumpets appealed as much for the amusement they gave the literati in imagining the vast extent of popular ignorance and priestly imposture as for their explanatory power. Hence, satirist Thomas Brown, in his walks around London at the turn of the eighteenth century, could observe of Quakers at a meeting that these nonsensical enthusiasts were "but the *Stentonorophonick Tubes*" of the noisy Spirit that spoke through them. The same gambit was evident in Voltaire's imagining of Catholic "speaking tubes" by which "celestial voices" were conveyed to the roofs of churches to cow devotees. As such technologized witticisms suggested, it was entertaining (as much as explanatory) to mechanize the vocality of popular piety, pagan and Christian alike. The very titillation of amusement made the explanation all the more attractive.[56]

The final piece of acoustic technology that loomed large in these discussions was just that sort of speaking tube to which Voltaire alluded. As Della Porta's description of a speaking statue suggested, the use of pipes for the conveyance of voices was a standard in natural magic, and Bacon incorporated such contrivances into his experimental program. Kircher even used a speaking tube in his quarters in the Jesuit College in Rome to communicate with the porter's lodge—an arrangement of no little astonishment to visitors. By the early nineteenth century, such acoustic tubes had become more of an architectural commonplace in public buildings. They were "extensively used," one handbook explained, "in coffee-rooms, hotels, business houses, counting-rooms, offices, and warehouses, for conveying orders to the attendants and journeymen situated in different parts of the establishment." Like the wooden-cylinder stethoscopes of the 1810s and 1820s, acoustic tubes offered the social utility of mediated distance. (Before he invented the stethoscope, R. T. H. Laënnec had been awkwardly—and reluctantly—pressing his head up against the bodies of his patients.) In placing his ears to the tin tubes and trumpets at an exhibition in 1803, one writer said he heard "a voice like that of a girl," the simile expressive of the disjoining of sound and body. "The voice," he reported—with a sense that any physical presence connected to it had been lost—"spoke English,—French and German." The speaking tube was a technology of disincarnation.[57]

That these acoustic tubes might be useful for exercising control through eavesdropping became widely acknowledged, so much so that Jeremy Bentham put them (as well as Morland's speaking trumpets) to extensive use in his notorious *Panopticon; Or, The Inspection House* (1791). In Michel Foucault's vision-dominated interpretation, it is the eye of surveillance that is internalized, but the wards of this inspection house also had the eavesdropping ear to contemplate: "To save the troublesome exertion of voice that might otherwise be necessary, and to prevent one prisoner from knowing that the inspector was occupied by another prisoner at a distance, a small *tin tube* might reach from each cell to the inspector's lodge. . . . By means of this implement, the slightest whisper of the one might be heard by the other." Bentham imagined using these "conversation-tubes" not only to turn prisoners (or laborers) into self-monitors through "the *apparent omnipresence* of the inspector," but also to issue orders to subordinates—a vocal technology to undergird "clock-work regularity" and "promptitude." Samuel Morland himself had anticipated the disciplining and distancing aspects of the new auditory technologies, remarking of

the stentorophonicon that "an Overseer of Works, of what kind soever, may by this give Order to many hundreds of Workmen, without once removing his station." Likewise, Bentham's contemporary Erasmus Darwin dreamed of building a speaking figure in such "a gigantic form" that it would be made loud enough "to command an army, or instruct a crowd." Bentham had plenty of company in his acoustic fantasies of mastery: these conveyances of sound were considered useful for detaching the utterance from the body that verbalized it and impersonalizing the voice of power.[58]

Bentham appealed to the effects of Enlightenment entertainments for validation that acoustic tubes would work effectively as part of the panopticon. "The power possessed by metallic tubes of conveying the slightest whispers to an almost indefinite distance," he reported, "can be of no secret to such readers as have seen any of the exhibitions of the speaking figures, whose properties depend upon this principle." That these amusements had the power to communicate a dread sense of surveillance was evident from the case reported by the early nineteenth-century French psychologist Jean Esquirol: a woman reportedly went mad after witnessing the Invisible Lady. Seeing in the amusement an emblem of invasive monitoring, she came to believe that "by some similar means, her lowest whispers may be heard at a distance." Pinchbeck confirmed these grim synergies, sliding effortlessly from his "observations on the acoustick temple and oracles" into espionage. In detailing "a certain mode of procedure by which the secret consultations of private societies may be made known," he appealed to the hidden tubes that were used in the Acoustic Temple. The ironies of such enlightened appropriations are worth savoring. Priestly powers of stealth and surveillance were first abominated, and then celebrated

14. Speaking Figure

The acoustic entertainments of the late Enlightenment inspired various caprices among the learned, including Jeremy Bentham's fantasies of eavesdropping, as described in his *Panopticon*. In this particular amusement, a hidden confederate in the ceiling, with the use of speaking trumpets, makes an ordinary doll appear to speak. The trick was easily turned around—from secretly conveying voices at a distance to clandestinely monitoring them from afar. From Philip Thicknesse, *The Speaking Figure, and the Automaton Chess-player, Exposed and Detected* (London: Stockdale, 1784), frontispiece. Courtesy of the Princeton University Library, Rare Books and Special Collections.

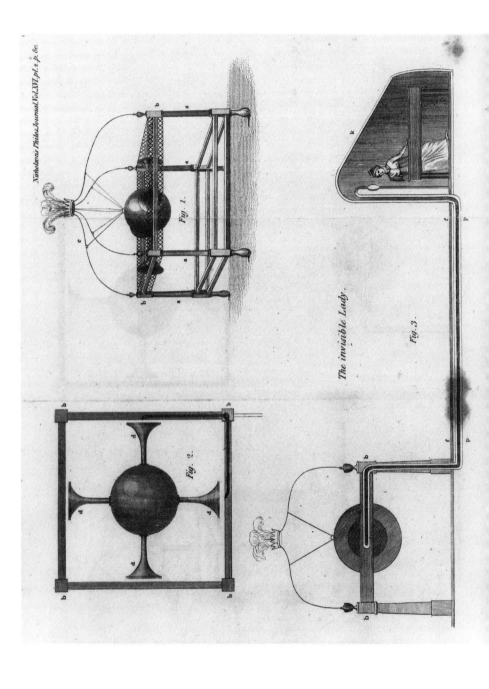

Fig. 1.

Fig. 2.

The invisible Lady.

Fig. 3.

for enhancing the exercise of modern statecraft and the efficiency of an industrializing economy.[59]

Generative for imagining new technologies of eavesdropping, amusements using acoustic tubes also became part of the literati's fantasies about the oracular and the revelatory. To listen to that latter-day amusement, the Invisible Lady, was once again to fathom how people had long been deceived into thinking that they heard the disembodied voices of the divine world. The Delphic oracle, one writer concluded bluntly in 1832, was "a piece of machinery, founded upon acoustic principles, similar to that of the invisible girl." Brewster went even farther, finding the Invisible Lady more alluring in its mechanical sophistication than the ancient oracles themselves, its male operators deftly managing—like the priests of old—the prescient voices of young women. Thanks in part to Brewster's widely disseminated descriptions, these entertainments lingered. Barnum and other showmen, such as John Henry Anderson and George Kirbye, were still cultivating mechanical imitations of the oracles in the 1850s—the whole gamut of acoustic temples, invisible ladies, speaking trumpets, and hidden tubes. The Hermetic dream of the animated statue found consummation in an extended series of edifying amusements that exposed the very emptiness of that ancient magic. All along, the lesson was not only retrospective: placing an ear to these tubes was imagined as an act of disengagement, a performance that distanced the hearer from those "traits of ignorance" among superstitious contemporaries who obstinately continued to accord supernatural power to "ominous sounds." Behind the transformation of the speaking statues of Hermes Trismegistus into the faint-voiced Invisible Lady was a larger significance: the education that such exhibitions offered in the pleasures of auditory suspicion.[60]

What, finally, were the religious implications of these varied efforts in natural philosophy to make sound yield up its secrets and to mechanize the oracular voice? While much of the acoustic program remained theologically routine—part of the wider fusion of Christian cosmology and

15. *The Invisible Lady*
These explanatory images of the acoustic deceptions of the "Invisible Lady" were later given wide circulation in David Brewster's *Letters on Natural Magic*, a consummate work of demystification. From "The Invisible Lady," *Nicholson's Journal of Natural Philosophy, Chemistry, and the Arts* 16 (1807): 80. Courtesy of the Library Company of Philadelphia.

16. A Listener to a Modern Oracle
During exhibitions and entertainments, listening at the end of acoustic tubes and trumpets created a new practice for hearing things. These staged modern oracles encouraged auditors to be both detached and amused; they invited listeners to acquire the habits of perceptual suspicion and impartial judgment that allowed penetration of the illusions of disembodied, revelatory voices. From "Exhibitions of Mechanical and Other Works of Ingenuity," Scrapbook, 1840, British Library, 1269.h.38. Courtesy of the British Library.

Baconian inquiry—the knowledge of sound was used to undercut certain kinds of devout experiences: the voices of demons, the power of priestly blessings, the magic of ringing bells, and the heavenly communications of the pietist. The awe over God's voice in the thunder, faring about as well as the providential interpretation of earthquakes, was perhaps the best example of a reimagined soundscape. Enlightenment natural philosophers pursued the physical causes of thunder and lightning with tenacity, and such learning carried important theological and emotional freight.

The American deist Elihu Palmer made the significance of this retuning very apparent in his *Principles of Nature*:

> In proportion as man makes progress in physical knowledge, he ceases to be the dupe of superstition, and what before appeared marvellous, now becomes plain and intelligible. In natural philosophy we may discover an hundred proofs of the truth of this assertion; the rapid lightning of Heaven, which darts with inconceivable velocity through the regions of space, was once considered a powerful weapon of destruction in the hands of God, and that no human power could controul it. This modification of physical energy, among enlightened minds, has lost all its terror.

One learned summary from 1830 noted, almost with a yawn, that the science of acoustics, with its knowledge of echoes and the velocity of sound, had arrived at "a perfect explanation" of thunder: "All the varieties of that awful Sound are easily accounted for." In his *Medical Inquiries* Benjamin Rush even went so far as to pathologize any lingering fear of thunder, expressly making it an "unreasonable" phobia for which he offered various practical remedies. Any emotional power that thunder continued to have for the literati was aestheticized, made an aspect of the sublime, comparable in imaginative force to the roar of a waterfall, not the voice of God.[61]

The science of acoustics gradually helped reframe the way a wide swath of the learned thought about oracular voices and portentous noises. Fontenelle, Trenchard, Palmer, Pinchbeck, and Brewster were exemplars; but another good one was Charles Page, a Harvard-educated inventor and lecturer, who took his knowledge of acoustics on the lyceum circuit in the 1830s before settling into the chemistry department at George Washington University in the 1840s. Noted for his experiments with electricity, Page wrote almost exclusively on scientific topics, but he did turn out one tract on religion, *Psychomancy: Spirit-Rappings and Table-Tippings Exposed* (1853).

That Page found Spiritualist claims unconvincing was not that surprising, but how he went about distancing himself from those experiences is revealing. At a number of points *Psychomancy* turned into a public lecture on acoustics in which such knowledge provided the means of "unravelling this imposture and illusion." Advising his readers to turn to Brewster's *Letters on Natural Magic,* Page adduced ventriloquism, speaking tubes, and the Invisible Lady by way of explaining "the machinery or instrumentality" that Spiritualist mediums used to make their revelatory sounds.[62]

A final example of how the learned used their knowledge of acoustics to refashion auditory experience is found in the exhibitions of British natural philosopher John Tyndall. A popular systematizer of acoustics, Tyndall was also a severe critic of Christian supernaturalism, all the way down to the routine practice of prayer. Notoriety as a freethinker hardly compromised his celebrity as a scientific performer (his itinerary included a wildly successful tour of the United States in 1872 and 1873). In a renowned series of lectures, Tyndall surrounded himself with all the new nineteenth-century instruments for picturing the mechanics and physiology of sound—everything from the kaleidophone to the laryngoscope. His demonstrations were among the grandest spectacles of the acoustic.

One of his exhibitions, showing "the action of hydrogen gas upon the voice," was especially suggestive. The vocal effects of inhaling this gas had been known since at least 1799 from a Genevan experiment, one of the innumerable studies investigating the impact of different media on the propagation of sound. Like the inhaling of nitrous oxide for purposes of scientific entertainment, Tyndall found that this hydrogen-gas discovery made quite a show: "You have already formed a notion of the strength and quality of my voice. I now empty my lungs of air, and inflate them with hydrogen from this gasholder. I try to speak vigorously, but my voice has lost wonderfully in power, and changed wonderfully in quality. You hear it, hollow, harsh, and unearthly: I cannot otherwise describe it." In another demonstration, Tyndall wryly remarked that "an uneducated person" might think a given effect was the product of "witchcraft," but the natural philosopher knew better. The unearthly alteration of voice—whether the hollow tones of the necromancer, the demonic utterances of the possessed, or the fiery tongues of the Spirit-filled enthusiast—had been absorbed into an entertaining demonstration of science's explanatory power, a diversion, like the Acoustic Temple, in which the mystery had been drained from the oracular voice.[63]

"Truth Changes from Day to Day—and So Do I": Elihu Vedder and the Desert Silences of the Oracles

The hollowness of the Acoustic Temple was reverberant. Enlightenment *philosophes* sought a quieter heaven—no ethereal, revelatory voices; no divine speech apart from the mechanisms of nature. And for those who inherited and improved on these "modern" assumptions, the universe could feel devocalized, a coldly unresponsive place. One Romantic answer was to seek Sibylline inspiration in art, especially in poetry and painting. The artist might be prophet and seer, might through the imagination recapture the oracular or through creative self-expression become the conduit of the transcendent. Some counter-Enlightenment critics, such as the Platonist Thomas Taylor and the essayist Thomas De Quincey, came to the explicit defense of the ancient oracles against "the spirit of triumphant ridicule" embodied in the work of van Dale and Fontenelle. One early nineteenth-century poet, Thomas Moore, even tried to use the Invisible Girl as an emblem of "consoling enchantment," a reverie on the "sweet spirit of mystery" and the renewed will to believe:

> They try to persuade me, my dear little sprite,
> That you're *not* a true daughter of ether and light,
>
> . . . . .
>
> But I *will* not believe them—no, Science, to you
> I have long bid a last and a careless adieu:
> Still flying from Nature to study her laws,
> And dulling delight by exploring its cause,
> You forget how superior, for mortals below,
> Is the fiction they dream to the truth that they know.

Even as various forms of fortunetelling continued to thrive at popular levels, highbrow efforts at oracular recovery often proved faint. Romantic visions, whether those of Wordsworth or Carlyle or Emerson (or, in this case, Thomas Moore), issued frequently in corroborating laments over the disenchantment of the world (a phrase that Max Weber, after all, borrowed from Romantic sources). As often as not, the result was a nostalgic picture of vanishing faith rather than the successful delivery of newborn bards of the Holy Ghost.[64]

The nostalgia for the oracular was given varied expression among American Romantics and Gothic reclaimers. In lamenting the lost resonance of Michelangelo's Sibyls, for example, the late nineteenth-century American artist John La Farge suggested that the oracles, alas, survived only decoratively—"the poetry, the charm, the intense importance has faded." For centuries the Sibylline verses "ran up and down the discussions of the Church. . . . Now we do not even know what is meant by a Sibyl." Shorn of the power of "prophetic confirmation," the Sibyls were now "merely names for the tag on the frame of a picture."[65]

The American visionary painter Elihu Vedder took a step beyond such nostalgia, especially in his early work of the 1860s, turning the loss of the oracular voice into material for his own arid dreamscapes. When combined with his autobiographical musings and his verse, stark images emerge of those oracular silences and longings. As Vedder observed late in life, "It is not for me to pass judgment on Doubt or Doubters, that concerns Philosophers and Theologians; but as a painter I can at least give its portrait with some hope of success, after an intimacy of many years standing." Vedder's religious wandering is a reminder of the very tangible effects of the Enlightenment's disenchanting powers, and his spiritual travails serve as an inlet into quintessential forms of modern hearing loss. To the extent that the stories of devocalization and rupture remain convincing narratives, they do so because of figures like Vedder.[66]

Growing up in Schenectady, New York, in the 1830s and 1840s, Vedder found himself in a world charged with the oracular, the marvelous, and the evangelistic. Raised in a Universalist home, he was spared the "nightmare" of Hell, but its "endless torture" still crowded in around him through those who "daily dinned [it] into my companions" and through those who railed against the Universalists for denying those very torments. Damnation and salvation encircled him in portentous combat: revival preachers, evoking macabre scenes of drunken desolation, pleaded with the young boys to sign temperance pledges, and old-time Dutch Calvinists, like one of his grandfathers, held out for the starkness of double predestination and for resignation to that divine decree. Sunday school seemed purgatorial—a place where he formulated questions about God "that have remained unanswered to this day" and where he felt "treated as if I were an imbecile." Relief came (at least once, anyway) when another boy found a particularly indelicate Bible verse and pointed it out to the teacher for elucidation.[67]

Greater mysteries than Sunday school and hellfire lurked around him. At one point his father was away on business for a considerable time, and, as the letters home grew ever more despondent, the family's straits seemed severe. So his mother "in her trouble" sought out a fortuneteller, and "now," Vedder wrote, "comes this strange thing":

> The Fortune-Teller told my mother that she had a husband over the water; that she had a letter saying he was coming home; but that a letter would arrive from him in a few days that would change all her plans; this letter would tell her that all was going well with him and that she and her children must go to him. All this came true,—every word of it.
>
> But this was not all. The Fortune-Teller told her that there seemed to be no reason why she should not live to a good old age, except that in a certain year all was very dark; could she get through that year alive, she would live a long time. She gave the year, and in that year my mother died.[68]

Even in his seventies, as he was putting together his digressive memoirs, Vedder remained burdened by this grim diviner, this dead-on voice of fortune.

Other childhood seers haunted him—one especially, his Aunt Eve. "I was growing up and filled with all the modern theories as to our relations with the Infinite, so my aunt seemed to me a being of another age. She never read the Bible, knowing it by heart." But it was not so much her intimacy with the Bible or even her deep conviction of her own sinfulness that lingered. "I have never lost the impression made on me when she related with deep emotion her last Vision," Vedder acknowledged. "She no more doubted the truth of these visions than I doubted the fact of my existence":

> She told me—they always came to her just before dawn. "I was standing in a barn with wonderful beams, and up in the beams it was full of beautiful little angels all singing softly and playing on curious instruments, and they made the sweetest music I ever heard, though I often hear sweet music. And a beautiful angel stood before me and said: 'Eve, I am told to ask you what is the dearest wish of your heart. You may tell me and it will be given to you.' And I answered: 'I want to look on the face of my Saviour.' Slowly a great light grew about me and I knew some one stood before me, and I knew it was the Lord, and I covered my face and did not look. I felt I was unworthy to look

on Him, or to speak to Him; and then the light went away and has never come back again."[69]

The auditory qualities of this "vision" are striking: Eve heard the singing, the heavenly instruments, the sweet music, and talked with the angel, but she could not bring herself to look upon the face of her Savior or to speak to him. It is no wonder that Vedder remembered this story vividly or that his own spiritual life should feel so flat in comparison.

For Vedder, religion became art, and art a religion. In school he had been exposed for the first time to William Blake, "the mad painter"; and Blake's visionary poetry absorbed him throughout his life, though Vedder baldly refused to fashion himself a mystic or a prophet. His remaking of one childhood story from a tale about Christianity to one about the aesthetic is suggestive of this creative translation. Relocated to Cuba because of his father's enterprise, Vedder was there "struck with the gorgeous ceremonials of the Church" and with "the legends of the Saints." As a schoolboy, he wanted to build his own shrine: "Collecting all the tinsel and most gaudy materials I could, and little highly coloured prints of Saints and gods and goddesses, and fashionable beauties, I erected an altar in a large unused room, and fitted it up beautifully with flowers and little candles, and then was ready for business. I formed my congregation by getting together all the little darkies of the neighbourhood, who came willingly enough to see the splendid sight." In a gesture that fused art, colonialism, and mission, Vedder thought that he would teach the "little darkies" how "to worship on bended knee" the gods of his own imagination.[70]

Instead Vedder found resistance from one of the boys, who refused to kneel at his altar (the boy likely found this playful manipulation of his own sacred materials offensive). With candles aflame, the altar, "a dream of beauty and magnificence," turned into "a general blaze" as a result of this defiant "beast of a boy-Luther" (Vedder, with his own religious identity slipping, tellingly transformed the boy into a raving Protestant). The aged Vedder mused that with better luck he "might have founded a cult of the beautiful, a religion of Art for Art's sake." "Who knows? I never tried it again," he concluded disingenuously, for much of his life was an effort to make art stand in for a visionary and oracular faith that had been emptied of significance. That hollowness was never satisfyingly filled, despite his ceaseless appropriations of the other, whether Catholic saints, Egyptian monuments, or Buddhist images.[71]

By the early 1860s, in his mid-twenties, Vedder was living meagerly in New York City and painting some of his most enduring works. Several entailed religious themes, and an arid silence hangs over many of them. In *The Lost Mind* (1864) a distracted woman wanders in the desert, the vacancy of soul mirrored in the barrenness of the landscape. The same wasteland was evoked in *Prayer for Death in the Desert* (1867), in which the kneeling supplicant gestures futilely to the parched heavens. The saint in the desert captivated the young Vedder, yet what mattered were not the visions found there but the silences, the lost seekers, the recluses without demonic or angelic visitors:

> We're never told of all those others
> Who fled the world their souls to save,
> Those poor wandering half-crazed brothers
> Who found in the desert but a grave.[72]

If Vedder was a visionary artist, he regularly painted against the grain of the mystical and the prophetic. As in *The Dead Alchemist* (1868), Vedder's seekers perished in the midst of their quest before any secrets could be communicated. For Vedder, there was always the foreboding of mystery, as in the fortuneteller's dark prognostications, but never the epiphany of Aunt Eve and her evangelical piety.

Vedder's most revealing painting of unrevealing oracles is *The Questioner of the Sphinx*, a work that drew on the popular fascination with Egyptian monuments and archaeology—an enchantment embodied in the Egyptian revival, which left its architectural mark across the United States in the first half of the nineteenth century. In the early 1860s Vedder had to rely on books, prints, and museums for his orientalist images of Egyptian exoticism (including a major exhibition at the New-York Historical Society in 1861). He would later travel to Egypt and become all the more absorbed, like other American and European tourists, by the "grandeur" of the architecture and the "silence" of the desert, "always the Desert—perhaps the best of all."[73] In the painting, the solitary wayfarer puts his ear to the stony lips of the Sphinx awaiting an oracular answer that does not come. Vedder underlined this unrequited listening by creating a second version of the same scene a decade later in which the wizened pilgrim has aged noticeably—as if he has grown old in God-forsaken waiting. As one American critic, James Jackson Jarves, interpreted the earlier version of the painting in 1864, the twilight inquirer confronts "the inscrutable statue, and asks to

17. *The Questioner of the Sphinx,* by Elihu Vedder, 1863
The nineteenth-century American artist Elihu Vedder, dwelling on desolate scenes of spiritual alienation, provided an extremely stark vision of the oracular silences that had descended on some modern listeners. Courtesy of the Museum of Fine Arts, Boston. Reproduced with permission. Copyright © 1999 Museum of Fine Arts, Boston. All rights reserved.

know the Great Secret of life, but receives no answer except the devouring silence, solitude, and death that encompass him."[74]

Vedder's Sphinx, like the stilled statue of Memnon, is mute and blank; no mysterious song, no esoteric utterance, is heard from the carved lips. Such silence recalls the treatments of Egyptian monuments in the commentaries of Salverte and Brewster, who relished showing how the ancient priests had achieved their jugglery, especially how they made the colossus of Memnon emit an awe-inspiring noise at the rising of the sun. Having solved to his satisfaction the puzzle of Memnon's miraculous sounds,

18. A Reprise of *The Questioner of Sphinx*, by Elihu Vedder, 1875
Vedder, in painting the same scene again twelve years later, aged the listener considerably and thus made all the more vivid the futility of waiting for a break in the silence. Courtesy of the Worcester Art Museum, Worcester, Massachusetts. Gift of Mr. and Mrs. Stuart Riley, Jr.

Brewster patted himself on the back: "It is curious to observe how the study of nature gradually dispels the consecrated delusions of ages, and reduces to the level of ordinary facts what time had invested with all the characters of the supernatural." Vedder's art reflects that stony demystification; the saints, the prophets, the oracles all seemed dead quiet. Such "pious tales" had been torn "to bits," Vedder said, and nature itself offered no pantheistic solace, only scorched wastes. The votary might still kneel at the statue's lips, desirous for a moment of Hermetic magic, but this waiting lacked even the consolation of a deftly manufactured voice. Nor was the silence pregnant with revelation in the way the quieted statue of Memnon had been for Saint Jerome, another hushed signal of the new birth made possible through Jesus Christ. Vedder, lost to that redemptive history, was hardly in a position to find comfort in the taciturn Sphinx.[75]

Orientalist imaginings of desolation—half-naked Egyptians kneeling before deanimated stones—allowed Vedder to dramatize his own prison-house interiors of an unsalvageable Christian faith. At about the time Vedder painted his first rendition of *The Questioner of the Sphinx*, he was getting by in shabby lodgings in New York City, often living hand-to-mouth between sales of his paintings: "It was in this bare room, kneeling at the window one night, that I made my great prayer—the last. I only asked for guidance, not for anything else, and it was an honest prayer. The only answer was—the brick walls and iron shutters." With self-contradiction, he did note that he prayed one more time later in life "in my deepest distress," but the result was the same. He prayed for "an innocent life; but it was found that the great laws could not be disturbed for such a small matter,—in fact were not disturbed in the least." In the one other passage in his autobiography where he takes up prayer directly, the conclusion is equally dark. This time, writing of his brother's anxious devotions, Vedder noted bluntly: "He wanted a direct answer from the Lord—and no answer came." *The Questioner of the Sphinx* was part of a memorial that Vedder built for his own unanswered prayers, a dreamscape not of revelation but of fatalistic silence.[76]

In a utopian or restorationist moment, Vedder had actually experimented with a mystical view of language, going so far as to invent a new hieroglyphic alphabet, "Alfaru," in which "each Sound had its proper Sign" and "each Sign did with Sound agree." Out of the chasms that yawned between voice and script, the sound and the signified, word and thing, Vedder dreamed of complete correspondence. With something of a Hermetic flourish, he imagined a language of religious immediacy in which "the 'divine afflatus'" would dwell unhindered. The prospect of undoing Babel, though, hardly transported Vedder as it had kabbalistic seekers of the Adamic language: Alfaru proved for him no more than a fleeting vagary of stabilized signs, a passing fancy of real presences. "Truth changes from day to day—and so do I," Vedder wrote in an epitaph for the joined modern displacements of God and personal identity.[77]

Vedder was left with "the Voice of Doubt which is never still" and at least a pair of divided interior voices—his own Dr. Jekyll and Mr. Hyde, he called them. He even saw in the initial letter of his last name a pictorialization of this very fracturing: "Thus I diverge on either hand. / An I—divided, cannot stand, / Falling apart it forms a V— / Which I much fear resembles me." Outside this fragmented interior he found only a faint echo of his own whispered longings—an Egyptian desert, which he first imagined and then came to know rather wanly as a tourist, where "ruined temples" and ancient monuments still sat in forlorn if "poetic" silence, just as he had already dreamed them in his younger days. Other voices he heard turned "the harmonious music of the Spheres" into an unsettling cacophony of shrieks: "Even while gazing at the starry sky, / Comes to his ears the agonizing cry / Of thousands of victims as they die."[78] Vedder managed to transfigure the loss of the revelatory voice into a visual art, but that seemed even to himself a rather empty comfort.

In 1896 the Pabst Brewing Company found another oracular use for Vedder's *Questioner of the Sphinx*—as an advertising image in which Vedder's spiritual thirsts became something easily quenched by a commodity of the American marketplace. The appropriation angered the artist not because of the commercial use—he had already lent his talents to manufacturers of comic valentines and Christmas cards—but because the company had not paid him for it (he eventually accepted $250 from Pabst as payment). That *The Questioner of the Sphinx* became an advertisement was fitting: in a world pictured as devoid of the oracular, advertising took on the aura of the vanished gods and made all kinds of new commodities the answering voice to these modern longings. Given Vedder's own gnawing doubts, the consumer culture may actually have arrived on an errand of mercy, providing at least a satisfying diversion. His desert pilgrim might not hear God, but at least he could have a beer.[79]

The clairaudient piety of Vedder's Aunt Eve or the oracular power of his mother's fortuneteller had lost place to the Baconian inquisition of nature in which the prophetic had been mechanized. As Bacon himself predicted in the *New-Atlantis,* "We do also declare natural divinations of diseases, plagues, swarms of hurtful creatures, scarcity, tempests, earthquakes, great inundations, comets, temperature of the year, and divers other things; and we give counsel thereupon what the people shall do for the prevention and remedy of them." The scientific and technological absorption of the oracular, its "natural divinations," had left Vedder's world hushed, but hardly tranquil. Within these modern silences the Enlightenment rescripting of the oracular tarried not so much as a politics of explanation, but as a hunger for meaning. An aesthetic of desire was a residue of the knowledge of power.[80]

Perhaps the convoluted history of the oracles themselves is warning enough not to dwell for too long on that vacant silence. While many "moderns," like Vedder, gave voice to despair and doubt, many more people have laid claim—through clairvoyants, mediums, fortunetellers, tongue-speakers, and prophets—to oracular powers. Fontenelle's depiction of the intermittence of the oracles in ancient history is true as well of the resilience of revelatory voices in nineteenth- and twentieth-century American culture: "*Oracles* were ruined for a certain time, and afterwards came into Credit again; for *Oracles* were subject to several Adventures and Misfortunes: And we ought not to believe them annihilated from the time of their being mute; for they might afterwards assume a Voice again and speak." Bacon's natural divinations have hardly had the last word.[81]

Still, that reversal of the Enlightenment's fortune sounds too effortless—as if the modern economy of credit and discredit could be suspended or ignored. The oracles of reason, exerting a dialectical pull, require a departing gesture. In 1945 Frederik Poulsen, a respected scholar of ancient Greek and Roman art who had already written a noteworthy book on Delphi, published an essay on talking statues in *Acta Archaeologica* with the subtitle, "A Chapter of the History of Religious Fraud." The piece turned out to be as much experimental report as historical rumination. Working hands-on with a chiseled bust, Poulsen actually refitted the sculpture with a long bronze tube and applied his own lips. Speaking into the tube—"we have tried this in practice"—he called the effect "powerful and strange," an altogether satisfactory reproduction of "god's voice." "The head acted as a veritable oracle, with a voice which would sound to an emotional mind both mysterious and weird," he averred. Fully at home with the explanatory categories of "oracle fraud" and "mere ventriloquism," Poulsen reenacted Kircher's natural magic, Fontenelle's history, Clarke's archaeology, and Pinchbeck's rational recreation for twentieth-century scholars.[82] The posture of suspicion was yet materialized in the very flesh of performance.

How to Become
a Ventriloquist

4 William Frederick Pinchbeck, expositor and mimic of the Acoustic Temple, was perhaps even keener on another vocal illusion: that of newfangled entertainers who called themselves ventriloquists. Just as he had journeyed to witness the philosophical fakery of a staged Egyptian oracle, Pinchbeck sought the earliest opportunity for hearing one of these new magicians of the human voice. That chance arrived with John Rannie, a Scottish-born juggler and actor, who was the first showman in the United States to promote ventriloquism as an amusement. Billing himself as "The European Ventriloquist," Rannie toured extensively across the early republic in the first decade of the nineteenth century, from Newburyport, Massachusetts, to Natchez, Mississippi. With public curiosity running high, Pinchbeck pursued Rannie's show in order to incorporate this illusion into his own published expositions of enlightened magic. The technologies of acoustic tubes and speaking trumpets had provided Pinchbeck with insight into the mechanisms of priestcraft, and ventriloquism offered another artifice that would help him "to convince superstition of her many ridiculous errors," as well as "to oppose the idea of supernatural agency in any production of man."[1]

Rannie's abilities were, to Pinchbeck, indicative of well-learned technique and daring enterprise, and the specific idea that there might be "diabolical agency" behind such doubled voices was laughable (even if some of the benighted still wanted to hear them that way). "What is there that a man cannot acquire by observation, assisted by good rules and proper application?" Pinchbeck speculated, his exposure to Rannie's "artificial voice" occasioning an ode to the progress made possible through philosophical ingenuity. And Pinchbeck was not misguided to see Rannie as an ally: the immigrant Scotsman was among the earliest entertainers to make a career in magic out of the pretense of dispelling religious superstition—a prominent cultural role later occupied by such showmen as P. T. Barnum and Houdini. Like his more famous contemporaries in France, Alexandre Vattemare and Louis Comte, Rannie the ventriloquist promoted himself as a picaresque voice of reason—well, actually, voices of reason. That shows like his had the power to capture the learned imagination was evident in the report of one Boston physician, who, in bragging of his assiduous dedication to science in a medical journal in 1824, suggested that his enthrallment with this rational amusement was even greater than Pinchbeck's: "Our constant devotion to anatomical pursuits has prompted us to improve every opportunity of witnessing these exhibitions, with the sole object of understanding the rationale." He estimated that, in his rounds, he had observed close to thirty different ventriloquists![2]

That ventriloquism should be turned to these enlightened ends was something of a marvel in itself. The term had long been deeply embedded in Christian theological debates over demonology—the entrancing wonder that some people became so possessed by the devil as to become his mouthpiece. As Joseph Glanvill commented in *Saducismus Triumphatus; Or, Full and Plain Evidence Concerning Witches and Apparitions* (1681), "For *Ventriloquy,* or speaking from the bottom of the Belly, 'tis a thing I think as strange and difficult to be conceived as any thing in Witchcraft, nor can it, I believe, be performed in any distinctness of articulate sounds, without such assistance of the Spirits, that spoke out of the *Dæmoniacks.*" It is all the more curious then that, by the late eighteenth century, ventriloquism, loosed from the confines of theological debate and biblical exegesis, had become a salient category in Enlightenment discussions of religion and had taken center stage as a form of rational entertainment. The expanded construction of ventriloquy provided a tangible way of thinking about oracular religion as rooted in illusion—that, indeed, various wonders of the devout ear had their origins in vocal deceptions that philosophers could pinpoint and magicians could demonstrate. In performative practice, the ventriloquist's art also shifted the focus of learned attention from the divine struggle over the soul to the protean malleability of personal identity, the fears and attractions of imposture, and the sheer pleasures of amusement. How ventriloquism came to have such multivocality for natural philosophers, how it was untethered from its religious moorings and turned into a rational recreation, is the express story this chapter tells.[3]

That distinct account, though, ripples out into a much larger series of circles. Just as the Enlightenment dismantling of the oracles condensed revised forms of history, politics, technology, and natural magic, the learned reconstruction of ventriloquism digested new understandings of entertainment, epistemology, anatomy, psychology, and the self. As with the display of the oracles, the revamping of ventriloquism was indicative of the crowded intersections of philosophy and performance, knowledge production and illusionist play, in the late Enlightenment. Within this tangled convergence, several key themes can be sorted out. The refashioning of ventriloquism suggests, first of all, how the literati went about making naturalistic, universal categories for explaining (away) religious phenomena—in this case, for exposing and disciplining the irrational voices of religious experience, whether close to home with enthused Protestants or farther afield with Eskimo shamans. Out of the confluence of learning, exhibition, and amusement emerged a knowledge of religion as an object of both study and suspicion. The turning of ventriloquism into a stage art was also indicative of the translation of religious practices into commercial entertainments, the absorption of the sacred and the magical into diverting, didactic spectacles. Such doubled voices eventually became so safe that various Christian entertainers embraced the ventriloquist's illusion as a form of evangelism.

Additionally, the way in which this auditory deception was handled in epistemological discussions, especially among the Scottish Common-Sense philosophers, opens a window on the larger education of the senses central to much of Enlightenment pedagogy. Improving the senses and building trust in their discriminating powers were fundamental to the advancement of the experimental philosophy, and ventriloquism was, perversely enough, pressed into service for the refinement of the ear. Beyond occupying a place in the learned's perceptual projects, these multiplicitous voices were also intertwined with the larger "rewriting" of the soul in terms of the fragmentations of the self.[4] As the philosophical lens shifted from the Christian drama of salvation to the phenomena of fissured and counterfeited identities, ventriloquists embodied that dislocation. Their protean act became an emblem of the culturally pervasive anxieties about personal identity, especially as those were magnified (and tamed) in the Scottish philosophy. Finally, this sportive knowledge of the slipperiness of the human voice intertwined with much wider anatomical and medical studies of auditory illusions, those thought to be a product of disease and madness.

What natural philosophers sought was a larger anatomy and psychology of hallucination for which the ricocheting voices of ventriloquism served as one small inlet—a madcap show of the terrible vulnerabilities of the human mind.

Vocal Artifice: An Enlightenment Theory of the Origins of Religion

From late antiquity through the early decades of the eighteenth century, ventriloquism was deeply embedded in Christian discourses about demon possession, necromancy, and pagan idolatry. The term itself, in its Latin derivation, meant literally "one who speaks from the belly," and it long held a place among many other specialized markers for different types of divination, prophecy, and conjuring. As Reginald Scot explained in *The Discoverie of Witchcraft* (1584), "Pythonists" or "Ventriloqui" speak in a "hollowe" voice, much different from their usual one, and are "such as take upon them to give oracles" or "to tell where things lost are become." In demonological discussions, such nomenclature was used to refer to those who were overcome by "a familiar spirit," who spoke during trances or fits in an apparently diabolical voice, or who claimed soothsaying powers.[5]

Much of the formative discussion of ventriloquy in the Christian tradition focused on the story of the Witch of Endor recounted in 1 Samuel 28, in which King Saul disguises himself and visits a sorceress in hopes of summoning up the ghost of Samuel and discerning the future of his battle against the Philistines. With the help of the necromancer, Saul hears the prophet Samuel speak from beyond the grave—an apparent success for the soothsayer that made for considerable anxious commentary in the patristic literature and long afterward: Why would God allow necromancy, a practice repeatedly abominated, to be used for divine purposes? Was this whole

19. The Witch of Endor ▸
The debate over ventriloquism was long grounded in Christian exegesis of the episode involving the Witch of Endor and the raising of Samuel's apparition. The seventeenth-century inquirer Joseph Glanvill was sure that the voice Saul heard was real—a technique of the devil perhaps, but not the mere vocal artifice of the conjurer. From Joseph Glanvill, *Saducismus Triumphatus; Or, Full and Plain Evidence Concerning Witches and Apparitions*, 2 vols. (London: J. Collins, 1681), vol. 1, frontispiece. Courtesy of the Princeton University Library, Rare Books and Special Collections.

And Saul perceiued that it was Samuel. and he stouped with his face to the ground. and bowed himself. 1ˢᵗ Samuel. Chap: 28: v. 14.

scene not accomplished through the power of the devil? Was this apparitional voice of Samuel real and prophetic, or only a diabolical illusion created by the enchantress to trick a weakened Saul? The story bundled many
crucial theological issues together, but among the most intriguing to centuries of interpreters was the question about the source of the ventriloquized
voice—namely, who was speaking and by what means or powers.[6]

In the early modern versions of this debate about Samuel's ghost, inter-
locutors swung, as in the larger controversies over witchcraft, between
those who saw the power of the demonic and the supernatural on display
and those who supported increasingly materialistic or skeptical explanations. Reginald Scot's work, a leading harbinger of dissent from long-standing demonic readings, shifted the blame, comparing the woman's powers
to that constant Protestant bugbear of Catholic "magic": "Let us confesse
that *Samuell* was not raised . . . and see whether this illusion may not be
contrived by the art and cunning of the woman, without anie of these
supernaturall devices: for I could cite a hundred papisticall and cousening
practises, as difficult as this, and as cleanlie handled." Amid his detailed explanations, Scot speculated that the diviner was a cunning ventriloquist
who "abused *Saule*" with her "counterfeit hollow voice." In the opposite
camp, Joseph Glanvill, who, as a member of the Royal Society, was committed to establishing an empirical base for the defense of Christian supernaturalism, argued that it was "a *real* Apparition" and thought that the
ventriloquial explanation was nonsense: "It cannot certainly in any reason
be thought, that the Woman could by a natural knack, speak such a Discourse as is related from *Samuel,* much less that she could from her Belly
imitate his Voice, so as to deceive one that knew him as *Saul* did." For
Glanvill—as with the Mathers, Henry More, and George Sinclair—the con-
tention that necromancers, witches, and demoniacs were mostly frauds
was mere sophistry. Diabolical as well as prophetic utterances were part of
a biblical world of spirits, apparitions, and wonders that Glanvill and his
various allies stood ready to defend against the incipient challenges of skeptical critics.[7]

The scriptural debate over the Witch of Endor and the sources of Samuel's voice had its lived counterpart in the "sacred theater" of possession
that haunted seventeenth-century Protestants and Catholics alike.[8] In the
context of such dramatic religious phenomena, "ventriloquy" was one of
the terms used to debate whether or not Satan was speaking through the
possessed. Was it a "familiar spirit" who made people roar out in low and

unnatural voices, speak in languages heretofore unknown to them, taunt ministers and godly neighbors, or mimic the cries of animals in what amounted to an infernal menagerie? Or were those afflicted with such voices, bellowings, and barkings fraudulent or diseased? As the Reverend John Whiting reported of a Hartford woman, Ann Cole, in 1662, she "was taken with strange fits, wherein she (or rather the devil, as 'tis judged, making use of her lips) held a discourse for a considerable time." One of the signs that the devil was indeed speaking "vocally" in another New England woman, Elizabeth Knapp, was that she often uttered her "reviling" expressions without "any motion at all" of her mouth and lips—"a clear demonstration," Increase Mather thought, "that the voice was not her own." Those who held to the supernaturalist position heard, in these "grum, low" voices from sometimes motionless lips, highly compelling evidence for the fearful presence of demons.[9]

Skeptics were inevitably contemptuous of all such trickeries of the voice, all the supposed fraud of demoniacs and soothsayers. In *A Perfect Discovery of Witches* (1661), Thomas Ady described ventriloquism as a commonplace scam used by impostors to make people "beleeve that they are possessed by the Devil, speaking within them, and tormenting them, and so do by that pretence move the people to charity."[10] In *Leviathan* (1651), Thomas Hobbes, arguing for the prevalence of religious impostures, was predictably scathing about vocal artifice, describing ventriloquism as a means by which enchanters were "able to make very many men believe" that their own voice "is a voice from Heaven." If the construct still required further sharpening, already it was being whetted for use against pious fraud. As another British exposer of demonic displays explained in 1718, "Some Counterfeits can speak out of their Bellies with a little or no Motion of their Lips. They can change their Voices, that they shall not be like their own. They can make, that what they shall say be heard, as if it was from a different Part of the Room, or as if it came from their own Fundament." "Such persons are call'd," he said, "*Engastriloques, or Ventriloquists.*"[11]

For all the sneering of skeptics, these discussions long remained torn. The lexicographer Thomas Blount captured this ambivalence in his entry under "ventriloquist" for his *Glossographia* (1656)—"one that has an evil spirit speaking in his belly, or one that by use and practice can speake as it were out of his belly, not moving his lips." In the late 1740s John Wesley, given his own first-hand experiences with the possessed and with exorcising prayer, easily placed the term in a frame similar to Glanvill's, suggest-

20. A Clever Invention

Joannes Baptista de La Chapelle, the consummate Enlightenment theorist of the vocal artifices used for religious impostures, honed his experimental skills through a variety of projects to aggrandize state power, including the development of a flotation device for the conveyance of soldiers across bodies of water. The fashionable touch of a swan headdress was designed to make the bobbing soldier less conspicuous. From Joannes Baptista de La Chapelle, *Traité de la construction théorique et practique du scaphandre, ou du bateau de l'homme* (Paris: Debure, 1775), plates III and IV. Shelfmark

ing that rationalistic critics who saw mere guile in extraordinary religion were wrongheaded. In one American replay of the debate in 1773, Congregationalist Ezra Stiles, a notable bearer of Enlightenment learning in New England, tried to convince a rabbi in Newport, Rhode Island, of the wisdom of a theatrical explanation for necromantic voices: "He had not heard of Ventriloquism before and still doubted it." In another American rendition in 1810, Frederick Quitman, a Lutheran minister who was ashamed of lingering Christian "superstitions," suggested that the Witch of Endor be interpreted as "a ventriloquist, who could speak in a manner unobserved by the spectators." Another preacher, Robert Scott, quickly countered Quitman's exegesis with a public rejoinder affirming the divine reality of the apparition and the voice. Ventriloquism remained embroiled in theological debates about the diabolical, the revelatory, and the magical, even as skeptics sought to turn it into a consummate example of staged religious imposture.[12]

The decisive turn toward the Enlightenment construction of ventriloquism was made in 1772 by Joannes Baptista de La Chapelle (1710–1792). That year, La Chapelle—mathematician, pedagogue, acoustician, and participant in the leading scientific societies of France and England—published his 572-page opus *Le Ventriloque, ou L'Engastrimythe* in London and Paris. Part of the much wider currents within the Enlightenment striving to establish a natural history of pious frauds, La Chapelle's treatise took its place in that stream of works fed by writers such as Hobbes, Fontenelle, van Dale, Charles Blount, John Trenchard, and David Hume. As a mathematician of respected standing and as an inventor who relished showing the practical applications of his learning, La Chapelle was well positioned to join the philosophical band in "the propagation of universal reason." Prior to this massive tome on ventriloquism, his most widely circulated work, the two-volume *Institutions de géométrie,* was a quintessential Enlightenment textbook and Cartesian blueprint. It presented the instruction of children in mathematics as the best means for enshrining the purity of reason and for inculcating the habits of exactitude that would lead to ever greater knowledge of nature. Though always wanting to restrain the vagaries of prejudice and the religious imagination, La Chapelle regularly gave free reign to his own technological fantasies, showing how mathematical reasoning issued in one solution after another for the operative needs of the state—in mining, communications, and warfare. His inventiveness included the grand design of a cork-filled flotation device that he labeled

L'homme-bateau, useful not only as a lifesaver for shipwrecked travelers, but also as a clandestine conveyance for soldiers.[13]

It was his applied geometry, notably his *Traité des sections coniques* (1765), that led La Chapelle into the domain of acoustics—a field in which he distinguished himself as an investigator of the physics of speaking trumpets, the main heir of Samuel Morland's mantle. His acoustic research on the improvement of these voice-carrying devices made him, in effect, a natural to take up the mechanics of deceptive religious voices. Scientific instruments could augment the range at which human utterances were heard; the voice was manipulable and extendable; it was capable of being duplicated and disjoined from the body of the speaker. The experimental knowledge behind a "machine" like the *Porte-voix* was apt preparation for a rationalistic interpretation of revelatory voices and mediumistic phenomena: the subtle art of propagating these mysterious sounds could likewise be penetrated. La Chapelle was well positioned to correct the defects of the ear, to become a consummate demystifier of the auditory.[14]

Though now all but forgotten—not gaining even a mention in any of the standard genealogies of the Enlightenment's production of a critical study of religion—La Chapelle's *Le Ventriloque* was a peculiarly influential work. It provided much of the basic analysis of these sorts of vocal phenomena across Europe and North America for the next century. Translated into Dutch (1774), Italian (1786), and Russian (1787), it was widely disseminated and even more widely abstracted. His book was the main source for the 1797 entry on ventriloquism in the *Encyclopaedia Britannica* (and its ensuing American incarnation); it was cited by Charles Brockden Brown as the background on the subject for his major fictional creation of Carwin, the rogue ventriloquist, in *Wieland* (1798) and in the serialized, fragmentary sequel *Memoirs of Carwin the Biloquist* (1803–1805); it provided all of the material for one of the first American expositions of the art, a small pamphlet published in Morristown, New Jersey, in 1799; it influenced a mix of philosophical interpreters, from Dugald Stewart to David Brewster to Eusèbe Salverte; and its stories even became staples of popular how-to guides by the mid-nineteenth century. La Chapelle, more than anyone else, reinvented ventriloquism as a generalized category for the rationalistic explanation of religion's most puzzling vocal phenomena. He gave it renewed currency as an idea; others would then turn his philosophical observations into a system of rational recreation, a widely recognized form of stage entertainment.[15]

La Chapelle, beginning his work in the skein of the age-old Christian debate about the Witch of Endor and the apparitional voice of Samuel,
wanted to cut through the whole theological tangle. Defending the view
that the soothsayer was a studied impostor with the ability to feign voices
and to pass them off as supernatural, La Chapelle expanded this archetypal
case of necromantic fraud into a blanket explanation that moved from the
artifice of the ancient oracles (following van Dale and Fontenelle) to the
credulity and fanaticism of his contemporaries. He moved the debate out
of the biblical narratives, the scriptural commentaries, and the theological
territory of demonology into the domains of experimental observation,
acoustic inquiry, and anatomical dissection. (It was the anatomy of the
mouth and throat, not the belly, argued La Chapelle, that deserved examination in the search for the "causes" of this vocal phenomenon.) Ventriloquism, he concluded, was an art, a practiced technique of modulation, misdirection, and muscular control; it required neither supernatural assistance
nor any special endowments of nature. Locating two contemporaries who
had developed ventriloquial skills for their own amusement—one a Vien-
nese baron who dabbled in puppetry and mimicry, and the other a local
grocer named Saint-Gille who always enjoyed a good practical joke—La
Chapelle built his explanatory framework on scientific report and empirical
observation, particularly of the grocer. To understand religious imposture,
La Chapelle did not need to view the possessed or the inspired; instead, all
he required was close observation of an impish illusionist. That was a fate-
ful shift of perspective.[16]

La Chapelle insisted that Saint-Gille was an honest man and hence a reliable source, but the shopkeeper certainly had a roguish streak, confounding people with his amateur illusions time and again. One story, aptly titled
"Les Religieux dupés," was particularly important for La Chapelle's purpose of establishing his point that ventriloquism was a generative force of
religious delusion, that it was an important technique for creating "an appearance of revelation." Taking refuge in a monastery during a storm,
Saint-Gille learns that the brothers are in mourning over the recent death
of one of their members; visiting the tomb in the church, Saint-Gille projects a ghostly voice purporting to be that of the dead friar—one that laments the indifferent prayers of his fellows for his suffering soul in Purga-
tory. Soon the ventriloquist has the whole community praying for
forgiveness, falling on the floor in fear and astonishment, and trying des-
perately to make amends to their lost brother. Overawed by the divine evi-

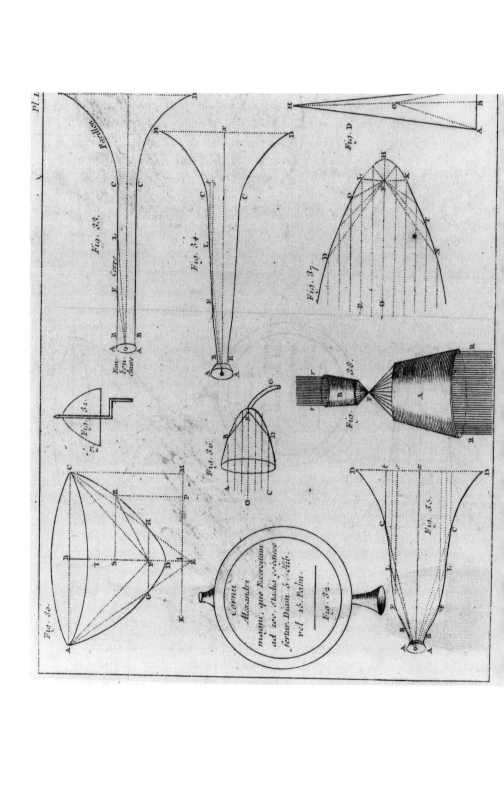

Fig. 33.

Fig. 34.

Fig. 31.

Fig. 30.

Fig. 36.

Fig. 37.

Fig. D

Fig. 38.

Fig. 32.

Fig. 35.

Cornu
Alexandri
magni, quæ Exercitum
ad 100. Stadia: vocisse
fertur Diam 5. Cub.
vel 16. Palm.

Poëllou

Corps

Embouchure

dences he finds in the spectral voice, the prior even tells Saint-Gille that such apparitions effectively put to flight all the skeptical reasonings of the philosophers. But then Saint-Gille, La Chapelle reports in all seriousness, lets the duped in on the trickery—telling them that it had all been done by the art of ventriloquy, that he himself is the all-too-human source of this oracle. In the consummate act of the enlightened magician, Saint-Gille takes the devout back to the church and turns it into the scene of their awakening from illusion, showing them his techniques of mystification. La Chapelle, reaffirming the ease with which the senses are deceived and the need for critical reason, drew out the doubled moral of the story: "The art of the ventriloquists is excellent for establishing and destroying superstition."[17]

That farcical story became La Chapelle's most renowned scene, reproduced from one commentary to another, with its anti-Catholic dimensions taking on an added edge when repeated in Britain and North America. La Chapelle's formal experiments with Saint-Gille, monitored by two other observers from the Académie Royale des Sciences, conjured up similar conclusions. In one test, Saint-Gille's talents were employed to convince a credulous woman that she heard the voice of a spirit, and then the researchers laboriously persuaded her of the real source of her illusion (the gendered aspects of this exhibition—the men of reason, the woman of superstitious faith—were all too transparent). To La Chapelle, the point of such demonstrations was that he had found one of the originating causes of religious phantasms and that now, so identified, ventriloquism could be turned with delicious irony from being a buttress of superstition to a tool of the Enlightenment. The study of nature had yielded up the secrets of the sorcerer's power, as well as the ancient springs of political and religious despotism, and now those demystified illusions could be turned into a Baconian theater, a didactic exhibition that would enact rationality's triumph over superstition and truth's routing of fraud. Other writers on the subject would improve the details of La Chapelle's anatomy and add to his data, but most

21. The Mathematics of Speaking Trumpets

La Chapelle, well schooled in acoustics, was one of the key eighteenth-century elaborators of the mechanics and mathematics of speaking trumpets. From Joannes Baptista de La Chapelle, *Traité des sections coniques, et autres courbes anciennes* (Paris: Debure, 1765), plate III. Shelfmark 1651-626. Courtesy of the British Library.

would repeat his basic conviction: ventriloquism was a primeval font of religious error that was capable of being turned from the purposes of occult mystery to modern *éclaircissement*.[18]

La Chapelle's experimental observations had immediate relevance to the much larger battle against religious enthusiasm. This was especially evident in appropriations among the Scottish Common-Sense philosophers. Dugald Stewart, in his *Elements of the Philosophy of the Human Mind* (3 vols., 1792–1827), placed his consideration of ventriloquism at the end of a long section on "sympathetic imitation" in which he considered the human propensity for copying others and the weighty influence that the imagination has on the body. Here, joining a train of medical writers, he took up "the contagious nature of convulsions, of hysteric disorders, of panics, and of all different kinds of enthusiasm" and turned to the joined importance of imitation and imagination to explain these varied phenomena. In crowded and noisy assemblies, whether political or religious, people were given to "spasmodic affections"; "their senses and their imagination" overstimulated, they were incapable of the "cool exercise" of the "reasoning powers." Animal magnetism was Stewart's leading example of people's susceptibility to such "theatrical representations," but that was part of a longer train of popular enthusiasms and religious frenzies (such as the Quakers, the French Prophets, and the massive evangelical revival at Cambuslang) for which sympathy, contagion, and "mechanical imitation" provided guiding categories of explanation. The Scottish Enlightenment was hardly any more moderate than the French when it came to efforts to retune the resonances of popular Christian piety.[19]

Ventriloquism was relevant to this discussion for Stewart because of the crucial role that "the imagination of the spectator or of the hearer" played in the human susceptibility to both deception and enthusiasm. Whereas some wanted to emphasize the formal acoustic dimensions of vocal illusions, for Stewart the point was the way in which the ventriloquist "manages the imaginations of his audience" through suggestion, misdirection, counterfeiting, and theater. Stewart accented the complicity of the deceived, the ways in which their own imaginations were excited, making up for any gaps in the artifice, finally yielding, "without resistance, to the agreeable delusions practised on [them] by the artist." The ventriloquist was thus like the mesmerist or the revivalist in bringing the imaginations of his spectators under his own skillful management. In his *Letters on Natural Magic,* David Brewster picked up on Stewart's point, attesting that the susceptibility of the human imagination to fall for such vocal illusions was immense, the superstitious person being "the willing dupe of his own judgment." "The influence over the human mind which the ventriloquist derives from the skillful practice of his art," Brewster concluded, "is greater than that which is exercised by any other species of conjuror." Stressing the ventriloquist's enormous power to manipulate people's superstitious imaginations, Brewster suggested that the accomplished artist had "the supernatural always at his command," being able to "summon up innumerable spirits" and to make them "unequivocally present to the imagination of his auditors." Such vocal artifice was, in short, the priest's treasure and the enthusiast's downfall.[20]

No one made more sophisticated use of La Chapelle's propositions about ventriloquism and religious illusion than did the American novelist Charles Brockden Brown, whose *Wieland; Or, The Transformation* and *Memoirs of Carwin, the Biloquist* centered on just such themes. Brown, like Tom Paine, journeyed from a Quaker upbringing into deistic skepticism, and Carwin's ventriloquist act was one emblem of Brown's religious disavowals. The Wieland family, steeped via their father in a long history of radical Protestant sectarianism, proves an easy target for Carwin's deceptions after his arrival at their tranquil home. Clara and her brother Theodore, for all their cultivation of republican virtue and education, retain active religious imaginations and are all too ready to attribute supernatural agency to Carwin's mysterious voices. The pious Theodore, after all, has long sought "the blissful privilege of direct communication" with God, "of listening to the audible enunciation" of divine speech. Clara, somewhat more cautious, is torn by the appearance of the marvelous, but ultimately lacks "grounds on which to build a disbelief." Carwin, too late, will provide the naturalistic basis for presuming "auricular deception" through his learned exposition of ventriloquy, or biloquism (Brown uses the two terms interchangeably). Earlier Carwin, tipping his hand, has tried to make the Wielands aware of "the power of mimicry," but they remained impervious to his "mode of explaining these appearances," incapable of absorbing such knowledge.[21]

Similar credulity within Carwin's own family started him in the cultivation of this art. "A thousand superstitious tales were current in the family," Carwin avers in the *Memoirs*. "Apparitions had been seen, and voices had been heard on a multitude of occasions. My father was a confident believer in supernatural tokens. The voice of his wife, who had been many years dead, had been twice heard at midnight whispering at his pillow." Seeing in such popular Christian beliefs an opening to manipulate his father, Carwin feels emboldened to move from simple mimicry and the ventriloquizing of distant voices to feigning utterances of the dead as well as the divine. Traveling through Spain, Carwin becomes a master at manipulating Catholic "superstitions," very much on the model of Saint-Gille, but his vocal artifice proves equally powerful over the imaginations of faithful Protestants. Put to the test, both his own family and the Wielands fail badly at suspicion; Carwin's studied art dupes them all (with bloody consequences for the Wielands, as Theodore is eventually thrown into such religious madness by this eruption of voices that he murders his wife and children). The whole violent mess, the apparently repentant Carwin tells Clara as he reveals his technical knowledge of natural magic, provides a potent "lesson to mankind on the evils of credulity," on the fatality of religious illusions.[22]

The reimagining of ventriloquism offered a way for rationalists and deists to scorn the continuing ferment of religious enthusiasm and prophecy—all the innovative voices of evangelical awakening, all the personal discoveries of divine calling amid these outpourings of the Spirit. "No other instrument" but deft ventriloquy was necessary to "institute a new sect," Carwin learns from a European mentor—a dismissive point that La Chapelle had made directly as well. "Can you doubt that these were illusions?" Clara's uncle asks her with appropriate skepticism after hearing about the voices. "Neither angel nor devil had any part in this affair." The philosophical knowledge of ventriloquism provided a basis for canniness and disbelief, an assumption of suspicion, as well as a game of disenchantment. It offered both a naturalistic vocabulary and a distancing amusement that helped support a stance of incredulity in the face of the clamoring voices of religious inspiration and the sweeping rise of revivalistic fervor. In this respect, at least, Brown's work was less a tale of Federalist alarm or Edwardsian depravity than one of solidarity with Jeffersonian suspicion over the perils of popular Christian piety.[23]

Brown, however, still played on both sides of the fence as he exposed the inner contradictions of the new learning: Enlightenment dreams that philosophical experiments with ventriloquism would unmask popular superstitions blended into the new masquerades made possible with such rational forms of recreation. The mesmerizing impostor Carwin was less interested in taming the enthusiastic imagination than in manipulating "the ignorant and credulous" for his own ends of wealth, power, and pleasure. In Carwin, Brown created the sort of charlatan who bared the irrationality

hidden in La Chapelle's embrace of the illusionist Saint-Gille as a philosophical ally. In this juggling of the Enlightenment and magic, reason easily
slipped into humbug, and such subversions from within made the natural
philosopher's hope of containing the eruptive voices of popular Christianity all the more a pipe dream.[24]

The uses to which La Chapelle's theory could be put ultimately extended far beyond such "local" applications within European and North
American Christianity. It offered a naturalistic lens on religions across the
board and came specifically to provide a way of making sense of indigenous conjurers encountered through colonial contact. La Chapelle and his
varied heirs had all seen ventriloquism as part of that ancient conspiracy of
priestly magicians, as one of the chief means employed among Egyptians,
Greeks, and other pagans to produce oracular illusions. Dugald Stewart,
though, made a significant extension of the construct by concluding his remarks on the subject in *Elements of the Philosophy of the Human Mind* with
an account of Captain George Lyon's travels among the Eskimos. Lyon's
story was then picked up by David Brewster in his *Letters on Natural Magic*,
quickly becoming part of the ventriloquist's echo chamber.

Stewart and Brewster read Lyon's "curious" narrative of exploration
with their new explanatory tools, ready to incorporate these "savages" and
their "male wizards" into the natural history of superstition. Lyon himself
had licensed this reading, finding "all the effect of ventriloquism" in the
various imitations that he saw enacted among the Eskimos by "an ugly and
stupid-looking young glutton." Speaking wryly of a diviner's possession by
a spirit named Tornga and the hollow voice that replaced the shaman's
own, Lyon reported what he heard in diction shaped by his knowledge of
ventriloquism: "Suddenly the voice seemed smothered, and was so managed as to sound as if retreating beneath the deck, each moment becoming
more distant, and ultimately giving the idea of being many feet below the
cabin, when it ceased entirely." Brewster, Stewart, and Lyon saw no mystery in the conjurer's powers, no threat of difference, no hint of the ecstatic
or the demonic, only the natural curiosity of the ventriloquist's illusion,
only what Euro-American stage magicians had by now rendered a harm-
less and humorous simulation. "The Eskimaux of Igloolik," it turned out,
were simply, as Brewster said, "ventriloquists of no mean skill." Philosopher and explorer joined together to make ventriloquism a vagrant hypoth-
esis available for explaining Eskimo "wizards" as readily as Delphic oracles
or sectarian enthusiasts.[25]

This rational recreation as a framework for encounter lingered. Decades later one of the major ethnographers among the Chukchees and Eskimos still included in his massive field report a section on "ventriloquism and other tricks" in his discussion of religious practices. "The Chukchee ventriloquists," he observed, "display great skill, and could with credit to themselves carry on a contest with the best artists of the kind of civilized countries . . . It is really wonderful how a shaman can keep up the illusion." As with the Enlightenment fabrication of shamanism and fetishism as global constructs, universalizing the category of ventriloquism allowed the learned to take "possession" of such indigenous practices in the stock terms of imposture and credulity. It enabled them to perform their own interpretive sleight-of-hand of transforming the strange into the familiar, ritual into art(ifice).[26]

As wildly vagrant as the excursions of Stewart and Brewster were, ventriloquism's use as a construct for advancing rationality and embarrassing superstition continued to widen. In a lengthy American tract called *Ventriloquism Explained* (1834), with a laudatory preface by the Amherst geologist Edward Hitchcock, the avowed hope was the further "diffusion of Scientific principles" of material causation and the negation of all the old wonders—ghosts, visions, voices, prognostications. The focus was especially on refining the judgment of the young, so that they would avoid being deceived by the slippery talk of mountebanks as well as the supernatural tales of "colored servants." Here, one more time, were La Chapelle's stories of Saint-Gille's religious dupes and Dugald Stewart's appropriation of Captain Lyon's travels. Some years later, in 1851, La Chapelle's abusive pranks were given an even more explicitly racial spin in the anecdote of one performer who supposedly disrupted a black revival meeting with a series of thrown voices. "Les Religieux dupés" had become, in this American incarnation, "Blitz and the Darkies," though, tellingly, illumination was not offered to the "cullered bredderen." Instead, the narrator invited his ostensibly white reader to share a good laugh at the irredeemably credulous; the ventriloquist, having broken up the meeting, left them with "their eyes rolled heavenward." Though one of the earliest ventriloquists, Richard Potter, was possibly the son of a slave mother and a white master, stage ventriloquism remained a predominantly Euro-American technique, a theatrical chiaroscuro in which the "white magic" of enlightened ingenuity was contrasted with "dark" superstition.[27]

The themes of priestly illusion and shamanistic deception kept sounding. This was especially the case in the bargain how-to guides on ventriloquy that began to appear in greater numbers after mid-century, such as *Everybody a Ventriloquist* (1856), *Ventriloquism Made Easy* (1860), *The Practical Magician, and Ventriloquist's Guide* (1876), or *How to Become a Ventriloquist* (1891). These little pop-culture books stood as the quintessential embodiments of the reduction of the necromantic voice to rational technique and boyish fun. That displacement was alive and well with L. Frank Baum's humbug wizard, the Great and Terrible Oz, who, as a master ventriloquist, uses an oracular head to cow the populace of the Emerald City. But the deceptive voice of priestly power now proves no match even for the Small and Meek Dorothy and her ragtag companions. With the curtain pulled back, the wizard's voice is reduced to a tremble, and the mystifying tricks of natural magic are turned, once again, into an edifying children's story.[28]

In 1900, another American writer, George Havelock Helm, offered a translation of a French essay on ventriloquism and prophecy by physiologist Paul Garnault that distilled this Enlightenment theory of the illusionist origins of religious voices. Roving from "primitives" in China back to the Witch of Endor and apostolic tongue-speaking, and then forward again to Spiritualist mediums, the American Helm echoed the French Garnault:

> It is through the prodigy of the dead being able to speak, which could not have been rendered patent and convincing except with the aid of ventriloquism, that people became imbued with a belief in the conversations of the dead, in spirits, gods, in short, in everything pertaining to inspiration and revelation. . . . Religious and artistic ventriloquism . . . are the first source of the belief in prophecy and divination, and it is from this source that all the superstitions and religions have grown out.[29]

La Chapelle's theorizing about religion and vocal deception cast a long shadow among philosophers and popularizers alike. As the current online *Britannica* still reports, "Many peoples are adepts in ventriloquism—e.g., Zulus, Maoris, and Eskimo."

Magic Shows; Or, How to Turn the Supernatural into Entertainment

When Francis Bacon, in *New-Atlantis*, presented his vision of the model college for increasing "the knowledge of Causes, and secret motions of things," he imagined magical performance as an instrument of the

experimental philosophy. Not the gnostic occultist but the common juggler would become part of the advancement of learning—his "deceits of the senses" mastered as a tool of natural philosophy.[30] Bacon's utopian dreams found partial fulfillment in the new celebrity magicians of the late eighteenth and early nineteenth centuries, many of whom presented themselves as wholly free of any "intelligence with supernatural beings" and as offering "a most agreeable antidote to superstition."[31] The old forms of magic—alchemy, astrology, palmistry, healing, and treasure seeking—persisted and often enough even flourished, but, from the late eighteenth century on, the magician increasingly appeared as one of the alluring celebrities of the Enlightenment, a wizard arrayed against wizardry, an exposer of "supernatural humbugs."[32]

Among the most renowned of these magicians were the operators of the phantasmagoria or the magic-lantern ghost show. Especially celebrated was the French magus Etienne Gaspard Robertson, who took a well-known technology from natural magic and widely popularized it in the late 1790s. Made spectacles across Europe, phantasmagoric exhibits were quickly exported by various performers to North America, flourishing in the United States in the first quarter of the nineteenth century (and well beyond that through ongoing reinvention and improvement). As had been the case in La Chapelle's account of Saint-Gille, Robertson chose a cloistered chapel surrounded by the tombs of monks for one of his grandest displays of simulated apparitions. That setting was crucial to Robertson's design of creating a sublime spectacle of both Gothic thrills and demystifying reason. An 1802 playbill of one of Robertson's imitators proclaimed that double purpose: "This SPECTROLOGY, which professes to expose the Practices of artful Impostors and pretended Exorcists, and to open the Eyes of those who still foster an absurd Belief in GHOSTS or DISEM-

22. Phantasmagoria

The magic lantern had long been an important instrument of natural magic, but at the end of eighteenth century it was transformed into one of the grand recreations of the late Enlightenment, the phantasmagoria. In a displacement vital to the imagination of the literati, the ghost show took place in a chapel turned theater. From Etienne Gaspard Robertson, *Mémoires récréatifs scientifiques et anecdotiques,* 2 vols. (Paris: n.p., 1831–1833), vol. 1, frontispiece. Courtesy of the Library of Congress.

BODIED SPIRITS, WILL, it is presumed, afford also to the Spectator an interesting and pleasing Entertainment."[33]

These spectral projections were not lost on deistic debunkers of revealed religion. In *The Age of Reason,* Paine latched onto such shows to illustrate his larger attack on prophecy and miracle: "There are performances by sleight-of-hand, and by persons acting in concert that have a miraculous appearance, which when known are thought nothing of. And besides these, there are mechanical and optical deceptions. There is now an exhibition in Paris of ghosts or spectres, which, though it is not imposed upon the spectators as a fact, has an astonishing appearance." Deistic skepticism about the divine showmanship of miracles found performative corroboration in the entrepreneurial showmanship of enlightened natural magicians like Robertson. Miracles were illusions and impostures, and magic shows were a medium of that insight.[34]

Ventriloquism was the close ally of the phantasmagoria. Its rise as a stage art was coeval with the ghost shows, coming into its own between 1795 and 1825. Before that, ventriloquial talents did not constitute a distinct performative genre, but mingled with the assorted entertainments at fairs and markets, the shows of acrobats, jugglers, mimics, freaks, musicians, mountebanks, and puppeteers.[35] Not that the new performers who now labeled themselves "ventriloquists" had any narrower range of talents and associations: they were adepts of mimicry, mastering impressions of multiple voices, natural sounds, and animal cries (in effect, re-creating the devil's menagerie of familiars in secular form). They were also experts at "throwing" their voice, making it seem to come from various distances and places (under the floor, from the ceiling, or out of a hat). Through clever misdirection and well-nigh motionless lips, stage ventriloquists brought all kinds of invisible beings into existence, badgering, flirting, and capering with them. They also created stage doubles by animating wooden dolls and automata (such "puppets" recalled those used in witchcraft and also foreshadowed the "dummies" that eventually became the *sine qua non* of vaudeville acts of the late nineteenth century). These varied entertainments made ventriloquists impresarios of the uncanny and bearers of auditory astonishment—of sounds uncertain and confounding. Some of the early ventriloquists such as John Rannie, Richard Potter, George Sutton, Jonathan Harrington, and John Wyman achieved considerable reputations in the United States, and a few adepts such as Alexandre Vattemare, William Love, and Antonio Blitz were internationally celebrated, touring in Britain, Europe, and North America.[36]

In the United States, ventriloquism became an established stage art in the first decade of the nineteenth century and remained a popular staple of antebellum theater and entertainment. Leading the way in this host of new performers in the early republic was Pinchbeck's idol, John Rannie.[37] Much of his variegated act was the usual juggler's show of card tricks, knife swallowing, and slack-wire walking, but he also stood out as an exemplar of stage magic's entanglement with rational religion. He commonly presented himself as a magician of the Enlightenment cultivating philosophical experiments, with ventriloquism as his most prodigious talent in that line. Ventriloquism, Rannie explained in a Boston advertisement in 1804, "is one of the most singular phenomena that has been contemplated by the most enlightened sages." He described the scriptural notion of familiar spirits and then informed his potential viewers that "when the witch at *Endor* raised the apparition of Samuel," it was "by the power of Ventriloquism" that the "artful woman" occasioned "a voice to come from the Ghost, which Saul took to be the voice of the prophet himself." How the woman "managed" this voice "as she pleased," Rannie promised, would be "clearly demonstrated in the course of this evening's exhibition."[38]

Such propositions evidently did not sit well with some of Boston's Protestant faithful, long accustomed as they were to opposing both players and jugglers as dissolute influences. Rannie was soon lamenting in his advertising how hard it was "to remove the cobwebs of imposition from the eyes of ALL mankind" and how his shows were being scorned by certain "disciples of illiberality." Comparing himself melodramatically to Copernicus in his confrontation with reigning orthodoxies, Rannie insisted that he had come "before the public, with both the ability and intention of exposing, and, if possible, exterminating the very dregs of fanaticism," only to find that many people had "the self-sufficience of an Ostrich," with their unseeing heads stuck in a bush. Like any showman worthy of the name, Rannie played up the controversy; he offered these poor "contracted spirits" a few more opportunities "to clear away the mists that have been cast over their understandings" and to dispel for good *the clouds of superstition.*" Rannie's apparent travails even caught the attention of one of America's few deistic papers, Elihu Palmer's *Prospect,* which took the occasion both to mock Christian benightedness and to promote Rannie's exposure of "the Apocryphal story of the Witch of Endor." (The magician's enactment meshed well with Palmer's own enjoyment in singling out the "foolish" tale of the Witch of Endor as a particular embarrassment to Bible-enchanted Christians.) Several years later Rannie was still playing the part of the enlightened magician as he toured New York, Philadelphia, and Boston, holding out his own peculiar light to the credulous. For a decade, Rannie's concert-hall exhibitions gave performative expression to the biblical hermeneutics of Scot and the natural philosophy of La Chapelle.[39]

Rannie had plenty of company. The multiplicitous William Love, for example, continued to trade on these learned associations in his variegated shows of the 1820s and 1830s. In one broadside he captured the basic tenor of how ventriloquism was promoted as a rational recreation, rightly pointing out that the art had been probed by "the most eminent Physiologists and Anatomists in Europe" and that the deception was widely recognized as an explanation for "the miraculous responses of the ancient Deities":

> Although the above Divertisement has been constructed principally with a view of creating a couple of hours' amusement, and exciting a laugh at the expense of some of the more prominent foibles and follies of human nature, it is presumed a higher and more important [aim] has been obtained.—To the historical Student and Antiquary Mr. Love's Entertainments cannot fail to prove a source of considerable interest and gratification, as he will fully elucidate the means which were resorted to, in remote ages, to impose upon the superstitious multitude by the Pythians, or Priestesses of Apollo, at Delphi; the ENGASTRIMANDI of the Greeks, mentioned by Oecumenius and St. Chrysostom, and by the Soothsayers, Magicians, and Sorcerers.

Lessons taught about the superstitious multitudes of the past were never far removed from messages about their credulous counterparts in the present, nor was natural philosophy remote from play. As the title of a favored pedagogic text of the 1820s and 1830s presented this common conjunction of amusement and instruction, *Philosophy in Sport Made Science in Earnest*.[40]

No religious group would feel the weight of this magical showmanship more than the Spiritualists, who became the greatest commodity in this ongoing commercial exchange between religion and stage magic, the always favored source for illusionist productions. (Mormons and Shakers, to be sure, drew their share of ballyhoo as well: Barnum at one point displayed in his American Museum six "SHAKING QUAKERS!" in "FULL SHAKER COSTUME! . . . SINGING, DANCING, WHIRLING," one of whom, "*a beautiful Lady,*" spun "round with the velocity of a Top!!"; and humorist Artemus Ward was celebrated for his "genial" representations of polygamous Mor-

23. Spiritualist Acoustics
The Spiritualists were a godsend for nineteenth-century stage magicians who made the unmasking of mediums a standard part of their repertory. Much of this exposure was acoustic, presenting all the auditory tricks, real and imagined, played on dumbfounded listeners in the dark environs of séances. From Jean Robert-Houdin, "The Secrets of Stage Conjuring," 1880, Magazine Magic, 8, Harry Price Library, University of London. Courtesy of the University of London Library.

mons.) But it was the Spiritualists, above all, who never escaped their stage doubles: hardly a showman missed the opportunity to exploit the fascination with Spiritualism through counter-demonstrations of how all this otherworldly contact was accomplished through various sleights.[41]

The science in magic could supposedly reproduce all of the séance's phenomena, from table tapping to spirit hands to levitation to cabinet tricks to acoustic effects. Barnum, Ward, Antonio Blitz, and George Kirbye, among numerous others, joined in on the American side; the French great Jean Robert-Houdin led the way in Europe; the British maestros John Henry

Anderson and John Nevil Maskelyne both performed and published extensively these Spiritualist debunkings. By the time Harry Houdini (whose stage name paid homage to Robert-Houdin) was crafting his own celebrity in tandem with such Spiritualist inquiries, the trick was truly old hat, so much so that turn-of-the-century trade catalogues for magicians carried a wide assortment of accessories for "Anti-Spiritualistic Illusions." (Sid Macaire's of Chicago, for example, carried forty-seven of these kits, all of which mimicked "the latest spirit sensations.") That hackneyed familiarity hardly slowed the luxuriant spread of magical suspicion in the twentieth century, conspicuous in John Mulholland's inheritance of Houdini's mantle and still evident in the current flourishing of *Skeptical Inquirer,* with its cadre of researchers who often double as magicians, such as James Randi and Joe Nickell.[42]

Among the devotees of this modern version of natural magic, ventriloquism was often near at hand to provide a rational accounting of spirit voices and rapping sounds. This was especially evident in the career of the Davenport brothers, two of the most renowned and controversial mediums, who were regularly charged with being mere conjurers. Ira Davenport, thrown into "a magnetic trance," would speak "not as from himself, or in his usual tone of voice or manner, but apparently as the forced proxy of some one else." Of the "deep, sepulchral, unnatural" voices heard at the Davenport séances, a defender admitted that "some will ask, Was not this ventriloquism? We answer emphatically, *No.*" Or, as one sympathetic biographer admitted of the brothers' vocal gift, "The first thing that occurs to every one is that it was the result of so common an art as ventriloquism."[43] This sort of critique—that Spiritualist voices, raps, and sounds were accomplished *"by the ordinary acoustic method of the ventriloquists"*—was prevalent enough that even the arch-Theosophist Madame Blavatsky dignified it with a biting response in *Isis Unveiled.* Dismissals notwithstanding, the charge remained hard to elude performatively. As the Victorian hypnotist Walford Bodie announced in his lecture "Spiritualism and Ventriloquism," "the spirit voices" were simply "the throwing of the voice by the medium or the exponent into another place, and the creation of the idea that the sound comes from some hidden spirit in that place." Bodie, who billed himself as "The Man with Twelve Voices," then claimed to show his audience how this was done. Saint-Gille was clearly flourishing as a huckster more than a century after the fact.[44]

When the charge of ventriloquism greeted female mediums, the battle became sharply gendered. As with other forms of stage magic, ventriloquism through the mid-nineteenth century was an exclusively male profession; such wizardry, like Masonic ritual, was a distinctly masculine preserve in which women seemed (quite literally) either to disappear or to be invisible. "There have been few female ventriloquists," one guidebook (misnamed *Everybody a Ventriloquist*) noted in 1856. "Effects produced by the female organs of speech have always manifested a deficiency of power." Such putative inadequacies did not keep acoustician Charles Page from discovering the ventriloquism of the Fox sisters, the founding mediums of the Spiritualist movement, when he went to observe them. Familiar with the explanatory schemes of Brewster's natural magic, Page became quickly convinced that the girls were cleverly misdirecting people's attention to get them to think sounds were coming from where they were not: "Our knowledge of ventriloquism," he said, "fortified us against this trick," and then he provided (via Brewster) a detailed excursus on the mechanisms of acoustic artifice. In Page's scripting, men like himself had the authoritative knowledge of natural magic (and implicitly the option to perform it for decent money); women had fraudulent gimmicks and sympathetic imaginations. When ventriloquism was seen as a biblical and spiritual form of deception, it was female; when it had market value and philosophical interest, it was male (indeed, exclusively so, since the female voice supposedly lacked the "power" for this public form of the art).[45]

For all the commercial potential of religion for nineteenth-century showmen, perhaps the most noteworthy dimension of this theater remained the sacred's strange disappearance under the cloak of entertainment. The Witch of Endor had a markedly different feel when the popular exegetes were showmen, not ministers or churchgoers. One of the compatriots of Rannie and Pinchbeck, a Mr. Martin, another operator of the phantasmagoria, advertised in June 1808 in New York that he was putting the devil on display in the Lyceum and that, despite some opposition, he would "show as many devils" as the people "may desire to see." An annoyed critic in the *Commercial Advertiser* derided Martin's exhibitions—"the devil dances on stilts to the tune of a hand organ"—but also made note of a troubling displacement: "The lyceum is a place converted from a church into a place of amusement for vulgar minds."[46] That little episode should hardly be taken as an emblem of any unilateral turn in this exchange between church and theater; the transactions have long flowed in both directions.[47] Still, it is hard not to see a taming in these new spectacles of the demonic, a soaking up of the fears of popular piety into the diversions of entertainment. What showmen provided were more and more opportunities to watch the flickering shadows of the supernatural, to relish the play of "special effects" rather than to contemplate the terrors of the soul. Barnum and his many compatriots knew this much: the consumer demands satisfaction, not deliverance.

Showmen not only tamed the spiritual realm through theatrical illusion; they even more clearly commodified magic and themselves, and, in that packaging, necromancy often lost much of its own enchantment, demonic and otherwise. Those religious resonances that remained once ventriloquism had been turned into a stage performance often seeped away, becoming an insignificant or nonexistent part of the ventriloquist's capers. An emblem of that blotting out can be discerned in one of Alexandre Vattemare's vocal illusions: "M. Alexandre will conclude," a London broadside from 1821 announced, "with causing A VOICE to proceed from the STOMACH of any one present." The belly-speaking demons were completely removed from earshot, even as this stage stunt eerily echoed them. One late nineteenth-century account of "Celebrated Ventriloquists" started with La Chapelle's proposition about the origins of the oracles, but then noted that the art, now shorn of any religious consequence, is, "happily, only the source of innocent amusement." Likewise, in an article entitled "How I Became a Ventriloquist," one practitioner explained in 1879 that there was nothing particularly mysterious about his multivoiced talents, that indeed a ventriloquist is "a very ordinary mortal," something any boy could become. Whereas Rannie, Vattemare, Comte, and Love were in the habit of promoting the Enlightenment significance of their performances (in addition to all the fun to be had), after mid-century few entertainers of this type bothered to advertise such learned connections. Their shows offered comic sketches, humorous imitations, and light-hearted fantasies—simply an evening to laugh away life's cares.[48]

That promotional shift need not be taken as a sign of the Enlightenment's failure; instead it can be seen as an indication of the thoroughness of this particular victory. Stage ventriloquism managed to submerge its oracular, demonic, and Christian precursor within the expanding culture of commodified leisure. The illusionist recreations of the Enlightenment, like the phantasmagoria, helped lay the groundwork for a whole complex of modern entertainments. Ventriloquism shared in this luxuriant growth;

as a commercial amusement, it passed into vaudeville, cinema, radio (incongruously enough), and television; it even became a pop-culture icon with Edgar Bergen and Charlie McCarthy.[49] Within this culture of showmanship, it takes something of an excavation to discern the old meanings of ventriloquism. As E. B. Tylor—in his monumental study *Primitive Culture* (1871)—remarked of the naturalistic abandonment of an animistic universe, in "old times" the ventriloquist "was really held to have a spirit rumbling or talking from inside his body"; now he was a stage entertainer, no longer a shaman but a showman. "How changed a philosophy it marks," concluded Tylor, a cultural evolutionist not known for his nostalgia, "that among ourselves the word 'ventriloquist' should have sunk to its present meaning."[50] The stage magician and his philosophical expositors made ventriloquism an easy and entertaining trick, a show of mastered simulation, available for the price of admission. In that, ventriloquism was indicative of the much larger absorption of religion into mediated, spectacular forms of modern consumption.

Contained in the reminiscences of Artemus Ward was a fitting epitaph for this passage of magic into entertainment: "The weird necromancer of the past and the prestidigitator of the present are very different sort of beings. All the atmosphere of supernatural solemnity which enveloped the sorcerer and the cabalist of ancient times has dissolved away. The conjuror of modern days is as commonplace and unromantic as the rest of his fellow-men; sometimes he is a little more so." Enlightened showmen exposed supernatural humbugs—with hollow oracles, faked voices, and projected spirits—but they also, perhaps even more effectively, unmasked themselves. As James Randi recently explained of his once priestly art, "The conjuror is a character actor, a juggler of the senses and a master of psychology, and makes no attempt to *be* a guru, saint, clairvoyant, or messiah. Entertainment is the goal."[51]

The demonic voices and the divine locutions of the old ventriloquism sounded incredibly docile once turned into an amusement. Just how safe that medium had become is indicated by the evangelical embrace of the art as an acceptable form of evangelistic entertainment over the past several decades. Now "gospel vents" have crowded onto the stage with their older vaudeville counterparts—stalwarts in a thriving evangelical subculture of entertainers, puppeteers, clowns, and magicians, most of whom aim their ministries at children and youth. This convergence, with roots at least as early as the 1920s, took firm hold by the 1950s with the formation of the Fellowship of Christian Magicians—a group that has been publishing a magazine for almost half a century called *The Christian Conjurer*. This trend in Christian entertainment has even resulted in dozens of little tracts such as *111 Ways to Use Ventriloquism in Church Work*, *The Gospel Ventriloquist*, and *Using Ventriloquism in Christian Education*. In the last-named pamphlet, from 1976, pastor Robert Blazek tells the story of how he "decided to pursue the knowledge and ability to use ventriloquism for Christ," how he turned himself and his dummy "Little Joe" into a winning tandem of evangelists. Perhaps, as is common in American religious history, the evangelicals are having the last laugh with the rise of "gospel ventriloquism," with the re-Christianization of this Enlightenment amusement, but the *philosophes* might well be laughing too at their success in turning a divine struggle into a didactic illusion.[52] Like La Chapelle going to watch a magician instead of to pray over the possessed, the spirits most familiar to modern culture prowl the cinema and Disney's Magic Kingdom as much as the souls of saints and sinners.

(Dis)Trusting the Ear; Or, How to Acquire a "New Kind of Experience"

With La Chapelle's expansive reformulation of ventriloquism, the art illumined many of the issues that were central to the culture of the Enlightenment. Prominent among these were the securing of knowledge and the education of the senses. Predictably the Scottish Common-Sense thinkers, whose arguments for the reliability of human perception were so prized for American Protestant didacticism, expressed particular concern about the art's apparent challenge to the trustworthiness of experience. Both Thomas Reid and Dugald Stewart addressed the issue in their massive philosophies of the mind—Reid briefly, Stewart at some length—and such devoted American followers as Benjamin Rush, Francis Wayland, and Thomas Upham followed suit in their own compendia of the intellectual powers.

Reid, Stewart, and company dealt with these vocal deceptions in the context of their larger ambitions to defang skepticism and to sharpen judgment. The impressions that the mind received through the senses, Reid acknowledged, were "limited and imperfect," but they were not inherently "fallacious," so experimental knowledge was both widely reliable and also capable of ongoing refinement. Against the varied philosophical traditions that emphasized distrust of the senses—Platonist, Augustinian, Cartesian, and Humean—Reid was affirming and optimistic. The senses, far from being marked by inherent defect or depraved by sin, were not "given to us by some malignant demon on purpose to delude us"; rather, they were provided "by the wise and beneficent Author of nature, to give us true information of things necessary to our preservation and happiness." Reid's confident pledge was that the power of deception and the excess of credulity diminished as experience deepened and learning grew.[53]

Such propositions make apparent why the education of the senses was so integral to the advancement of this sanguine version of the Enlightenment, crucial for everything from forming proper habits of experimental observation to establishing precise discriminations of taste. For improvements in accuracy and reliability, the ear was especially marked for reformation because of its complicity in that hallmark of superstitious credulity, the gullible acceptance and repetition of hearsay. Those who "believe and report every thing they hear," in Benjamin Rush's phrase, were the object of repeated concern in Common-Sense regimens. Such unbounded credulity, undercutting any knowledge gained through human testimony, played into the hands of skeptics and required policing. Rush, who had been educated at Princeton and Edinburgh, thought the acceptance of untested hearsay such a profound disorder that he even labeled it a disease of the mind. Wholly confident in his abilities to contain both hearsay and auditory illusions, Rush was as enamored as anyone with the progressive prospects for improving the bodily senses. This was so much the case that he was ready to dispense outright with those spiritual senses that "some Christian philosophers" had imagined opening up "in a future state of existence." "The addition of these new senses will be unnecessary," Rush believed, if "the five senses we possess" already were "extended and improved" in the ways that he knew were possible through careful refinement.[54]

The acoustic deceptions of ventriloquists were understood within these epistemological debates about improving, correcting, and ordering the habits of perception. Writing in 1785, before ventriloquism had been formalized as "an engine for drawing money," Reid admitted that he (unlike La Chapelle) had not had "the fortune to be acquainted with any of these artists," but nonetheless hazarded that the vocal illusions possible were "only such an imperfect imitation as may deceive those who are inattentive, or under a panic." The powers of impersonation paled before the minute discriminations of "an attentive ear," always "able to distinguish the copy from the original." Human senses, if imperfect, emerged from these vocal tricks unscathed, perhaps even sharpened in their discernment. In the 1797 edition of the *Encyclopaedia Britannica,* another learned project coming from Edinburgh, the moral of La Chapelle's inquiry was taken to be that it provided observers with a new "ground of suspicion." After repeated study of Saint-Gille, La Chapelle gradually saw through these tricks, no longer hearing the voices as if they came from rooftops or cellars: "Our author, well acquainted with the powers of the ventriloquist, and having acquired *a new kind of experience,* at once referred [the voice] directly to the mouth of the speaker."[55]

Dugald Stewart came to the same conclusion. After frequenting a number of ventriloquists' exhibitions (and still pining to see more, especially those of the celebrated Alexandre Vattemare), Stewart decided that deceptions of this variety finally had "but narrow limits," at least for the philosophically disciplined viewer: "In the progress of entertainment, I have, in general, become distinctly sensible of the imposition; and have sometimes wondered that it should have misled me for a moment." Benjamin Rush followed a similar track in his own speculations on "the deceptions of ventriloquists." It was, he insisted, "the want of experience" that allowed these artificial voices to "deceive the ear." What Reid, Stewart, Rush, and their varied allies imagined was a fine-tuned discipline of listening, a carefully trained ear that would minimize the power of both "acoustic illusions" and "wonderful relations," that would, in effect, keep people from hearing things in gullible ways. The perceptual habits acquired through penetrating the ventriloquist's deception embodied an auditory culture of seasoned judgments, reliable inductions, and dependable words. These vagabond voices were, ironically, made another listening exercise for ordering the well-regulated mind.[56]

Brockden Brown's use of ventriloquism in *Wieland* played off these epistemological assurances. Henry Pleyel, despite the careful education of his senses, is all too ready to credit the flimsiest of hearsay about Clara's character—"a midnight conference" of defaming voices that Carwin creates. In his haste, Pleyel blunders in failing to weigh this hearsay properly—that is, by exercising critical reason and by "comparing the evidence of sight with that of hearing." In the disciplines of Common-Sense philosophy, these were two of the most important admonitions: use one sense to correct the shortcomings or misperceptions of another and be extremely vigilant in inductive reasoning, since the problem was usually not so much sensory imperfection as it was rashness of judgment in making erroneous chains of connection. In the darkness, though, Pleyel's ears are at the mercy of Carwin's deceptions: "My sight was of no use to me. . . . Hearing was the only avenue to information," Pleyel explains of his enraged leap to the wrong conclusion.[57] While Brockden Brown seemed to relish exploring this skeptical challenge to the optimism of Reid's epistemological propositions, he himself still relied on such perceptual principles to explore how it was the Wieland household went so wrong.

Benjamin Rush, displaying little of Brockden Brown's playful engagement with skepticism, drew more staunchly on these perceptual precautions in disciplining the senses. Certain, like Reid and Stewart, that the right education would remove the prejudices of superstition and enthusiasm, Rush committed himself to the Scottish system for acquiring reliable knowledge—the tripartite "marriage" of the senses, reason, and human testimony: "What God has joined together, let no man put asunder," Rush solemnly vowed. Using the popular belief in apparitions as an example, he noted that the rule of employing one sense to correct another should in itself dispel such specters. "Ghosts, it has been said, have been *seen* and *heard;* but never *handled,*" Rush noted; and this, he thought, perfectly illustrated the way in which one sense would help protect others from error—in this case, touch ensuring "the correctness of seeing and hearing." Rush then went on with his argument. Apparitions were also "contrary to *reason*" and "to one of the laws of *testimony,* which requires the congruence of several witnesses." Spirits were generally seen "by one person only," who invariably suffered from a "defective education" and who was usually "under influence of great terror." Here was Rush's bottom line: the ear, like the other organs of perception, could be trusted, but only under a system of vigilant management—that is, with the senses trained to monitor one another, with reason disciplined against superstitious judgments and unruly passions, and with hearsay held in check through the carefully regulated acceptance of human testimony.[58]

Rush exemplified a far-flung educational enterprise. Whether at Princeton, Harvard, Brown, or Bowdoin, the Scottish pedagogy of the senses was widely inherited and elaborated among American philosophers of the mind in the first half of the nineteenth century. Establishing trust in the ear and its sensuous counterparts required the formation of a well-ordered mind, with its carefully acquired habits of perception. The proper education of the senses, along with the other faculties, needed to begin with young children at home and school. "Children should be taught from their earliest years to use their senses intelligently and habitually," Princeton's James McCosh was still instructing in his book *The Senses* in 1882. The training of children's eyes and ears in the practices of careful observation was integral to the progress of scientific knowledge. At the same time, the successful formation of such perceptual routines demanded, in Thomas Upham's phrase, the containment of "imperfect and disordered sensations," including those "connected with the sense of Hearing." "The ear may be trained to habits," Upham related, and the right training still involved, for this Bowdoin philosopher, penetrating the auditory deceptions of ventriloquists.[59]

Improving the ear on these Common-Sense terms almost inevitably implied a religious corollary—namely, the mastery of the sundry misperceptions that plagued the hearing of the warmly devout. Though a convert to Holiness theology as well as a student of contemplative spirituality, Thomas Upham found at best modest space for "a living mental intercourse with heaven" amid the laws of his philosophy of the mind. In his classification of disordered auditory sensations, he invoked as an example those misguided souls whose "ears are affected with what they imagine to be the voices and songs of celestial beings." Even when drawn to Catholic mystics such as Catherine of Genoa and Jeanne Marie Guyon, Upham first had to turn them into careful guards against the illusions of the external senses. With the "natural principles" of his mental philosophy close at hand, Upham cleaned up Guyon's religious experiences of "sights seen and sounds heard." Saint Catherine, too, became an alert manager of "defective experience." As Upham observed, "She distrusted, in particular, every thing of the nature of visions, of revelations, and of remarkable impressions." Confidence in the reliability of the senses was never a simple proposition, even for Common-Sense philosophers. To trust the ear always meant knowing very precisely what experiences to distrust.[60]

"Shivered into Pieces": Voices, Impostors, and the Puzzle of Personal Identity

All along, ventriloquism fascinated as well because of its way of imagining personal identity. After Locke had made the question of the continuous self one of consciousness, and after Hume, among others, had shown just how flimsy that proposition was, many were left to wonder how to shore up the old religious anchors—the substantial permanence of the soul and the final accounting of the Last Judgment—in the face of these philosophical buffetings. Such theological twisting had its cultural counterpart in the effects of the expanding market economy and democratic solvents, both of which ate away at the fixedness of social hierarchies and made for new improvised dramas of self-fashioning. In a commercial culture, as historian Jean-Christophe Agnew has argued, the self came to be seen as increasingly performative and polymorphous, one more commodity in a mercurial economy of exchange. The widespread political and religious concerns with dissimulation and hypocrisy, with the gaps between outward displays and inward realities, were further indices of the anxieties over the manipulation and impermanence of the self. Amid this social, economic, and religious fluidity, getting a "fix" on personal identity became one of the most absorbing and intractable problems in the making of modernity, and the literati's uneasiness with the metamorphosing power of religious voices needs to be interpreted against that anxious backdrop.[61]

Into the breach of dissolving identity stepped, once again, the Scottish Common-Sense thinkers. That the self was one, not many; that personal identity was built on sameness and continuity; that personality was indivisible and whole—these were the weighty affirmations, based on underlying Christian views of the soul and moral responsibility, that Thomas Reid and his lieutenants were especially intent on sustaining. Indeed, like the assumption about the universality of the moral sense or conscience, the presupposing of personal identity was a first principle for the Scottish philosophy. In insisting on the tenacious verities of the self, Reid argued that Locke had gone awry in grounding the stability of personal identity in consciousness and memory. These, ever "flowing like the water of a river," were too shifting and transient; "one intelligent being," Reid feared, might then "be two or twenty different persons, if he shall so often lose the consciousness of his former actions." For Reid, the Common-Sense principle of personal identity admitted of "no ambiguity"; "the notion of it is fixed and precise"; it was a given truth that simply could be assumed in the face of whatever questions sophistic skeptics might raise against it. The coherence of personal identity was seen as essential to an orderly and rational Christian universe, to the provident justice of ultimate rewards and punishments, to the preservation of moral accountability and individual rights, and to the disciplined integrity of a well-regulated mind.[62]

Not surprisingly, just under the surface of such bald affirmations of unified selfhood were anarchic fears of dissolving identities—as in Reid's alarmed image of some "lunatics" who "seriously believed themselves to be made of glass; and, in consequence of this, lived in continual terror of having their brittle frame shivered into pieces." For Reid, the ventriloquist entered as one emblem of the perils of unhinged identity, irresponsibility, and roguish impersonation. If such a performer could carry his deception "to perfection" (which Reid asserted, on faith, could not be done), "a gastriloquist would be as dangerous a man in society" as someone who "could make himself invisible." Ventriloquism, successfully practiced, would permit a disappearing act, an altered or undercover identity, a spectral being without any fixed signs of character. One British ventriloquist, in describing his talents in 1798, conjured up this very horror: he claimed to speak "in a voice apparently detached from his Person, distinct from his natural Tone of Speech." Even as this new rational amusement offered a handy way of deriding religious enthusiasm and demonism, it appeared to work against one of reason's dearest adjuncts, a controlled, unified, well-bounded self. Such divided, disconnected voices seemed, indeed, the carnivalized inversion of that crystalline "inner voice" through which the universality and univocality of the moral sense was imagined.[63]

These vocal impostures were all the more suggestive for thinking about the dangerously protean qualities of the self because the voice had long been considered one of the most dependable markers of identity. As Robert Boyle had observed in the late seventeenth century of the particularity of voices, "Notwithstanding the multitude of persons, which a man . . . is wont to exchange words with, there is scarce ever any one, that he cannot by his voice distinguish from every other that he has held discourse with, and this though the same party speaks sometimes louder, sometimes lower, sometimes faster, sometimes slower, &c." Equally notable, Boyle thought, was the fundamental gendering of voices—that "one may very well distinguish the voice, whether the person that he hears, but does not see, be a man or a woman, notwithstanding the almost numberless differing voices that each of the sexes affords." The Common-Sense thinkers concurred: Thomas Reid, trying again to tweak the skeptics, pointed to the ability "to distinguish all our acquaintance . . . by their voice" as "a wonderful instance of the accuracy, as well as of the truth of our senses, in things that are of real use in life." One of Reid's faithful American disciples, Francis Wayland, likewise counted on this vocal distinctiveness in praising the ear's reliable discriminations: "The voice of every human being may easily be distinguished from that of every other."[64]

David Brewster went farther in identifying the voice with a continuous self, even avowing the "immutability" of "the human voice": the features of the face and the form of the body may change with time, but the voice always "supplies us with the full power of recognition." The very sounds of speech were impressed with "the permanence of character," Brewster averred, anticipating the idea of a voiceprint. That the voice was intimately connected to the continuities of personal identity, to the trustworthiness of social perception, and to the essentials of gender made the slippery, slithering multiplicity of ventriloquized voices, whether mediumistic or staged, all the more dangerous—and alluring. The ventriloquist flouted the pious assurances of durability and discernment, playing artfully with the referential reliabilities of the voice and teasingly subverting the comfortable essentialism of Common-Sense thinkers.[65]

Stage magicians, unlike necromancers or demoniacs, were clearly in control of a technique, so their vocal versatility was viewed as less a threat than a game—a little dangerous perhaps, but also an amusing way of externalizing these anxieties over interior diversity, of turning those divided inner voices into a skillful entertainment. In this regard, Walter Scott wrote a telling tribute in 1824 to ventriloquist Alexandre Vattemare:

> Of yore, in old England, it was not thought good
> To carry two visages under one hood;
> What should folks say to you, who have faces such plenty,
> That from under one hood you last night show'd us twenty?
> Stand forth, arch deceiver! and tell us, in truth,
> Are you handsome or ugly? in age, or in youth?
> Man, woman, or child? or a dog, or a mouse?
> Or are you, at once, each live thing in the house?

The ventriloquist, embodying dissimulation and multiplicity, made Scott ask "above all, are you one individual?" or "a troop—an assemblage—a mob"? The ventriloquist's act imagined personal identity, in effect, as a kaleidoscope (a popular device invented by David Brewster a few years before Monsieur Alexandre wowed Britain; "this system of endless changes is one of the most extraordinary properties of the Kaleidoscope," Brewster noted). The performer offered a many-visaged and ever-changing "assemblage"—an image of the self which Scott at once delighted in and feared, wondering indeed whether he needed to call in "the sheriff" to control this riotous "mob."[66]

Vattemare, who chose the itinerant life of the showman after studying for both the priesthood and medicine, was an archetypal chameleon, and, in this, he was representative of his guild. His "quick transitions of voice," his cosmopolitan ability to perform interchangeably in several languages, and his polymorphous illusions made him a latter-day Proteus (a classical allusion that came readily to mind for several who witnessed his performative powers). "The rapidity with which he effects the transformations is so inconceivable," exulted one London devotee, "as to excite continual doubts in the minds of the audience, whether the various personages who appear before them, can possibly be embodied by the same man." Important, too, were the quick changes of costume and character, the transgressive play of "age, youth, sex, gesture," of "beasts, men, women, in confusion." One Scottish theatergoer captured the lingering memories of Vattemare's act in a suggestive turn of phrase: "You may forget us—we'll not you; / For in all sorts of things around / Some fragments of you will be found."[67] In Vattemare's performances the artist seemed to dissolve into the objects around him, slivered through a series of mimetic projections. Vattemare was everyone and no one, pieces and splinters, anything and everything, as he offered up a picture of personal identity almost endlessly recombinant. To affirm the indivisibility of the self seemed a rather weightless proposition when faced with performers of such protean forms and voices. "The change of face and figure on the part of the ventriloquist," Brewster marveled with an open-mouthed astonishment dangerous for a Scottish natural philosopher, "was so perfect, that his personal identity could not be recognised in the *dramatis personae*."[68]

What ventriloquists like Vattemare and William Love presented in playful form was the dread picture of personal identity most notoriously depicted by Hume. Where Common-Sense theorists assumed constancy, intelligibility, and clarity in the idea of the self, Hume found only a chaos of shifting sensations and passions. "There is no such idea" as personal identity, he said—only "a bundle or collection of different perceptions, which succeed each other with an inconceivable rapidity, and are in a perpetual flux and movement." Personal identity was a metaphysical fiction, Hume testified: "The mind is a kind of theatre, where several perceptions successively make their appearance; pass, re-pass, glide away, and mingle in an infinite variety of postures and situations." Ventriloquy was an ideal stage art to embody such a theatrical model of multiplicity and variability. Here was not a troupe of performers all in their distinct roles, but a lone player who was a whole cast in himself, rapidly gliding between voices and identities, splitting himself again and again through mimicry, dialogue, and puppetry. Whether to exalt Hume's "discovery" of inner fragmentation or to shudder at the loss of a solid and substantial self was a quintessentially modern question (one that postmodernists and the transgendered multiples of cyberspace now seem endlessly to rediscover as peculiarly their own). Vattemare, his admirers, and his imitators came close to celebrating Hume's multivalent self.[69]

Ventriloquism also suggested, as did other stage arts, that selves were constituted in performance and through imitation, through the mimetic copying of others—what Dugald Stewart termed "the *dramatic effect* of human character and of human life." This aspect of identity hinged not on the interiors of memory and consciousness, but on the exteriors of manners, presentation, and interaction. The ventriloquist's power of impersonation suggested the strength of these imitative capacities, the proclivity for self-fashioning through mimesis, as well as the multiple ruses of social encounters. However much Stewart wanted to move from the "pliableness and mobility" of childlike imitations to the "fixed" and "disciplined" character of the well-molded adult, he remained deeply drawn to these "counterfeiting" dimensions of psychosocial life. He marveled time and again at the human capacity for mimicry, such as that of a renowned colleague who could do an unerring impersonation of Adam Smith, including "the very tones of his voice" and "all the peculiarities of his look and manner." (The imitation was actually so compelling it gave Stewart a ghostly *frisson*.) "We copy instinctively the voices of our companions, their tones, their accents, and their modes of pronunciation," Stewart observed. In this endless process of social copying, mimicry, and exchange, where did the self leave off and the selves of others begin? Imitation, Edmund Burke said in inquiring into its pleasures and uses, "forms our manners, our opinions, our lives," and it was a point that Stewart (fittingly) copied into a footnote. Ventriloquists called attention to the mimetic constitution of the self, to all the impersonation and counterfeiting that was inescapable in social (and intellectual) life.[70]

Ventriloquists helped the learned turn concerns over self-fashioning and imitation into a rational diversion, but these entertainers could not completely escape the disreputable consequences of their performances of destabilized identities. Ventriloquism was always seen as a likely art for the rogue and the cheat. Among La Chapelle's most popular tales was one he collected of a sixteenth-century impostor, Louis Brabant, who supposedly counterfeited the voices of the dead in order to swindle his way to his desired bride and a fortune, and anecdotes of such European charlatans served as the most common form for brokering the art to American audiences. The first of these appeared in the *Massachusetts Magazine* in 1790; it related the story of a French ventriloquist who assumed the garb of piety to deceive a devout family and wheedle his way through faked divine voices into a very lucrative marriage. This tale, along with Brabant's and others in the same vein, found regular repetition in the American press between 1790 and 1830.[71]

These European stories were made indigenous with Brockden Brown's Carwin, a knave whose powers of vocal deception, however sportive, were terribly dangerous. Endlessly inscrutable and shifty, Carwin was without solid identity, and the impact of such mutability on moral responsibility was, as Reid would have predicted, anarchic and contagious: lacking the clear inner voice of conscience, Carwin wreaks havoc on Theodore Wieland's own psychic integrity.[72] The same sort of knavery was evident in milder form in the artist Raphaelle Peale's dabbling with ventriloquism; his vocal impostures discomfited his learned father, Charles Willson Peale (part of a larger pattern, as in the stories of both Carwin and Brabant, in which young men subverted patriarchal authority with this trickery).[73] In the early republic, tales of the rogue ventriloquist served as one of the prototypes for the confidence man—a fun-house mirror for reflecting the cultural problematics of imposture and identity. Melville, indeed, would draw directly on this literary reservoir when writing *The Confidence-Man* (1857)—his own classic depiction of the slipperiness of human voices and the fragility of social trust.[74]

With such ominous confusions of identity in mind, the *Encyclopaedia Britannica* even had some misgivings about the dissemination of this technical knowledge. Perhaps this expertise should remain esoteric, reserved for the *illuminati*: "We should hardly have described the practical rules of the art to the public; for though it is proper to make the existence of such an art universally known, it will readily occur to every reflecting mind, that the attainment of it should not be rendered easy to those who, like Louis Brabant, might make it subservient to the purposes of knavery and deception."[75] As the fate of the Wielands suggests, this Enlightenment proposi-

24. Ventriloquist Louis Comte and a Speaking Pig
One of the most commonly advertised ploys of the early ventriloquists was the terrorizing of the superstitious and the credulous. In this instance the French ventriloquist Louis Comte made a mockery of rustics by creating the illusion of a speaking pig—a feat that villagers supposedly explained as a wonder of the devil. From *Voyages et séances anecdotiques de M. Comte* (Paris: J. G. Dentu, 1816), opposite p. 33. Harry Price Library, University of London. Courtesy of the University of London Library.

tion about ventriloquism—that the knowledge of how impostures were accomplished would lead to a stabler, more rationalistic and disciplined culture—was always shaky, even perilous. Certainly, almost all the theatrical ventriloquists were renowned for practical jokes and roguish deceptions *off* the stage; in many ways, their self-promotion depended on stories of day-to-day social disruptions, successful masquerades, and cruel tricks. John Rannie, for example, boasted of creating through ventriloquism the impression of a prophecy in Portland, Maine, in which the town would be "swallowed up by an earthquake, in the course of three days." The credulous, Rannie claimed with delight, left town in "great numbers."

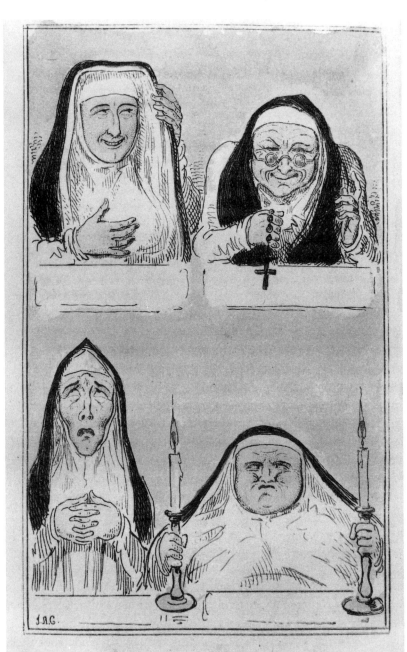

MONS^R ALEXANDRE.

as Sisters.

Celestine.   Mumble.
Doleful.   Lamberte.

Vattemare, too, was famed for his off-stage tricks, for breaking up church services and terrifying "superstitious rustics" with heavenly and diabolical voices; and so was his counterpart Louis Comte. The pursuit of demystification almost always included the abuse of the credulous.[76]

Perhaps fittingly, ventriloquists were often undone by their own magic as their performances of mutable, mimetic identities came back to stalk them. Several ventriloquists were plagued by impersonators, by other traveling players who tried to pass themselves off as one of the more renowned performers. In his tour in 1810, Rannie complained of another person billing himself as "Mr. Rannie, a Ventriloquist," when of course he himself was "the only *real Ventriloquist.*" Jealous to protect his market from "pretenders," he lamented in his American travels "the many impostors which infest this country" and disavowed "all connection with every person who may have hitherto imposed on the world with the shadow for the reality." William Love involved himself in similar spectacles, denouncing the "many pseudo-ventriloquists" and "unblushing plagiarists" who borrowed his material and even "HIS NAME." They were "the IMITATION," while he was the "genuine artist." Love's host of quick "transformations," his "dozen or twenty" voices, clearly laid the groundwork for his own impersonation, for the instability of his own identity. He billed one of his pieces as "LOVE IN ALL SHAPES," promised in another to "personate Eight different characters at the same time," and in yet another cast himself as "The Wolf in Sheep's Clothing." Amid such *"Extraordinary Illusions,"* it seemed only fair to ask: Was there a real Love from which the counterfeits could be distinguished?[77]

Trying to protect—or recover—a reliable identity could be draining. One ventriloquist, Signor Blitz, grew exhausted by others presenting themselves as "the *original* Blitz" or even "Signor Blitz, The Great Original." "Frequently my identity has been disputed when I have visited the different towns and cities professionally . . . there being not less than thirteen people travelling the country using my name and profession, circulating a verba-

---

🖑 **25.** *Monsieur Alexandre as Sisters*
The religious were a common object of the ventriloquist's burlesque. The supremely popular Alexandre Vattemare, who fashioned himself a friend of the literati, slid his way through multiple personae, including the roles of various nuns. From William T. Moncrieff, *The Adventures of a Ventriloquist; Or, The Rogueries of Nicholas* (London: Duncombe, 1822), opposite p. 31. Courtesy of the Princeton University Library, Rare Books and Special Collections.

tim copy of my handbill and advertisement." Through these "impostors," he sighed, "I have been denied my own personality, and termed 'Bogus.'" He thought them a very sad commentary on the all too mutable adaptability of "character" in the American marketplace. For men who made their living as chameleons (the English-born Blitz, after all, had refashioned himself as an "exotic" wizard from Moravia), it was hard to credit their sudden discovery of the inimitable integrity of personal identity or their own clarity about the line between the genuine and the fake. Their own voices were too shifty, and their own social identities too artificial, to give such protestations solidity.[78]

What had been most interesting about ventriloquism in 1680 was the question of divine presence: Could the demonic speak in the human? Could the vocal chords be taken over by another entity beyond the person? In 1830, after the passing of the Enlightenment, that question remained in force, but what had emerged alongside the theological frameworks were several parallel tracks—in effect, the philosophy, psychology, and sociology of the self. These altered voices were now part of the theater of identity, and in that auditorium they sounded vastly different. There were now whole new discursive domains in which to reposition the voices of possession, conversion, and ecstasy—those of personal identity, double consciousness, dissociation, and memory. At best, the voices became useful repertories for pious self-fashioning; at worst, dangerous scripts for self-disintegration.

The fate of the evangelical visionary Ansel Bourne was symptomatic of these relocations. As an itinerant preacher, Bourne had been called in 1857 by direct commission from God: "Settle up your worldly business, and go to work for me. . . . Go, open your mouth and I will fill it. Go, tell the world what . . . your ears have heard." Yet Bourne ended his life famed instead for a two-month episode of altered identity: in William James's *Principles of Psychology,* under the heading "Consciousness of Self," he is memorialized as a textbook example of the divided personality. (Bourne, by the way, received no compensatory attention in *The Varieties of Religious Experience.*) As James noted, whether personal identity was a unified whole or a Humean "stream" of fragments was "the most puzzling puzzle with which psychology has to deal," a riddle made all the more profound by James's own infatuation with the serialization of "social selves."[79]

The Common-Sense philosophy of mind, in which a central concern was the stabilization of personal identity, provided a crucial foundation for that psychological transformation. The dominant concerns about interior voices were no longer theological, let alone devotional, but instead centered on masking the rifts of interior fragmentation. The focus was on preventing the splintering of "our personality into remote and unrelated fragments" (as Thomas Upham described the dreaded disordering of personal identity). Who could really desire these voices when the bounded solidity of personal identity was so prized and yet so fragile, when the well-regulated mind required so much steadiness, self-control, attention, and sensory discipline? The new laws of consciousness and perception could hardly permit these unpredictable sounds within the borders of the continuous self.[80] The construction of an autonomous modern subject, at once certain of an authentic voice and ever afraid of falling to pieces, turned the noises of an eruptive divine world into dangerous signs of inward multiplicity. The formative concern with the problem of personal identity, from Locke to Reid and far beyond, provided a context in which the charged presences of divine voices slid into the feared absences of a unified self.

"The Diseased Ear" and the Unsound Mind: The Anatomy and Psychology of Auditory Hallucinations

The uncertainties about personal identity were connected with more material questions about anatomy and medical psychology. It was hardly surprising that La Chapelle saw his investigation of vocal artifice as, in part, an anatomical project—that is, a description of the bodily mechanisms of these doubled voices. Anatomists, like the Boston physician who went to see those thirty ventriloquists in the early 1820s, found in the human voice and its counterpart, the ear, resources for endless dissection. Might these performers possess "a double or triple larynx"? Could the ancient assumptions about this speech being generated in the stomach be completely laid aside? Why was the location of sounds sometimes so hard for the ear to determine? Could the ear's limitations be overcome through artificial devices or surgical intervention? Could researchers devise medical instruments that would allow the recesses of the ear and the throat to be visually inspected? Such questions galvanized late eighteenth- and early nineteenth-century anatomists, and ventriloquists provided a few sparks for their wide-ranging imaginations. At least one researcher had conducted physical examinations of live ventriloquists; a French physiologist experimented on his own body after learning the art for himself; still another

584 · Of the inward Eare. 8.Booke

Tab. 10. sheweth the eares and the diuers internall parts thereof.

Figure 1. sheweth the whole externall eare, with a part of the Temple bone.

Figure 2. sheweth the left bone of the Temple diuided in the middest by the instrument of hearing, whereabout on either side there are certaine passages heere particularly described.

Fig. 3 & 4. Sheweth the three little Bones.

Fig. 5. sheweth a portion of the bone of the temples which is seene nere the hole of Hearing diuided through the middest, whereby the Nerues, Bones & Membrans may appeare as Vesalius conceyneth of them.

Fig. 6. sheweth the Vessels, Membranes, Bones & holes of the Organ of Hearing, as Platerus hath described thē.

Fig. 7, and 8. sheweth the little bones of the hearing of a man and of a Calfe both ioyned and separated.

Fig. 9. v sheweth the Muscle found out by Aquapendent.

a, The lower eare or the lap of the eare,
bb, The circumference of the eare cald in Greeke Helix.
ce, the interior protuberation or swelling of the eare called Anthelix,
d, The boate of the outward eare.
e, the Goates beard called Tragus, wherein are haires growing.
f, The place against the Goats beard called Antitragus.   Figure 2.
A. A part of the yoke bone.
B. The sinus or bosome whereinto the lower iaw is articulated.
CC, the stony bone swelling within the Scull.
D. The second hole of the bone of the Temples for the passage of the sleepy Artery.
E, A little scale or thin bone betwixte this hole and the first cauity.
FFF, the porosity or spongines of the stony bone.
aa, The externall hole of the eare.
bb, The bony canale of that passage.
c, the Tympane or Drumme is here placed at the passage.
d, the interiour hole into which the nerue is inserted.
ef. Heere also is the stony bone perforated.
ggg, A canale of the auditory Nerue from e to g, in the bone of the Temples, yet this Canale is described by it selfe at the side of the bone aboue the fift Figure.
a, β, Two holes in the beginning and ending of this Canale.
γ, A, Two other holes in the externall and internall part.
b, The first cauity, according to some the second, reaching from e to E.
ii, two canals or pipes of the fyrst cauity.
k, the higher hole which is shut with the stirrop.
l, The lower hole alwayes open.   (bone
mm, The second cauity in the bone.
1,2,3. Three litle burrows or holes of the second cauity described apart.
n, the third cauity lying vnder this supersycies.
Fig: 3. 4. o 3. A long bone representing a pyramide.
p 3,4 the membrane of the drum,   (dal Figure
q 3,4. A bony ring at the Tympane described also by it selfe.   r, 4. the Mallet or hammer.
s, The Anuile.   t the Stirrop.   *Figure 5.*
A, A part of the hole of hearing.
B. A membrane couering the hole ouerthwart.
C. The bone of hearing likened to a hammer.
D, the auditory Nerue.   (hearing.
G, His distribution through the great hole of
E, A branch of this nerue going through a darke hole vnto the Temples.
F. Another branch falling through the hole wher by a veine doth enter in.
H, I. A round cauity in the fore-part whereof is placed, the bone noted with I.   *Fig. 6.*
aa The fyrst hole of the Organ of hearing.

TABVLA. X.

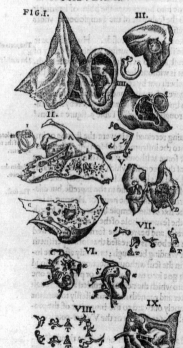

FIG.I.
II.
III.
IV.
V.
VI.
VII.
VIII.
IX.

where it passeth through the fourth hole. β The auditory Nerue diuided into two partes, cauity. δ, where it passeth through his second hole neere to A. ε An artery entring that cauitie thorough the third hole, and a nerue falling through the same hole. H. the same artery falling through the fyst hole, n, the lower part of the 5.nerue reaching vnto the 2 & 3.cauity. θθ, A higher part of the 5.nerue broght through the scruing canale or pipe vnto s where it falleth out. x, the Tympane or Drum shutting the fist cauity. λ, the three little bones of hearing ioyned together. μ, the third cauity or the Trumpet of the organ of hearing. V the second cauity or the mettali mine running out with three burroughs. ξ, ϖ, The Canale or watercourse carrying a Nerue and an artery, opening it selfe with two holes. Figu: 7 & 8, ρ The Hammer σ, the Anuile, τ, The Stirrop.

anatomist seemed hopeful about solving his lingering questions through dissection (though cadavers of ventriloquists were obviously even harder to locate than their voices).[81]

The anatomy of an illusion like ventriloquism was a sideshow in a much grander exhibition: the wholesale display of human and comparative anatomy since the Renaissance—a vast "culture of dissection" that has been variously credited with the discovery of interiority, the fragmentation of knowledge, and the mechanization of the body. Every part of the human frame came in for scrutiny among the Italian anatomists, including famed inquirers such as Andreas Vesalius and Gabriele Fallopius, and the ear itself had received extensive exploration by the middle of the sixteenth century. (We still carry these learned conquests in our own ears—evident, for example, in the Eustachian tube, a name that comes from the sixteenth-century Italian anatomist Bartolomeo Eustachio.) In *Microcosmographia* (1615), Helkiah Crooke, a leading English anatomist, surveyed the "intricate Meanders" of the ear, attempting to bring order to its convolutions through the analogies of "a Market place," "the cavitie of a metall Mine," and "a Watercourse." Such mappings had become all the more precise and extensive by the late seventeenth century, epitomized by Thomas Willis' *Two Discourses Concerning the Soul of Brutes* (1672), Joseph-Guichard Du Verney's *Traité de l'organe de l'ouïe* (1683), and Günther Christoph Schelhammer's *De auditu* (1684).[82]

Du Verney's study emerged as a pivotal early Enlightenment text on the ear's anatomy and became a standard work in British medicine, especially after its English translation in 1737. Part of that "inquisitive Search into the Organs of our Senses," Du Verney's book marked out the ear as a specialized object of study and strove for a comprehensive understanding that penetrated all "the Minuteness and Delicacy" of the ear's structures. Attentive in the first section of his treatise to the anatomy of the external and internal ear (the cochlea, the tympanum, the malleus and incus, and so on, all

26. Anatomy of the Ear
The ear was "so full of intricate Meanders," Helkiah Crooke noted in his anatomy, that it was "very hard to be diciphered." To help bring intelligible order to its labyrinthine parts, Crooke mapped out the ear as a marketplace, a series of canals, and a metal mine. From Helkiah Crooke, *Microcosmographia: A Description of the Body of Man* (London: Laggard, 1615), 584. Courtesy of the Princeton University Library, Rare Books and Special Collections.

Plate I.

Fig. I.

Fig. II.

B. Cole Sculp.

graphically laid bare in *"Sixteen Curious Copper-Plates"*), Du Verney proceeded in the second part to consider the mechanics of hearing and finished in the third with the diseases of the ear as well as the standard remedies available. In this last discussion, Du Verney presented a classical array of treatments—bleedings, purgings, painkillers, and injections—many of which were, not surprisingly, on the order of that reported in an English treatise in 1713: for "Ulcers in the Ears . . . some inject with the Urin of a young Child."[83]

This threefold division of knowledge—the anatomy, mechanics, and diseases of the ear—was still very much present in early nineteenth-century medical texts. These included notably John C. Saunders' *The Anatomy of the Human Ear* (1806), John Curtis' *Treatise on the Physiology and Diseases of the Ear* (1817), Jean Antoine Saissy's *An Essay on the Diseases of the Internal Ear* (1819), Thomas Buchanan's *An Engraved Representation of the Anatomy of the Human Ear* (1823), David Tod's *The Anatomy and Physiology of the Organ of Hearing* (1832), Joseph Togno's *A Popular Essay on the Laws of Acoustics, and on the Anatomy and Physiology of the Ear* (1834), and Joseph Williams' *Treatise on the Ear* (1840). For an important swath of medical men, European and American alike, these were the focal questions through which to think about hearing: the structures, workings, and infirmities of the ear. In the permeable, encyclopedic intellectual worlds that the Enlightenment furthered, such knowledge easily moved beyond those circles, taking its place as another gentleman's performance: for example, Edinburgh professor of medicine Alexander Monro gathered a considerable group of his colleagues, including professor of moral philosophy Dugald Stewart, in the city's Anatomical Theatre in 1794 to observe his dissections of the ear. In such visual displays, the mechanisms of hearing were made a spectacle for the philosopher's observing eye through the probing touch.[84]

A common Christian response to all the new knowledge of the body's

27. The Orifice of the Ear

Joseph-Guichard Du Verney's *Traité de l'organe de l'ouïe* (1683), in its precise charting of the external and internal ear, was indicative of the growing specialization of anatomical knowledge in the early Enlightenment. Du Verney presented the outer ear as a shell-like covering for the dark "Orifice of the Auditory Passage." From Joseph-Guichard Du Verney, *A Treatise of the Organ of Hearing: Containing the Structure, the Uses, and the Diseases of all the Parts of the Ear* (London: Baker, 1737), plate I. Courtesy of the Firestone Library, Princeton University.

interior was, predictably, to redouble the praises of God's creation. An early eighteenth-century Anglican clergyman and fellow of the Royal Society, William Derham—in reviewing the newly detailed anatomies of the ear by Willis, Du Verney, Schelhammer, and Valsalva, among others—found in these works only further evidence of God's intricate design of the human body. "Who can reflect upon all this curious Apparatus of the *Sense of Hearing,* and not give the great Creator his due Praise!" he marveled, easily incorporating the ear's microscopic anatomy into natural theology. Nearly a century later William Paley made the same move, using the bodily mechanisms of the ear as an illustration to inspire an adoring contemplation of God's intricate designs. His famed opening analogy, which made the point that the machinery of a watch required a watchmaker, distracted from his real theological absorption: the human body and comparative anatomy.[85]

Paley's commonplace perspective about the ear was even more eloquently presented by another late eighteenth-century Anglican minister, John Trusler, in a sermonic meditation on the sense of hearing:

> Were I to lay open to your view the formation of the ear, and explain to you its mechanism so wonderfully constructed, and so admirably adapted to the purposes of hearing; were I to shew you that He created even the air, proportionate to this design, it being through this medium that the surprising end is brought about, . . . you would naturally cry out with the Psalmist, "Lord how manifold is Thy goodness!"

In this providential anatomy, even earwax shared in the benevolence of divine purpose, a bitter substance that guarded the entrance of the ears, "nauseous to all kind of insects that creep into holes, and who might otherwise lodge themselves there and obstruct our hearing." As Trusler concluded, "To study Anatomy, is to study Divinity, and nothing but downright

28. The Labyrinth of the Ear 🖙

Du Verney's formative work moved only modestly beyond the convoluted anatomy of hearing into a psychology of auditory misperception, but the latter domain would receive growing attention among medical pathologists in the late Enlightenment. The cavernous windings of the ear itself would become an emblem of hearing's oracular deceits. From Joseph-Guichard Du Verney, *A Treatise of the Organ of Hearing: Containing the Structure, the Uses, and the Diseases of All the Parts of the Ear* (London: Baker, 1737), plate X. Courtesy of the Firestone Library, Princeton University.

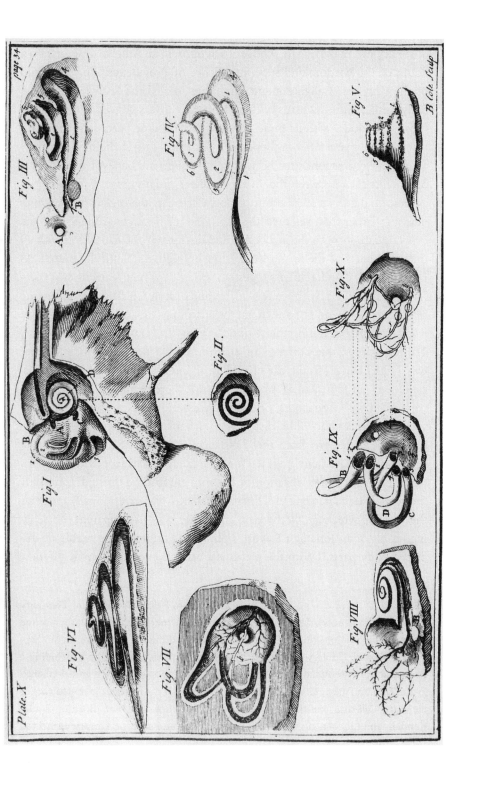

Plate. X.

Fig. III.

Fig. IX.

Fig. V.

B. Cole Sculp

Fig. I

Fig. II.

Fig. X.

Fig. IX.

Fig. VI.

Fig. VII.

Fig. VIII.

obstinacy can make a man, who looks at himself, an Atheist, or leave him a doubt of the wisdom and superintendence of Providence." In this strand of the Christian Enlightenment, the more refined the knowledge of the body's minute mechanisms became (and the ear was viewed as among the most marvelous, with its minuscule and labyrinthine parts), the more admirable the divine Artificer appeared. Christians saw in the new anatomy an ancient correspondence between God's supreme benevolence and the body's intricacy, between the divine Architect and his greatest temple.[86]

Despite the mechanistic drift of post-Cartesian anatomists (the body as machine rather than vessel of the soul), the religious consequences of the growing attention to the structures and diseases of the ear (along with all the other parts of the body) were, often enough, theologically muted. As Derham, Paley, and Trusler suggested, most of the new learning was comfortably assimilable within a reasonable and orderly Christianity. Still, some cracks were evident. For one thing, the anatomies took some cleaning up (a small example: in noting the salubrious view that earwax repelled insects, Trusler ignored the warnings of anatomists that this "glutinous Matter" was a filthy danger to the ear's health in all kinds of other ways). "The diseased ear," in John Curtis' phrase, was not a pretty sight: "morbid Ears" were filled with discharges, oozings, abscesses, funguses, worms, tumors, violent pains, and horrible "distempers." It took a highly selective vision to draw roseate lessons from these modern anatomies that were, after all, driven by a materialist engine (fundamentally discordant with Trusler's larger Neoplatonist celebration of the soul enraptured through sound). If the consecrated anatomy of Christian theology was exceptionally resilient, the somatic wreckage of the new anatomies was also apparent, portending, in historian Jonathan Sawday's phrase, a "fragmentary rubble of displaced body parts." With the piecemeal dissection of the senses, the new

29. William Paley's Anatomical Theology ⟩

The expanding knowledge of the ear's microscopic mechanisms regularly inspired Christian meditations on the Creator's benevolent design of the universe. William Paley's *Natural Theology* was primarily a work in Christian anatomy, including a comparative contemplation of the ear's instrumentation in humans and elephants. From William Paley, *Natural Theology; Or, Evidences of the Existence and Attributes of the Deity, Collected from the Appearances of Nature* (London, 1802; Boston: Gould, Kendall, and Lincoln, 1837), plate V. Courtesy of the Firestone Library, Princeton University.

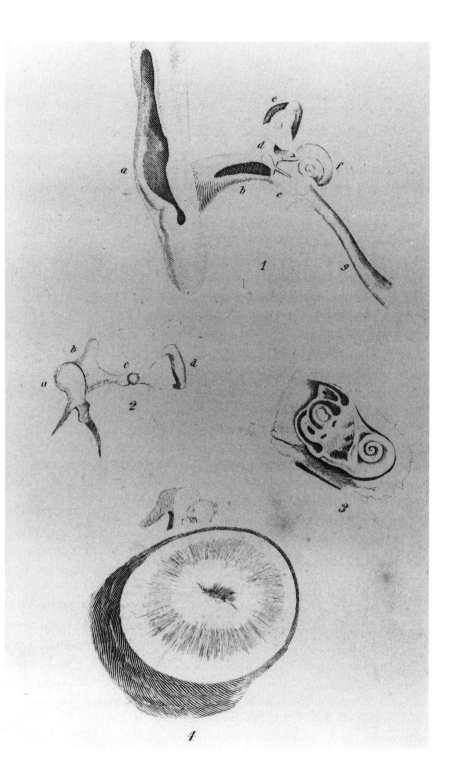

knowledge augured, in particular, a medical disassemblage and dispersal of the Christian sensorium.[87]

Anatomists, from Du Verney to Saunders to Williams, rarely indulged in homilies on the beauty, perfection, astonishing design, and ecstatic transports of the ear. They seemed, if anything, committed to the promethean project of improving and mending God's handiwork through a host of devices to salvage the mechanism of hearing—including, by the 1810s, a range of artificial ears that extended well beyond the ear-trumpet. Whatever their own deficiencies, these "mechanical contrivances," these imitative "substitutes," these "French ears" in a handy carrying case, certainly highlighted the limitations of the "natural ear." With attention riveted on the material etiology of disease, the human ear seemed sadly feeble, marked by defect and deafness, in need of prosthetic assistance, preyed on by quacks and prayed over by those left, in desperation, to "the care of Providence."[88] Artificial ears, their effectiveness clearly a gamble for the hard of hearing, did not inspire trust, but neither did the ravaged hearing of the diseased ear. The promised perfections of the spiritual ear, caught in a progressive technological ethos at odds with eschatological deferral, lost ground to more immediate remedies for hearing's incapacities—the mechanical surrogates of prosthetic ears.

Another fissure of greater consequence was the anatomical account of the ear's distempered illusions. Most of the diseases that Du Verney studied were those physical ills that diminished the capacity to hear, but there was another hybridized category of infirmity that blended body and mind, sensation and perception. Within that class fell those disorders that rendered "the Ear sensible of Noises which are not in reality, or which are not external." Du Verney insisted on a whole range of perceived sounds that "may be produc'd without any Wind being in the Ear, or without Matter which strikes the Membranes externally"—that is, people were plagued by "an infinite Number" of whistlings, murmurings, buzzings, and tinklings that had no material basis, no objective correlate. Du Verney drew attention to an illusory realm of internal sounds that accompanied various infirmities and accentuated how "the Hearing is deprav'd in mistaking these Noises as coming from some external Object." These false perceptions were often the symptoms of graver ills, Du Verney observed, and common accompaniments included delirium, frenzy, and swooning. At this point Du Verney's auditory inquiry swerved out of "the Disorders of the Ear" into "the Disorders of the Brain," so that at the end of his treatise he approached the vortex of the "deprav'd Imagination," the enthusiast's prime malady.[89] While Du Verney himself did not make the connective leap to religious phantasm, he marked hearing with an illusory interiority that pointed ahead to the accounts of auditory hallucinations which would proliferate in the late Enlightenment. Sick people often heard things that had existence only in their own minds—that, disconnected from the mechanisms of air, vibration, and sensation, resided in a delusive subjectivity.

Subsequent anatomists of the ear's diseases were similarly intent on confronting the unreal noises that their patients experienced—rustling, singing, hissing, ringing, whispering—and on administering the right therapies. The causes assigned for tinnitus and allied complaints ranged from intestinal maladies to obstructed Eustachian tubes to disorders "under the vague term nervous," and it was within this last grouping that anatomy and psychology became fully reciprocal, that somatic debility merged with mental hallucination. Physician Joseph Williams—who, in his *Treatise on the Ear*, also concerned himself with ventriloquism, the Invisible Girl, and speaking trumpets—made the connection to mental disorder directly: the troubling experience of illusory sounds had multiple potential sources, but "it frequently arises from an altered function of nerves, and is often induced by the depressing passions, and . . . is much complained of by hypochondriacs, dyspeptics, and hysterical females, whose imagination sometimes converts these noises into *whispers*, proving a source of great disquiet, and amounting, in some instances, to complete hallucination." Williams went on to associate these auditory illusions—"the *supposed* unearthly whispers and anomalous sounds"—with lunacy, and suggested that the ear's treacheries were especially linked to mental alienation.[90]

For this nexus, Williams pointed back in a footnote to John Haslam's *Observations on Insanity* (1798); following that lead would have pulled the reader into a labyrinthine literature intent on detailing, quantifying, diagnosing, and remedying the false perceptions of mania, particularly what were then coming to be labeled visual and auditory hallucinations. The anatomies of the diseased ear paled before the proliferating studies of insanity in medicalizing hearing's illusions (though dissection, it should be noted, all along remained the absolutely inseparable counterpart to these studies). Haslam, working from his experience with several hundred patients, noted that they often "heard those things, which really did not exist at the time." He attributed many of these false perceptions to failed education, to the need to remove prejudices and "discipline the intellect." Other-

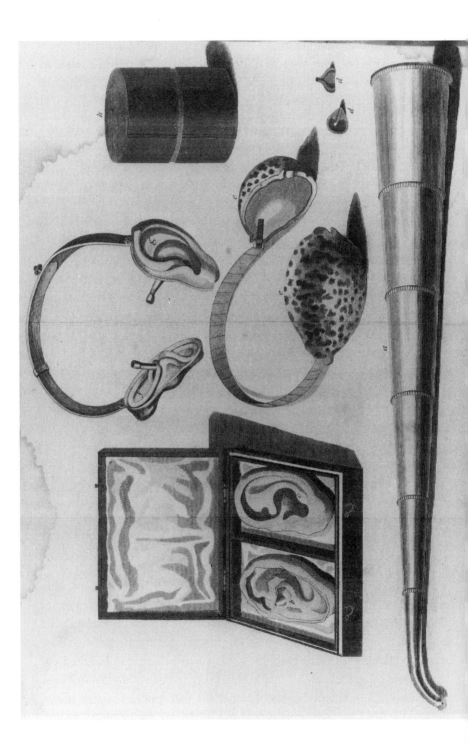

wise, "the belief in the powers of witchcraft, and in ghosts, and superstitions of every denomination . . . grasp strongly upon the mind and seduce its credulity." He pointed directly to "religious terror" as one of the causes of insanity, and, as a case in point, described a twenty-seven-year-old woman whose mental disorder stemmed from "religious enthusiasm, and a too frequent attendance on conventicles." Her symptoms included terrible fears over her soul's salvation (especially for the transgression of having once "said the Lord's Prayer backwards") and a disturbing habit of nocturnal devotions: "She alternately sang, and cried the greatest part of the night." She died five months after entering Haslam's hospital, and he accordingly dissected her body in an attempt to anatomize further her "disorder."[91]

Medicalizing religious enthusiasm—there was nothing particularly novel in Haslam's efforts to do that, though his itemized intrusion into the very routines of popular Christian piety was noteworthy. Since at least the middle of the seventeenth century, materialist models for explaining spiritual disorders had been gaining ground among the learned, and, by the early eighteenth century, that medical strategy had been fully deployed against unruly sectarians, especially the French Prophets, and thereafter always stood ready for redeployment. Enlightenment epistemologies (whether Lockean, Common-Sense, or Kantian) demanded the disciplining of religious enthusiasm, a confinement of those "ungrounded fancies of a man's own brain" within a secure domain from which reason and the state might avoid contamination. The senses, properly trained and cultivated, formed the basis for a well-ordered mind, one protected from the chimera of "frequent communications from the Divine Spirit." Medical psychology,

30. Artificial Ears

Complications for pious estimates of the ear appeared in the expanding pathologies of the organ's diseases, illusions, and defects. The medical pursuit of artificial ears, for example, heightened attention to the natural weaknesses and limitations of human hearing. Physician John Curtis noted several of the prosthetic instruments that had crowded onto the medical scene, including the old stand-by of a hearing trumpet (a) and its case (h), French artificial ears (b and c) with gold tubes (d), a Spanish version (e), and a German counterpart (f and g). From John Harrison Curtis, *A Treatise on the Physiology and Pathology of the Ear* (London, 1817; London: Longman, Rees, Orme, Brown, and Green, 1831), frontispiece. Courtesy of the Firestone Library, Princeton University.

a knowledge produced in part to contain the delusions of religious fervor, proved a formidable adversary for traditional forms of Christian devotionalism—a foe that, often as not, wore the garb of a rational, enlightened faith and that thus worked to transform Christianity from within.[92]

In the late eighteenth and early nineteenth centuries, the institutional resources in England, France, and the United States devoted to policing the shifting boundaries between the sane and the insane mushroomed, as was evident in the ascent of asylums. Through those institutions and the medical learning upon which they fed, through the vision of moral reform and religious placidity they sought to concretize, hallucinatory diagnoses crept into ever wider realms of Christian experience and practice. By the estimate of one census in antebellum America, close to 8 percent of the cases of confinement to asylums resulted from "religious excitement"—that is, mostly from the enthusiastic excesses of revivals. As Alexis de Tocqueville summarily concluded, "Religious insanity is very common in the United States," a view that echoed those of leading American alienists, including Amariah Brigham and Pliny Earle, who helped oversee the expanding network of asylums. To combat this raging source of insanity, reasonable medical men imagined a Christianity of quiet and calm—no bodily ecstasies, no revival meetings, no terror, no mortifications of the flesh, no gulping of eucharistic wine, no outcries, no demonic agency, no hallucinatory provocations. (The imagined "stillness" even extended to the "noise" of church bells; perceiving them as a public health problem, Brigham dreamed "a good and great reform, . . . a total relinquishment of bells on the Lord's day.") Those mentally deranged by the clamor of evangelical fanaticism were to be taken out of the world of camp meetings and put into a setting of isolated retreat, where religious worship itself was to embody the noiseless regimen of reason, and where a cure was to be effected through habits of industry, courtesy, and self-control. To a remarkable degree, the antebellum asylum was imagined as the obverse of the revival.[93]

The intellectual underpinning for this confinement of the religiously insane was built less on the classical categories of "melancholy" and "enthusiasm" than on diagnostic schemes that focused on perceptual errors and on curative regimens that would then offer better management of these misperceptions. William Battie's *Treatise on Madness* (1758) was formative in identifying lunacy essentially with "false perception," especially with disordered experiences of sound and sight. Included among these delusions, for

Battie, were those religious "extasies" that led some of the devout to believe they had "frequent conversations with Angelic ministers of grace."
The emphasis on false perception provided an important springboard for
subsequent theorists, who, by the end of the eighteenth century, had made
"illusion" and "hallucination" recognized classifications among the interrelated diseases of the sensory organs and the brain. In the 1790s, physicians
Erasmus Darwin and Alexander Crichton utilized these notions as inter-
changeable terms in the diagnosis of mental delusion, and both employed
numerous religious examples to show the regress of "diseased perceptions." In these reports, the delirium of the devout often seemed less
horrific than trivial; Crichton pointed, for example, to a divinity student
who "mistook the noise of flatulency with which he was troubled, for an
evil spirit who infested him." (For Crichton, *daemonomania*—a patient's belief in "the immediate communication with spirits" or in "the power of
working miracles"—was actually a definable subspecies of "HALLUCINATIO,
or ILLUSION.") In the early decades of the nineteenth century, hallucination
was increasingly distinguished from illusion and became the stronger category within medical psychology: illusions were taken to be sensory
misperceptions of actual phenomena, while hallucinations were those
phantasms of the brain that had no correlation with external realities.[94]

Charles Brockden Brown's exploration of religious enthusiasts not only
as victims of imposture but also as subjects of hallucinatory voices was indicative of the expanding reach of these diagnostic tools. In describing Theodore Wieland's madness, his violent derangement through assuming God
was speaking to him, Brown pointed in a footnote to Erasmus Darwin's
Zoonomia (1794–1796) and its account of *mania mutabilis*, a form of "delirium" or "hallucination" in which patients confused "imaginations for realities." For Darwin, natural philosopher and Methodist debunker, "superstitious hope," bodily mortification, and "the fear of hell" all constituted
discrete sources of insanity, prominent springs of "maniacal hallucination."
Darwin's examples of those afflicted with mutable madness included a
young woman who thought she had seen an angel "who told her, that she
need not eat." He also included another woman who "imagined she heard
a voice say to her one day, as she was at her toilet, 'Repent, or you will be
damned'"—a hallucination that left her unsettled for two years. (Darwin,
not incidentally, was among those who had experimented hands-on with
the illusions of speaking machines, creating one "with lips of soft leather"
that was capable of producing a few words with "so great nicety as to de-

ceive all who heard it unseen." His desire to command the mechanisms of artificial voices meshed neatly with his ambition to master the psychology of auditory hallucinations: together these gave him the magician's complement of powers to deceive and undeceive.) With blunt specificity, Darwin, like Haslam, redefined the intimate voices of evangelical piety as dangerous illusions that, left untreated, led to mental disintegration and self-destruction.[95]

Brockden Brown dramatized these very dangers, turning Wieland's religious fanaticism into an opportunity to explore the explanatory force of Darwin's theories of "insane perceptions" and "maniacal illusions." The final ventriloquized voice of Carwin (whose name curiously echoed Darwin's) manages to jar Wieland back into reality: "'Man of errors! cease to cherish thy delusion: not heaven or hell, but thy senses have misled thee to commit these acts. Shake off thy frenzy, and ascend into [the] rational and human. Be lunatic no longer.'" His madness demystified, Wieland is left with no more "blissful visions," no more divine communications, only "uninterrupted silence." Sunk now in a disenchanted madness, voiceless, he has become the precise opposite of the self-mastering ventriloquist: "His lips moved, but no sound escaped him." In this vacancy, Wieland commits suicide, perhaps a necessary end to one so disordered by religious insanity, certainly one that Darwin and his colleagues Haslam and Crichton would have predicted. After all, the young woman who had been instructed to fast by an angel eventually starved herself to death. The literati tirelessly underscored this point: the violence—to self and other—that experiences of divine speech engendered, the cruelty that shadowed the very presumption of revelation.[96]

The medical work of Benjamin Rush represented a further extension and indigenization of such theorizing in the early republic. His *Medical Inquiries and Observations upon the Diseases of the Mind* (1812) included a chapter entitled "Of Illusions"; notable among those suffering from this disease of "false perceptions" were those "superstitious people" who "fancy they hear voices" (indeed, Rush pinpointed the ear as the primary seat of diseased perception). Of fifty patients he surveyed in Pennsylvania Hospital, he determined that the cause of mental derangement in five of them—or 10 percent of his cases—was "erroneous opinions in religion." Still, as a gentlemanly defender of true Christianity, schooled in Common-Sense verities and Hartleyan syntheses, Rush reassured his readers that real religion was not responsible for producing the insanity of "supposed visions and revelations." Equally, he reassured them that "this explanation of illusions" did not "invalidate accounts that are given in the Old and New Testaments of the supernatural voices" heard by the prophets and the apostle Paul. While such numinous experiences among his contemporaries were amenable to explanation by "natural causes"—namely, "a change in the natural actions of the brain, or of the organs of hearing"—the biblical world of immediate revelation remained comfortably exempt. Despite the obvious rejoinders of radical deists and skeptics, it was a miraculous preserve that Rush thought defensible. He tried to use the new knowledge conservatively—namely, to advance the stolid Reformed proposition about the closed world of biblical inspiration and to pathologize anew sectarian visionaries. But illusion and hallucination proved highly absorbent categories, and the respectable Christianity that Rush represented served far more as a stimulus than a curb to their thirst. By 1840, when Thomas Upham was exploring "Diseased Auditory states of Mind" and the illusions connected with "excited religious feeling," the psychological sanctuary still preserved for the "spiritual communications" of Christian devotion was so rickety as to be insupportable.[97]

What would have passed as commonplace expressions and instructive experiences in Methodist class meetings or evangelical memoirs, what would have been devotionally intelligible within the main currents of contemplative Christianity from Augustine to Wesley, sounded vastly different in the multiplying pages of medical psychology. Alexandre Brierre de Boismont's *Des Hallucinations* (1845), published in translation in Philadelphia in 1853 and offering what he called a "rational history" or "medical history" of religious experience, encapsulates these trends. Still striking a deferential tone toward "the apparitions of Holy Writ," he viewed the rest of history and his own culture as a vast psychiatric hospital. In dismissing imposture as mostly an inadequate explanation for the oracular dimensions of religious experience—that people are but the dupes of priestly charlatans—he insisted that the real domain for such inquiry was medical psychology, not politics. While Brierre de Boismont adopted the moderate position that hallucination was not identical with lunacy but could coexist with sanity, he nonetheless spent most of his time on the pathology of hallucinations—that is, the diagnosis, confinement, and treatment of those who suffered from these disturbances. Even as he granted reason to heroic historical personages from Socrates to Luther to George Fox despite their illusory voices (a generosity by no means shared by all of his medical colleagues), he viewed the experiences of "hallucinated persons" in the contemporary culture as primarily an aspect of insanity in need of remedy. Fortunately, science had learned that hallucinations were "susceptible of treatment and cure, and that this desirable end could be accomplished by attacking them boldly, harassing them incessantly, and forcing them to acknowledge themselves beaten."[98]

Brierre de Boismont's very temperateness toward Christianity makes his conclusions about voices and hearing all the more telling. In the grand mapping of modern delusions, he too found that "hallucinations of hearing" were "the most common," estimated as "comprising two-thirds of the whole," and his collection of cases illustrating this point was, by any measure, impressive. Every aspect of devout hearing was reworkable within this hallucinatory context. The dialogues of prayer and meditation, for example, sounded far different after a description of the mind's illusory exchanges—of how "the hallucinated" held interiorized conversations "with the creations of their brain," how these murmurings took on the appearance of involving "two beings." Brierre de Boismont's Christian rationalism, likewise, made earthly intimations of heavenly music and angelic song the fantasies of the hallucinating imagination, and visits with the devil were predictably shunted into the same category. To preserve the sanity of Luther, for example, Brierre de Boismont turned a midnight disputation with Satan into a symptom of Luther's "tension of mind, the pictured reflex of his thoughts."[99]

In the elusiveness of all these voices, ventriloquism was not forgotten, continuing to carry imaginative force for the learned. At one point Brierre de Boismont explicitly pictured some of his patients as ventriloquists, and he often sounded less like a medical observer than like a spectator at a ventriloquist's show, almost amused by the range of auditory illusions: "Sometimes the voices are close at hand, sometimes far off, and in different directions. They may be concealed above the head, under the floor, may come from a neighboring house, from the chimney, from a bedpost, a bureau, a bed, or anything. . . . Voices may proceed from heaven." The performances and technologies of natural magic slid into medical case studies of the devoutly disordered; among Brierre de Boismont's sources was Brewster's *Letters on Natural Magic*. When, for example, one of Brierre de Boismont's patients reported seeing demons and other fiends approaching her, he depicted her as under assault from "horrible phantasmagoria"; when one woman told him of hearing voices "far off in the fields," he pictured her replying to them "as if she had a speaking-trumpet." The rational recreations of the Enlightenment lingered as the mechanical voices of speaking automata slipped into the verbal automatisms of the mind that had lost rational control of itself. After half a century of medical theorizing, the term "illusion" had effectively crossed from the magical into the psychological. By 1850 religion still had a considerable future as an illusion, but that future also had a very particular past.[100]

Even starker examples of how the psychological shift in perspective remade the oracular dimensions of Christian piety appear in the work of Brierre de Boismont's illustrious compatriot Etienne Esquirol, whose book *Des Maladies mentales* was translated for American audiences in 1845 and whose *Aliénation mentale: Des Illusions chez les aliénés* (1832) helped to differentiate fully the categories of hallucination and illusion. In both of these volumes, he presented the case of a "very devout" Catholic woman who was haunted by religious voices, and the fate of this "hallucinarian" (Esquirol's term for visionary) proved coldly instructive about the peculiar auditory confinements of the asylum. Called by her wardens "the 'Mother of the church,' because she spoke incessantly on religious subjects," the woman "fancied she had in her belly all the personages of the new testament," and out of her stomach even came voices dramatizing the Crucifixion, fitting perhaps for a woman who seemed doubly crucified by her own afflictions and the demystified rationality of her keepers. "Nothing could dissipate these ludicrous illusions," her physician reported, and after she died in 1816 he dissected her abdomen, searching for the anatomy of ventriloquism gone mad. The belly-speaking demons had been renamed, the heavenly voices completely repositioned, and what was left was an uncontainable welter of auditory hallucinations and terribly divided selves.[101]

The American translation of Esquirol's *Des Maladies mentales* appeared in the wake of the Millerite movement, an apocalyptic storm that swept the United States in the early 1840s and that served as a prime index for American alienists of the pressing need to tame religious hallucinations. For those medical men who turned to Esquirol for perspective, they must have nodded while reading of the hospitalized apocalypticist who believed Christ's return was imminent: "Many times I saw John the Baptist in heaven, in a chariot drawn by seven horses, from whence I believe he was preparing with angels, the events that are to precede the coming of Christ." The asylum provided for the complete recontextualization of the revelatory strands of Christian piety, eerily evident in another of this man's "hallucinations" from 1821 (Esquirol insistently switched back to this term, though his patient used the term "vision" and poignantly prayed to him at one point "to believe that my visions are true"): "About midnight, I heard a loud voice proceeding from heaven, which uttered words which I cannot repeat, for I did not comprehend them. A little after, I heard a loud cry, and saw demons, who were suffering the chastisements of God. On hearing this voice I arose and hastily prayed. The next day I gave my money to the poor." To the voices of reason, the asylum would be the salvation of God's disordered listeners; it would give them the "moral and intellectual habits" that would cure their diseased perceptions and reorder their vagrant religious imaginations. One reordering it definitely accomplished: hearing things became a quintessential earmark of modern insanity.[102]

The distinctions fashioned in the late Enlightenment to delimit rational perception long ramified. The very categories "hallucination" and "illusion" became common intellectual property in the second half of the nineteenth century, often giving the whole of religious experience the appearance of being merely the fantastic projections of the unsound mind. "Hallucination is perception without an object," went a standard psychological definition in the 1880s, the framework of delusional subjectivity having been reduced to a terse formula. It is this breakage of the sign, the loss of any presence in these experiences, that marks the real undoing of God's listeners. No one was speaking to them or within them, and to retain the marks of sanity, to keep their distance from the archaic and the ecstatic (evident in E. B. Tylor's image of "the primitive ventriloquist," so remote from the modern West), they needed to affirm that absence—an unreality that was itself also a construction, however natural or real or required it had come to seem.[103] When objects survived at all in the hallucinatory imagination, they did so as sensory illusions—the light that becomes a numinous angel, the rustling leaves that become whispering voices, the statue that comes to life. But mostly they magically disappeared into a sphere of sounds without speakers—disembodied voices that had no actuality except in the memories, imaginations, desires, and agonies of those who heard them. Nowhere did divine words lose their presences more thoroughly than in asylums. The normalization of God's silence, if far from total, had found its métier.

Voices from Spirit-Land

5 In 1696 John Aubrey, a fellow of the Royal Society, published in London a book entitled *Miscellanies*, "a collection of *Hermetick Philosophy.*" "*Natural Philosophy* hath been exceedingly advanced within Fifty Years last past," he began, "but methinks, 'tis strange that *Hermetick Philosophy* hath lain so long untouch. It is a Subject worthy of serious Consideration." There followed his observations on, among other things, astrology, omens, dreams, apparitions, visions, oracles, crystal gazing, and ecstasies. Aubrey also had a whole chapter on voices, ranging from Augustine's "Take, read," to a personal acquaintance of his own who had twice heard an ethereal command to translate Luther's *Tischreden* into English. Another section of Aubrey's compendium took up the knockings of spirits on bedsteads and walls—phenomena for which Puritan Richard Baxter's *Certainty of the Worlds of Spirits* (1691) was the leading source. (The extent of such lore is a reminder of the larger history behind the "audible realities" and "peculiar noises" of mid-nineteenth-century Spiritualism, all those portentous "knockings, rappings, jarrings, creakings, tickings" that aroused so much Victorian wonder.) A little later in the volume, Aubrey offered a chapter entitled "Converse with Angels and Spirits" in which one "Angelical Revelation" after another was recounted. The rubric was conventional—Heinrich Cornelius Agrippa's *Three Books of Occult Philosophy*, for example, had a section called "Of the Tongues of Angels, and of Their Speaking amongst Themselves, and with Us."[1]

Aubrey's umbrella for all these wonders was Hermetic philosophy, a designation derived from the ancient writings attributed to the Egyptian magus Hermes Trismegistus, whose wisdom was taken to be a primeval anticipation of the highest truths of Christian revelation and pagan philosophy. Through Renaissance rediscovery and reworking, the Hermetic tradition, evident in Aubrey's usage, had come to embrace a loose combination of

Christian, Neoplatonist, biblical, and kabbalistic elements. Among its hybrid components was a desire to know the hidden speech of angels and spirits, to enter the sensorium of the celestial world. Aubrey's piety, very much akin to John Beaumont's contemplation of seraphic sounds, included an affirmation of an arcane acoustics in which celestial voices, angelic conversations, mystical words, and heavenly harmonies were avidly pursued.

Though Aubrey felt that Hermetic philosophy was falling out of favor with the ascent of the new natural philosophy, it would prove highly adaptable and almost endlessly renewable. In contrast to the Baconian and Lockean cultivation of the bodily senses as the experimental avenue for the advancement of knowledge, these esoteric currents regularly overflowed conventional sensory channels. Interested less in the management of the senses than in their transformation, these mixed Hermetic, Christian, and kabbalistic streams emphasized the supreme reality of the celestial world and the practices by which that realm was penetrated, its influences attracted, or its inhabitants invoked. These multilayered traditions flourished beside, within, through, and beyond the Enlightenment. Esoteric books of mystical illumination circulated widely on both sides of the Atlantic, and their influence was evident around almost every bend, from the alchemical, Pythagorean fascinations of Newton to the cosmological visions of Joseph Smith. Hermetic dreams hardly slumbered in the modern aftermath (fittingly, a new edition of Aubrey's *Miscellanies* appeared in 1857 and another in 1890). The aural arcana of that harmonial world formed, as this chapter will show, a persistent counterpoint to the increasingly demystified acoustics of the new natural philosophy.[2]

Such inquiries, especially those into the speech of angels and into the spiritual senses beyond the body, were massively extended by one of the Enlightenment's own, the Swedish natural-philosopher-turned-Christian-mystic Emanuel Swedenborg (1688–1772). In a portentous move in the 1740s, Swedenborg shifted from the learned theaters of anatomy and mechanical invention to the heavenly spheres of angelic conversation and apocalyptic unfolding. Operating within the severe limits imposed by the Lutheran establishment, Swedenborg published all of his religious writings beyond Sweden's borders (especially in the freer climes of London and Amsterdam) and gathered almost no following in his homeland during his lifetime. Instead, a considerable audience for his memorable accounts arose in England and the United States, where his ideas steadily percolated in the

1780s and 1790s and became an especially strong brew in the first half of the nineteenth century. Spawning a vast publishing enterprise and an extended network of adepts and dabblers, Swedenborg became one of the era's consummate bearers of immediate revelation and an inspiration for several of America's homegrown revelators. Eventually, he even became for some an angelic spirit guide, a dead-yet-living contact for heavenly wisdom.[3]

He and his Anglo-American progeny, who crystallized into the Church of the New Jerusalem (or "New Church"), were particularly savvy synthesizers of natural philosophy and immediate revelation. More eclectic than most evangelicals, Swedenborgian seekers fused the empiricist exactitude of experimental philosophy to a dualistic spiritualizing of the scriptures, the body, the senses, animals, dreams, landscapes. Everything harbored hidden correspondences; all the world was a hieroglyph. To Swedenborg and those who followed his lead, the trick to reharmonizing the universe was not to ignore the materialistic, rationalistic, and experimental dimensions of the Enlightenment, but to transmute them into a spiritual inquiry every bit as thorough, substantial, and precise. Versed in Hermetic cosmologies and kabbalistic hermeneutics, Swedenborg sought to throw open the arcana of scripture and the mysteries of the heavenly world to rational understanding and empirical report. Resisting the deistic separation of reason and immediate revelation, he offered religious enlightenment by way of the Enlightenment.[4]

The opening up of the interior senses—for example, to speak inwardly with angels, as Swedenborg did—was, by the mid-nineteenth century, rarely sufficient. The voices from spirit-land that people desired were increasingly materialized and incarnated, though devoted leaders of the New Church mostly opposed this turn (as a betrayal of Swedenborg's authority, as well as his sharp dualism). For many, transcending the bodily senses was finally not as satisfying as having the physical evidence at hand. One avenue, with decidedly evangelical and eschatological valences, was the gift of speaking in tongues, which received a burst of attention from the 1830s into the 1850s. Could the Holy Spirit (or good spirits) descend upon people and make the human tongue the passive vehicle of heavenly communications? Spiritualist mediumship often edged into tongue-speaking, and there was a lively exchange in popular religion (Mormon, Shaker, Spiritualist, and evangelical) over the presences of these spectral voices long before the rise of Pentecostalism. An episode of tongue-speaking among some Scottish Presbyterians in the early 1830s, along with its Congregationalist reverberations in New England, is used here to explore the reach of those fascinations.

The restoration of this apostolic gift of speaking in unknown languages proved to be merely one repercussion among many in this "new age" of spirit presences and angelic conversations. (The "new age" was, by the way, an apocalyptic designation pushed especially by nineteenth-century Swedenborgians.)[5] Sometimes the spirits provided catchy choruses for singing in earthly circles; sometimes the angels dictated entire books through automatic writing; and sometimes heavenly voices were even mediated through speaking trumpets, as the acoustic recreations of the Enlightenment were dramatically reenchanted. Eventually, as spirits even took up the telephone, the acoustic technologies of modernity seemed to have been turned completely against the Enlightenment uses of Fontenelle and Brewster, made part of a communications network in a wonderland of good vibrations.

Talking with Angels; Or, The End of Artifice

Swedenborg's religious experiences over the last three decades of his life are as richly documented and intriguingly complex as any figure of the eighteenth century. Through dreams, visions, and voices, through prayer, meditation, and eucharistic participation, through bodily denials and sexually charged spiritual unions, Swedenborg turned inward, seeking the Lord and his angels and warring with Satan and his sirens. It was a contemplative struggle on the grandest scale, worthy of a desert saint, a medieval recluse, or, more proximately, a pietist mystic like Jacob Boehme. Drawn, as was John Wesley, to the Moravians and their devotionalism, Swedenborg remained deeply marked by such pietistic strains within his native Lutheranism (he was the son of a wonder-guided Lutheran bishop). After 1743, though, he gradually moved beyond these more familiar forms of devotionalism through studied techniques of slowed breathing and through the progressive opening of his "spiritual sight." From the mid-1740s to the end of his life, he developed the ability to "converse with angels and spirits in the same manner as I speak with men," and a hallmark of his piety became a near endless stream of communications with angels. (The angels were understood to be the spirits of people who had once lived on earth and who were now arrayed in various habitations, kingdoms, and spheres in heaven.) Despite a considerable doctrinal and exegetical corpus,

Swedenborg captured the attention of his British and American readers above all through these memorable relations of things heard and seen in the spiritual world.[6]

The attention these experiences garnered him was as much negative as positive. As early as Immanuel Kant's *Träume eines Geistersehers* (1766), Swedenborg's familiarity with angels met a gush of ridicule and made him a leading exhibit in medical psychology. One of Swedenborg's staunchest defenders in antebellum America, George Bush—a graduate of Princeton Seminary, a former tutor at the nearby college, and a professor at New York University—knew that vindicating Swedenborg meant defending both his motives and his sanity. The common view, Bush noted, was that the Swede's revelations were either "designed imposture" or "unconscious illusion," especially the latter. His spiritual travels were thus widely dismissed as "a strange medley of hallucinations," a product of "religious mania," "the fruit of a distempered brain." As critic Enoch Pond concluded summarily, "His mind was disordered; it had become unbalanced; and he was, to a degree, *insane*. There can be no reasonable doubt of it." No matter how wide open the religious world of the early republic seemed, talking with angels carried a steep price. Benjamin Rush, in his *Medical Inquiries and Observations upon the Diseases of the Mind,* specifically pathologized those who "see and converse with angels." Accordingly, Swedenborg was regularly read out of the ranks of the reasonable.[7]

By the 1830s and 1840s, these prominent Enlightenment ways of explaining Swedenborg's religious voices were as likely to surface in popular settings as learned ones. Hence, in 1842 in Indiana a New Church preacher found himself in a formal debate with a Presbyterian minister on the bumptious resolution that "Emanuel Swedenborg was an insane person, or a blasphemer and a knave."[8] John Wesley, in particular, had been crucial for blessing this interpretive course in evangelical circles, largely sidestepping the theological content of Swedenborg's visions by recycling suspect accounts of the mystic's fevered mind. Diagnoses of mental malady—calls for the "shutting up of Swedenborg in a madhouse"—weighed very heavily on New Church evangelism, on anyone who wanted to take these religious experiences seriously. So desperate were apologists to establish Swedenborg's rationality that they went to extreme lengths even to deny his basic pietism, publishing articles proclaiming "Swedenborg Not a Visionary" and "Swedenborg Not a Mystic." Hardly a testimonial came from the press that did not bespeak the necessity of confronting the charge of insanity, of denying that these revelatory encounters were "the effects of a disordered state of the brain, which the science of physiology professes to explain." The New Church battle with materialist explanations was not abstract but highly personal, deeply bound up with feelings of disrespect and insult.[9]

Swedenborg proved hard to confine, though, because of certain social advantages. An aristocratic cosmopolitan, he carried the respected standing of a natural philosopher, and these badges of genteel credibility helped his experimental reports of angelic conversations gain a hearing that they would have otherwise been denied. A scion of the Enlightenment and the right social circles, he was hard to dismiss as a vulgar enthusiast, one of the weak-minded and credulous. Certainly those Americans who "received" Swedenborg's teachings, as did the scholar George Bush, almost invariably made this point about his learning (and, implicitly, the social position that went with it). For example, Margaret Hiller, a New England convert at the turn of the nineteenth century, singled out Swedenborg's "extensive erudition," his uniting of philosophical learning with religious vision, as a principal attraction.[10] Emerson, both hagiographer and critic of this "colossal soul," was similarly drawn to Swedenborg's preparations "in shipyards and dissecting-rooms." "One is glad to learn that his books on mines and metals are held in the highest esteem by those who understand these matters," Emerson remarked dryly.[11] Because Swedenborg had first been a student of astronomy and anatomy, a Cartesian rationalist, a productive mathematician, an improver of mines and trade, a cognoscente of air-pumps and microscopes as well as of speaking trumpets and acoustic tubes, his admirers were able to accrue greater credit for him as a visionary. Because Swedenborg was clearly as committed as anyone to the advancement of knowledge, because he brought all of his energies for precise mapping and classification to his grand tours through heaven and hell, his followers were able to present this kabbalistic mystic and pietist pilgrim as, through it all and at bottom, a man of science.[12]

Beyond his conversations with angels and beyond his hybridity as natural philosopher and Christian visionary, Swedenborg offered other attractions. Among his biggest allures was as an inspired guide to scriptural interpretation, with much of his theological writing taking the form of extended commentaries on the hidden spiritual meanings of biblical texts, recondite correspondences beneath the literal words. "*He* will furnish you with a *key* to unlock the holy treasures of Divine Wisdom contained in the written

Word of the Lord"—so claimed convert Elizabeth Jones in 1816 in a letter to her Presbyterian pastor in Newburgh, New York, on her reasons for switching to the New Church. Carrying this weapon into exegetical combat, Jones, an "unlearned female," was able to "forget my own inferiority" and stoutly defend Swedenborg's views of scripture as well as his Christ-centered views on the Trinity. In a heavily Protestant culture, riven with strife over biblical subtleties, inspired commentaries like those of Swedenborg (or, later, Mary Baker Eddy) carried the hope of finding a solid foundation beneath all the disputes. Though new prophets necessarily only added to the scriptural melee, the hope was always one of interpretive healing. "The right of private judgment in the interpretation of Scriptures, which is the first principle of Protestantism, has introduced a perfect anarchy into the Christian world," despaired a Swedenborgian preacher in Boston in 1818. "Every year, every day, may give birth to new sectaries and new creeds. Where is the umpire? where is the judge?" The New Church, like those who later turned to Joseph Smith and the *Book of Mormon*, thought they had that final referee—a new key to the scriptures in the form of Emanuel Swedenborg's inspired glosses.[13]

Swedenborg was also well tailored for the American religious milieu in many of his liberal doctrinal emphases, which were easy to make part of a mounting anti-Calvinist polemic. (In one of his visions, Swedenborg actually encountered Calvin in the spirit world, and it turned out the reformer had been spending altogether too much time in an otherworldly brothel.)[14] On original sin, predestination, and the damnation of infants, Swedenborg adopted sharply anti-Calvinist views, in keeping with wider Enlightenment currents.[15] Much of his theological work was infused with liberal predilections—the hallowing of charity, free will, usefulness, marriage love, and progress through education (the angelic tutelage of children was a prominent activity of heaven). Sharing in wider universalistic currents, he opened salvation to all those, inside or outside the church, who sustained a regenerate life of active benevolence and loving affections toward their neighbors. His realized eschatology, in which the Last Judgment had already been accomplished in the spiritual world in 1757, invited dreams of a new era of millennial progress in which the advancement of learning, technology, and civil liberty could be enfolded as evidence of the dawning of the New Jerusalem.[16] Likewise, his reinterpretation of the Trinity in terms of the oneness of Christ played to Enlightenment sentiments (the belief that such three-in-one mathematics would never add up), and so did his dismissal of tangible miracles as illusory. His American disciples became adroit at such maneuvers. "The age of *external* miracles has doubtless passed away," Margaret Hiller noted, but, at the same time, Swedenborg's experiences "exhibited a species of *internal,* or *spiritual miracle,* absolutely *new* and truly *astonishing.*" Swedenborg, often reduced now to a metaphysical bridge into Spiritualism, offered many attractions to his Anglo-American audiences.[17]

For all his liberal affinities, Swedenborg talked with angels, matched wits with evil spirits, dreamed extraordinary dreams, and pored over the Apocalypse. Whatever else gained him his considerable readership (by the 1820s, *Heaven and Hell* was already an American bestseller, rivaling the novels of James Fenimore Cooper and Walter Scott for sales), the leading impetus was surely the mystic's numerous points of connection with popular forms of supernaturalism.[18] Swedenborg was both symptom and spur of the oracular mode in the early republic. As was evident in the earlier examination of evangelical narratives, mystical auditions and epiphanic dreams were Protestant commonplaces, part of a religious culture of divine intimacy cultivated through biblical immersion, prayer, meditation, and revival. *An Account of a Trance or Vision of Sarah Alley,* published in Poughkeepsie in 1798, was representative. Taken on an out-of-body tour of heaven and hell by an angel serving as guide, Alley even encountered Jesus himself. "Christ told me I could not enter there yet," she said—"that I must return to the world, and warn the people thereof to repent."[19] Swedenborg's encounters with everyone from Moses and Aristotle to the apostles and Luther, with angels and spirits of all kinds, were received within this culture of visions, dreams, and voices, a world in which it was not especially unusual for God "to make extraordinary discoveries and revelations to particular persons."[20] Many came to see Swedenborg as embodying a new epoch of "a more intimate fellowship with saints and angels," an imminent time of restoration when "angels shall converse with men as familiarly as they did with Adam before the fall."[21]

31. A Swedenborgian Angel

Of the many wonderful relations of mystic Emanuel Swedenborg, among the most alluring to English and American audiences were his manifold encounters with angels. From Emanuel Swedenborg, *The Joys of Heaven* (Manchester: Davis, 1814), frontispiece. Courtesy of the Swedenborg Library, Bryn Athyn College of the New Church, Bryn Athyn, Pennsylvania.

And I beheld and heard an Angel
flying through the midst of Heaven.
saying with a loud voice Woe. Woe. Woe.
Rev. VIII. 13.

What precisely did people learn about the speech of angels through all of Swedenborg's interior discoveries? On the face of it, the auditory world of the angels sounded a lot like the earthly world. As Swedenborg related in *Heaven and Hell*, at the opening of his chapter on the speech of angels: "The Angels converse together, as we do on earth, and in like manner on various subjects, whether of a domestic, civil, moral, or spiritual nature. . . . The speech of angels is equally divided into words with our's, and alike sonorous and audible, for they have mouths, tongues and ears, as we have." But these close correspondences between earthly and spiritual realms hid fundamental differences. To begin with, the speech of the angels was cosmopolitan and unified: "There is but one language used throughout heaven, so that all of every society, however distant, understand one another." It was also exceedingly condensed and precise, such that angels were "able to express more in one word than we can do in a thousand." Against the deistic suspicion of the artificiality of all human language and hence all revelation—that no words could ever match the purity, universality, or exactitude of nature's geometry—Swedenborg heard a celestial language of just such clarity and scope. In Baconian and Cartesian frameworks, mere words were impugned for their inconstancy, frailty, and vernacular provinciality, and whole new classificatory and experimental languages were dreamed to help deliver the learned out of such contingency into universal knowledge. From this "want of a universal language," Paine would draw the skeptical conclusion as crisply as anyone: "Human language, whether in speech or in print, cannot be the vehicle of the Word of God." In talking with angels, Swedenborg discerned a rejoinder to the absorption of revelation into the language of nature, to the very dismissal of the oracular power of words.[22]

Swedenborg embraced the philosophical ambition for a universal language, but he kept that dream within the frameworks of Christian eschatology and Adamic restoration. The exalted range of angelic speech stemmed not from such sources as abstracted mathematical formulas or cleverly designed ideographs, but instead from a knowledge of the secrets embedded in scripture. Those mysteries, including the esoteric significance of biblical numbers and the Hebrew alphabet, shaped angelic expression, infusing both its oral and written forms. Much of the potency of heavenly communications grew out of the access that the angels had to these divine encryptions, the copious meanings hidden in "the very flexures and curvatures" of the Hebrew letters, as well as "the sounding of them." Such angelic words, imbued with presence, transcended the philosophical suspicions that gnawed at the trustworthiness of ordinary words, those arbitrary signs that seemed ever harder in the eighteenth century to shore up with a divine origin. For the undisciplined mutability and estranging localism of human languages, Swedenborg offered a religious balm: angelic fluency, not pure mathematics or learned ingenuity, would reverse the consequences of Babel. The lexicons of natural philosophy, however important, ultimately paled before the condensed surpluses of heavenly wisdom.[23]

Among the most crucial ways that the speech of angels differed from human speech was in the fate of artifice. Swedenborg, one in a great company of early modern moralists who inveighed against hypocrisy and dissimulation, found in the spiritual world a realm where guile was consistently undone, where aristocratic masks and courtly intrigues fell away. Mutterers and whisperers, for example, fared poorly in heaven, and those spirits who remained inclined to conceal their real thoughts with a calculated softness of voice were exposed by the very nature of heavenly communication. "Such speech is heard at greater distances and more loudly than open speech," Swedenborg reported happily. Also, flatterers and wheedlers—all "those who speak differently from what they think"—were subject to unmaskings of various kinds. One hypocrite, for example, was presented as a spiritual dartboard in which arrows rained down upon his head until his pretense was punctured, thus revealing his "true character." In Swedenborg's heaven, the senses of the angels were exquisitely discerning, and their fine-tuned ears, in particular, permitted them to make a complete register of the inner lives of others through perceiving subtle "variegations in the voice." "The angels know the disposition and qualities of another from his speech, his affection from the sound of his voice," Swedenborg related. "I have heard the angels declare what life another person has led from only hearing him speak."[24]

At times, the capacity of the angels to penetrate the hearts and minds of others appeared sinister, even inquisitorial. In this Christian vision of total exposure, nothing remained hidden. The deceitful, the seducing, the backbiting, the cajoling, and the fraudulent were turned inside out; they were bared of all casuistic reserve and equivocation—"not the least room is left for evasion or denial." So thoroughgoing were the probings of the angels that Swedenborg, the dissecting anatomist, described their discriminating powers as a kind of autopsy of the spiritual body: "When all that a man had done here in his natural body is made manifest to him after death, then the examining angels inspect his face, and commence their inquest, which begins at the fingers of each hand, and is from thence continued throughout the whole body." Putting an end to artifice and deceit would not be accomplished without merciless invasions of body and spirit. A heaven of such relentless honesty—where every tone of the voice, where every look of the face, automatically opened the recesses of the soul to inspection—was not without its terror. Was it any wonder that those hypocrites who tried forlornly to persist in their disguises began, Swedenborg reported, to feel "anguish and pain, to change countenance, and to be struck in a manner lifeless"? With an Augustinian or Kantian absolutism, Swedenborg's heavenly kingdom tolerated no secrets and no lies, and few pains were spared in rooting them out. His angelic societies, endlessly purifying themselves of artifice, had a dystopic underside.[25]

The heart of Swedenborg's mystic listening centered on the speech of the spiritual and celestial angels. The universal language of the angels was not "learnt" but "natural"; it flowed "spontaneously from their affections"—indeed, the very sound of their voices corresponded completely with their affections, so that their language "may be called a sounding affection, and a speaking thought." There were no gaps, no slippages, no broken signs, no arbitrary conventions, "it being impossible for them to utter any thing which does not correspond with their affection." In an evocative turn of phrase, Swedenborg described the speech of one angel as so harmonious and delightful that it was "as if Love itself had spoken with a tongue."[26] At another point, caught up in the sheer purity of angelic speech, he experienced these words in incarnational form as "a virgin who was dressed beautifully in a robe of white neatly gathered at the breast, and who was graceful in the movements of her body" (in the same vision, the speech of evil spirits was represented to him as "the hind-quarters of a horse").[27] For the subsequent imagining of a Romantic self—one absorbed with spontaneous expression and pure sincerity—Swedenborg's celestial angels would provide an exalted model. "These angels are without any garment or covering, for nakedness corresponds to Innocence," the seer related. Their childlike simplicity and artlessness, embodied in their Edenic nudity, put an end to the artifices of social life and imagined the ultimately transparent self.[28]

Swedenborg's most empyrean conversations with the angels performed important cultural work in the here and now. American followers took his lessons about angelic speech to heart and dreamed new kinds of intimacies and interiors through them. As New Churchman Richard DeCharms explained in 1856, "the external man is now too generally a hypocrite, and speaks a language which the soul does not feel"; and again, "the internal man is now so hid under feigned and false appearances, which we are taught from infancy to assume, that the expressions of the external man are no longer the natural language of the soul." In the world of the angels, DeCharms explained, "thoughts themselves would speak . . . communicated by undulations of the heavenly aura, as sounds are in our own air." American adepts took special delight in Swedenborg's rendering of angelic speech, in all those pure spirits who were incapable of thinking one thing and speaking another: "They do not know what hypocrisy is, and what fraudulent disguise is, and deceit." With their complete restoration of the unity of feelings and words, interiors and exteriors, Swedenborg's angels offered an idealized remaking of the self—pure and genuine, plainly expressive of loving affections, wholly open in character. These angels, tearing away all the masks of polite society, proved very easy to transpose into American middle-class saints of authenticity.[29]

Bodies, Spirits, Senses: The Penetrating Eye, the Obedient Ear, and the Tasteless Angel

Swedenborg's proficiency in talking with angels and in describing their speech was enmeshed in a highly complicated sensorium. No other Christian visionary paid such close, dissecting attention to the bodily and spiritual senses, and this intensive inquiry flowed out of Swedenborg's natural philosophy, especially his work as an anatomist. The seer had studied the five senses at length, composing a whole disquisition upon them as well as writing separate essays on the ear and the eye. Synthesizing the experiments of others and pursuing his own probings of the body, he was bent on an ambitious Cartesian project of arriving at "knowledge of the soul" through "anatomical experience."[30] Though Swedenborg was following standard cosmological models of microcosm and macrocosm in imagining the whole of heaven as a human body, it was his own physiological learning that allowed him to detail with unusual precision the different organs of that Grand Man. The very "Form of Heaven," he noted trenchantly in *Heaven and Hell*, corresponded to "the structure of the human body, as viewed and examined by a skilful anatomist."[31] Swedenborg emerged from the anatomy theaters of the early Enlightenment and remade himself as the dissectionist of heaven's sensorium. His unrivaled ability to map that spiritual body, in turn, would deeply mark his American followers.

Swedenborg shared most of the assumptions about the senses current in the wider experimental philosophy. He was interested, for example, in how the bodily senses could be "sharpened"—that is, how they could be improved, trained, and managed. He was convinced of the utility of empirical demonstration and desired to provide just this sort of evidence of the spiritual realms. "I am well aware of the fact that many people will say nobody can possibly speak to spirits or angels as long as he is living in the body, and that many will call it delusion," Swedenborg confessed early on in the *Arcana Coelestia*, before offering his usual empiricist rebuttal. "But none of this deters me; for I have seen, I have heard, I have felt." The seer exuberantly affirmed the testimony of his own senses and took that sensationalism with him into heaven, pointing to a spiritual world where the senses were all the more delicate and vigorous: "Let people beware of falsely assuming that spirits do not possess far keener sensory powers than they did in the life of the body," Swedenborg warned. "From thousands of experiences I know that the reverse is true." As with hearing's grand enhancements among the angels, Swedenborg found in heaven the consummate refinement of the senses. "This spiritual body is most perfectly organized," one American adherent elaborated, "having all the organs and senses of the material body, but inconceivably more acute, exquisite, and perfect." In Swedenborgian circles, the careful education of the senses—not least the proper formation of the ear—became a given. "That the ear is highly susceptible of improvement," a writer in *New Jerusalem Magazine* concluded in 1838, "and that it will well repay a judicious cultivation, there can be no doubt."[32]

Like most of his Enlightenment contemporaries, Swedenborg's epistemology remained hybrid. Along with the experimental philosophy, he had also deeply imbibed a Neoplatonist as well as a Cartesian distrust of the bodily senses. The fallacies and illusions to which the senses were subject made reason's disciplines—the seasoned judgment that allowed for the correction of sensory error—extremely crucial, and Swedenborg rarely missed an opportunity to disparage the shortcomings of the bodily senses and the dangers of mere sensualism. Swedenborg so avidly pursued the body and the senses not as ends, but in search of a vehicle by which to refute all those "scientific and philosophic reasonings" that called "the life of a spirit or a soul" into question. "The senses are too strong for the soul. Our senses barbarize us"—so Emerson claimed, and it is not surprising that he and other American transcendentalists saw in Swedenborg a harbinger of their own revolt against "the despotism of sense." However analogous the bodily and spiritual senses were, Swedenborgian attention was ultimately riveted on cautioning the former against material illusions and opening up the latter to the really real.[33]

Perhaps Swedenborg was most in synchronicity with his philosophical colleagues in according particular privileges to the eye. At the outset of his treatise on the five senses, for example, he imagined all of knowledge in visual terms and made clear his desire for a panoramic view—the surveying of the world as if "from the top of a mountain" or "from a high tower." In the *Arcana Coelestia* he likewise elucidated the higher perfection of one spiritual realm over another by comparing sight's superior sweep to hearing's limits: "For that which hearing is able to take in through an hour of speech may be presented to the sight within a minute, such as for example, views of plains, palaces, and cities." Though Swedenborg cultivated a multi-sensory spiritual discipline, he often used the eye to stand for all the senses. In his memorable relations it was, first and foremost, his "spiritual sight" that was opened. "The eye is the noblest region of the face, and surpasses the other senses," Swedenborg wrote in his *Spiritual Diary,* and his American heirs readily embraced that incomparability. Caleb Reed, for example, echoed the seer's view in a lecture entitled "The Senses" in Boston in 1838, noting succinctly that "the sense of sight," corresponding to the understanding, "is the highest or noblest of the senses." Within the Swedenborgian sensorium—like its Aristotelian, Cartesian, Lockean, and Common-Sense counterparts—sight was the most honored sense.[34]

At the other end of the sensory hierarchy was taste, so thoroughly linked with the material body that it could not be freed for spiritual transformation. Taste, indeed, was the one sense that the angels did not have, at least not in any way comparable to its bodily counterpart. "Spirits have every sense except taste; but taste they have not," Swedenborg wrote in his *Spiritual Diary* in 1748. "It is now manifest to me that they are delighted with man's spiritual food, thus with the knowledges of truth and good. But they do not insinuate themselves into taste, which is a sense properly dedicated to corporeal food, or to the nourishment of the body, in which they have no delight."[35] The barring of taste from heaven suggested something of its earthly allure and power. One of the seer's earliest visions related to those who were "devoted to conviviality in eating" and to indulging "their appetites." "In the middle of the day at dinner an angel spoke to me, and told me not to eat too much at table," Swedenborg wrote. It was his own "unseemly appetite" for sumptuous dining that had to be "cast out of my body" like a demon; the craving had to be "burnt up" and "cleansed." This visionary lesson about taste and "overloaded stomachs" helped shape the bodily habits of temperance cultivated by Swedenborg's Anglo-American progeny. As Caleb Reed proclaimed in his Boston lecture, "taste is the lowest of the senses; and the love of indulging it is the grossest form of sensualism."[36]

Both smell and touch, falling in between vision and taste in the hierarchy of the senses, had a place in heaven. Following common anatomical models, Swedenborg considered touch the most comprehensive sense, the one underlying the rest, the very basis of all sensation. "The touch, therefore, which is extended over the whole body, is the common or universal sense, to which the others refer themselves," Caleb Reed averred in familiar terms. Though physical touch carried many of the same carnal dangers that hampered taste, the angels nonetheless retained this sense, often to an exquisite degree. Swedenborg himself was allowed repeatedly to witness the tactility of the spiritual world, including the delicate touch of spirit hands and the feel of angelic clothes (remember, only the celestial angels were naked). Despite the conventional denials of bodily cravings, the Swedenborgian spiritual world possessed a distinctly sensuous feel. Whether exercised in the intimacies of true marriage love or in the palpable enjoyments of otherworldly festivities, a transformed sense of touch clearly occupied a fundamental place in this angelic sensorium.[37]

Smell was packed with still greater import, especially because of the way its precise discriminations were joined to determinations of virtue and piety. In keeping with long-standing Christian perceptions of ethereal scents, Swedenborg's heaven abounded in pleasant fragrances—for example, floral perfumes of endless variety, and the redolence of those living in faith and charity. More than the aromatics, the very specific stenches by which the angels sniffed out dangerous spirits were especially critical to the social workings of the spiritual world. "The horrid stench of wall lice" revealed those who had persecuted the innocent; "that of a stinking mouse" corresponded to the avaricious; that of excrement, to adulterers. The smells of fetid water, vomit, carcasses, and burned bread all exhaled their own unmistakable character references as well. It was fitting that, according to Swedenborg's exegesis, the mark of Cain was not a visual emblem but an odor placed upon him that kept him eternally other—"such an odour so that there was nowhere that he could wander, because men would want to drive him away." Odors were crucial to the social imagination of the Enlightenment and the rising bourgeois culture, and the spiritual senses that Swedenborgians so eagerly anticipated showed how deep these sensory orderings of social, moral, and religious differentiation went. Spiritual odors, Caleb Reed explained, allowed angels to judge "the quality of a spirit . . . at a great distance"—that is, to avoid the proximity of those who were defiling or who were simply of a "lower" sphere. The smells of heaven and hell were so loaded with nuances that Swedenborg finally despaired of describing them fully, suggesting it would require a whole volume to set out the moral economy of odor.[38]

And then there was the ear, second to the eye in nobility, but showered with every bit as much attention from Swedenborg as its more exalted counterpart. "How vast a science and knowledge is this unique sense," he commented, and spared little of his immense energy for anatomy in pursuing this organ. Knowledgeable about the various acoustic experiments of his day—those on echoes, the velocity of sound, the mathematics of harmony, and the physics of speaking trumpets, for example—Swedenborg followed Hooke and Newton (among other natural philosophers) into a speculative labyrinth in which sound vibrations were explored as a master key to the animation of matter. "It is in the sense of hearing, above all other senses, that we may most advantageously observe the real nature of tremulation," Swedenborg noted in a treatise on the radiating force of vibrations in 1719. In his anatomical inquiries into the ear, he even confronted (like Du Verney before him) the prospect of auditory illusions, the internal sounds that had no connection to external sensation: "In fantastic imaginations," he observed, "persons are able to hear various sounds and connected conversations, so that they sometimes persuade themselves that a spirit is speaking with them. I have spoken with a woman, who every day continually heard the singing of hymns within her." Obviously undeterred by the auditory dangers of the enthusiastic imagination, Swedenborg would never waver in insisting on the supreme verity of the internal sounds that he discovered through the opening of his spiritual hearing. Of this he was certain: the internal perceptions behind and beyond bodily sensations belonged to a higher reality.[39]

Exploring the microscopic secrets of the ear's anatomy provided Swedenborg with various tools for his religious imagination, one of which was conceiving the actuality of the normally inaudible world of spirits:

> I have spoken to spirits about the fact that few people probably are going to believe that so many things exist in the next life, the reason for that unbelief being that man has no more than a very general and hazy concept, amounting to none at all, about his life after death, a concept which people have confirmed for themselves from the fact that they do not see the soul or spirit with their eyes. . . . Spirits whom I have spoken to have been amazed that man should be like this, even though he knows that nature itself and each of its kingdoms contain so many wonderful and varied things of which he is ignorant. Take just the human ear, for example. A whole book could be written about the remarkable and unheard of aspects of it, in whose existence everybody has faith. But if anything is said about the spiritual world, the source of every single thing in the realms of nature, scarcely anyone believes it.[40]

Swedenborg's explorations of the ear, a part of the body that was notorious for its minutely hidden mechanisms, prepared him for his soundings in the world of spirits and angels. Its elusive recesses, like the arcana of the human body more generally, served as one vehicle by which he moved from material to spiritual senses.

Throughout Swedenborg's vast corpus, the ear's primary associations were with the obedience of dutiful listening and with the will and the affections. While the ear also remained a conduit of rational learning, it was—at an almost structuralist level—the other with respect to the understanding and independence of the eye. Swedenborg made these correspondences recurrently, often with the simplicity of an equation: "By the ear and by hearing is signified hearkening and obedience; . . . by 'giving ear to any one' is signified to obey," and the eye was, with equal terseness and repetitiveness, linked to rational understanding. As a universalized and cosmological anatomy, the opposition was inscribed in the very body of the Grand Man: those angels who resided in the eyes corresponded to analytic discernment; those in the ears, to hearkening obedience.[41] An American follower elaborated this basic sensory distinction in an article in *New Jerusalem Magazine* in 1834: "The two senses of seeing and hearing . . . differ from each other in a manner corresponding to the difference between the understanding and the will." When the object of inquiry was critical appraisal, "the most direct way is through the eye," but when the hope was lifted affections, the best route was through the ear. Caleb Reed evoked the same correspondences in his lecture "The Senses" in 1838: "The sense of hearing has more relation to the will, and corresponds to obedience . . . so the faculty of hearing is peculiarly a receptive faculty. And as such it is not active, investigating, questioning, penetrating, like the eye, but quiescent and passive." No more basic distinction existed in the Swedenborgian sensorium than this one, between the rational, inquisitive eye and the emotive, obedient ear.[42]

The opposition of the understanding and the will, along with that of the eye and the ear, was inevitably joined, in turn, to the differentiation of the male and the female. In the Swedenborgian economy of gender, the roseate vision was one of a grand, conjunctive union of the sexes in self-completing love, but that ultimate wholeness still presupposed, as one American follower put it in 1855, "a species of dominion belonging to the male over the female."[43] That privilege depended on the same advantage the eye enjoyed over the ear: in men, the understanding and rationality predominated; in women, the will and the affections—and such distinctions, however harmoniously conjoined, very much followed the couple into the blisses of the perfected marriage. As a corollary of these gendered assumptions, it was unimaginable within Swedenborg's vision that women might serve as preachers. Those women who invaded this public domain of masculine understanding lost their essential "feminine nature"—in this case, that of the affective yet obedient listener.[44] Given these classical oppositions at the heart of the Swedenborgian system, the eye appeared unassailable in its power and nobility; the ear, tied dangerously to passivity, irrationality, and femaleness.

Yet in the highest heaven, that of the celestial angels, hearing became the preeminent sense. "It is worthy of being noticed here," Swedenborg remarked in *Heaven and Hell*, "that the Angels of the Third Heaven advance in Wisdom by hearing, and not by sight; for what they hear from preaching enters not into the memory, but immediately into their perception and will, and so into the form of their life." In the most exalted heaven, for all its dazzling light, the ear was the perceptual center. There reasoning and understanding were absorbed into a higher wisdom; there the gap between reflection and action closed into immediate obedience and unquestioning love. These celestial angels, vastly excelling their counterparts in the spiritual kingdom in wisdom and glory, "know immediately by Influx (in-spiration) from the Lord whether that which they hear be true or not." When the Lord's words come to them, they indulge in no rational calculation; "for as soon as they hear them, they immediately will and do them, without having any occasion to . . . reason upon [them]." Hearing, precisely because of its associations with both the affections and submission, embodied this most inward way of angelic wisdom. And since in this Swedenborgian sensorium of the spirit all were to aspire toward this perfected practice of divine love, the hearkening of the celestial angels—the way they lent their ears to the Lord and to one another—served as an exalted model of Christian obedience in which listening and loving converged. For such a spiritual life, the reasoning, mas-culine eye was not so noble or so powerful or so enthroned, since all the ce-lestial angels, male and female alike, progressed on notably feminine terms. In this Christian practice, in which obedience to God was ultimately more important than the understanding of God, the ear finally displaced the eye.[45]

Another acoustic model, that of musical harmony, provided the consummate representation of the unity, submission, and love that were dominant in the highest heaven. The ear's connection to the affections had always been marked most insistently through music, and the joys and delights of heaven were, for Swedenborg, as for most in the Christian tradition, dreamed especially through harmonious sounds. "Today, I heard angels of the interior heaven, of whom there were very many in consociation, forming a hymn which was plainly audible to me," Swedenborg noted in his *Spiritual Diary* in 1748. Through the alchemy of hymn singing, the angels "had been forming a golden crown with diadems about the head of our Saviour." What most caught Swedenborg's attention was not this bejeweling spectacle, but instead the wonders of how all the angels sang together: "No one leads the choir, but all together lead each other mutually." Such was the blessedness of this celestial harmony, Swedenborg discovered, that no one can be among the angels "who wants to act from himself and to command the others, and is unwilling to suffer himself to be led." Spontaneous in their affections, yet marked by unanimity, those who performed these canticles were utterly devoid of self-love. Sometimes the delights of these harmonies were so overwhelming as to be entrancing, leaving the angels in "a delightful stupor," one of utter stillness. In this representation of the heavenly choirs,

Swedenborg offered a model of the self's engulfed subjection to the divine whole, and an exaltation of Christian mutuality over rational autonomy. Through devout listening Swedenborg imagined the soul's submission to God, as well as the rapt emotions of that obedience.[46]

Beyond the mystical enchantments of hearing, what Swedenborg and his progeny ultimately dreamed was a synesthesia of the eye and the ear, and, with that merging, a reunion of the understanding and the will as well as of the male and the female. That sensory recombination was made manifest in Swedenborg's shifting descriptions of angelic speech: the aural and the visual crossed each other in "a shining vibration." "The speech of angels," Swedenborg related, "is sometimes made to appear visually in the world of spirits, and thus before the interior sight, as shimmering light or a brilliant flame." On another occasion, he said, the spirits spoke to him "by means of purely visual representatives, by presenting flames varying in colour, by lights, [by] clouds rising and descending." These synesthesias of seeing and hearing mirrored the true marriages of heaven, in which the understanding of the husband joined in complete harmony with the will of the wife. Such heavenly unions, mutualities, and reciprocities were imagined in part through reconciling the gendered structures of the eye and the ear. With the advent of the New Jerusalem, one American writer explained in 1839, "the will and the understanding and the eye and the ear will not have separate interests and ends," but will be "made one," a restoration of the primordial unities of the Most Ancient Church. In Swedenborg's heaven, three interrelated marriages were performed —those of the understanding and the will, the male and the female, and the eye and the ear.[47]

Throughout all of his vast experiences, Swedenborg tested a mystical sensorium—Christian, kabbalistic, and Hermetic—in the crucible of the Enlightenment. By exhaustively exploring the spiritual senses in anatomical terms, he ushered a mystical strand of Christian devotionalism through the age of reason. To be sure, much of his vision was deeply traditional in its pietistic emphases (closer to Fletcher and Edwards than to Reid and Rush), and this included the routine regulation of sensory pleasures. As one Swedenborgian pastor, John Clowes, noted in his *Letters on the Human Body* (1826), there was still a pressing need to impose order on "the otherwise uncontrollable, fascinating, and dangerous misrule of our *senses*"—that is, to place the dangerous seductions of the bodily senses in a *"state of submission"* to the purities of the spiritual senses. In a standard devotionalist conceit, Clowes pictured the bodily senses as animals that needed to be bridled before the spiritual senses could be spurred. One American New Churchman, likewise, praised Jeanne Marie Guyon for her contemplative teachings on the "death of the sensual," the mortification of the "outward senses," which "have always been among the chief occasions of sin." The spiritual senses of the mystic were still opened through a denial of the merely sensuous. Swedenborg's angels, after all, had been purged of the erotic allures of taste.[48]

But the seer's heaven was also one of floral gardens, brilliant colors, sumptuous homes, and ecstatic harmonies, so it remained easy for his followers to make him the broker of more indulgent sensibilities in which the spiritual senses invited not so much bodily renunciation as somatic celebration. Very much at home with genteel refinement, Swedenborg and his more affluent disciples comfortably blessed the pleasures that accompanied wealth, just so long as this love of the world did not eclipse the love of God (a notoriously difficult line to draw). With the coming of the New Church, Caleb Reed explained, Christians no longer needed to be "cut off" from their bodily senses, because the spiritual and the material, the internal and the external, could now be brought into harmonious correspondence. As the New Jerusalem progressively unfolded, Christians would "learn to cultivate the senses, and take pleasure in their perfection," by appreciating music, art, and architecture. The restored purity of the senses was a common Swedenborgian theme across a wide social spectrum; but for those, like Reed, who were especially concerned with respectability, the deliverance of the senses almost inevitably ended up being imagined in terms of genteel elegance. The taste of polite culture was fully redeemable, even in itself redemptive, and the refined senses of the New Jerusalem came to reflect those aesthetic sensibilities.[49]

Within the Swedenborgian restoration of Christian sensuousness hovered one especially momentous supposition. In the Most Ancient Church the bodily senses had been wholly at one with the spiritual senses, and, as a result, people had communicated openly with angels, living in full awareness of "both worlds at the same time." And it was to this time of "open communication" that many in the New Church imagined returning—not just in heaven, but soon in a new era of "a more free intercourse with Heaven." In contrast to more temperate Protestant perspectives that treated the apparitions of angels as parallel to miracles—that is, phenomena useful to the foundation of the church, but now unnecessary and vulnerable to Catholic superstitions—many Swedenborgians hungrily pursued the ancient intimacies with angels. "What then hinders our conversing with angels now, as the patriarchs and prophets did of old?" asked one expectant devotee. "That intercourse with the spiritual world is now becoming and will soon be more common than it has been, we have no doubt," wrote another in 1828. Any realization of such desires depended on an axial proposition about human perception—namely, that people are "endowed with spiritual senses, and that these senses may be opened by the Lord while man lives upon earth, so as to make him sensibly acquainted with the things of the spiritual world." But whose unlocked senses were to be trusted? Only Swedenborg's, or those of any and every mystic? In the heady atmosphere of antebellum America, the opening of the spiritual senses became an extremely contentious issue.[50]

Talking with Swedenborg; Or, The Problem of Authority

Swedenborg's followers had a love-hate relationship with immediate revelation. On the one hand, they celebrated the seer's heavenly conversations and the hovering nearness of angels, ever guiding and comforting. Some even rhapsodized about angels speaking to them in visions or in "the mystic land of dreams"; others told extraordinary tales of deathbed illuminations or epiphanic conversions. One Hoosier, for example, wrote to the *New Church Repository* in 1851 to recast his youthful conversion experience in a Swedenborgian light: with head bowed to "listen undisturbed" to a sermon, "*I lost my outer consciousness! My spiritual sight was opened!* . . . With great wonder and astonishment I exclaimed—it is Jesus! Jesus! . . . As I gazed intently upon the Divine, just above me, a little at the right, a voice, as of an angel, was heard in mine ear." More distinctively, a few devotees were even blessed with a manifestation of Swedenborg himself. One told of a "remarkable dream"—"so lively, so real, . . . that I had some doubts whether I could pronounce it to be a dream"—in which he met Swedenborg as an angel of approval and blessing. Another humble devotee had the angelic Swedenborg thank him directly for going to the expense of displaying his framed portrait as "a family picture"—the image serving, in effect, as a materializing aid to the voice of Swedenborg's angel. As with Ann Lee's visionary presence among the Shakers, the seer was, on occasion at least, apotheosized into an angelic being of unsurpassed wisdom and beauty, a source of continuing inspiration.[51]

On the other hand, many Swedenborgians were defensive about their reputation for holding "a constant intercourse with angels and deceased persons," a "popular error," *New Jerusalem Magazine* lamented in 1829, that had made its way into the first volume of the first edition of the *Encyclopaedia Americana*. The same journal had complained the year before that misinformation of this sort was epidemic: How often had believers faced such misbegotten inquiries as to "whether we do not set chairs and dishes for our friends who have left the natural body"? It was all so galling, "for at the very threshold of the system we learn that it is impossible for spirits to be seen by the natural eye—to be heard by the natural ear—to sit in material chairs, and to eat material food."[52] Besides these basic affronts to their respectability and to their dualism of matter and spirit, American followers were also well aware of Swedenborg's more cautionary statements about the demonic dangers that shadowed direct spiritual intercourse. Evil spirits were just as real and prevalent as angels, and the ingrained fear of necromancy made many New Church leaders extremely harsh critics of Spiritualism. Most of all, the seer's devotees were apprehensive about maintaining the singular authority of his writings amid all this talk of spirits and angels. Here was the underlying dilemma: Was Swedenborg a final word or an open door?[53]

Long before the Rochester rappings effectively inaugurated the Spiritualist movement, Swedenborgians were enmeshed in a world of angels both eruptive and divisive. From early in the movement's rise in England, many followers were drawn to Swedenborg not only for the luminosity of his experiences but also as a bridge to their own mystical confirmations. "Several persons in Manchester," an observer noted of one of the foundational New Church societies in 1784, "are having open communication with the spiritual world and receive ocular and auricular proofs of the statements of Swedenborg."[54] The Anglican and Swedenborgian John Clowes, though himself of a visionary turn, was nonetheless alarmed in 1820 when a woman, "who was a receiver of the New Doctrines, asserted in the most solemn manner, that she had immediate open communication with heaven, that she frequently saw and conversed with the Lord Himself, and that she was expressly commanded by Him to establish a New Church, which was to be called the *New Church New*, to distinguish it from what was commonly called the New Church." The woman managed to gather a handful of converts before the official opposition of Clowes and others in the New Church silenced this oracle of the New Church New.[55]

The issue was recurrent. For example, James Johnston, a British Swedenborgian and a common laborer, conversed with angels from 1817 to his death in 1840 and left a monumental diary record of those exchanges. The chief apologist of this "Celestial Representative," John Martin, came to the United States (at the bidding of his own angels) shortly after Johnston's death and decided that America would be "the best place" to publish this diary of revelations. A copy of the manuscript, and soon the original itself, made the transit to a New York circle of Swedenborgians and mediums—one of whom began to channel Johnston's spirit voice through her body. After circulating in manuscript and by word of mouth, Johnston's "Intercourse with Angels" appeared in two printed excerpts in New York in 1866, under the aegis of an anonymous editor who had come across a handwritten copy in Westchester County in 1863. A hybrid of scriptural commentaries, millennial speculations, and prophetic denunciations (of slavery and class exploitation, for starters), Johnston's revelations insisted that the fullness of time had arrived in which people on earth would again be in "regular communication with the angels." And he had this on good authority: Swedenborg, now "an angel of heaven," told him that all the preparations were set for this reopened intercourse and that Johnston's own conversations were but the "first bud" in the flowering of "Communication with the Angels in Heaven and men on earth." Though kept on the edges of the New Church, Johnston's talks with angels (including with Swedenborg) enjoyed a clandestine circulation, and the shadowy travels of his manuscript were indicative of the unquelled yearnings for renewed conversation with angels in this subculture—desires that were always hard to keep from surfacing anarchically.[56]

The constitution of religious authority, everywhere a problem in antebellum America, was specifically refracted through the Swedenborgian senses. Take the vignette of Samuel Worcester and his circle of followers, for whom a small cache of manuscripts survive from the mid-1840s under the auspicious title, "Sundry Papers Regarding the Opening of the Spiritual Senses." On a visit to New York in June 1844, six months before his death, Worcester, who was a prominent New Church minister from Massachusetts, reported having his spiritual senses opened, upon which he was enabled to see and converse with Swedenborg and other spirits. Going into a meditative state during worship in which the very light of his face and "the tones of his voice" made evident the nearness of "heavenly beings," Worcester was permitted to give "many truths direct from Swedenborg"—an angelic presence so "gentle and sweet" that it moved him to tears. Necessarily wary of the devil's illusions, he performed a battery of ritual tests, "calling the name of the Lord, repeating portions of the Word, making the sign of the Cross, &c &c," all of which these spirits passed. Soon others in the New York fellowship, quickly labeled the New Era movement, also had their spiritual sight and hearing opened. The conclusion these experiences pushed Worcester, family, and friends toward was that Swedenborg "is the *present* as well as the *past* revelator" to the New Church. For reasons large and small—for the Holy City to come down out of heaven, for the cure of rheumatism, for the right order of baptism, for the proper education of children, for the minute rules of Sabbath observance—Swedenborg had to become a living voice again.[57]

Many in the New Church were roused to excoriate Worcester and his circle for the supposed madness and indecorum of their "Necromantic Orgies," and the critics largely succeeded in shunting the group to the margins of an already small church.[58] Was not this, critics railed, the exact sort of auditory challenge to the anchor of canonical texts that should alarm anyone concerned about stabilizing church authority? The often accommodating George Bush warned against those who were "prone to say, 'I have a higher authority than that of any written record. I have a voice direct from the spirit-world itself. Is not this the head-quarters of truth? . . . A new era is being ushered in.'" Within these subcultural debates, it was not natural philosophy, not theories of imposture and illusion, but ecclesial strictures that proved the gravest speech impediment that the angels faced. Though the flexible charges of insanity, hallucination, and priestly machination could still be invoked by one New Churchman against another (Richard DeCharms did this to Worcester, for example), the debate pivoted on ecclesiological concerns. Since within Swedenborgian circles the possibility of angels speaking was assumed, the question centered on the parameters and the trajectories of that communication. It was religious authority trying to maintain some semblance of authority, not the acids of the Enlightenment, that set the sharpest limits on angelic speech.[59]

The Swedenborgian yearning for angels hardly led to a free-for-all, however eruptive the voices of these visitants seemed. The New Era advocates, as much as their opponents, had to draw discernible boundaries, had to police the line between "orderly and disorderly open intercourse." The question was not whether, but when to restrain the spiritual senses, how to close or narrow the openings. "You are all too desirous of new revelations, to permit those that are already given to do their work," so admonished Swedenborg the angel in one of the more ironic messages that Samuel Worcester received. Read the Bible, read my writings—those are already filled with immediate presence, Swedenborg instructed from heaven. Once his spiritual hearing was opened, Worcester claimed that he spoke to no other spirits besides Swedenborg's without first getting permission from the seer. And the climax of Worcester's visionary experiences was his priestly ordination at the hands of the angelic Swedenborg, which he said that he received "spiritually kneeling." However dissolvent of authority the opening of the spiritual senses appeared, Worcester and company extended their perception only to underline the authority of Swedenborg and his ministers.[60]

The leading spokesman for the New Era, Silas Jones, a former lecturer on phrenology, performed the same kind of dance with authority, trying valiantly to set out the rules for orderly angelic visits, even as he welcomed the spirits. Those communications which reinforced the authority of the Lord, scripture, and Swedenborg and those which celebrated charity, humility, and conjugal love were orderly. Those which embraced fortunetelling, evil spirits, and sexual promiscuity, as well as the magical search for "the philosopher's stone," "the elixir of life," and "worldly riches," were disorderly. These latter promptings very much required resistance, Jones claimed, no doubt because they exercised an allure within this fluid fellowship. The authorization of certain experiences demanded the delegitimation of others—in this case, occultist elements that swirled around the New Era group and that other New Churchmen used to tar them. In a modest way, Jones was attempting for New Era Swedenborgians what Jonathan Edwards had essayed for New Light evangelicals—the sorting out of the reliable and illusory signs of genuine religious experience.[61]

The New Era coterie walked a tightrope. They needed the angels (especially the angelic Swedenborg) to bring form to a fellowship that was inchoate, as well as to confer authority on their priesthood and their sacraments, but they also dreaded the seductions of disorder that shadowed the spirits. As Silas Jones confessed in 1848, "It has pleased the Lord in his divine providence to lead the writer where he has seen much of

THE LITTLE MESSENGER.

VOLUME I.   PHILADELPHIA, NOVEMBER 15, 1868.   NUMBER

ANGELIC CARE.

ALREADY we have invited you to think of divine protection; let us now turn your thoughts to angelic care. It is in a great measure by means of angelic care that divine protection is exercised. When we sleep and when we are awake angels are near us. Good thoughts come into our minds when we are awake through the ministry of the angels of the Lord; and when we sleep we have pleasant and instructive dreams, because angels are doing their work for us while we rest under the auspices of the Lord, who never slumbers nor sleeps. We might indeed dream, like the young girl represented in our picture, that an angel came into our chamber and hovered over our pillow; but that angels are near us is no dream. It is written in the Psalms: "He shall give his angels charge concerning thee;" and though the highest meaning of these words is in regard to Him who came down from heaven, it is true that all whom he came to lead to heaven are objects of divine protection, and thus of heavenly care. We may say heavenly care or angelic care, for heavenly and angelic mean the same thing. Let us think of a few particulars of angelic care for us.

In the Psalms the angels of the Lord are called his ministers that do his word, hearkening unto the voice of his word. The things that we learn in the sacred Scriptures, the angels love more and understand better than we do ourselves, and we are taught in the Church that when we read the Scriptures, angels know what we read and what we think while we read. Our ideas of what we read are to their ideas like the founda-tions of a house to the house itself. If there were none in the world who were able to form some idea of what the Scriptures mean, the angels would have no subjects for thought. So the Lord takes care that there shall always be some men who read and love, and to some extent un-derstand, his word. There have been times when the knowledge of the Lord has been very nearly lost in the world, but he has interposed and prevented it from going tirely out of sight of men. Th was such a time just before came as a little child; and t he came, and men saw him ing according to the Scriptu and in many ways fulfilling the and evil ones who hated m and tried to make them fo God, knew him as well as m For we are told that when was casting out devils, some them said to him: "We k thee, who thou art." And was tempted, and an evil one cited to him passages of the cred Scriptures, and tried make him act according t false meaning of them. Y can read all about this in M iv. 1-11; and in Luke iv. And it is because you can the Scriptures in the same as he used them then, in def ing yourselves from evil, th have reminded you of this p of the life of our Lord in world.

The angels hearken to voice of the word of the Lo they knew when Jesus tempted, and they knew w things he said in speaking truth when the tempter speaking falsely. And just they knew he was tempted, that he was fighting the tle of temptation by means truths in the holy word, t know when we have evil thoughts come into minds, and they help us by suggesting good o And they do it mostly by means of what we t remember of the words of the Scriptures. have a strong inclination to do what we ou not to do, or a disinclination to perform duty, and then we remember something in Scriptures, and we feel that we cannot do w we ought not, nor fail to do what we ought,

25

open intercourse with the spiritual world. Much of what he has seen has been altogether disorderly." Still, Jones and Worcester, like others in this fellowship, desired the angels, longed to live "in perpetual society" with them, and dreamed of their consolation and love. They yearned, too, for the living presence of the absent dead (especially deceased family members, as well as Swedenborg himself); they sought to erase loss and separation. "Why should not the man of the church have open intercourse with angels?" Jones pined, even after all his sorting out of the unruly. He chided those "who are satisfied with their day of small things," those who did not seek "the opening of their internal sight and hearing," those who knew Swedenborg only as past and not a present revelator. Aware of the contradictions over authority he could hardly resolve, he nonetheless expressed bewilderment at those who "hatch out rules of order" and lose sight of this ultimate desire, "a state of oneness with an angel." The senses, their opening and closing, were fiercely embattled in these circles, vexed by questions of authority, yet ever laced with longing for "the privilege of hearing and conversing with those in heaven."[62]

That Swedenborg had come back to life as the angel of the New Era, speaking to people and performing ordinations, was not at all comforting to clericalists within the New Church. Always wary of the artful disguises of evil spirits, pastor Benjamin Barrett warned of hell-bent Swedenborg impersonators, those whose malignant design it was "to personate him in the most perfect and satisfactory manner" and thus to be all the more effective in leading people away from the true church. Filling the spiritual world with deceitful beings who eagerly wanted to assume Swedenborg's voice, Barrett warned that a fake Swedenborg would be likely to tell a self-conceited dupe "that the Lord had chosen him to be the medium of some new and important instruction to His church, and that his spiritual senses had been opened for that purpose." If a clerical hierarchy was to be sustained and routinized, the treacheries of the spiritual senses needed to be recognized and Swedenborg's angel kept quiet. Key New Church

32. *Angelic Care*

Angels possessed an animating power in the pious desires and dreams of those within the New Jerusalem Church; they were bearers of protection, consolation, purity, and authenticity. From "Angelic Care," *Little Messenger*, 15 November 1868. Courtesy of the Swedenborg Library, Bryn Athyn College of the New Church, Bryn Athyn, Pennsylvania.

leaders, such as Richard DeCharms, were all too happy to sacrifice the hope of restored converse with angels to the requirements of ecclesiastical government, middle-class respectability, and intellectual solidity. Swedenborgians, DeCharms said, "are thought to be visionaries, enthusiasts, sight-keepers and sign-demanders," but against such "popular prejudice" he insisted that New Churchmen "are preeminent over all other men for cool-headed, common-sense intellection, and the utmostly practical utilitarianism." Keeping people from talking to Swedenborg's angel was part of creating that image of order, refinement, and rationality.[63]

The New Church was a small pond, and in the larger waters of American religion these particular ecclesial restraints made few ripples. Swedenborg's angelic form was a favorite guide among clairvoyants, mesmerists, and Spiritualists, and the New Church could do nothing to keep him quiet in those circles. Within the induced trances and clairvoyant healings of animal magnetism, the visions of Swedenborg were refracted through the hypnotic lens of Franz Anton Mesmer, the late eighteenth-century Austrian physician whose techniques proved so wonderfully popular in antebellum America. One wayfarer, Louisa Ogden, who moved from the Episcopal Church to the New Church in 1844, made her story of reidentification hinge on her witnessing the public exhibition of "a magnetic somnambulist." Ogden was soon conducting hypnotic experiments on her sister, and the sensory effects produced offered her "a proof that there existed a medium of communication to our spirits, other than that of our own material senses." It was through mesmeric sleep that Ogden was prepared for Swedenborg's sensorium, that she came to believe in "a still higher state of magnetism" in which people's "spiritual senses" were "so thoroughly opened, as to communicate with spirits." George Bush made the same correlations, joining Swedenborg to Mesmer and discussing Swedenborg's spiritual senses under the rubrics of "magnetic vision" and "magnetic hearing." Bush specifically credited Swedenborg with discovery of "the law of spiritual acoustics"—that is, his description of angelic speech corresponded to "the mode of hearing in the Mesmeric state." Swedenborg's understanding of the spiritual senses, closely bound to scriptural exegesis and contemplative practice, remained yoked to time-worn Christian emphases, but with these magnetic translations those ties were increasingly loosened.[64]

The ability of the New Church to control Swedenborg's angelic voice slipped all the more, once mesmerists had seized hold of the seer's understanding of internal perception. One of the most renowned clairvoyants and magnetic healers, Andrew Jackson Davis, featured Swedenborg prominently among his spirit guides (alongside the ancient physician Galen). Davis, known as the Poughkeepsie Seer, was led into Swedenborgian circles in the mid-1840s through his stage exhibitions of animal magnetism, in which he dictated wisdom from the spirits and offered medical diagnoses through his clairvoyant sight into bodies. A Pythagorean who listened for "the music of the spheres" and delved into "the secrets of harmony," Davis developed his own spiritual acoustics, which he termed "psychophonetics," and thus remade the Swedenborgian sensorium in the terms of his own system. "A most exquisite insight into the laws of psychophonetics is indispensable to a correct comprehension of the wonders heard by the spiritual tympanum," Davis instructed. Sailing on "a boundless ocean" of "soul-sounds" that were "absolutely inaudible to the physical ear," he filled his autobiography with episodes of mysterious voices and strange music. In a curious moment of reenchantment, he even taught himself "a sort of ventriloquism" by which he imitated the "Aeolian harmony" of the heavens, a "purling symphony" that he claimed to manage by "breathing through the epiglottis and pharyngeal passages."[65]

Davis was exactly the terror that New Churchmen like Richard DeCharms and Benjamin Barrett feared—a clairaudient for whom Swedenborg was one inner voice among several and who was not beholden to basic propositions of theirs about the Bible and the Trinity. For them, the Poughkeepsie Seer showed all that was wrong with talking with Swedenborg's angel: mediated through the mouths of such latter-day trance-speakers, the spirit of Swedenborg was regularly forced to acknowledge the errors in his own revelations, those that resulted from "the prevailing theology" and "the popular religion of his day." To Barrett and DeCharms, Davis and his ilk were no friends of Swedenborg; rather, they were a distraction, diminishing the true seer's "authority as the Lord's official expositor of his Word." "In all time past, and in all time to come," DeCharms exulted after debunking Davis' revelations, "there could not and cannot possibly be more than one Swedenborg, and no other man could or even can arrive at the same kind or degree of spirituality as his." The opening of the spiritual senses had become a minefield littered with the explosive issues of religious authority, and those who talked with Swedenborg's angel as well as those who refused this listening crystallized these problems as clearly as anyone did.[66]

Of Tongue-Speaking and the Gifted Hearer

In the midst of all this antebellum ferment over the voices of spirits and angels, Swedenborgians, like other American Christians, also faced a heightened interest in the gift of tongues. A small hint of these concerns was evident in Swedenborg's own accounts of angelic speech: when angels and spirits spoke to him, he reported not only hearing it as an internal operation upon his ear, but also feeling it as "some gentle vibrations" upon his tongue. When a revival of this ecstatic speech was kindled in Scotland and London in the early 1830s, *New Jerusalem Magazine* took up the question of the gift's restoration in an extended editorial. Drawn into the reports of tongue-speaking during prayer and worship, the author tried to cut through the "ridicule" of such learned journals as the *Edinburgh Review*, which had so thoroughly stigmatized these "prophetical hieroglyphics" as a "wild waste of human breath." For someone versed in the harmonies of angelic canticles, what was to be made of these "gifted" persons, whose "tones and voice become perfectly harmonious" when they were "singing in the spirit"? For someone who knew how closely angels and spirits attended to people in this world, and who expected that intimacy to become all the more apparent as the New Jerusalem descended, what was to be said of this restored manifestation of the Holy Spirit? Not wanting "to judge rashly or hastily of a thing in itself so difficult to be comprehended," the writer tentatively decided against these gifts, largely because of the unintelligibility of this speech. One thing New Churchmen presumed from Swedenborg was the utter perspicuity of heavenly language.[67]

This New Church rejection of the gift of tongues was far more evenhanded than the standard dismissals among the literati and establishment-minded Christians. Take, for example, the eighteenth-century churchman Conyers Middleton, one of those reasonable men who found imposture to be the most compelling explanation for miracles past and present. The managed art of ventriloquism seemed to him, as it had for Thomas Hobbes, a perfectly good way of fathoming how "weak and ignorant people" might be led to believe that they heard "the *voice of a Spirit or Daemon*." Not surprisingly, given the general deceptiveness of oracular voices, Middleton did not think highly of ancient Christian claims of speaking in tongues. Indeed, he thought that, of all the gifts professed in the early church—such as healing the sick, casting out demons, seeing visions, and prophesying—this was the one "most evidently and confessedly withdrawn, in the earliest ages of the Church." This so-called gift had quickly and completely fallen away, in Middleton's view, because the priestly artifice involved was especially difficult to sustain. Tongues were so safely removed from the church's life and so hard to counterfeit that Middleton was even ready to throw down the gauntlet before contemporary enthusiasts like the Methodists: "If, in the list of their extraordinary gifts, they cannot shew us this, we may fairly conclude, that they have none else to shew, which are real and genuin[e]." In hindsight, this seems like one of the more naive, even credulous moments for a learned advocate of the imposture thesis. It was decidedly the wrong kind of challenge to issue to all those "Sects of Christians, of our own times," with their "boasted gifts" of *"pretended revelations, prophetic visions, and divine impressions."*[68]

Middleton's history, like most of these Anglican and Reformed models of miraculous cessation, was wishful history. It was a model of the mannerly, hierarchic decorum that ecclesial Protestants and moderate Enlightenment gentlemen hoped would govern religious and social life—that indeed they stood ready to enforce against a vast welter of "impostors" and "enthusiasts," such as Quakers and Methodists. In that way, Middleton's history of tongue-speaking was a fantasy of order, a history of desire. In actuality, he would not have had to look far for "the least hint" of the gift's renewal among latter-day Christians. Just a few decades before Middleton penned his inquiry in the 1740s, that apocalyptic group, the French Prophets, had been notorious for including among their ecstasies the gift of tongues. One inspired leader, for example, lapsed into Latin and had his tongue taken over by the Spirit; the very tone of his voice was altered *"several times such, that naturally he is not capable of."* Other pietist sects, including the Moravians, reported episodes; Wesley, curious himself about these extraordinary gifts, openly dismissed Middleton's account.[69]

The situation soon got a lot worse for Middleton's version of church history. Ann Lee and the Shakers, for example, made speaking in tongues a recurrent manifestation, part of a wider piety of spiritual gifts that permeated the group from its late eighteenth-century founding right through the antebellum period.[70] By the 1830s, Mormons, too, had fully restored the ancient gifts of visions, healings, tongues, and prophecy. In the first years of the movement, Brigham Young, along with ordinary followers, prayed in unknown tongues, and Joseph Smith endorsed such inspired utterances as "the pure Adamic language."[71] By the 1850s, Spiritualists—drawing on scripture, Swedenborg, animal magnetism, clairvoyance, and popular ghost lore—had made spirit voices and unknown tongues a common part of their own distinct Pentecost.

The limits of cessationist history were increasingly felt even in those Reformed circles that had long been among its primary bearers. The episode to which the editorial in *New Jerusalem Magazine* was responding made that especially clear. In 1832, *Fraser's Magazine* ran a series of three articles by a renowned Scottish Presbyterian minister, Edward Irving, under the heading, "Facts Connected with Recent Manifestations of Spiritual Gifts." In an atmosphere charged with millennial expectancy and evangelical revival, Irving conveyed to a wide audience "the tidings of the restoration of the gift of tongues," "the great event of the Holy Spirit's again making his voice to be heard"—a recovery that had begun in the west of Scotland in 1829 and then spread to his fashionable congregation in London. Devout women, Irving noted, were the initial bearers of this gifted speech. "The Holy Ghost came with mighty power upon the sick woman as she lay in her weakness," Irving related of one saint, "and constrained her to speak at great length, and with superhuman strength, in an unknown tongue, to the astonishment of all who heard."[72]

Deathbed weakness was integral to these early stories: the reopening of this "channel of communication," the Pentecostal speech in strange tongues, was founded on a loss of autonomy and agency, a carnivalized inversion of the canons of the modern self. "I was made to speak," said one follower typically; the voice "fell upon me as a supernatural utterance."[73] "It is Jesus . . . occupying the speech," Irving explained, "and using the tongue of his servant to speak the things which he desireth at that time to be spoken and heard."[74] In a posture that cut against Enlightenment understandings of independent rationality as well as Romantic notions of artistic genius, the inspired ostensibly forfeited the freedom of self-expression to become the passive vehicles of divine speech. The gifted were God's fleshly instruments, God's own speaking trumpets: *"We have no more power over it than a trumpet has over its sounds,"* one of the blessed explained. As an "ear witness" to such utterances, Irving was convinced that he heard the very sounds of the Spirit's indwelling presence.[75]

The Irvingites brought out the debunkers in droves, ecclesial and enlightened alike, who paraded the explanations of imposture and illusion to considerable marginalizing effect. The contempt of the *Edinburgh Review*, rekindled by a friendly biography of Irving, was typical: "There was nothing miraculous in the gift of tongues. It was from beginning to end a gross delusion; in some cases a shallow imposture." The Reformed and Anglican conviction that such extraordinary gifts had been closed off after the biblical epoch was readily joined to Enlightenment constructions of hallucination, credulity, sympathetic imitation, and fanaticism to fend off this latest challenge. Irving himself was made to pay dearly for his support of the tongue-speakers. He was summarily removed from the Presbyterian ministry for encouraging the hubbub and died a couple of years later in 1834, minister to a remnant of believers.[76]

Still, the effects of these manifestations, which generated wide (if mostly critical) attention in Protestant circles, lingered in the air. Take William Watson Andrews, a young Connecticut man, fresh out of Yale, enamored of Coleridge's *Aids to Reflection* and earnestly preparing himself for the ministry (and the millennium). Harboring an esoteric streak, he noted in a letter to classmate Noah Porter, "I am now busy in deciphering the enigmas, and phantasies, and devotional flights of Jacob Böhme." A short time later, amid such mystical excursions, he read an article that changed his life: "It was immediately after leaving Yale, in the autumn of 1831, that my attention was arrested by a letter taken from *Fraser's Magazine,* giving an account of the utterances in tongues and prophesyings by holy men and women of the Kirk of Scotland," he recalled. Made aware of this restoration of tongues, Andrews was never quite right again as a Congregationalist.[77]

His interest in tongues led him down a path of intense study of biblical prophecy and the abiding gifts of the Holy Spirit (fascinations which friends lamented and foes lambasted). Eventually Andrews simply withdrew from the Congregationalist ministry to join what remained of the Irvingite movement, a small and eclectic body known as the Catholic Apostolic Church, which managed to combine the gifts of the Spirit, including tongues and the interpretation of tongues, with a hierarchic ecclesiology and a full-orbed sacramentalism. (The nineteenth-century scholar Philip Schaff called the group "one of the unsolved enigmas of Church History," combining "a high order of piety" with "astounding assumptions.") Before a gathering of his reverend colleagues in 1849, Andrews outlined his reasons for leaving them:

It is many years since I heard with joy of the revival of the supernatural gifts of the Holy Ghost in the land of our fathers. Such an interposition of God in a time of great spiritual decay and abounding ungodliness, and full of signs of approaching judgment, seemed to give such promise of deliverance to the Church, that I could not, as many did, reject the report without examination. I saw from the Scriptures that the promise of the Holy Ghost was without limitation, and that there was nothing presumptuous in desiring and praying for those spiritual manifestations which made the primitive age so glorious. And all that I could learn of the gifts alleged to be now revived—as the truth and holiness expressed in prophetic utterances, and the general zeal and faithfulness of those who recognized in them the voice of the Spirit of the Lord—gradually led me to the conviction that God was truly reviving his ancient work.

After further contact with "ear witnesses," as well as a subsequent visit "to the churches where the Holy Ghost was thus manifesting Himself," Andrews had been convinced. He became, in the very heart of New England, an evangelist for this restored church and an American apologist for Irving and the enfleshed gifts of Pentecost.[78]

Not a few of his friends wondered why Andrews, a sensible and very well-connected Congregationalist clergyman, would throw aside his natural alliances for this apparent babbling. Andrews, with eschatological and devotional urgency, was drawn to the sign, to the token of incarnational presence, to the very mystery of hearing the Spirit's voice enunciated through the organs of otherwise ordinary people. He reported with reverence the testimony of one of those so gifted: "The moment I am visited with the Spirit, and carried out to God in a tongue which I know not, it is as if a deep covering of snow had fallen on all the country round, and I saw nothing but the object of my desire, and the road which leadeth unto it. I am more conscious than ever to the presence of God. He and He only, is in my soul." Like Irving himself, Andrews was a listener, not a vehicle of such vocalized presence. Compelled by his desires for a tangible sign, and at the same time steeped in Christian yearnings for transcendence, Andrews found the ears to hear. And in this spiritual economy of intuitive discernment, that perhaps was the most important gift. Andrews followed Irving in turning what this "generation of mockers" heard as screaming, crying, or "unmeaning gibberish" into "the most majestic and divine utterance," "a present God speaking by his Spirit." Andrews' description of Irving's inflexible commitment to this "sign of the presence" stands aptly for his own: "That voice, which to many wise and good men was a jargon, or a mere outbreak of excited feeling, was to him the utterance of the Holy Ghost, and he dared not silence it."[79]

The effects of the Pentecostal revival of 1829–1832 were evident as well on a far more renowned American theologian, Horace Bushnell. Despite at one point cautioning Andrews directly to mute his "peculiar notions," Bushnell swirled in the same currents.[80] "What, then, . . . has become of these miracles, these tongues, gifts of healing, prophecies? what, also, of dreams, presentiments, visits of angels?" Bushnell asked in *Nature and the Supernatural* (1858), before going on to conclude that conventional Protestant arguments for the discontinuation of such spiritual gifts were inadequate. To Bushnell the choice seemed clear: either find room for these signs and wonders or succumb to the triumphant march of "mere naturalism." Bushnell knew all too many people (both within and outside the churches) who seemed "to ache" under a pained "sense of vacuity," and, to his mind, Protestant Christianity had become part of the problem, reduced to a redundant echo of reason, science, and mechanistic order.[81]

After surveying the long stream of Christian history in an attempt to explode the cessationist view, his leading contemporary example was that of Irving and "the recurrence of tongues" in Scotland and London. Despite the widespread dismissal of these cases by "thinking men" as "mere hallucinations"—"the illusions . . . of ignorant minds, weakened by superstition, heated by religious enthusiasm"—Bushnell, like Andrews, was ready to credit these ecstatic utterances:

> For this gift of tongues, representing the Divine Spirit as playing the vocal organs of a man, . . . is designed to be a symbol to the world of the possibility and fact of a divine access to the soul, and a divine operation in it—a symbol more expressive than any other could be. And then it is the more exactly appropriate in its adaptation, that it wants another gift in the hearer, exactly correspondent, to understand it or give the interpretation.

If somewhat tamed by Bushnell, who presented it more as a Romantic symbol than an oracular practice, this "gift of tongues" still had the power to open up cracks in the well-ordered mind. Paired with a "gift in the hearer," tongues had the potential to disrupt the Baconian and Lockean education of the senses. While Bushnell acknowledged that "nothing is farther off from the christian experience of our New England communities, than the gift of tongues," he nonetheless was able to point out just such an unexpected episode in a little group gathered in private for prayer. He was drawn to these small ruptures as a way to unsettle the tidy habits of a well-ordered mind—an attempt, however faltering, to break his own "latent subjection to the conventionalities of philosophy."[82]

Bushnell knew that his own desires for "the immediate, living realities of religion" were the same longings which drove others "to the badly written, silly oracles of our new-discovered, scientific necromancy"—that there was a fundamental affinity between his own poeticized rendering of the gift of tongues and the Pentecostal profusion of voices in Spiritualist circles.[83] The historian's temptation has long been to sketch a lineage from Irving to the Holiness movement and then to Pentecostalism, but the more immediate fruition of the renewed interest in tongue-speaking was among Spiritualists. Not Bethel Bible college, not the Azusa Street revival—the places usually hailed for the modern renewal of the gift of tongues—but the Spiritualist circle was the contiguous Pentecost. If the theological assumptions of Irving, Andrews, and Bushnell diverged sharply from those of most Spiritualists (evident in Bushnell's snide dismissal), they were bound together by the reclamation of this spiritual gift—the materializing embodiment of the Spirit's voice.

In the same year that Bushnell published the first edition of *Nature and the Supernatural,* John Edmonds issued a little Spiritualist tract called *Speaking in Many Tongues.* The ostensible inspiration for its publication was a Spiritualist circle that had been caught up in discussing 1 Corinthians 12, "where Paul speaks of the diversity of spiritual gifts." The group interpreted the passage in light of Spiritualist manifestations, and made the new languages gained by mediums the analogue of the apostolic gift of tongues at Pentecost. Concentrating mostly on the sudden reception of foreign languages (from French, Italian, and Latin to Chinese and Chippewa), Edmonds ran off example after example of such gifts in Spiritualist circles. His own daughter had a Spirit speak through her in nine or ten "different tongues," including French, of which he noted proudly that it was not "a *wretched patois*" but "pure Parisian." As in the Irvingite revival, trance-speakers among the Spiritualists alternated these unknown tongues with patches of English. Though displaying little of the eschatological urgency that drove Andrews, Edmonds took these "external manifestations" as an embodied sign to awaken people to "the religion of spiritual intercourse."[84] As the specific immanence of the Holy Spirit was diffused into the presence of various voices from spirit-land, the shadow of Swedenborg was again apparent (Edmonds predictably paid the Swedish mystic high homage). The gift of tongues, too, was readily absorbed into the surplus wisdom of the angels.

Viewed now from the edge of the twenty-first century, the "gift of tongues" is supremely important in highlighting the distance between the present religious reality and the past of the Enlightenment dream. No other gift, not even the current profusion of angels, makes Middleton's history of imposture appear so outmoded and uninstructive. As Pentecostalism has ascended across the United States and around the globe into a massively popular form of Christianity, these episodes of the 1830s through the 1850s take on all the more symbolic importance as tiny harbingers of the undoing of modernity's devocalized history. If the convictions of Edward Irving and William Watson Andrews, beleaguered by the power of Reformed Protestantism and the persuasiveness of learned diagnoses, were kept marginal for almost another century, who can afford to cackle now? Sometimes those whom the Holy Spirit agitated with irrepressible sounds laughed uncontrollably. It does not take a gifted hearer to imagine that hilarity as prophetic—a last laugh of vindication at the retreat of the voices of reason and their ecclesiastical allies.

Sacramental Technologies: The Failed Acoustics of Modernity?

Thomas Lake Harris was another of those nineteenth-century American mystics who talked with Swedenborg's angel. In an extraordinary career as a poet, visionary, exegete, and community-builder, Harris sought both to emulate and surpass the Swedish seer in offering his own revelatory commentary to unveil the arcana of scripture. Sharing in much of the "spiritual Harmonialism" that animated Andrew Jackson Davis, Harris tuned his body to celestial sound as well as to angelic speech: "The universe moves in music. . . . Every heart in Heaven beats in music." Anxious in the 1850s about the buffetings of the New Church amid controversies over Spiritualism, Harris received reassurance directly from "the Spirit Swedenborg": "Dear brother, have no fear concerning the New Church. . . . America shall become, in progress of events, one cosmopolitan temple of the New Church." This prophecy about the New Church sounds, in retrospect, about as accurate as Jefferson's prediction of the triumphant rule of Unitarianism. Still, American religion did become an ever more cosmopolitan temple, and this nineteenth-century renaissance of spirits, angels, and ancient harmonies—of which Harris was an avatar—helped lay the groundwork for a pastiche of New Age pieties that flourish at the new millennial threshold. Getting "in tune with the infinite," discovering "the power of vibration," and "going into the 'silence'" are quests that today's seekers have inherited from the nineteenth century.[85]

The mystic Harris suggested how the Enlightenment dream of a demystified acoustics was frustrated. In one of his visionary journeys, Harris toured a heavenly city where he "saw marble statues, such as no sculptor's art could equal"—statuary of the apostles, the Virgin Mary, and the woman at the well of Samaria. Then, coming into a mystery more wonderful than any other yet made known to him, he learned from his angel guide that these were "living statues." "Speak to the marble, and see it will answer you," advised the angel. And indeed the statues "breathed and spoke," becoming the pulsing media "for the voices of the Angels," the living embodiments of "the truths of the Word." In realizing the Hermetic aspiration of an animated statue, Harris imagined a thoroughly enchanted universe in which divine presences permeated everything, in which "a spiritual creation" saturated "marble effigies." The speaking statues were not artifices, but emblems of a world alive with God's spirit, charged with voices. "Listen," the angel instructed Harris. "I did so," the mystic responded, "and I heard a sweet voice proceeding apparently from every tree." The hidden wisdom that Harris garnered from the angels included how people have "lost the faculty of hearing in its finer sense" and how in the ultimate heaven they would have "new auditory organs" opened. In learning how to hear things on Hermetic and Swedenborgian terms, Harris brashly turned the acoustics of modernity inside out.[86]

Amid Harris' visionary soundscape, no stethoscope was at hand with which to correct his perception of living statues, and, even if one had been available, in this transformed sensorium of the spirit it would have been of little help. As the new era of angels and spirits descended upon America, the very technologies of natural philosophy were readily turned against the materialistic, objectifying dimensions of modern science. "To listen attentively to the finest and least obtrusive sounds, as with the stethoscope to the murmurs in the breast," Garth Wilkinson explained in a popular mid-nineteenth-century biography of Swedenborg, "needs a hush that breathing disturbs; the common ear has to die, and be born again, to exercise these delicate attentions." Rather than an instrument of the experimentally disciplined senses, the stethoscope became a symbol of a Romantic spirituality finely tuned to make the inaudible audible.[87]

Even the oracular technologies that the learned thought they had fully absorbed into the rational recreations of the Enlightenment began to slip from their grasp. Topsy-turvy, the speaking trumpet itself came alive as a medium of celestial voices. In one Spiritualist circle in Ohio in the early 1850s, for example, angels began "speaking through a trumpet," using this device to mediate their message of harmony and divine love, even singing and delivering lectures to crowded audiences through this venerable technology. The old acoustic illusions, though still on display as magical amusements, now had competition from the entertainments of séances and the mysteriously propagated voices to be met there: "All being seated and quiet, a trumpet was taken down from the wall, by the spirits," so went one account, "and we were greeted with, 'Good evening, friends, we are happy to meet you here.'" This sort of mediumship, already common in the 1850s, remained so into the 1910s and 1920s, including the Michigan seer Etta Wriedt, who simply referred to herself as a "trumpet medium." Her gift included amplifying the voices of the dead through a special megaphonic instrument that was "raised into the air by an invisible power" and that rendered audible what otherwise would have remained imperceptible. Here was another reversal for the Enlightenment: Fontenelle's favored mechanism of priestcraft was reenchanted as Spiritualists seized hold of Samuel Morland's stentorophonicon. Trumpet mediums effectively snapped the link between the mastery of sound and the advance against ghostly superstitions.[88]

The Enlightenment brief, from Fontenelle to Brewster, had been dedicated to the proposition that the technological disembodiment of the voice and the artificial propagation of sound were useful means of exposing the absences in the oracular. Twisted around, mechanical mediation became instead a vehicle of presences, a salvific force alive with vibrational and telegraphic connections. "Truth's speaking trumpet" is the expression that Henry David Thoreau used periodically to describe the inspiration he discovered through sound and silence, "the true Delphi and Dodona."[89] In rapt awe of the nobility of listening—"The five senses are but so many modified ears," he wrote in his *Journal* in 1838—Thoreau found sonorous revelations pouring forth from crickets, roosters, brooks,

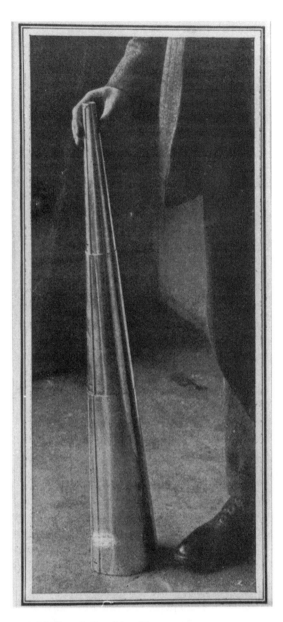

33. A Medium's Speaking Trumpet

Etta Wriedt, an early twentieth-century medium from Michigan, continued a practice that had already emerged among Spiritualists in the 1850s—namely, materializing spirit voices through a speaking trumpet. This is the instrument that she employed to produce those sacramental effects. From "Through the Trumpet,"
London Magazine (1915), Psychical Research Files, Harry Price Library, University of
London. Courtesy of the University of London Library.

bells, and whippoorwills: "I whose life was but yesterday so desultory and shallow—suddenly recover my spirits—my spirituality through my hearing."[90]

Even more fundamentally, Thoreau discerned a universal harmony, a music of the spheres, through telegraph posts and wires. Listening attentively to the sounds of the strung wire, and often applying his ear directly to telegraph posts in order to hear the hum in the very "entrails" of this "oracular tree," Thoreau divined within the vibrations of this technology "the sound of a far off glorious life." In the delicacy of this new practice of listening, he heard an augury of "finer senses." In effect, he transformed the commercial web of the telegraph into a spiritual opening, hearing through the new wires an "undecayed oracle" of the transcendent: "I make my own use of the telegraph—without consulting the Directors—like the sparrows which I perceive use it extensively for a perch." Thoreau's transfigured telegraph became another of Truth's speaking trumpets: "This wire is my redeemer," he exulted. "It stings my ear with everlasting truth."[91]

Thoreau's harmonic convergence of the telegraph and Delphi was hard to equal, but the telephone sometimes came close, readily evoking its own versions of technological sacramentalism. Once again, the connection was especially evident among Spiritualists, a few of whom used the telephone as a tool for materializing the speech of the disincarnated and for imagining a distinctly modern system of celestial communication. Inventors of one of these "spirit telephones," which they called the "psychophone," claimed to have a created a transmitter capable of receiving "supernormal voices." In one photograph from the early 1920s, the originators listened together, by all appearances enthralled with their own mechanical and mystical breakthrough. Among the initial whispers heard through the ear-pieces of the psychophone was the distinctly Swedenborgian affirmation, "We are your angel friends." The technologies of the disembodied voice were thus turned from exposing the illusions of supernatural voices to providing acoustic proof of them. Certainly, the very real power of the telephone to make present the voice of the absent was a sacramental effect even more striking than that of the phonograph. Thomas Edison himself, while he dismissed "the childish contraptions" of Spiritualist inventors as "so unscientific" and "so silly," shared in the metaphysical excitement surrounding the telephone and hoped for an apparatus that would ultimately bridge this world and "another world."[92]

The affinities between the telephone and spirituality were also very

35. Psychophone
Some Spiritualists took the telephone's sacramental potential for transforming absence into presence to its logical conclusion, making the instrument into a technology of spiritual immediacy. In this case, the inventors of the "psychophone" listen with a mix of scientific intensity and mystic awe to the friendly voices of spirits. From George H. Lethem, "The Spirit Telephone," *London Magazine* (1921), Psychical Research Files, Harry Price Library, University of London. Courtesy of the University of London Library.

34. The Sacramental Powers of the Telephone
The telephone's ability to make present the disembodied voice of the absent evoked technological awe. Imagined here in miraculous terms, the apparatus (itself magically hidden from view) allows the spiritualized voice to walk on water. Through mechanical invention, these ethereal bodies attain the very touch of an angelic connection. From Robertson T. Barrett, *The Telephone's Message* (n.p.: n.p., 1931), 11, illustration by Franklin Booth. Courtesy of the Firestone Library, Princeton University.

much on display with Alexander Graham Bell's chief assistant, Thomas Watson. An ardent Spiritualist, Watson secretly sought out the advice of a medium at a critical juncture in Bell's experiments, in hopes that the spirits might "give the telephone a boost." The more important lift that Watson provided for the telephone, though, was the role he played early on in staged exhibitions of the technology. A favorite part of the show was Watson's singing of popular revival hymns, borrowed from Dwight L. Moody and Ira Sankey, into the telephone. The apparatus, he said, gave his voice "a mystic touch." Though Watson himself had grown far removed from his Baptist upbringing, the evangelical trace in his performances is suggestive of how technological sacramentalism extended well beyond Spiritualist circles.[93] As one woman wrote more recently of her placement of Jesus' picture in her home, "I always had Sallman's head of Christ in my living room by the telephone. Always reminding me that I can call on Jesus at all times." Rather than accentuating the bodily absence underlying this presence, the telephone was transmuted into a material mooring for imagining the immaterial listening of Jesus, a Savior who hears and answers prayers.[94]

All along, these technologized voices represented the double fate of the Enlightenment; they were signs not only of its failure, but also of its triumph. The inventors of the psychophone were, after all, scrambling for science's prestige, even as titans like Edison withheld it from them. The experimental pursuit of the spiritual senses through modern anatomy and technology led a long way from the theological ground of Jonathan Edwards and John Fletcher, let alone Augustine and Hildegard of Bingen. The very proliferation of angelic speech was, from one perspective, another victory for the modern privatization and fragmentation of religious authority. People all had their own angels, and the enlightened could now step back and let the ensuing religious factionalism police itself. Already the biblical text as an anchor of authority had proven impossible to stabilize, but the living voice was even more fractious—something members of the New Church found out painfully once their seer started speaking again as an angel. Thomas Lake Harris could be left to waft through the celestial spheres, chatting up the spirit Swedenborg, as an individual eccentricity. An animated universe was made a solitary option, leaving the public culture of government, science, and education to work in its rationalized ways. Even then as some seekers mystified modern acoustic technologies, the alienating effects of disenchantment continued to be readily apparent. One Christian contemplative, trying to cultivate a quiet life of devotion against a backdrop of "fax machines, cellular phones and pagers, call forwarding, call waiting, and caller ID," observed that she first had to silence the telephone ringer. It kept breaking her "solitude into a thousand pieces."[95]

As this woman's struggle with the telephone suggests, long-standing cultural ambivalences over the relationship between piety and technology have hardly gone away. The movie *Contact* serves as a neat capsule of those ongoing tensions and negotiations. "I think it's great that you listen. Most people don't do that anymore," a colleague tells the scientist Ellie Arroway (played by Jodie Foster). Though ostensibly indifferent to questions about God, Arroway nonetheless fervently pursues extraterrestrial intelligence through radio transmissions. And for all her hardboiled empiricism and mathematical precision, it is soon evident that her zeal is grounded on deeper religious yearnings, especially an underlying Spiritualist quest for contact with her mother and father, who both died when she was little. Hollywood does its viewers the favor of filling in "the holes in our lives" brought on by lost faith, by absence and loneliness, turning Arroway into a Swedenborgian traveler in the heavens, an awed mystic whose eyes and ears are dramatically opened. In ultimately rewarding Arroway's many years of unrequited listening, the film seems to decide the case against the acoustics of the Enlightenment, making radio the latest sacramental technology.[96] Still, the explanations of hoax and hallucination undercut the authority of Arroway's experience upon her return, and the policymakers of the state sweep her experiences into the safe margins of private fantasy. And—a point not to be forgotten—*Contact* is spiritual hearing as spectacular entertainment, rather than contemplative practice. It should be clear by now that turning the revelatory voice into a mediated diversion was an old Enlightenment illusion.

Epilogue

> In a cedar-shake shack on a cliff—but we all live like this—is a
> man in his thirties who lives alone with a stone he is trying to
> teach to talk. . . . What have we been doing all these centuries
> but trying to call God back to the mountain, or, failing that,
> raise a peep out of anything that isn't us? . . . You empty your-
> self and wait, listening.
>
> —Annie Dillard, "Teaching a Stone to Talk"

The desire for a "holy listening" has hardly subsided in American culture. If
anything, the noisier and more frenetic the contemporary world is perceived as being, the stronger that spiritual longing becomes. The popularity of music therapies among alternative healers—many of whom offer up
a "mystical acoustics" by which body, mind, and cosmos are harmo-
nized—is certainly one example of this yearning for attunement. Another
is the heightened attention to contemplative silences, evident in New Age
appropriations of Zen Buddhism and Eastern Orthodoxy, as well as in the
growing rediscovery of devotional practices internal to Western Christianity. These desires are apparent too in the current passion for angels and
their whispers of consolation—a notable revitalizing of Swedenborgian
mysticism. The seer appears frequently, for example, in Sophy Burnham's
bestselling *Book of Angels*.[1]

For all the vigor of these contemporary pieties, most of them still entail
a sense of loss, the nostalgic feeling of never quite overcoming the
disaggregations of modernity. In Annie Dillard's story, the man on the cliff
who is trying to teach a stone to talk is left, despite his daily rituals of devotion, in an unyielding silence: "You wait, you give your life's length to listening, and nothing happens." The Enlightenment, whatever its failings
and overturnings, continues to shadow today's spiritual hearers. As devotional writer Barbara Brown Taylor asks in *When God Is Silent* (1998),

"Whatever happened to the talkative God of the Bible? What wouldn't we give for one comforting word in the garden in the cool of the evening?"[2]

Psychotherapist Dianne Skafte's *Listening to the Oracle,* a recent spiritual guidebook, is typical in locating itself in the penumbra of an Enlightenment cloud that stubbornly refuses to disperse. It assumes that Americans are in the midst of a "spiritual renaissance," manifest in the growing interest in "angels, miracles, apparitions" as well as "the beauty of simple ritual and devotional practices." It assumes, too, that Americans as "carriers of modern culture" remain suspicious of sacramental signs and portents, aloof from meditative retreat and holy listening. Skafte's assumption is that the oracles (and all the enchanted ways of knowing which they symbolize) have been lost, and are having a very hard time making their way back into the modern world. She feels compelled to tiptoe up to her own captivation with channeling and those ventriloquized voices of wise spirits that double and split the channeler's own voice. However much the American religious scene seems to partake of a postmodern turn, Jefferson's oracle of reason still sounds as a cultural clarion—one that can never quite be escaped even by those who are most desirous of slipping its bonds.[3]

"*Listen* is such a little, ordinary word that it is easily passed over," writes Margaret Guenther, an Episcopalian spiritual director. "Yet we all know the pain of not being listened to, of not being heard. I feel a clutch at my heart whenever I see a child who is desperate, inarticulate with grief, crying for his preoccupied parent to listen to him." One of the most striking aspects of contemporary American spiritualities is how much they invest in the gifts of the patient listener and the voicings of feeling and memory. As Guenther starkly concludes, "In a way, not to be heard is not to exist." This therapeutic impulse is of no small power and poignancy—one evident in everything from Pentecostal testimonials to feminist blessings of relational selves, from the tearful confessions of Promise Keepers to Bill Clinton's telegenic empathy ("I feel your pain"). The very desire for so much intimate listening is laced with sorrow and vulnerability. "You heard me. You heard me all the way. . . . You heard me to my own story," a woman told a small group in which feminist theologian Nelle Morton participated. Yet disappointment often trails the promise that the fragile self will discover wholeness through various talking cures. As Morton acknowledged, many fail to find the attentive listener they seek, where the "loving ear" turns hearing into "a direct transitive verb that evokes speech—new speech that has never been spoken before."[4]

Perhaps one of the things being commented upon in these contemporary pieties of listening is the missing ear of God, the diminished hearing of Jesus, Mary, angels, or the saints, the need to find a therapeutic replacement for the absences in prayer. If God truly listened, let alone spoke, would religious people need to talk themselves, often with such painful urgency and volubility, into their own existence? Would intimacy depend on self-realization? "When I really hear someone," psychotherapist Carl Rogers related, "it is like listening to the music of the spheres." Such cosmic listening—long familiar to Neoplatonist, Jewish, and Christian mysticisms and still very much evident in the nineteenth-century harmonialism of Andrew Jackson Davis, Henry David Thoreau, and Thomas Lake Harris—has come to depend increasingly on the perceived quality of interpersonal relationships. "I believe I know why it is satisfying to me to hear someone," Rogers continued. "When I can really hear someone it puts me in touch with him. It enriches my life." If listening still leads to "the universal," as Rogers affirmed, that ascent is now regularly thought to be achieved through a resonant exchange with another person.[5] Religion as a private affair, concerned with the tangibles of this-worldly relationships and distanced from a dialogic God—surely Tom Paine and his compatriots would have seen a family resemblance.

Paine and company would no doubt find even more of a resonance with the ways that the auditory has been redefined in political terms. The distinctly modern quest has been to gain a hearing through democratic association, through a secular polity in which having a voice is equated with voting and political participation. Hearing and being heard stand as a crucial modern idiom through which to explore the empowerment of the subject (and the subject of empowerment). "Hearing to speech is political. . . . Hearing to bring forth speech is empowering," Nelle Morton wrote, again with pointed eloquence. Like the translation of the Christian history of the oracles into a secular history of tyranny and freedom, modern dreams about listening, even many religious ones, hinge on the political. The stories that hold the imagination are about the opening of communicative spaces within local and national communities—discursive spheres in which the people, all the people, will finally have a voice and be heard. Such humanistic dreams circle back to John Dewey's sense of "the connections of the ear" to the formation of a vibrant public culture. Recall his dictum: "Vision is a spectator; hearing is a participator."[6]

Not only the dreams but also the nightmares of contemporary listening are deeply political. "You open wide the portals [*pavillons*] of your ears to admit the State," Jacques Derrida writes in *The Ear of the Other*, in what is by now a familiar interrogation of the totalizing powers of ostensibly democratic governments. The freedoms pledged, academic and otherwise, are exposed as ruses, and modern citizens become no more than the "phonograph dog" obeying the master's voice. Jacques Attali's *Noise*, a political economy of music, is laden with a similar alarm about the monologic apparatus of the state—one undergirded by the bourgeois enshrinement of a tedious harmony, so hard to disrupt, so repressive of the body, so pervasive in its Musak-like commodification. To Attali, the modern state has become "a generalized eavesdropping device" that wields technologies of listening out of the deeper and more sinister ambition to create a culture of self-surveillance.[7]

It now hardly requires the invocation of French poststructuralists to conjure up such political dystopias. Americans lived through one of their own in the late 1990s, thanks to Linda Tripp's covert tape-recordings, Kenneth Starr's desire to tap the President through a wired Monica Lewinsky, and the state's intrusion into the phone sex of the state's own representatives. What kind of listeners did the scandal rely on (a scandal in which there was, after all, so little to see and so much to hear)? Neither liberated nor subjugated auditors, but still politically tuned ones, lending ears that were, alternately, appalled and amused, disengaged and titillated. The scandal prospered in a culture of commodified eavesdropping, where surveillance merges into entertainment, where listening thrives on mediated distance. Certainly, William Frederick Pinchbeck and Jeremy Bentham, students of the Acoustic Temple and the Invisible Lady, anticipated the pleasures and powers of that culture, if not its disillusionments. The scandal flourished as well in a culture still charged with Christian eschatology. Perhaps Kenneth Starr's desire for total exposure, for the elimination of all equivocation, has its strongest echo in religious yearnings for the moral transparencies of heaven and hell. It was not Bentham's acoustic tubes but Swedenborg's celestial angels that promised complete access into every nook and cranny of the liar's body and soul.

Religion is absorbed into the discourses of politics and therapy: now, *there's* a narrative with a familiar ring. Does this story, like all those stories about modern hearing loss, have to end on a note of religious absence or displacement? Even though that sort of closure has proven endlessly attractive as a form of cultural criticism, it needs to be resisted, for all the reasons that arise from religion's multiform presences in contemporary American society, for all the weaknesses that inhere in overdrawn narratives of modern secularism. It would not take much interpretive dexterity or ethnographic immersion to qualify, complicate, or even cancel these supposed absorptions and attenuations of religion. (What, after all, would American politics be like without evangelicalism? And would the culture of therapeutic well-being be half so powerful without religious forms of mind cure?) A quick return to the gifted hearers of Pentecostalism, in all their profusion, would be enough to circumvent any story line about rationalization and the untuning of the sky. To the end, the narratives about rupture, silence, and devocalization remain narrow and inadequate stories.

Still, these clear limitations do not negate the various cultural locations in which the history of the Enlightenment sensorium, including its demystified acoustics, remains pivotal. Prominent among those sites is the critical study of religion and its disciplinary unfolding. A forceful reminder of this particular Enlightenment legacy can be seen in the work of one of the nineteenth century's leading philosophical critics of religion, Ludwig Feuerbach, whose remarkable understanding of the senses appeared at the outset of this book as an epigraph. Insisting on the fundamental sensuousness and imaginative fabrication of all religion, Feuerbach lavished an excess of suspicion upon the sense of hearing and the psychological deceptions to which it was prone. At stake, in particular, for Feuerbach was Christianity's misplaced reliance upon listening to God's words, notably Protestantism's heightened spiritualization of hearing. The eardrum, he observed in *Das Wesen der Religion* (1845), was "the sounding board" of the religious illusion, and "the ear the womb of the gods." In a turn of argument that makes sense only in light of the larger Enlightenment campaign against the mystic's ear, Feuerbach was ready to embrace all the other senses as allies of skeptical rationality, while casting the ear aside as irredeemable: "The only fearful, mystical, and pious sense is that of hearing."

Intent on maintaining the vast superiority of the eye's critical judgment over the ear's "spook realm" of unmanly dependency, Feuerbach underlined the point through an aphorism: "An eyewitness is worth more than a thousand auditory witnesses." The Enlightenment anatomies of pious fraud still resonated in Feuerbach's attack on the ear as the primary organ of religious fears and figments. His naturalistic vision remained deeply allied to a chain of associations about hearing that left the ear especially vulnerable to suspicion and that made it useful for the very enfleshment of a natural history of religion. The ear was mystical; the ear was female; the ear was obedient, timid, exploitable, weak, and untrustworthy. The development of a philosophical critique of religion was joined to a specific pedagogy of the senses in which the reeducation of the Christian ear was axiomatic. The history of the critical study of religion is also a history of the senses.[8]

The literati's body of knowledge about auditory hallucinations, fragmented identities, politicized voices, (de)mystified powers, illusory projections, emptied presences, and unreliable words has hardly yet dissipated in the academic winds of postmodernism. For all the light the *philosophes* shed on religion—indeed, because of that light—they inched the clock toward the "midnight of absence" that now haunts much of religious studies and the humanities generally. The most skeptical strands of the Enlightenment have their intensification, not their undoing, in a broad swath of poststructuralist criticism: the politics of unmasking the metaphysics of presence, the play amid the flutter of artificial signs.[9] Those who are most intent on burying the self-assured rationality of the Enlightenment often stay to ventriloquize the ghosts of absence, illusion, and simulation. It requires no theological leap, only historical canniness, to suggest that suspicion be turned on the suspicious. Watch the lips. The voices of reason, up to their old artifices, are heard even in their postmodern disappearance, still speaking without appearing to speak.

Notes

Introduction

1. This description of Joe Nickell's work is based on an extended conversation that I had with him on 19 November 1997, as well as on Joe Nickell, *Looking for a Miracle: Weeping Icons, Relics, Stigmata, Visions, and Healing Cures* (Buffalo: Prometheus, 1993); Joe Nickell, *Entities: Angels, Spirits, Demons, and Other Alien Beings* (Amherst, N.Y.: Prometheus, 1995); Joe Sharkey, "Hold This Page Sideways and You Can See Elvis. Really," *New York Times*, 24 August 1997, sect. IV, 2. Nickell is a complicated shape-shifter, also in keeping with the tradition of Enlightenment magic: a Ph.D. in English, a poet, a detective, a professional magician, and a highly productive skeptic. This particular episode with Nancy Fowler is also a typically gendered combat in which "male" skepticism confronts "female" credulity. On this last point, see David J. Hess, *Science in the New Age: The Paranormal, Its Defenders and Debunkers, and American Culture* (Madison: University of Wisconsin Press, 1993), 108–113.

2. Richard C. Cabot, *Physical Diagnosis,* 4th ed. (New York: Wood, 1910), 143–144. See Stanley Joel Reiser, *Medicine and the Reign of Technology* (Cambridge: Cambridge University Press, 1978), 23–44; Malcolm Nicolson, "The Introduction of Percussion and Stethoscopy to Early Nineteenth-Century Edinburgh," in W. F. Bynum and Roy Porter, eds., *Medicine and the Five Senses* (Cambridge: Cambridge University Press, 1993), 134–153. For a case in which the stethoscope symbolizes the improvement of acquired perceptions, see Francis Wayland, *The Elements of Intellectual Philosophy* (Boston: Phillips, Sampson, 1855), 83–84. On the formation of these auditory habits, see Henry I. Bowditch, *The Young Stethoscopist; Or, The Student's Aid to Auscultation* (New York: Langley, 1846), v–vii, 13–16.

3. On managing the senses, see Alexander Crichton, *An Inquiry into the Nature and Origin of Mental Derangement,* 2 vols. (London: Cadell, 1798), 1: 264–265, 311. On the flea and the improved ear, see William Gardiner, *The Music of Nature* (London, 1832; Boston: Ditson, 1837), 18–21. In thinking about the refinement of sense experience in seventeenth- and eighteenth-century natural philosophy, I have been influenced especially by Steven Shapin, *The Scientific Revolution* (Chicago: University of Chicago Press, 1996), 93–96; and by Steven Shapin, *A Social History of Truth: Civility and Science in Seventeenth-Century England* (Chicago: University of Chicago Press, 1994). I have drawn as well on those studying disciplines around medical training and musical listening. See Susan C. Lawrence, "Educating the Senses: Students, Teachers, and Medical Rhetoric in Eighteenth-Century London," in Bynum

and Porter, eds., *Medicine and the Five Senses*, 154–178; and James H. Johnson, *Listening in Paris: A Cultural History* (Berkeley: University of California Press, 1995), 195–196, 228–236. On interconnections of the experimental philosophy with the critique of religious enthusiasm, see Michael Heyd, *"Be Sober and Reasonable": The Critique of Enthusiasm in the Seventeenth and Early Eighteenth Centuries* (Leiden: Brill, 1995), 157–163, 243. Critical, too, have been my ongoing conversations with Ann Taves on the history of religious experience and its psychologies. Her ability to hold both naturalistic explanation and visionary experience together in one narrative is exemplary. See Ann Taves, *Fits, Trances, and Visions: Experiencing Religion and Explaining Experience from Wesley to James* (Princeton: Princeton University Press, 1999). For another ingenious model of this double enterprise, see Phillip H. Wiebe, *Visions of Jesus: Direct Encounters from the New Testament to Today* (New York: Oxford University Press, 1997).

4. John Beaumont, *An Historical, Physiological and Theological Treatise of Spirits, Apparitions, Witchcrafts, and Other Magical Practices* (London: D. Browne, 1705), A3, 177, 393–394.

5. Joseph Glanvill, *Saducismus Triumphatus; Or, Full and Plain Evidence Concerning Witches and Apparitions (1689)*, ed. Coleman O. Parsons (Gainesville, Fla.: Scholars' Facsimiles and Reprints, 1966), xvi. This quotation is from a report Glanvill made to the Royal Society in 1668; he himself was closer to Beaumont than Hume in his inquiry into the land of spirits.

6. Beaumont, *Treatise of Spirits*, 210–211.

7. Ethan Allen, *Reason the Only Oracle of Man*, ed. John Pell (Bennington, Vt., 1784; New York: Scholars' Facsimiles and Reprints, 1940), 231; Thomas Paine, *The Age of Reason*, in *The Complete Writings of Thomas Paine*, ed. Philip S. Foner, 2 vols. (New York: Citadel, 1945), I: 596–597.

8. On the impact of these didactic strands on the working out of the American Enlightenment, see Donald H. Meyer, *The Instructed Conscience: The Shaping of the American National Ethic* (Philadelphia: University of Pennsylvania Press, 1972); Henry F. May, *The Enlightenment in America* (New York: Oxford University Press, 1976); Mark A. Noll, *Princeton and the Republic, 1768–1822: The Search for a Christian Enlightenment in the Era of Samuel Stanhope Smith* (Princeton: Princeton University Press, 1989); Mark A. Noll, "The Rise and Long Life of the Protestant Enlightenment in America," in William M. Shea and Peter A. Huff, eds., *Knowledge and Belief in America: Enlightenment Traditions and Modern Religious Thought* (Cambridge: Cambridge University Press, 1995), 88–124; Theodore Dwight Bozeman, *Protestants in an Age of Science: The Baconian Ideal and Antebellum American Religious Thought* (Chapel Hill: University of North Carolina Press, 1977); Douglas Sloan, *The Scottish Enlightenment and the American College Ideal* (New York: Teachers College Press, 1971); Daniel Walker Howe, *The Unitarian Conscience: Harvard Moral Philosophy, 1805–1861* (Cambridge, Mass.: Harvard University Press, 1970).

9. Shapin, *Scientific Revolution*, 93–94. Emerson noted this etymology of "our word Mystic" in his essay on Swedenborg. See Ralph Waldo Emerson, "Swedenborg, or the Mystic," in *The Collected Works of Ralph Waldo Emerson*, ed. Wallace

E. Williams and Douglas Emory Wilson (Cambridge, Mass.: Harvard University Press, 1987), 4: 55.

10. Walter J. Ong, *The Presence of the Word: Some Prolegomena for Cultural and Religious History* (New Haven: Yale University Press, 1967), 72; Henry D. Thoreau, *Journal*, vol. 5, ed. Patrick F. O'Connell (Princeton: Princeton University Press, 1997), 469.

11. The historical literature on the intersections of entertainment, education, and natural philosophy is notably rich. See Barbara Maria Stafford, *Artful Science: Enlightenment Entertainment and the Eclipse of Visual Education* (Cambridge, Mass.: MIT Press, 1994); Barbara Maria Stafford, "Instructive Games: Apparatus and the Experimental Aesthetics of Imposture," in Walter Pape and Frederick Burwick, eds., *Reflecting Senses: Perception and Appearance in Literature, Culture, and the Arts* (Berlin: Walter de Gruyter, 1995), 223–249; Robert Darnton, *Mesmerism and the End of the Enlightenment in France* (Cambridge, Mass.: Harvard University Press, 1968), esp. 27–33; Grete de Francesco, *The Power of the Charlatan*, trans. Miriam Beard (New Haven: Yale University Press, 1939), 229–249; Richard D. Altick, *The Shows of London* (Cambridge, Mass.: Harvard University Press, 1978), 3–4, 64–76, 81; Simon Schaffer, "The Consuming Flame: Electrical Showmen and Tory Mystics in the World of Goods," in John Brewer and Roy Porter, eds., *Consumption and the World of Goods* (New York: Routledge, 1993), 489–526; James W. Cook, Jr., "From the Age of Reason to the Age of Barnum: The Great Automaton Chess-Player and the Emergence of Victorian Cultural Illusionism," *Winterthur Portfolio* 30 (Winter 1995): 231–257; Thomas L. Hankins and Robert J. Silverman, *Instruments and the Imagination* (Princeton: Princeton University Press, 1995).

12. William James, *The Varieties of Religious Experience* (New York: Penguin, 1982), 12; D. T. Suzuki, *Swedenborg: Buddha of the North,* trans. Andrew Bernstein (West Chester, Penn.: Swedenborg Foundation, 1996). Swedenborg's insecure place in a shifting canon was at its firmest in the middle decades of the nineteenth century. In R. A. Vaughan's influential compendium *Hours with the Mystics* (1856) he was favored with his own distinct section—a structuring device not accorded the likes of Bernard of Clairvaux and John of the Cross. See Robert Alfred Vaughan, *Hours with the Mystics: A Contribution to the History of Religious Opinion,* 2 vols. (London, 1856; London: Slark, 1888), 2: 319–335. Henry Corbin exemplifies the subsequent comparativist and phenomenological embrace of Swedenborg. See Henry Corbin, *Swedenborg and Esoteric Islam,* trans. Leonard Fox (West Chester, Penn.: Swedenborg Foundation, 1995).

13. The Vermont *philosophe* Ethan Allen is another good example of these exchanges. Raised in "the Mountanious wilds of America," Allen considered the opinions of "the independent literary Gentlemen of France" to be the measure of his deistic theology, bravely sending off his work to "the Academy of Arts and Sciences at Paris." See John J. Duffy, ed., *Ethan Allen and His Kin: Correspondence, 1772–1819,* 2 vols. (Hanover, N.H.: University Press of New England, 1998), 1: 190–191, 230–231. For Franklin's interest in speaking machines, see Hankins and Silverman, *Instruments and the Imagination,* 197.

14. For the state of the literature on the American side, see David D. Hall, *Cultures of Print: Essays in the History of the Book* (Amherst: University of Massachusetts Press, 1996).

15. See notably Kenneth Cmiel, *Democratic Eloquence: The Fight over Popular Speech in Nineteenth-Century America* (New York, 1990; Berkeley: University of California Press, 1991); Jane Kamensky, *Governing the Tongue: The Politics of Speech in Early New England* (New York: Oxford University Press, 1997); Harry S. Stout, *The New England Soul: Preaching and Religious Culture in Colonial New England* (New York: Oxford University Press, 1986); Emily Ann Thompson, "'Mysteries of the Acoustic': Architectural Acoustics in America, 1800–1932," Ph.D. diss., Princeton University, 1992.

16. The mystical connections for music have been especially prominent in the work of Joscelyn Godwin. See, for example, Joscelyn Godwin, ed., *Music, Mysticism and Magic* (London: Routledge and Kegan Paul, 1986); Joscelyn Godwin, *Harmonies of Heaven and Earth: The Spiritual Dimension of Music from Antiquity to the Avant-Garde* (London: Thames and Hudson, 1987). For comparative perspectives in the history of religions, see Lawrence E. Sullivan, ed., *Enchanting Powers: Music in the World's Religions* (Cambridge, Mass.: Harvard University Press, 1997).

17. Alain Corbin, *Village Bells: Sound and Meaning in the Nineteenth-Century French Countryside,* trans. Martin Thom (New York: Columbia University Press, 1998), xi. Appearing quite recently and of note alongside Corbin's work are the literary soundings of Bruce R. Smith, *The Acoustic World of Early Modern England: Attending to the O-Factor* (Chicago: University of Chicago Press, 1999).

18. Martin Luther, *Luther's Works,* vol. 29: *Lectures on Titus, Philemon, and Hebrews,* ed. Jaroslav Pelikan (Saint Louis: Concordia, 1968), 224.

19. Louise Vinge, *The Five Senses: Studies in a Literary Tradition* (Lund, Sweden: Gleerup, 1975), 128; William A. Graham, *Beyond the Written Word: Oral Aspects of Scripture in the History of Religion* (Cambridge: Cambridge University Press, 1987), esp. 141–144.

20. William C. Chittick, ed., *The Sufi Path of Knowledge: Ibn al-'Arabi's Metaphysics of Imagination* (Albany: State University of New York Press, 1989), 213. Another important point of dialogue would be the emphasis on hearing over vision in modern Jewish philosophy from Hermann Cohen to Emmanuel Levinas, an expanse of issues relating to ethics, aesthetics, and monotheism. For entry into that larger conversation, see Leora Batnitzky, *Idolatry and Representation: The Philosophy of Franz Rosenzweig Reconsidered* (Princeton: Princeton University Press, 2000).

1. Hearing Loss

1. Constance Classen, *Worlds of Sense: Exploring the Senses in History and across Cultures* (London: Routledge, 1993), 28.

2. Anthony Synnott, "Puzzling over the Senses from Plato to Marx," in David Howes, ed., *The Varieties of Sensory Experience: A Sourcebook in the Anthropology of the Senses* (Toronto: University of Toronto Press, 1991), 61–76 (quotations of Aris-

totle on pp. 63–64); Anthony Synnott, *The Body Social: Symbolism, Self and Society* (London: Routledge, 1993), 128–155; Louise Vinge, *The Five Senses: Studies in a Literary Tradition* (Lund, Sweden: Gleerup, 1975), 15–21; P. Christopher Smith, "From Acoustics to Optics: The Rise of the Metaphysical and the Demise of the Melodic in Aristotle's *Poetics*," in David Michael Levin, ed., *Sites of Vision: The Discursive Construction of Sight in the History of Philosophy* (Cambridge, Mass.: MIT Press, 1997), 68–91. In the Aristotelian corpus, the critical works for the ordering of the senses are *On the Soul* and *Sense and Sensibilia*. See Jonathan Barnes, ed., *The Complete Works of Aristotle*, 2 vols. (Princeton: Princeton University Press, 1984). For Christian interactions with these classical discourses, see David Chidester, *Word and Light: Seeing, Hearing, and Religious Discourse* (Urbana: University of Illinois Press, 1992). Chidester points to a prevailing Christian preference for the eye over the ear, from Augustine to Bonaventure, though noting some auditory dissenters, including Meister Eckhart and then, predictably, Protestants such as Luther and Melancthon. For other advocates of the minority position of elevating the ear over the eye, see Thomas Frangenberg, "*Auditus visu prestantior:* Comparisons of Hearing and Vision in Charles de Bovelles's *Liber de sensibus*," in Charles Burnett, Michael Fend, and Penelope Gouk, eds., *The Second Sense: Studies in Hearing and Musical Judgement from Antiquity to the Seventeenth Century* (London: Warburg Institute, 1991), 71–89; Vinge, *Five Senses*, 36–37, 58–59.

3. Jacques Ellul, *The Humiliation of the Word,* trans. Joyce Main Hanks (Grand Rapids, Mich.: Eerdmans, 1985), 2; Martin Jay, *Downcast Eyes: The Denigration of Vision in Twentieth-Century French Thought* (Berkeley: University of California Press, 1993), 45, 64, 69, 85; John Locke, *An Essay Concerning Human Understanding*, ed. Peter H. Nidditch (Oxford: Clarendon, 1975), 146. Jay's care in qualifying these conclusions should be emphasized—as, for example, in his recognition of "the complexity of the modern scopic regime, both in theoretical and practical terms, even at its moment of apparent triumph in the Enlightenment"; but such qualifications are finally peripheral to his larger argument about ocularcentrism (p. 105). For additional samplings of this extensive literature on modern visuality, see David Michael Levin, ed., *Modernity and the Hegemony of Vision* (Berkeley: University of California Press, 1993); Jonathan Crary, *Techniques of the Observer: On Vision and Modernity in the Nineteenth Century* (Cambridge, Mass.: MIT Press, 1990); Levin, ed., *Sites of Vision;* Teresa Brennan and Martin Jay, eds., *Vision in Context: Historical and Contemporary Perspectives on Sight* (London: Routledge, 1996). For a strong, if rare, "auditory" challenge to these visualist constructions, see Steven Connor, "The Modern Auditory I," in Roy Porter, ed., *Rewriting the Self: Histories from the Renaissance to the Present* (London: Routledge, 1997), 203–223.

4. Lucien Febvre, *The Problem of Unbelief in the Sixteenth Century: The Religion of Rabelais*, trans. Beatrice Gottlieb (Cambridge, Mass.: Harvard University Press, 1982), 423–442; Robert Mandrou, *Introduction to Modern France, 1500–1640: An Essay in Historical Psychology*, trans. R. E. Hallmark (New York: Holmes and Meier, 1976), 49–50. On the philosophical uses and contexts for the French history of the senses, see Jay, *Downcast Eyes*, 34–36.

5. Alain Corbin, *Time, Desire and Horror: Towards a History of the Senses,* trans. Jean Birrell (Cambridge: Polity Press, 1995), 181–192; Alain Corbin, *Village Bells: Sound and Meaning in the Nineteenth-Century French Countryside,* trans. Martin Thom (New York: Columbia University Press, 1998), esp. 298–308; Alain Corbin, *The Foul and the Fragrant: Odor and the French Social Imagination,* trans. Miriam L. Kochan (Cambridge, Mass.: Harvard University Press, 1986). For a work that helpfully broadens interpretation of the sense of smell both temporally and culturally, see Constance Classen, David Howes, and Anthony Synnott, *Aroma: The Cultural History of Smell* (London: Routledge, 1994).

6. Eliot quoted in Glenn Willmott, *McLuhan, or Modernism in Reverse* (Toronto: University of Toronto Press, 1996), 225; Walter J. Ong, *Faith and Contexts,* ed. Thomas J. Farrell and Paul A. Soukup, 3 vols. (Atlanta: Scholars Press, 1992–1995), 1: 218; 2: 162; 3: 73. For analysis of the impact that the modern print culture had on the aurality of sacred texts, see William A. Graham, *Beyond the Written Word: Oral Aspects of Scripture in the History of Religion* (Cambridge: Cambridge University Press, 1987), esp. 19–44.

7. Walter J. Ong, *The Presence of the Word: Some Prolegomena for Cultural and Religious History* (New Haven: Yale University Press, 1967), 9, 14, 64–73, 174. Ong laid the foundation for this larger history through his study of sixteenth-century Ramist logic in which diagrammatic, spatialized, printed knowledge displaces dialogic ways of knowing. That Ramist reorientation of the intellectual world ends in "the elimination of sound and voice from man's understanding of the intellectual world" and in "the silences of a spatialized universe." See Walter J. Ong, *Ramus, Method, and the Decay of Dialogue* (Cambridge, Mass.: Harvard University Press, 1958), 318. See also Walter J. Ong, *Interfaces of the Word: Studies in the Evolution of Consciousness and Culture* (Ithaca: Cornell University Press, 1977); Walter J. Ong, *Orality and Literacy: The Technologizing of the Word* (London: Routledge, 1982). Penelope Gouk has also recently underlined the shortcomings of Ong's linear model of visualist ascendancy. See Penelope Gouk, *Music, Science and Natural Magic in Seventeenth-Century England* (New Haven: Yale University Press, 1999), 18.

8. Marshall McLuhan, "Inside the Five Sense Sensorium," *Canadian Architect* 6 (June 1961): 54; Marshall McLuhan, *The Gutenberg Galaxy: The Making of Typographic Man* (Toronto, 1962; New York: Signet, 1969), 39. The historian who has done the most to give grounding and nuance to these mythic assessments of the print revolution is Elizabeth Eisenstein. For a summary volume of her research, see Elizabeth L. Eisenstein, *The Printing Revolution in Early Modern Europe* (Cambridge: Cambridge University Press, 1983).

9. McLuhan, *Gutenberg Galaxy,* 27–39, 45–48; Marshall McLuhan, *Understanding Media: The Extensions of Man* (New York: McGraw-Hill, 1964; rpt. 1965), 15–16; McLuhan, "Inside the Five Sense Sensorium," 49–54. McLuhan was heavily influenced in these oppositional constructions of ear and eye cultures by J. C. Carothers, "Culture, Psychiatry, and the Written Word," *Psychiatry* 22 (November 1959): 307–320.

10. McLuhan, *Gutenberg Galaxy,* 27–39, 45–48, 59, 87; McLuhan, *Understanding Media,* 16; McLuhan, "Inside the Five Sense Sensorium," 49–54.

11. McLuhan, *Understanding Media*, 15, 298; McLuhan, *Gutenberg Galaxy*, 68; Edmund Carpenter, *Eskimo Realities* (New York: Holt, Rinehart, and Winston, 1973), 33–34. For a recent example of how these sensory distinctions continue to structure cultural differentiation, see Constance Classen, *Inca Cosmology and the Human Body* (Salt Lake City: University of Utah Press, 1993), 5–7. On the use of primitivism in McLuhan's thought and his visual-acoustic dichotomies, see S. D. Neill, *Clarifying McLuhan: An Assessment of Process and Product* (Westport, Conn.: Greenwood, 1993), 67–71; Willmott, *McLuhan*, 119–134.

12. Also valuable is the work of Constance Classen, though, unlike Corbin, she reiterates as much as complicates the ocularcentric narrative about the Enlightenment and modernity: "Modern Western culture is a culture of the eye." See Constance Classen, *The Color of Angels: Cosmology, Gender and the Aesthetic Imagination* (London: Routledge, 1998), 1.

13. Francis Bacon, *The Works of Francis Bacon*, ed. James Spedding, Robert Leslie Ellis, and Douglas Denon Heath, 14 vols. (London, 1857–1874; Stuttgart: Frommann, 1963), 3: 162–164.

14. Bacon, *Works*, 2: 389, 408, 430, 434.

15. Robert Boyle, *Works*, ed. Thomas Birch, 6 vols. (Hildesheim, Germany: Olms, 1966), 6: 199; Narcissus Marsh, "An Introductory Essay to the Doctrine of Sounds, containing some Proposals for the Improvement of Acousticks," *Philosophical Transactions* 14 (1684): 472–473, 481–483, 486.

16. *Edinburgh Encyclopaedia*, 18 vols. (Philadelphia: Parker, 1832), 1: 106. I delineate the secondary literature on acoustics in chapter 3 at n. 36.

17. *Encyclopaedia Americana*, 13 vols. (Philadelphia: Carey and Lea, 1829–1833), 1: 35. On the Hooke experiments as a precedent for Chladni's, see Penelope Gouk, "The Role of Acoustics and Music Theory in the Scientific Work of Robert Hooke," *Annals of Science* 37 (September 1980): 581–582. On anatomy, see, for example, Barbara Maria Stafford, *Body Criticism: Imaging the Unseen in Enlightenment Art and Medicine* (Cambridge, Mass.: MIT Press, 1991); David Hillman and Carla Mazzio, eds., *The Body in Parts: Fantasies of Corporeality in Early Modern Europe* (New York: Routledge, 1997); and the last section of Chapter 4, below. For the pictorialization of sound, see R. Murray Schafer, *The Tuning of the World* (New York: Knopf, 1977), 127–128; Thomas L. Hankins and Robert J. Silverman, *Instruments and the Imagination* (Princeton: Princeton University Press, 1995), 130–133.

18. Galileo Galilei, *Mathematical Discourse Concerning Two New Sciences*, excerpted in R. Bruce Lindsay, ed., *Acoustics: Historical and Philosophical Development* (Stroudsbourg, Penn.: Dowden, Hutchinson, and Ross, 1973), 59.

19. Newton cited in Sigalia Dostrovsky, "The Origins of Vibration Theory: The Scientific Revolution and the Nature of Music," Ph.D. diss., Princeton University, 1969, 236–237; David Hartley, *Observations on Man, His Frame, His Duty, and His Expectations*, 6th ed. (London: Thomas Tegg and Son, 1834), 121–124; John Elliot, *Philosophical Observations on the Senses of Vision and Hearing* (London: Murray, 1780), 11–15, 42; Eric Carlson, Jeffrey L. Wollock, and Patricia S. Noel, eds., *Benjamin Rush's Lectures on the Mind* (Philadelphia: American Philosophical Society, 1981), 574. Hartley and Elliot pursue music-color, sound-sight correspondences from their

reading of Newton, whose Pythagorean and acoustic sources are outlined in Penelope Gouk, "The Harmonic Roots of Newtonian Science," in John Fauvel, Raymond Flood, Michael Shortland, and Robin Williams, eds., *Let Newton Be!* (Oxford: Oxford University Press, 1988), 102–125; Gouk, *Music, Science and Natural Magic*, 224–257. For the color-tone debates, see Hankins and Silverman, *Instruments and the Imagination*, 74–77. Within its visualist focus, Barbara Stafford's *Body Criticism* contains various reminders of the sensorial complexity of the Enlightenment. See, for example, her reflections on smell on pp. 428–430.

20. Adam Phillips, "Introduction," in Edmund Burke, *A Philosophical Enquiry into the Origin of Our Ideas of the Sublime and the Beautiful* (Oxford: Oxford University Press, 1990), xi; Etienne Bonnot de Condillac, *Condillac's Treatise on the Sensations,* trans. Geraldine Carr (London: Favil, 1930); Elisabeth de Fontenay, *Diderot: Reason and Resonance,* trans. Jeffrey Mehlman (New York: Braziller, 1982), 157, 166; Hartley, *Observations on Man,* 147. Hartley's upending of the eye came in the context of a discussion of music and the passions it stimulated; Hartley emphasized "religious contemplations" as one of music's primary associations (p. 267).

21. Carlson, Wollock, and Noel, eds., *Benjamin Rush's Lectures,* 33–35, 256, 339, 346, 350–352, 357, 361, 587.

22. Ibid., 336. See the discussion of Bentham's acoustics in Chapter 3, below. For Foucault's elision of eavesdropping in his emphasis on the interiorized gaze of surveillance, see Jay, *Downcast Eyes,* 411n; Michel Foucault, *Power/Knowledge: Selected Interviews and Other Writings, 1972–1977,* ed. Colin Gordon (New York: Pantheon, 1980), 154–155. For critical analysis of such auditory forms of surveillance from one of Foucault's poststructuralist compatriots, see Jacques Attali, *Noise: The Political Economy of Music,* trans. Brian Massumi (Minneapolis: University of Minnesota Press, 1985), esp. 5–8.

23. Thomas Paine, *The Complete Writings of Thomas Paine,* ed. Philip S. Foner, 2 vols. (New York: Citadel, 1945), 1: 466, 505; 2: 786–787, 793.

24. Andrew Pollack, "Sound Bites and Then Some," *New York Times,* 21 April 1997, D1, D8.

25. Michel de Certeau, *The Practice of Everyday Life,* trans. Steven Rendall (Berkeley: University of California Press, 1984), 137.

26. John Hollander, *The Untuning of the Sky: Ideas of Music in English Poetry, 1500–1700* (Princeton: Princeton University Press, 1961), 19; Schafer, *Tuning of the World,* 258–262; Ellul, *Humiliation,* 195–196; Corbin, *Village Bells,* 306–307. "Soundscape" is a term that Schafer develops, and my usage is picked up from him, though others have also adopted the term. It anticipates Corbin's "auditory landscape." For a more recent extension of Schafer's soundscape experiments, which shares in his sense of diminished sacrality, see J. Douglas Porteous, *Landscapes of the Mind: Worlds of Sense and Metaphor* (Toronto: University of Toronto Press, 1990), esp. 50–51. For a widely read account of the lost oracular voice, built from a perspective of evolutionary neuropsychology, see Julian Jaynes, *The Origin of Consciousness in the Breakdown of the Bicameral Mind* (Boston: Houghton Mifflin, 1976).

27. Nicholas Wolterstorff, *Divine Discourse: Philosophical Reflections on the Claim that God Speaks* (Cambridge: Cambridge University Press, 1995), 49, 273.

28. Ibid., 273–274.

29. Ong, *Orality and Literacy,* 72, 75. For a counterpart to Ong's consecration of the spoken word, one that helpfully places the impulse within larger counter-Enlightenment currents, see Harold Stahmer, *"Speak That I May See Thee!": The Religious Significance of Language* (New York: Macmillan, 1968).

30. Edward Herbert, *The Autobiography of Edward, Lord Herbert of Cherbury,* ed. Sidney Lee (London: Routledge and Sons, 1886), 133–134; Bernard Whitman, *A Lecture on Popular Superstitions* (Boston: Bowles and Dearborn, 1829), 29–30. Note also the resonant voice in "Echo in a Church," in Edward Herbert, *The Poems English and Latin of Edward Lord Herbert of Cherbury,* ed. G. C. Moore Smith (Oxford: Clarendon Press, 1923), 47–48. For his view on oracles, see Edward Herbert, *Pagan Religion: A Translation of De religione gentilium,* ed. John Anthony Butler (Ottawa: Dovehouse, 1996), 285–301, 337–338.

31. Margaret Gordon, *The Home Life of Sir David Brewster* (Edinburgh: Edmonston and Douglas, 1869), 17–18, 293–295, 312–314; David Brewster, *Letters on Natural Magic* (London, 1832; London: Murray, 1842), 351. For his religious context, see Paul Baxter, "Brewster, Evangelism and the Disruption of the Church of Scotland," in A. D. Morrison-Low and J. R. R. Christie, eds., *'Martyr of Science': Sir David Brewster 1781–1868* (Edinburgh: Royal Scottish Museum Studies, 1984), 45–50; Richard Westfall, "Introduction," in David Brewster, *Memoirs of the Life, Writings, and Discoveries of Sir Isaac Newton* (New York: Johnson Reprint, 1965), xix–xxi. Gordon's memoir is the best source on Brewster's private life and beliefs, most of his papers having been destroyed in a fire.

32. Peter Harrison, *'Religion' and the Religions in the English Enlightenment* (Cambridge: Cambridge University Press, 1990), 16, 73–77; Thomas Hobbes, *Leviathan,* ed. Richard Tuck (Cambridge: Cambridge University Press, 1991), 70.

33. Chidester, *Word and Light,* xiv. It should be noted that Chidester had particularly compelling reasons for this shift of perspective, having moved from the University of California at Santa Barbara to the University of Cape Town. Still, his reorientation is indicative of a much larger redirection in religious studies and the humanities generally toward widely shared poststucturalist questions about the power/knowledge complex. Though this critical perspective is still sometimes presented as an insurgency against phenomenological essentialists and protectionists within religious studies, it verges, by now, on an orthodoxy. See, for example, Russell T. McCutcheon, *Manufacturing Religion: The Discourse on Sui Generis Religion and the Politics of Nostalgia* (New York: Oxford University Press, 1997).

34. James Elkins, *The Object Stares Back: On the Nature of Seeing* (New York, 1996; San Diego: Harcourt Brace, 1997), 11–12, 44–45, 72. For a crucial work for this reappraisal of the animism of images in the West, see David Freedberg, *The Power of Images: Studies in the History and Theory of Response* (Chicago: University of Chicago Press, 1989). For incisive analysis of the "interactivity" of popular religious images in American culture, see David Morgan, *Visual Piety: A History and Theory of Popular Religious Images* (Berkeley: University of California Press, 1998), 50–58. For three works in phenomenology that address specifically the intersubjectivities of listening and speaking, see (hear) Don Ihde, *Listening and Voice: A Phenomenology of*

Sound (Athens, Ohio: Ohio University Press, 1976); David Michael Levin, *The Listening Self: Personal Growth, Social Change, and the Closure of Metaphysics* (London: Routledge, 1989); Bruce R. Smith, *The Acoustic World of Early Modern England: Attending to the O-Factor* (Chicago: University of Chicago Press, 1999), esp. 6–29.

35. Consider, for example, the gendered images of seeing and hearing in Philo of Alexandria—images in which sight is active and hence male, hearing passive and hence female. See Chidester, *Word and Light*, 32–33; Vinge, *Five Senses*, 24–25. Also see the example from Meister Eckart in Margaret Miles, *Image as Insight: Visual Understanding in Western Christianity and Secular Culture* (Boston: Beacon Press, 1985), 100–101.

36. Hans Jonas, *The Phenomenon of Life: Toward a Philosophical Biology* (New York: Harper and Row, 1966), 139; John Dewey, *The Public and Its Problems* (New York: Henry Holt, 1927), 218–219.

37. Maurice Merleau-Ponty, *The Visible and the Invisible,* trans. Alphonso Lingis (Evanston, Ill.: Northwestern University Press, 1968), 144–145, 264–265; Freedberg, *Power of Images,* 28. See also Levin, *Listening Self,* 166–182, 223–235; Jay, *Downcast Eyes,* 101–103, 298–328.

38. Levin, *Listening Self,* 272.

39. Augustine, *Confessions,* trans. R. S. Pine-Coffin (New York: Viking Penguin, 1978), 211–212. On the spiritual sense of hearing, see Elizabeth Sears, "The Iconography of Auditory Perception in the Early Middle Ages: On Psalm Illustration and Psalm Exegesis," in Burnett, Fend, and Gouk, eds., *Second Sense,* 19–42 (Augustine's idea of the interior ear is cited on p. 28).

40. Herman Melville, *Pierre; Or, The Ambiguities* (New York: Library of America, 1984), 240, 244–245; Robert Frost, *Collected Poems, Prose, and Plays* (New York: Library of America, 1995), 307.

2. Sound Christians

1. For rich descriptions of the travails of itinerancy, see Nathan Hatch, *The Democratization of American Christianity* (New Haven: Yale University Press, 1989); Christine Leigh Heyrman, *Southern Cross: The Beginnings of the Bible Belt* (New York: Knopf, 1997); Russell Richey, *Early American Methodism* (Bloomington: Indiana University Press, 1991); Donald E. Byrne, Jr., *No Foot of Land: Folklore of American Methodist Itinerants* (Metuchen, N.J.: Scarecrow, 1975); John H. Wigger, *Taking Heaven by Storm: Methodism and the Rise of Popular Christianity in America* (New York: Oxford University Press, 1998). For a fine overview of the Methodist movement in international perspective, see David Hempton, *The Religion of the People: Methodism and Popular Religion, c. 1750–1900* (London: Routledge, 1996).

2. E. F. Newell, *Life and Observations of Rev. E. F. Newell* (Worcester, Mass.: Ainsworth, 1847), 87.

3. Jarena Lee, *The Life and Religious Experience of Jarena Lee, a Coloured Lady* (1836) in William L. Andrews, ed., *Sisters of the Spirit: Three Black Women's Autobiographies of the Nineteenth Century* (Bloomington: Indiana University Press, 1986), 35–36, 44.

4. John Fletcher, "On Evangelical Mysticism," in *The Works of the Reverend John Fletcher, Late Vicar of Madeley*, 4 vols. (New York: Lane and Scott, 1851), 4: 7–13.

5. Fletcher, "Six Letters on the Spiritual Manifestation of the Son of God," in *Works*, 4: 277.

6. Timothy Walker, *The Way to Try All Pretended Apostles* (Boston: Green, 1743), 6, 8–9, 21. On debates over itinerancy, see especially Timothy D. Hall, *Contested Boundaries: Itinerancy and the Reshaping of the Colonial American Religious World* (Durham, N.C.: Duke University Press, 1994). Hall discusses the opposition to these inward calls on pp. 47, 63. There are several fine studies of the ministry in early America, especially in New England. Most deal with the issue of calling and ministerial calls at least in passing, though rarely at length. See Donald M. Scott, *From Office to Profession: The New England Ministry, 1750–1850* (Philadelphia: University of Pennsylvania Press, 1978), 6–8, 84–85; David D. Hall, *The Faithful Shepherd: A History of the New England Ministry in the Seventeenth Century* (Chapel Hill: University of North Carolina Press, 1972), 10–12, 19–20, 31–32; J. William T. Youngs, Jr., *God's Messengers: Religious Leadership in Colonial New England, 1700–1750* (Baltimore: Johns Hopkins University Press, 1976), 11–39; Harry S. Stout, *The New England Soul: Preaching and Religious Culture in Colonial New England* (New York: Oxford University Press, 1986), 162–164, 207–211; Sidney E. Mead, "The Rise of the Evangelical Conception of the Ministry in America, 1607–1850," in H. Richard Niebuhr and Daniel D. Williams, *The Ministry in Historical Perspectives* (New York, 1956; San Francisco: Harper and Row, 1983), 231–233. The fullest analysis of call stories, especially of the visionary force of them among evangelical women preachers, is in Catherine A. Brekus, *Strangers and Pilgrims: Female Preaching in America, 1740–1845* (Chapel Hill: University of North Carolina Press, 1998), 162–193. See also Earl Kent Brown, *Women of Mr. Wesley's Methodism* (New York: Edwin Mellen, 1983), 16–19; Paul Wesley Chilcote, *John Wesley and the Women Preachers of Early Methodism* (Metuchen, N.J.: Scarecrow, 1991), 77–83, 141–145.

7. William Perkins quoted in Paul Marshall, *A Kind of Life Imposed on Man: Vocation and Social Order from Tyndale to Locke* (Toronto: University of Toronto Press, 1996), 41. Marshall's is an excellent overview of this Protestant teaching, and I have relied on his careful account of the social and economic dimensions of this doctrine. Especially noteworthy are the intricate accommodations of calling to social mobility and voluntarism on the part of some Puritans, but, as Marshall makes clear, the grounding of this Reformed doctrine remained conservative (even into the most influential twentieth-century formulations).

8. Charles Chauncy, *Enthusiasm Described and Caution'd Against* (Boston: Draper, 1742), 12.

9. John Wesley, *The Works of John Wesley: Sermons IV, 115–151*, ed. Albert C. Outler (Nashville: Abingdon, 1987), 82.

10. John Calvin, *Institutes of the Christian Religion*, trans. John Allen, 2 vols. (Philadelphia: Presbyterian Board of Publication, 1844), 2: 267–268.

11. Quoted in James L. Ainslie, *The Doctrine of Ministerial Order in the Reformed Churches of the Sixteenth and Seventeenth Centuries* (Edinburgh: T. and T. Clark, 1940), 141.

12. Calvin, *Institutes*, 2: 267; Ainslie, *Doctrine*, 142–143.

13. Hall, *Faithful Shepherd*, 19, 31, 270. See also Youngs, *God's Messengers*, 11, 24, 38–39.

14. George Fox, *The Journal of George Fox*, ed. John L. Nickalls (Cambridge: Cambridge University Press, 1952), 7, 11, 19.

15. John Woolman, *The Journal and Major Essays of John Woolman*, ed. Phillips P. Moulton (New York: Oxford University Press, 1971), 40, 58, 151, 185–186, 314.

16. Thomas Brown, *The Works of Mr. Thomas Brown, Serious and Comical, in Prose and Verse*, 7th ed., 4 vols. (London: Edward Midwinter, 1730), 1: 107–108.

17. See John Bunyan, *Grace Abounding to the Chief of Sinners*, ed. Roger Sharrock (Oxford: Clarendon, 1962), 82–95. For seventeenth-century Baptist views of divine calling to the ministry, see W. Clark Gilpin, *The Millenarian Piety of Roger Williams* (Chicago: University of Chicago Press, 1979), 89–95, 141–146.

18. Calvin, *Institutes*, 2: 263. See also Hall, *Faithful Shepherd*, 11–12.

19. Wesley, *Works of John Wesley: Sermons IV*, 115–151, 75–84.

20. Adam Clarke, *A Letter to a Preacher* (1800) in Adam Clarke and Thomas Coke, *The Preacher's Manual* (Nashville: Stevenson, 1857), 98–102; John Wesley to Mary Bosanquet, 13 June 1771, in John Telford, ed., *The Letters of the Rev. John Wesley, A. M.* (London: Epworth, 1931), 5: 257.

21. An unidentified churchman of "high standing" quoted in Andrew Manship, *Thirteen Years' Experience in the Itinerancy* (Philadelphia: Higgins and Perkinpine, 1856), 361. Wesley's model ministerial biographies are more circumspect in their descriptions of the call than many of their American counterparts. See John Wesley, ed., *The Experience of Several Eminent Methodist Preachers* (Chambersburg, Penn.: Yeats and Johns, 1812).

22. On the gendered dimensions of the call stories and the discouragements women faced, see Brekus, *Strangers and Pilgrims*, 162–193. For an example of official discouragement (at least initially), see George White, *A Brief Account of the Life, Experience, Travels, and Gospel Labours of George White, an African* (1810) in Graham Russell Hodges, ed., *Black Itinerants of the Gospel: The Narratives of John Jea and George White* (Madison: Madison House, 1993), 59, 65–66.

23. William Swayze, *Narrative of William Swayze, Minister of the Gospel* (Cincinnati: Methodist Book Room, 1839), 58.

24. Billy Hibbard, *Memoirs of the Life and Travels of B. Hibbard, Minister of the Gospel* (New York: Totten, 1825), 42.

25. Lorenzo Dow, *History of Cosmopolite* (Wheeling, Va.: Martin, 1848), 19–21, 27–29.

26. Joshua Marsden, *Grace Displayed: An Interesting Narrative of the Life, Conversion, Christian Experience, Ministry, and Missionary Labours of Joshua Marsden* (New York: Paul and Thomas, 1813), 101–105, 108. The larger tensions over the necessity of formal theological training only grew in Methodist circles. For one call narrative especially marked by this conflict, see B. M. Drake, *A Sketch of the Life of Rev. Elijah Steele* (Cincinnati: Methodist Book Concern, 1843), 15–30.

27. "John Smith" to John Wesley, 21 August 1747, *The Works of John Wesley: Letters II, 1740–1755*, ed. Frank Baker (Oxford: Clarendon, 1982), 259.

28. Mary Fletcher, *The Life of Mrs. Mary Fletcher, Consort and Relict of the Rev. John Fletcher, Vicar of Madeley*, ed. Henry Moore (New York: Mason and Lane, 1837), 44.

29. Jesse J. Goben, *The Writings of Jesse J. Goben* (Middletown, N.Y.: Beebe's Sons, n.d.), 38–40.

30. Michael J. Crawford, ed., "The Spiritual Travels of Nathan Cole," *William and Mary Quarterly* 33 (January 1976): 96; Jonathan Edwards, *Letters and Personal Writings*, ed. George S. Claghorn (New Haven: Yale University Press, 1998), 797. The oracle trope for the scriptures was a commonplace, used equally by Anglicans, Puritans, and evangelicals (whether Thomas Shepard, Richard Allestree, Cotton Mather, John Wesley, or John Fletcher).

31. John McLean, comp., *Sketch of Rev. Philip Gatch* (Cincinnati: Swormstedt, 1854), 18.

32. Fanny Newell, *Diary of Fanny Newell* (Boston: Peirce, 1848), 124. For a wider range of examples of this reiterative auditory spirituality, see Katherine M. Faull, ed., *Moravian Women's Memoirs: Their Related Lives, 1750–1820* (Syracuse: Syracuse University Press, 1997), 13, 20, 40, 102; Diane Sasson, *The Shaker Spiritual Narrative* (Knoxville: University of Tennessee Press, 1983), 52–55.

33. Clarke and Coke, *Preacher's Manual*, 142–143. For the Wesley example, see David Lyle Jeffrey, ed., *A Burning and Shining Light: English Spirituality in the Age of Wesley* (Grand Rapids, Mich.: Eerdmans, 1987), 242. On the longer history of bibliomancy, see Keith Thomas, *Religion and the Decline of Magic* (New York: Viking Penguin, 1971), 51, 139–140.

34. Woolman, *Journal*, 27.

35. Hibbard, *Memoirs*, 119–122.

36. Jacob Young, *Autobiography of a Pioneer; Or, The Nativity, Experience, Travels, and Ministerial Labors of Rev. Jacob Young* (Cincinnati: Cranston and Curts, 1857), 52–53.

37. James B. Finley, *Autobiography of Rev. James B. Finley; Or, Pioneer Life in the West*, ed. W. P. Strickland (Cincinnati: Methodist Book Concern, 1855), 177.

38. Elizabeth Sears, "The Iconography of Auditory Perception in the Early Middle Ages: On Psalm Illustration and Psalm Exegesis," in Charles Burnett, Michael Fend, and Penelope Gouk, eds., *The Second Sense: Studies in Hearing and Musical Judgement from Antiquity to the Seventeenth Century* (London: Warburg Institute, 1991), 26.

39. Richard Brathwaite, *Essaies upon the Five Senses* (London: Whittaker, 1620), 57, 116. For discussion of this tradition of a moral spirituality of the senses, see Louise Vinge, *The Five Senses: Studies in a Literary Tradition* (Lund, Sweden: Gleerup, 1975), 84–85, 95, 122–124. For extreme unction as an example of the "obsessive distrust of the senses" in the Western tradition, see Elisabeth de Fontenay, *Diderot: Reason and Resonance*, trans. Jeffrey Mehlman (New York: Braziller, 1982), 160.

40. John Bunyan, *The Pilgrim's Progress* (Oxford: Oxford University Press, 1984), 10, 22, 74; Brathwaite, *Essaies*, 9–10.

41. For perceptive analyses of this theme in early modern discourse, see Carla Mazzio, "Sins of the Tongue," in David Hillman and Carla Mazzio, eds., *The Body*

in *Parts: Fantasies of Corporeality in Early Modern Europe* (New York: Routledge, 1997), 52–79; Jane Kamensky, *Governing the Tongue: The Politics of Speech in Early New England* (New York: Oxford University Press, 1997), 17–42.

42. Clarke, *Letter,* in Clarke and Coke, *Preacher's Manual,* 103.

43. Boston King, *Memoirs of the Life of Boston King, a Black Preacher* (1798), in Vincent Carretta, ed., *Unchained Voices: An Anthology of Black Authors in the English-Speaking World of the Eighteenth Century* (Lexington: University Press of Kentucky, 1996), 352.

44. Newell, *Life,* 66. See also William Law, *A Serious Call to a Devout and Holy Life* (London, 1728; London: Dent, 1906), 74, 147–148.

45. Dow, *History of Cosmopolite,* 19; *The Groans of the Spirit* (1652) quoted in Helen C. White, *English Devotional Literature (Prose), 1600–1640* (Madison, 1931; New York: Haskell, 1966), 152.

46. George Whitefield, *George Whitefield's Journals, 1737–1741,* ed. William V. Davis (Gainesville, Fla.: Scholars' Facsimiles and Reprints, 1969), 31, 36; Woolman, *Journal,* 5, 75–76; Jeanne Marie Guyon, *The Life and Religious Experience of the Celebrated Lady Guion* (New York: Hoyt and Bolmore, 1820), 47; John Wesley, *A Plain Account of Christian Perfection,* in *The Works of John Wesley,* 14 vols. (London, 1872; Grand Rapids, Mich.: Baker, 1986), 11: 366–367; Wesley, *List of Works Revised and Abridged from Various Authors,* in *Works,* 14: 204, 208–209. For discussions of the influence of Thomas à Kempis on Wesley and on the larger traditions of Wesleyan spirituality, see Frank Baker, "John Wesley and the 'Imitatio Christi,'" *London Quarterly and Holborn Review* 166 (January 1941): 74–87; Robert G. Tuttle, Jr., *Mysticism in the Wesleyan Tradition* (Grand Rapids, Mich.: Francis Asbury, 1989), 58–63, 138–139.

47. On the failure of the New England Puritans to issue the book (despite considerable continuities between their own devotional manuals and their Catholic parallels), see Charles Hambrick-Stowe, *The Practice of Piety: Puritan Devotional Disciplines in Seventeenth-Century New England* (Chapel Hill: University of North Carolina Press, 1982), 28, 267.

48. James Penn Pilkington, *The Methodist Publishing House,* 2 vols. (Nashville: Abingdon, 1968), 1: 87–89, 92, 102; Hibbard, *Memoirs,* 81; W. P. Strickland, *The Life of Jacob Gruber* (New York: Carlton and Porter, 1860), 29.

49. Protestant devotionalism has received growing attention. See Hambrick-Stowe, *Practice of Piety;* Frank C. Senn, ed., *Protestant Spiritual Traditions* (New York: Paulist, 1986); Bradley C. Hanson, ed., *Modern Christian Spirituality: Methodological and Historical Essays* (Atlanta: Scholars Press, 1990); Louis Dupré and Don E. Saliers, eds., *Christian Spirituality: Post-Reformation and Modern* (New York: Crossroad, 1989); Gordon S. Wakefield, *Methodist Devotion: The Spiritual Life in the Methodist Tradition, 1791–1945* (London: Epworth, 1966); Tuttle, *Mysticism;* Jeffrey, ed., *Burning and a Shining Light;* Leigh Eric Schmidt, *Holy Fairs: Scottish Communions and American Revivals in the Early Modern Period* (Princeton: Princeton University Press, 1989), 115–168.

50. Wesley, *A Farther Appeal to Men of Reason and Religion,* in *Works,* 8: 190.

51. Wesley, *List of Works,* in *Works,* 14: 207.

52. Thomas à Kempis, *An Extract of the Christian's Pattern; Or, A Treatise of the Imitation of Christ*, ed. John Wesley (Philadelphia: Dickins, 1794), 9, 42, 48, 187.

53. Ibid., 19; John Wesley to Philothea Briggs, 16 October 1771, in Telford, ed., *Letters*, 5: 282–283.

54. Kempis, *Christian's Pattern*, 83, 109–110.

55. Ibid., 110–111, 182. On the speaking-hearing dialectic in early modern mystical texts, see Michel de Certeau, *Heterologies: Discourse on the Other*, trans. Brian Massumi (Minneapolis: University of Minnesota Press, 1986), 88–91.

56. Fletcher, *Works*, 4: 7–13, 21, 275–277, 284–285, 288. For the larger history of this mystical language, see Bernard McGinn, *The Presence of God: A History of Western Christian Mysticism* (New York: Crossroad, 1991–), 1: 121–124, 239–240; 2: 185–190, 254–255; 3: 77–78, 155–156; Karl Rahner, "Le Début d'une doctrine des cinq sens spirituels chez Origène," *Revue d'ascétique et de mystique* 13 (April 1932): 113–145; Rosemary Drage Hale, "'Taste and See, for God is Sweet': Sensory Perception and Memory in Medieval Christian Experience," in Anne Clark Bartlett, ed., *Vox Mystica: Essays on Medieval Mysticism* (Cambridge: D. S. Brewer, 1995), 3–14; Constance Classen, *The Color of Angels: Cosmology, Gender and the Aesthetic Imagination* (London: Routledge, 1998), esp. 13–20. Fletcher's *Six Letters* was published in his *Posthumous Pieces*, a work that went through five American editions between 1793 and 1824. These letters were also available in the various editions of his complete works. His writings were well known and commonly cited. See Hibbard, *Memoirs*, 81, 128; Young, *Autobiography of a Pioneer*, 51.

57. Fletcher, *Works*, 4: 11, 275–277, 280, 284; Jean McMahon Humez, ed., *Gifts of Power: The Writings of Rebecca Jackson, Black Visionary, Shaker Eldress* (Amherst: University of Massachusetts Press, 1981), 202–203, 243–249.

58. Lee, *Life*, 35, 48; King, *Memoirs*, 358; Hibbard, *Memoirs*, 39.

59. Guyon, *Life*, 526–527; Nicholas Constas, "The *Conceptio per Aurem* in Late Antiquity: Observations on Eve, the Serpent, and Mary's Ear," unpublished manuscript; Thomas Boslooper, *The Virgin Birth* (Philadelphia: Westminster, 1962), 59.

60. Fletcher, *Works*, 4: 276, 283; James P. Horton, *A Narrative of the Early Life, Remarkable Conversion, and Spiritual Labours of James P. Horton* (n.p.: n.p., 1846), 23; Guyon, *Life*, 79.

61. Jean Libby, ed., *From Slavery to Salvation: The Autobiography of Rev. Thomas W. Henry of the A.M.E. Church* (Jackson: University Press of Mississippi, 1994), 7, 10–11, 14.

62. Benjamin Abbott, *Experience and Gospel Labours of the Rev. Benjamin Abbott* (New York: Waugh and Mason, 1832), 12–13; Lee, *Life*, 30, 35.

63. Newell, *Diary*, 73–75.

64. Manship, *Thirteen Years' Experience*, 50.

65. Swayze, *Narrative*, 81–82.

66. Dan Young, *Autobiography of Dan Young: A New England Preacher of the Olden Time*, ed. W. P. Strickland (New York: Carlton and Potter, 1860), 48–49. On seeing the devil's visible form, see Heyrman, *Southern Cross*, 28–33, 57–58, 70–73.

67. Orange Scott, *The New and Improved Camp Meeting Hymn Book* (Brookfield,

Mass.: Merriam, 1830), 16. Writing of Puritan Samuel Sewall's sense of hearing, historian David D. Hall has observed, "Any encounter with thunder, trumpets, or shrill cries in everyday life stirred associations in Sewall's mind with their meaning in Revelation. Abrupt sounds were the sensate medium of God's anger." See David D. Hall, *Worlds of Wonder, Days of Judgment: Popular Religious Belief in Early New England* (New York: Knopf, 1989), 225. Those signals clearly remained equally powerful among evangelicals.

68. Zilpha Elaw, *Memoirs of the Life, Religious Experience, Ministerial Travels and Labours* (1846), in Andrews, ed., *Sisters of the Spirit*, 65–66; Anne Crooke, "American Camp-Meetings," 13 September 1806, in William Graham Campbell, *The Apostle of Kerry; Or, The Wonders of the Irish General Mission* (Toronto: Wesleyan Methodist Conference, 1869), 305–306.

69. Donald E. Byrne, in his study of the folklore of Methodist itinerants, labels this story "the most widely-told Dow anecdote." See Byrne, *No Foot of Land*, 286.

70. Lorenzo Dow, *Works: Travels, Providential Experience, &c. &c. of Lorenzo Dow in Europe and America*, 2 vols. (Dublin: John Jones, 1806), 2: 82–83.

71. Manship, *Thirteen Years' Experience*, 18–19; Edgar Allen Poe, "The Bells," in Philip Van Doren Stern, ed., *The Portable Edgar Allen Poe* (New York: Viking, 1945), 634–637.

72. Young, *Autobiography of Dan Young*, 112–113.

73. Increase Mather, *Remarkable Providences* (London: Smith, 1856), 51–95; Cotton Mather, *Magnalia Christi Americana; Or, The Ecclesiastical History of New England*, 2 vols. (Hartford: Andrus, 1853), 2: 361–372. For the continuation of such uses, see James Allin, *Thunder and Earthquake, a Loud and Awful Call to Reformation* (Boston: Rogers, 1727), 3–17.

74. Hibbard, *Memoirs*, 154.

75. Abbott, *Experience*, 118–119; Hibbard, *Memoirs*, 154; Newell, *Life*, 98–99. For other examples of this stock-in-trade evangelism, see Heyrman, *Southern Cross*, 75; Stout, *New England Soul*, 190. This is an important context for understanding the centrality of thunder for visionary Rebecca Cox Jackson. See Humez, ed., *Gifts of Power*, 15, 71–72, 178–179, 200, 243–249.

76. Jonathan Edwards, *Ethical Writings*, ed. Paul Ramsey (New Haven: Yale University Press, 1989), 378n, 380n; Scott, *New and Improved Camp Meeting Hymn Book*, 131, 137.

77. Law, *Serious Call*, 202–204; Elaw, *Memoirs*, 73–74.

78. John Wesley to Charles Wesley, 20 October 1753 and 31 October 1753, in Wesley, *Works: Letters II, 1740–1755*, 526, 528; Dow, *Works*, 1: 142; Hempton, *Religion of the People*, 33–34.

79. Newell, *Diary*, 110–111.

80. Finley, *Autobiography*, 166–167, 179–180.

81. Charles Chauncy, *Seasonable Thoughts on the State of Religion in New-England* (Boston: Rogers and Fowle, 1743), 78, 80, 100, 104–106, 126; Frances Trollope, *Domestic Manners of the Americans*, ed. Pamela Neville-Sington (New York: Penguin, 1997), 130; Jacques Ellul, *The Humiliation of the Word*, trans. Joyce Main Hanks (Grand Rapids, Mich.: Eerdmans, 1985), 13.

82. Etienne Bonnot de Condillac, *Condillac's Treatise on the Sensations*, trans. Geraldine Carr (London: Favil, 1930), 47–52, 55. On the politics of musical harmony, see Jacques Attali, *Noise: The Political Economy of Music*, trans. Brian Massumi (Minneapolis: University of Minnesota Press, 1985).

83. Constance Classen, *Worlds of Sense: Exploring the Senses in History and across Cultures* (London: Routledge, 1993), 81–82 (Orwell is quoted on p. 82).

84. Benjamin Bayly, *An Essay on Inspiration* (London, 1707; London: J.M., 1708), 398, 401; Brown, *Works*, 3: 257; Thomas Paine, "Worship and Church Bells," in *The Complete Writings of Thomas Paine*, ed. Philip S. Foner, 2 vols. (New York: Citadel, 1945), 2: 758, 760.

85. Walker, *Way to Try*, 5, 29.

86. McLean, *Sketch*, 14; Henry Boehm, *Reminiscences, Historical and Biographical, of Sixty-Four Years in the Ministry* (New York: Carlton and Porter, 1865), 131; Abbott, *Experience*, 187.

87. W. J. T. Mitchell, *Picture Theory: Essays on Verbal and Visual Representation* (Chicago: University of Chicago Press, 1994).

88. Manship, *Thirteen Years' Experience*, 56–57, 89; Joseph Travis, *Autobiography of the Rev. Joseph Travis* (Nashville: Stevenson and Owen, 1856), 87, 96; White, *Brief Account*, 75.

89. Michel de Certeau, *The Practice of Everyday Life*, trans. Steven Rendall (Berkeley: University of California Press, 1984), 162–164.

90. Newell, *Diary*, 77–80. For a similar intermingling of the voices of the saints and that of God speaking and calling at a camp meeting, see Elaw, *Memoirs*, 81–82.

91. Chauncy, *Seasonable Thoughts*, 86, 130–131.

92. Ibid., 218.

93. Bayly, *Essay on Inspiration*, 27–29.

94. On Protestant cessationist views, see Michael Heyd, *"Be Sober and Reasonable": The Critique of Enthusiasm in the Seventeenth and Early Eighteenth Centuries* (Leiden: Brill, 1995), esp. 18–20, 30–31, 38; Robert Bruce Mullin, *Miracles and the Modern Religious Imagination* (New Haven: Yale University Press, 1996), 9–30.

95. Jonathan Edwards, *Religious Affections*, ed. John E. Smith (New Haven: Yale University Press, 1959), 131–135, 195, 260, 272–275. Edwards is a scholarly industry unto himself, and that vigorous enterprise includes his intricate understanding of the spiritual sense(s). For a good recent overview, see Michael J. McClymond, *Encounters with God: An Approach to the Theology of Jonathan Edwards* (New York: Oxford University Press, 1998), 9–26.

96. Edwards, *Religious Affections*, 142–145, 288.

97. Ibid., 149, 207, 219–221, 223, 279–280, 290.

98. Calvin, *Institutes*, 2: 259; Mather, *Manuductio*, 31, 103.

99. Stout, *New England Soul*, 91–92, 163–165, 220 (Adams is quoted on pp. 91–92).

100. George Whitefield, *Sermons on Important Subjects* (London: Fisher and Jackson, 1828), 330–331; Daniel Burgess, *Rules for Hearing the Word of God* (London: Field, 1757), 8, 12; Cotton Mather, *The Echo's of Devotion* (Boston: Fleet and Crump, 1716), 31. For another colonial take on how to listen to sermons—caught between traditional models of submission and widening Enlightenment suspicions of priest-

craft—see Jonathan Mayhew, *Sermons upon the Following Subjects, viz. On Hearing the Word* (London: Millar, 1756), 2–39.

101. Finley, *Autobiography*, 167; Hibbard, *Memoirs*, 137–138; Ned Landsman, *From Colonials to Provincials: American Thought and Culture, 1680–1760* (New York: Twayne, 1997), 57–59; David Jaffee, "The Village Enlightenment in New England, 1760–1820," *William and Mary Quarterly* 47 (July 1990): 327–346; Stephen H. Bradley, *A Sketch of the Life of Stephen H. Bradley, from the Age of Five to Twenty-Four Years* (Madison, Conn.: n.p., 1830), 6; Alexis de Tocqueville, *Democracy in America*, 2 vols. (New York: Vintage Books, 1945), 2: 4, 10, 142.

102. Amanda Berry Smith, *An Autobiography: The Story of the Lord's Dealings with Mrs. Amanda Smith, the Colored Evangelist* (Chicago: Meyer, 1893), 132–133, 147–148.

103. Oral Roberts, *The Call* (Garden City, N.Y.: Doubleday, 1971), 22, 33–35.

3. Oracles of Reason

1. William Frederick Pinchbeck, *The Expositor; Or, Many Mysteries Unravelled* (Boston: n.p., 1805), 28–38, 81–82, 90–91; "Astonishing Invisible Lady: The Acoustic Temple, and Incomprehensible Crystal," Wilmington, Delaware, 1804, Broadsides Collection, American Antiquarian Society, Worcester, Mass.; William Frederick Pinchbeck, *Witchcraft; Or, the Art of Fortune-Telling Unveiled* (Boston: n.p., 1805), 46–49, 81. See also James M. Barriskill, "The Newburyport Theatre in the Eighteenth Century," *Essex Institute Historical Collections* 91 (October 1955): 339–342; James M. Barriskill, "Newburyport Theatre in the Federalist Period," *Essex Institute Historical Collections* 93 (January 1957): 12–14.

2. "Astonishing Invisible Lady," broadside; Pinchbeck, *Expositor*, 25, 91; Pinchbeck, *Witchcraft*, 7–18.

3. Pinchbeck, *Witchcraft*, 46–49; "Astonishing Invisible Lady," broadside; "The Mystery of the Invisible Lady Unfold[e]d and Explained," Salem, Mass., 1805, Broadsides Collection, American Antiquarian Society, Worcester, Mass.

4. Pinchbeck, *Witchcraft*, 13, 48–49.

5. "Mystery of the Invisible Lady," broadside.

6. For a very useful compilation of commentary and primary sources, see Georg Luck, ed., *Arcana Mundi: Magic and the Occult in the Greek and Roman Worlds* (Baltimore: Johns Hopkins University Press, 1985); Lucan is quoted on p. 283. See also H. W. Parke, *Greek Oracles* (London: Hutchinson University Library, 1967); David Frankfurter, *Religion in Roman Egypt: Assimilation and Resistance* (Princeton: Princeton University Press, 1998), 145–197.

7. Jonathan Edwards, *A History of the Work of Redemption*, ed. John F. Wilson (New Haven: Yale University Press, 1989), 392–393.

8. H. W. Parke, *Sibyls and Sibylline Prophecy in Classical Antiquity*, ed. B. C. McGing (London: Routledge, 1988), 169–170; Parke, *Greek Oracles*, 144–148; James H. Charlesworth, ed., *The Old Testament Pseudepigrapha*, 2 vols. (Garden City, N.Y.: Doubleday, 1983), 1: 317–326, 345, 426. The intricacy of Jewish adaptations of the Sibylline tradition is explored in John J. Collins, *Seers, Sibyls and Sages in Hellenistic-*

Roman Judaism (Leiden: Brill, 1997), 181–197. For the ongoing vitality of Christian Sibyllinism, see Bernard McGinn, *Visions of the End: Apocalyptic Traditions in the Middle Ages* (New York: Columbia University Press, 1979), 18–21, 40, 43–50, 130–133. For eighteenth-century uses, see John Floyer, *The Sibylline Oracles Translated from the Best Greek Copies, and Compar'd with the Sacred Prophesies, especially with Daniel and the Revelations, and with So Much History as Plainly Shews, that Many of the Sibyls Predictions Are Exactly Fulfill'd* (London: Bruges, 1713); William Whiston, *A Vindication of the Sibylline Oracles* (London: n.p., 1715).

9. I have relied on the following secondary accounts for contextualization of the debate over the oracles in the French Enlightenment: Marcel Bouchard, *L'Histoire des oracles de Fontenelle* (Paris: Sfelt, 1947), 75–104; Alain Niderst, *Fontenelle à la recherche de lui-même* (Paris: Nizet, 1972), 284–302; Gianni Paganini, "Fontenelle et la critique des oracles entre libertinisme et clandestinité," in Alain Niderst and Jean Mesnard, eds., *Fontenelle* (Paris: Presses Universitaires de France, 1989), 333–349; Frank E. Manuel, *The Eighteenth Century Confronts the Gods* (Cambridge, Mass.: Harvard University Press, 1959), 47–53, 65–70. For further contextualization within Enlightenment debates about religion, see Peter Harrison, *"Religion" and the Religions in the English Enlightenment* (Cambridge: Cambridge University Press, 1990), esp. 77–92; J. Samuel Preus, *Explaining Religion: Criticism and Theory from Bodin to Freud* (New Haven: Yale University Press, 1987), 47–55; J. A. I. Champion, *The Pillars of Priestcraft Shaken: The Church of England and Its Enemies, 1660–1730* (Cambridge: Cambridge University Press, 1992); Jonathan Z. Smith, "Religion, Religions, Religious," in Mark C. Taylor, ed., *Critical Terms for Religious Studies* (Chicago: University of Chicago Press, 1998), 269–284. Harrison and Manuel both contain especially cogent descriptions of the "imposture thesis" and the "twofold philosophy."

10. *Encyclopaedia Britannica; Or, A Dictionary of Arts, Sciences, and Miscellaneous Literature,* 18 vols. (Edinburgh, 1797; Philadelphia: Dobson, 1798), 13: 367; Theodoret, *Ecclesiastical History* (London: Bagster and Sons, 1843), 318–319; Kenneth Gross, *The Dream of the Moving Statue* (Ithaca: Cornell University Press, 1992), 51.

11. Reginald Scot, *The Discoverie of Witchcraft* (London, 1584; rpt. London: Rowan and Littlefield, 1973), 128–133; Thomas Ady, *A Perfect Discovery of Witches* (London: R.I., 1661), 29, 42–43, 65–66; Edward Herbert, *Pagan Religion: A Translation of De religione gentilium,* ed. John Anthony Butler (Ottawa: Dovehouse, 1996), 345–349. Peter Harrison has labeled this pervasive disputational rhetoric *paganopapism.* See Harrison, *"Religion" and the Religions,* 9, 144–145. See also Michael Heyd, *"Be Sober and Reasonable": The Critique of Enthusiasm in the Seventeenth and Early Eighteenth Centuries* (Leiden: Brill, 1995), 61–63.

12. For the revival of classical theories of religion during the Enlightenment, see Harrison, *"Religion" and the Religions,* 14–18.

13. Lucian, *Alexander; Or, The False Prophet,* trans. Charles Blount, in *The Works of Lucian, Translated from the Greek by Several Eminent Hands,* ed. John Dryden (London: Briscoe, 1711), 148, 151–158, 161, 165, 172.

14. Charles Blount, *The Oracles of Reason* (London: n.p., 1693), B5; Lucian, *Alexander,* 144, 155, 166; David Hume, *An Enquiry Concerning Human Understanding,* ed.

Eric Steinberg (Indianapolis: Hackett, 1977), 80–81. See also Voltaire, *Philosophical Dictionary*, in *The Works of Voltaire*, 42 vols. (Akron, Ohio: Werner, 1905), 12: 103–104. Not surprisingly, Alexander shared the company of the prophet Muhammad, who had long served as an exemplar of religious cunning in the Western imagination. More threateningly, the most radical skeptics extended the impostor model to Moses and Jesus. On this radical strand, see especially Silvia Berti, Françoise Charles-Daubert, and Richard H. Popkin, eds., *Heterodoxy, Spinozism, and Free Thought in Early-Eighteenth-Century Europe: Studies on the Traité des trois imposteurs* (Dordrecht, Holland: Kluwer, 1996). On American appropriations of the biographies of Muhammad as impostor, see Robert J. Allison, *The Crescent Obscured: The United States and the Muslim World, 1776–1815* (New York: Oxford University Press, 1995), 35–46. For commentary on the prophet-as-impostor trope in American journalism, see Mark Silk, *Unsecular Media: Making News of Religion in America* (Urbana: University of Illinois Press, 1995), 91–105. On the social dimensions of trust and credit among the learned, see Steven Shapin, *A Social History of Truth: Civility and Science in Seventeenth-Century England* (Chicago: University of Chicago Press, 1994).

15. Whiston, *Vindication*, 81; David Blondel, *A Treatise of the Sibyls* (London: T.R., 1661), 9, 15, 49, 57–63, 70, 148.

16. *Encyclopaedia Britannica*, 17: 455. For a contemporary summary of the array of modern critics, see John Beaumont, *Gleanings of Antiquities* (London: J. Roberts, 1724), 55–68. See also Lynn Thorndike, *A History of Magic and Experimental Science*, 8 vols. (New York: Columbia University Press, 1923–1958), 8: 476–479. For one belated attempt to recover the devotional use of these texts, see Alfred Canon White and Mariana Monteiro, *"As David and the Sibyls Say": A Sketch of the Sibyls and the Sibylline Oracles* (Edinburgh: Sands, 1905).

17. Pierre Bayle, *Oeuvres diverses*, 5 vols. (The Hague, 1725; Hildesheim, Germany: Georg Ols, 1964), 1: 4–7; Voltaire, *Philosophical Dictionary*, in *Works*, 12: 94, 97–98. On the relationship of van Dale's work to Fontenelle's, see Bouchard, *L'Histoire*, 92–104. For a critical edition of Fontenelle's text, including a table comparing the contents of van Dale, Fontenelle, and Jean Baltus, see Bernard de Fontenelle, *Histoire des oracles*, ed. Louis Maigron (Paris: Cornély, 1908). For van Dale's reservations about the liberties Fontenelle took with his work, see Antonius van Dale, "Lettre de Monsieur van Dale à un de ses amis," *Nouvelles de la république des lettres* 4 (May 1687): 459–487. For examples of how this scholarship flowed into English deism and latitudinarianism, see John Toland, *Letters to Serena* (London: Lintot, 1704), unpaginated preface and letter III; Conyers Middleton, *An Examination of the Lord Bishop of London's Discourses Concerning the Use and Intent of Prophecy* (London: Manby and Cox, 1750), title page, 107–111; Conyers Middleton, *A Free Inquiry into the Miraculous Powers* (London: Manby and Cox, 1749), 232.

18. Jean Baltus, *An Answer to Mr. de Fontenelle's History of Oracles* (London: W.B., 1709), unpaginated preface, 4–7. See also Jean Baltus, *A Continuation of the Answer to the History of Oracles* (London: W.B., 1710), iv–vi. Baltus, a Jesuit, offered the fullest Christian response to the new history, and English Protestants appropriated his

works, with due notation of where his Catholicism led him astray, to defend a view of history that largely overarched the Protestant-Catholic divide. For the French editions, see Jean Baltus, *Réponse à l'histoire des oracles, de Mr. de Fontenelle, de l'Académie Françoise* (Strasbourg, 1707; Strasbourg: Doulssecker, 1709); Jean Baltus, *Suite de la réponse à l'histoire des oracles* (Strasbourg: Doulssecker, 1708). I am using the English translations of the period, where available, because these are more indicative of how these ideas flowed into Anglo-American discourse; at the same time, I have consulted the French versions.

19. Bernard Le Bovier de Fontenelle, *The History of Oracles, and the Cheats of the Pagan Priests* (London: n.p., 1688), unpaginated preface, 155; Antonius van Dale, *De oraculis veterum ethnicorum dissertationes duae* (Amsterdam, 1683; Amsterdam: Boom, 1700).

20. *Lettres édifiantes et curieuses, écrites des missions étrangères*, 25 vols. (Paris: Merigot, 1780–1783), 11: 42–79; Baltus, *Continuation*, 195–197. For the Incan case of oracular suppression, see Constance Classen, *Worlds of Sense: Exploring the Senses in History and across Cultures* (London: Routledge, 1993), 106–120 (quotation from Garcilaso de la Vega is on p. 113). For the missionary argument, see also J. S. Forsyth, *Demonologia; Or, Natural Knowledge Revealed; Being an Exposé of Ancient and Modern Superstitions, Credulity, Fanaticism, and Imposture* (London: Bumpus, 1827), 160–161. For a wider context, see Kenneth Mills, *Idolatry and Its Enemies: Colonial Andean Religion and Extirpation, 1640–1750* (Princeton: Princeton University Press, 1997), esp. 215–216.

21. Fontenelle, *History of Oracles*, 4.

22. Blount, *Oracles*, B2, 38–40, 167–171. For the joining of the critique of oracles to that of biblical prophecy, see also Middleton, *Examination*, 107–111.

23. Ethan Allen, *Reason the Only Oracle of Man*, ed. John Pell (Bennington, Vt., 1784; New York: Scholars' Facsimiles and Reprints, 1940), esp. 200–232, 256–258, 283–285; John Stewart, *The Moral or Intellectual Last Will and Testament of John Stewart, the Traveller, the Only Man of Nature that Ever Appeared in the World* (London: n.p., 1810), 372; John Stewart, *The Sophiometer; Or, Regulator of Mental Power* (London: Gosnell, 1812), 6–9, 75–76, unpaginated appendix; John Stewart, *Opus Maximum; Or, the Great Essay to Reduce the Moral World from Contingency to System* (London: Ginger, 1803), frontispiece, 10, 18, 53, 120–121; Thomas Jefferson to Miles King, 26 September 1814, in Thomas Jefferson, *Jefferson's Extracts from the Gospels: "The Philosophy of Jesus" and "The Life and Morals of Jesus,"* ed. Dickinson W. Adams (Princeton: Princeton University Press, 1983), 360.

24. Allen, *Reason*, 211, 232; Anthony Ashley Cooper, *A Letter Concerning Enthusiasm* (London: J. Morphew, 1708), 70–71, 77; "A True and Genuine Account of a Wonderful Wandering Spirit," *General Magazine, and Historical Chronicle* 1 (February 1741): 120–121. For Dutch Protestant struggles with prophesying and direct inspiration, the immediate religious context out of which van Dale's original attack on the oracles emerged, see Andrew C. Fix, *Prophecy and Reason: The Dutch Collegiants in the Early Enlightenment* (Princeton: Princeton University Press, 1991), 161–184 (a note on van Dale's earlier critique of free prophecy is on p. 180).

25. John Trenchard, *The Natural History of Superstition* (London: Baldwin, 1709), 8–10, 20–21.

26. John Trenchard and Thomas Gordon, *Cato's Letters; Or, Essays on Liberty, Civil and Religious*, 4 vols. (London, 1720–1723; London: Wilkins, 1733), 1: 82–88, 2: 155, 3: 113–114, 4: 254–255; John Trenchard and Thomas Gordon, *The Independent Whig; Or, A Defense of Primitive Christianity*, 4 vols. (London, 1720–1721; London: Peele, 1732–1747), 1: 133, 186; *Encyclopaedia Britannica*, 6: 77.

27. Walter Anderson, *The History of Croesus, King of Lydia* (Edinburgh: Hamilton, Balfour, and Neill, 1755), 21; Thomas Paine, *Rights of Man*, in *The Complete Writings of Thomas Paine*, ed. Philip S. Foner, 2 vols. (New York: Citadel, 1945), 1: 277; Joel Barlow, *The Political Writings of Joel Barlow* (New York: Mott and Lyon, 1796), 41–43. See also David Brewster, *Letters on Natural Magic* (London, 1832; London: Murray, 1842), 4; Elihu Palmer, *An Enquiry Relative to the Moral and Political Improvement of the Human Species* (New York: Crookes, 1797), 25–26; *Prospect; Or, View of the Moral World*, 22 September 1804, 330–333; "Craft," *Temple of Reason*, 20 February 1802, 31; "Oracles," *Temple of Reason*, 18 September 1802, 234–235. The republican political uses of the critique of imposture and priestcraft are highlighted in Champion, *Pillars of Priestcraft*, 9–12, 133–169, 174–179.

28. Elias Smith, "'The Oracle . . . Explained," *Herald of Gospel Liberty*, 31 March 1809, 64.

29. Eusèbe Salverte, *The Occult Sciences: The Philosophy of Magic, Prodigies, and Apparent Miracles*, trans. Anthony Todd Thomson, 2 vols. (New York: Harper and Brothers, 1847), 2: 228; Eusèbe Salverte, *Des Sciences occultes; Ou Essai sur la magie, les prodiges et les miracles* (Paris: Sédillot, 1829); P. T. Barnum, *The Humbugs of the World* (New York: Carleton, 1866), 387–400. For this popularization, see also Forsyth, *Demonologia*, x, xvi, 159.

30. For other possibilities beyond Clarke, see the varied allusions to "the researches of modern antiquaries and travellers" in the chapter on oracles in Richard A. Davenport, *Sketches of Imposture, Deception, and Credulity* (Philadelphia: Zieber, 1845), 21, 23–24, 28; and also in D. P. Kidder, *Remarkable Delusions; Or, Illustrations of Popular Errors* (New York: Lane and Scott, 1852), 169–171. See also Henry Cockton, *Life and Adventures of Valentine Vox the Ventriloquist* (London, 1840; New York: Burt, n.d.), 145–156. In this novel, the antiquities, thanks to collectors like Clarke, have been brought home to the skeptical viewer in the British Museum, who is sure that "there is nothing . . . that can have so great a tendency to prove the rapid progress of the human intellect as an oracle" (p. 148).

31. Edward Daniel Clarke, *Travels in Various Countries of Europe, Asia and Africa*, 6 vols. (London: Cadell and Davies, 1811–1823), 2: 239–240; 3: 677–678; 4: 179–180.

32. Clarke, *Travels*, 3:678–679. Clarke's tours were on the front edge of antiquarian and archaeological exploration of oracle shrines and temples, most of which began to be seriously excavated only in the late nineteenth century. It is worth noting that the archaeological evidence suggests that various devices were used in antiquity to create speaking statues, but any reading of this evidence which focuses on fraudulence obviously remains far more indebted to the Enlightenment history

than a careful reconstruction of the multilayered significance of oracular practices at ancient shrines. Compare, for example, the following: Frederik Poulsen, "Talking, Weeping and Bleeding Sculptures: A Chapter of the History of Religious Fraud," *Acta Archaeologica* 16 (1945): 178–195; and Frankfurter, *Religion in Roman Egypt*, 150–152, 158–159, 176–179.

33. Salverte, *Occult Sciences*, 1: 149. For a typical chain running from the oracles through Catholics to Mormons, see Kidder, *Remarkable Delusions*, 167–195.

34. Salverte, *Occult Sciences*, 1: 13, 239; 2: 7; Brewster, *Letters*, 195; "Magic," *Hogg's Weekly Instructor*, 27 September 1845, 65–67.

35. Francis Bacon, *The Works of Francis Bacon*, ed. James Spedding, Robert Leslie Ellis, and Douglas Denon Heath, 14 vols. (London, 1857–1874; Stuttgart: Frommann, 1963), 2: 390, 397, 436; 3: 162–163; *Encyclopaedia Americana*, 13 vols. (Philadelphia: Carey and Lea, 1829–1833), 1: 38.

36. Marin Mersenne, *Harmonie universelle*, 7 vols. (Paris: n.p., 1636–1637); Joseph Saveur, *Principes d'acoustique et de musique* (Paris, 1701; Geneva: Minkoff, 1973), 1. Acoustics has received a fraction of the scholarly attention that optics has garnered, but the literature has been growing of late. Appearing quite recently is Penelope Gouk, *Music, Science and Natural Magic in Seventeenth-Century England* (New Haven: Yale University Press, 1999), the fulfillment of her prior studies of seventeenth-century English acoustics and a good place now to begin. Other leading works include: Dayton Clarence Miller, *Anecdotal History of the Science of Sound to the Beginnings of the Twentieth Century* (New York: Macmillan, 1935); Frederick Vinton Hunt, *Origins in Acoustics: The Science of Sound from Antiquity to the Age of Newton* (New Haven: Yale University Press, 1978); R. Bruce Lindsay, ed., *Acoustics: Historical and Philosophical Development* (Stroudsbourg, Penn.: Dowden, Hutchinson, and Ross, 1973), a basic compendium of primary materials with historical commentary; Sigalia Dostrovsky, "The Origins of Vibration Theory: The Scientific Revolution and the Nature of Music," Ph.D. diss., Princeton University, 1969; Emily Ann Thompson, "'Mysteries of the Acoustic': Architectural Acoustics in America, 1800–1932," Ph.D. diss., Princeton University, 1992, the best source for developments on the American side; Penelope M. Gouk, "Acoustics in the Early Royal Society, 1660–1680," *Notes and Records of the Royal Society of London* 36 (February 1982): 155–175; Penelope Gouk, "The Role of Acoustics and Music Theory in the Scientific Work of Robert Hooke," *Annals of Science* 37 (September 1980): 573–605; Penelope Mary Gouk, "Music in the Natural Philosophy of the Early Royal Society," Ph.D. diss., Warburg Institute, University of London, 1982; Peter Dear, *Mersenne and the Learning of the Schools* (Ithaca: Cornell University Press, 1988), esp. 117–169; H. F. Cohen, *Quantifying Music: The Science of Music at the First Stage of the Scientific Revolution, 1580–1650* (Dordrecht, Holland: Reidel, 1984); Charles Burnett, Michael Fend, and Penelope Gouk, eds. *The Second Sense: Studies in Hearing and Musical Judgement from Antiquity to the Seventeenth Century* (London: Warburg Institute, 1991), a superb collection of essays that helps place early modern acoustics in classical, patristic, and medieval frames of reference; Alistair C. Crombie, "The Study of the Senses in Renaissance Science," *Proceedings of the International Congress of the*

History of Science 1 (1964): 93–114, an excellent review of early modern anatomies of the ear; Albert Cohen, *Music in the French Royal Academy of Sciences: A Study in the Evolution of Musical Thought* (Princeton: Princeton University Press, 1982), esp. 3–40; Thomas L. Hankins and Robert J. Silverman, *Instruments and the Imagination* (Princeton: Princeton University Press, 1995), esp. 178–220; Stephan Vogel, "Sensation of Tone, Perception of Sound, and Empiricism: Helmholtz's Physiological Acoustics," in David Cahan, ed., *Hermann von Helmholtz and the Foundations of Nineteenth-Century Science* (Berkeley: University of California Press, 1993), 259–287. The works of Miller, Lindsay, and Hunt remain useful internalist histories by three men who were actively involved in the further professionalization of the field in the twentieth century.

37. Matthew Young, *An Enquiry into the Principal Phaenomena of Sounds and Musical Strings* (Dublin: Joseph Hill, 1784), 1; Mersenne is quoted in Dostrovsky, "Origins of Vibration Theory," 147. See also Mersenne, *Harmonie,* 3B: 81–85. On Fontenelle's support, see Dostrovsky, "Origins of Vibration Theory," 250–251; Cohen, *Music in the French Royal Academy,* 18, 24–25. On Franklin's interest in the velocity and air-as-medium questions, see Benjamin Franklin, *Experiments and Observations on Electricity* (London: Henry, 1769), 435–437; Benjamin Franklin, *The Papers of Benjamin Franklin,* ed. Leonard W. Labaree (New Haven: Yale University Press, 1959–), 3: 337; 10: 130–132.

38. Saveur, *Principes,* 1–3, 58; Robert Hooke, *The Posthumous Works of Robert Hooke* (London: Smith and Walford, 1705), xxiii, 39. For Bacon's comments on "an ear-spectacle," see Bacon, *Works,* 2: 434–435.

39. Bacon, *Works,* 2: 397, 3: 162–163; Samuel Rush, *A Discourse on the Moral Influence of Sounds, Delivered before the Chester County Cabinet of Natural Science, January 18th, 1839* (Philadelphia: J. Perry, 1839), 5. On this drive for practical improvements in acoustics within the Baconian tradition, see Gouk, "Acoustics in the Early Royal Society," 156–159, 163–165.

40. For the specific links between acoustics and natural magic, see especially Hankins and Silverman, *Instruments and the Imagination,* 4–5, 13, 178–220; Gouk, *Music, Science and Natural Magic.* For classic works on the much debated exchange between Renaissance magic and the rise of modern science, see Frances A. Yates, *Giordano Bruno and the Hermetic Tradition* (London: Routledge and Kegan Paul, 1964); Paolo Rossi, *Francis Bacon: From Magic to Science,* trans. Sacha Rabinovitch (Chicago: University of Chicago Press, 1968), esp. 1–35; Charles Webster, *From Paracelsus to Newton: Magic and the Making of Modern Science* (Cambridge: Cambridge University Press, 1982).

41. Bacon, *Works,* 2: 413, 425; 3: 162–164. Mersenne raised the same question about ventriloquial charlatanry. See Mersenne, *Harmonie,* 3B: 54–56. On Bacon's acoustic art, see Gouk, *Music, Science and Natural Magic,* 158–169.

42. *Encyclopaedia Britannica,* 1: 91–92; *Edinburgh Encyclopaedia,* 18 vols. (Philadelphia: Parker, 1832), 1: 117–119.

43. See, for example, Dear, *Mersenne;* Gouk, "Role of Acoustics," 593; Gouk, "Music in the Natural Philosophy," 9–10, 21–23, 154–162, 352–356.

44. On Mersenne's calculations, see Mersenne, *Harmonie*, 1A: 38; Hunt, *Origins*, 86–87; on Kircher, see the account in P. Conor Reilly, *Athanasius Kircher, S.J.: Master of a Hundred Arts, 1601–1680* (Wiesbaden: Edizioni del Mondo, 1974), 175; and Athanasius Kircher, *Phonurgia nova* (Kempten, Germany: Rudolph Dreherr, 1673), 113–115; on Bacon's observations, see Bacon, *Works*, 2: 414–415; on Marsh's, see Narcissus Marsh, "An Introductory Essay to the Doctrine of Sounds, containing some Proposals for the Improvement of Acousticks," *Philosophical Transactions* 14 (1684): 477. For a recent exploration of Christian underpinnings to technological dreams, see David F. Noble, *The Religion of Technology: The Divinity of Man and the Spirit of Invention* (New York: Knopf, 1998).

45. Walter Scott, ed., *Hermetica: The Ancient Greek and Latin Writings which Contain Religious or Philosophic Teachings Ascribed to Hermes Trismegistus*, 4 vols. (Oxford: Clarendon, 1924), 1: 339–341. See also Yates, *Bruno*, 18, 35–41, 67–68, 132–133. For the kabbalistic elements within these early modern Hermetic aspirations of animation, see Moshe Idel, *Golem: Jewish Magical and Mystical Traditions on the Artificial Anthropoid* (Albany: State University of New York, 1990), esp. 177–180.

46. Heinrich Cornelius Agrippa, *Three Books of Occult Philosophy* (London: R.W., 1651), 77–78; Montfaucon de Villars, *The Count of Gabalis; Or, the Extravagant Mysteries of the Cabalists, Exposed* (London: B.M., 1680), 85. The latter, though ostensibly a satire of magical traditions, remains a good source on those very traditions. On the seriousness with which voices and oracles were taken by early modern Hermeticists, see Agrippa, *Three Books*, 411–413, 499–519; Villars, *Count of Gabalis*, 62–99.

47. Giambattista Della Porta, *Natural Magick* (London: Young and Speed, 1658), 385–386. Important for pulling natural magic further into the mechanical arts was the revival of the knowledge of ancient hydraulics and pneumatics, both of which overlapped with the mechanization of statues and voices. On these issues, see Yates, *Bruno*, 147–149; Frances A. Yates, *The Rosicrucian Enlightenment* (London, 1972; Boulder, Colo.: Shambhala, 1978), 11–13, 59; Frances A. Yates, *Theatre of the World* (Chicago: University of Chicago Press, 1969), 26–33.

48. *Encyclopaedia Britannica*, 1: 91; William Hooper, *Rational Recreations in Which the Principles of Numbers and Natural Philosophy Are Clearly and Copiously Elucidated*, 4 vols. (London: Davis, 1774), 1: i–iv; 2: 202–204, 220–223; *The Oracle of the Arts; Or, Entertaining Expounder of the Wonders of Science* (London: Bumpus, 1824), 27–30; Kircher, *Phonurgia nova*, 113, 152–153, 161–163. For the larger reworking of natural magic, see Wayne Shumaker, *Natural Magic and Modern Science: Four Treatises, 1590–1657* (Binghamton: Medieval and Renaissance Texts and Studies, 1989), 126–202; Thorndike, *History of Magic*, 7: 273–322, 590–621. On Kircher and his influence in the invention of these acoustic technologies and illusions, see Joscelyn Godwin, *Athanasius Kircher: A Renaissance Man and the Quest for Lost Knowledge* (London: Thames and Hudson, 1979), esp. 66–74; Reilly, *Kircher*, 35–36, 135–144, 175; Thorndike, *History of Magic*, 8: 224–226; Yates, *Bruno*, 421–423; Gouk, *Music, Science and Natural Magic*, 101–107. For the wider courting of illusion and play in Kircher, among others, see Paula Findlen, "Jokes of Nature and Jokes of Knowledge: The

Playfulness in Scientific Discourse in Early Modern Europe," *Renaissance Quarterly* 43 (Summer 1990): 292–331.

49. Fontenelle, *History of the Oracles*, 43–44, 118; Johann Beckmann, *A History of Inventions and Discoveries*, trans. William Johnston, 4 vols. (London: Longman, Hurst, Rees, Orme, and Brown, 1817), 3: 270.

50. Jacques de Vaucanson, *An Account of the Mechanism of an Automaton*, trans. J. T. Desaguliers (London: Parker, 1742), 17; Edgar Allen Poe, "Maezel's Chess-Player," in Philip Van Doren Stern, ed., *The Portable Edgar Allen Poe* (New York: Viking, 1945), 510; Wolfgang von Kempelen, *Le Mécanisme de la parole, suivi de la description d'une machine parlante* (Vienna: Bauer, 1791), viii–ix, 394–464. On efforts to create talking automata, see Alfred Chapuis and Edmond Droz, *Automata: A Historical and Technological Study*, trans. Alec Reid (New York: Central, 1958), 320–326; Homer Dudley and T. H. Tarnoczy, "The Speaking Machine of Wolfgang von Kempelen," *Journal of the Acoustical Society of America* 22 (March 1950): 151–166; Silvio Bedini, "The Role of Automata in the History of Technology," *Technology and Culture* 5 (Winter 1964): 38; Hankins and Silverman, *Instruments and the Imagination*, 186–198; John Nevil Maskelyne, "Natural Magic: Acoustics" (1878), and "Automata" (1879), Magazine Magic, Harry Price Library, University of London.

51. Charles Wheatstone, *The Scientific Papers of Sir Charles Wheatstone* (London: Taylor and Francis, 1879), 348–367; Account of Wheatstone lecture, May 1835, in "Exhibitions of Mechanical and Other Works of Ingenuity," Scrapbook, 1840, British Library, 1269.h.38; Alexander Graham Bell, "Prehistoric Telephone Days," *National Geographic Magazine* 41 (March 1922): 233–237; Théodose du Moncel, *The Telephone, the Microphone, and the Phonograph* (New York: Harper, 1879), 11.

52. "The Talking Phonograph," *Scientific American* 22 (December 1877), 385 (emphasis added). On the phonograph, see especially Andre Millard, *America on Record: A History of Recorded Sound* (Cambridge: Cambridge University Press, 1995); Emily Thompson, "Machines, Music, and the Quest for Fidelity: Marketing the Edison Phonograph in America, 1877–1925," *Musical Quarterly* 79 (Spring 1995): 131–171; Michael Taussig, *Mimesis and Alterity: A Particular History of the Senses* (New York: Routledge, 1993), 193–235; William Howland Kenney, *Recorded Music in American Life: The Phonograph and Popular Memory, 1890–1945* (New York: Oxford University Press, 1999).

53. Samuel Morland, *Tuba Stentoro-Phonica, an Instrument of Excellent Use, as well at Sea, as at Land* (London: W. Godbid, 1672), 11, 14. On the speaking trumpet, see Gouk, "Acoustics in the Early Royal Society," 164–165; Gouk, "Music in the Natural Philosophy," 104–107; Hunt, *Origins*, 121–129; H. W. Dickinson, *Sir Samuel Morland, Diplomat and Inventor, 1625–1695* (Cambridge: Newcomen Society, 1970), 40–45; Young, *Enquiry*, 49–57. On the Kircher-Morland dispute, see especially Beckmann, *History of Inventions*, 1: 152–166.

54. Fontenelle, *History of Oracles*, 103, 107, 109, 131; Fontenelle, *Histoire des oracles*, 109. Van Dale also discussed the use of speaking trumpets and other acoustic devices, though without naming Morland. See van Dale, *De oraculis*, 195, and the commentary to the plates adjoining pp. 141, 195.

55. Baltus, *Answer*, 119, 127, 147–153.

56. Ibid., 149–153; Baltus, *Continuation*, 197, 209–211, 217–219; Thomas Brown, *The Works of Mr. Thomas Brown, Serious and Comical, in Prose and Verse*, 7th ed., 4 vols. (London: Edward Midwinter, 1730), 3: 257; Voltaire, *Philosophical Dictionary*, in *Works*, 12: 92, 98.

57. E. Cobham Brewer, *Sound and Its Phenomena* (Boston: Ditson, 1885), 123–124; Joseph Farington, *The Farington Diary*, ed. James Greig, 8 vols. (London: Hutchinson, 1922–1928), 2: 116. For Brewer's extension of this knowledge to the oracles, see pp. 126, 165. For this technology's expansion in the early decades of the nineteenth century, see also John Ayrton Paris, *Philosophy in Sport Made Science in Earnest*, 3 vols. (London: Longman, Rees, Orme, Brown, and Green, 1827), 2: 219; W. H. C. Bartlett, *Elements of Natural Philosophy* (New York: Barnes, 1852), 91. For Kircher's bellwether use of the speaking tube as a mechanism of both access and distance, see Paula Findlen, *Possessing Nature: Museums, Collecting, and Scientific Culture in Early Modern Italy* (Berkeley: University of California Press, 1994), 107, 121, 128. For Laënnec's description of his sense of the social awkwardness of applying his own ear and his desire for a mediating instrument, see R. T. H. Laënnec, *A Treatise on the Diseases of the Chest, in Which They Are Described According to Their Anatomical Characters and Their Diagnosis Established on a New Principle by Means of Acoustick Instruments*, trans. John Forbes (London: Underwood, 1821), 284–285.

58. Jeremy Bentham, *Panopticon; Or, The Inspection-House*, in *The Works of Jeremy Bentham*, ed. John Bowring (Edinburgh: Tait, 1843), 4: 41, 44–45, 66, 84–85; Morland, *Tuba Stentoro-Phonica*, 14; Erasmus Darwin, *The Temple of Nature; Or, the Origin of Society: A Poem, with Philosophical Notes* (London, 1802; London: Jones, 1824), 98.

59. Bentham, *Panopticon*, 4: 41, 44–45, 66, 84–85; Jean Etienne Dominique Esquirol, *Mental Maladies: A Treatise on Insanity*, trans. E. K. Hunt (Philadelphia: Lea and Blanchard, 1845), 40; Pinchbeck, *Witchcraft*, 70–71. On the use of acoustic tubes in entertainments in the decade before Bentham's work, see Philip Thicknesse, *The Speaking Figure, and the Automaton Chess-Player, Exposed and Detected* (London: Stockdale, 1784), 4–8.

60. William Gardiner, *The Music of Nature* (London, 1832; Boston: Ditson, 1837), 361–364; Brewster, *Letters*, 158–164. See also Day Francis, *New Hocus Pocus; Or, The Whole Art of Legerdemain* (Philadelphia: Nathaniel Hickman, 1818), 6–7; John Millington, *An Epitome of the Elementary Principles of Mechanical Philosophy* (London: Simpkin and Marshall, 1830), 209–210; "Eusèbe Salverte on the Occult Sciences," *North British Review* 3 (May 1845): 23; George W. Kirbye, *Origin and History of Ventriloquism, with Full and Comprehensive Instruction in the Art* (Philadelphia: Brinckloe, 1861), 35, 40–42; John Henry Anderson, *The Fashionable Science of Parlour Magic* (London: Strand, 1855), vi, 39. The Invisible Girl, along with other speaking figures and automata, is discussed in Richard D. Altick, *The Shows of London* (Cambridge, Mass.: Harvard University Press, 1978), 67–68, 352–356.

61. Elihu Palmer, *Principles of Nature* (London: Carlile, 1823), 71; J. F. W. Herschel, "Sound," in Edward Smedley, ed., *Encyclopaedia Metropolitana; Or, Universal Dictionary of Knowledge*, 2 vols. (London: Baldwin and Cradock, 1829–1830), 2: 753–754; Benjamin Rush, *Medical Inquiries and Observations upon the Diseases of the Mind* (Philadelphia: Kimber and Richardson, 1812), 330–331; Edmund Burke, *A Philo-*

sophical Enquiry into the Origins of Our Ideas of the Sublime and Beautiful, ed. Adam Phillips (Oxford: Oxford University Press, 1990), 75; Gardiner, *Music of Nature,* 25.

62. Charles G. Page, *Psychomancy: Spirit-Rappings and Table-Tippings Exposed* (New York: Appleton, 1853), 9, 42, 55, 58–59. On the acoustic lectures of Page and others, see Kenneth Walter Cameron, ed., *The Massachusetts Lyceum during the American Renaissance* (Hartford: Transcendental Books, 1969), 16–18, 51, 124–125, 127, 195.

63. John Tyndall, *Sound* (New York: D. Appleton, 1867), 9, 81. On hydrogen gas experiments, see "Des Effets du gaz hydrogène sur la voix," *Journal de physique, de chimie, d'histoire naturelle et des arts* 48 (1799): 459; Herschel, "Sound," 766. For discussion of Tyndall's views on prayer and miracles, see Robert Bruce Mullin, *Miracles and the Modern Religious Imagination* (New Haven: Yale University Press, 1996), 40–46. On his lectures, see Charles A. Taylor, "John Tyndall's Demonstrations on Sound, 1854–1882," *Proceedings of the Royal Institution of Great Britain* 48 (1975): 37–62; Miller, *Anecdotal History,* 80–81. On nitrous oxide demonstrations, see Ellen Hickey Grayson, "Social Disorder and Psychological Disorder: Laughing Gas Demonstrations, 1800–1850," in Rosemarie Garland Thomason, ed., *Freakery: Cultural Spectacles of the Extraordinary Body* (New York: New York University Press, 1996), 108–120.

64. Thomas Moore, *The Poetical Works of Thomas Moore,* 10 vols. (London: Longman, 1840), 2: 32–35; Thomas De Quincey, *Essays on Christianity, Paganism, and Superstition* (New York: Hurd and Houghton, 1878), 465–532 (quotation is on p. 497). On Moore's poem, see also Altick, *Shows,* 353.

65. John La Farge, *The Gospel Story in Art* (New York: Macmillan, 1913), 19–20, 50.

66. Elihu Vedder, *Doubt and Other Things* (Boston: Porter Sargent, 1922), 21. The key secondary work on Vedder, which includes a complete catalogue of his paintings, is Regina Soria, *Elihu Vedder: American Visionary Artist in Rome, 1836–1923* (Rutherford, N.J.: Fairleigh Dickinson University Press, 1970). See also Regina Soria, Joshua C. Taylor, Jane Dillenberger, and Richard Murray, *Perceptions and Evocations: The Art of Elihu Vedder* (Washington, D.C.: Smithsonian Institution Press, 1979); Nola H. Tutag, "A Reconstruction of the Career of Elihu Vedder Based upon the Unpublished Letters and Documents of the Artist, His Family, and Correspondents Held by the Archives of American Art," Ed.D. diss., Wayne State University, 1969; Abraham A. Davidson, *The Eccentrics and Other American Visionary Painters* (New York: E. P. Dutton, 1978), 63–66, 77–83; Gail Gelburd, *Elihu Vedder: Mystic Figures of the Nineteenth Century* (Hempstead, N.Y.: Hofstra Museum, 1989). Vedder's papers, consisting mostly of correspondence, drafts of his literary manuscripts, family photographs, and miscellaneous clippings, are in the Archives of American Art, Smithsonian Institution, Washington, D.C. The few journals (for 1878, 1882, 1889–1890) add little to our understanding of his religious life; they are mostly terse jottings about travels, visitors, the weather, and the like.

67. Elihu Vedder, *The Digressions of V.* (Boston: Houghton Mifflin, 1910), 42–44, 48, 64–65.

68. Ibid., 19–20.

69. Ibid., 40–41.

70. Ibid., 61, 75–76.

71. Ibid., 75–76.

72. Vedder, *Doubt,* 140.

73. Vedder, *Digressions,* 451–454. On the New-York Historical Society exhibition, see Joshua C. Taylor, "Perceptions and Digressions," in Soria, Taylor, Dillenberger, and Murray, *Perceptions,* 58. More generally, see Richard G. Carrott, *The Egyptian Revival: Its Sources, Monuments, and Meaning, 1808–1858* (Berkeley: University of California Press, 1978); Timothy Mitchell, *Colonising Egypt* (Cambridge: Cambridge University Press, 1988), esp. 1–33. For a tourist's fascination with the Sphinx and the desert (and specifically with Vedder's imagination of both), see Amelia B. Edwards, *A Thousand Miles Up the Nile* (London: G. Routledge and Sons, 1891), xvi–xvii, 489–492.

74. James Jackson Jarves, *The Art-Idea,* ed. Benjamin Rowland, Jr. (Cambridge, Mass.: Harvard University Press, 1960), 200.

75. Elihu Vedder, *Miscellaneous Moods in Verse* (Boston: Porter Sargent, 1914), unpaginated (poem 16); Vedder, *Digressions,* 452; Vedder, *Doubt,* 44; Brewster, *Letters,* 234–240. On the sounds and silence of the statue of Memnon, see G. W. Bowersock, "The Miracle of Memnon," *Bulletin of the American Society of Papyrologists* 21 (1984): 21–32; Gross, *Dream of the Moving Statue,* 163–166.

76. Vedder, *Digressions,* 89, 197. There is also a scarcely whispered prayer in Vedder, *Miscellaneous Moods,* poem 63.

77. Vedder, *Doubt,* 42, 136; Vedder, *Miscellaneous Moods,* unpaginated (poem 60 and author's note to "Phonetics").

78. Vedder, *Digressions,* 42, 136, 318–320, 451; Vedder, *Doubt,* 42, 51, 53; Vedder, *Miscellaneous Moods,* unpaginated (poems 16 and 30).

79. On the Pabst episode, see Soria, *Elihu Vedder,* 246; Tutag, "Reconstruction," 244, 246–247, 249; Elihu Vedder to Caroline Vedder, 25 February 1896, 5 March 1896, 8 March 1896, 19 March 1896, 11 April 1896, Vedder Papers.

80. Bacon, *Works,* 1: 166.

81. Fontenelle, *History of the Oracles,* 164.

82. Poulsen, "Talking, Weeping and Bleeding Sculptures," 182–185. In his book on Delphi, Poulsen had downplayed the political trickery of "shrewd priests" and relied instead on the psychology of "hysterical affections, which in every religion make women serviceable media." See Frederik Poulsen, *Delphi,* trans. G. C. Richards (London: Gylendal, 1920), 24–25.

4. How to Become a Ventriloquist

1. William Frederick Pinchbeck, *The Expositor; Or, Many Mysteries Unravelled* (Boston: n.p., 1805), A2, 31–35, 38–40, 53–60, 81–82, 90–91 (quotations are on pp. A2, 35). For the geographic range of Rannie and other performers, see Charles Joseph Pecor, *The Magician on the American Stage, 1752–1874* (Washington, D.C.: Emerson and West, 1977).

2. "Voice," *Boston Medical Intelligencer,* 22 July 1823, 39; "Ventriloquism," *Boston Medical Intelligencer,* 31 August 1824, 67; Pinchbeck, *Expositor,* 53–54, 60.

3. Joseph Glanvill, *Saducismus Triumphatus; Or, Full and Plain Evidence Concerning Witches and Apparitions,* 2 vols. (London: J. Collins, 1681), 2: 64. Ventriloquism's history has been told primarily by practitioners. By far the best example of that genre is Valentine Vox, *I Can See Your Lips Moving: The History and Art of Ventriloquism* (Tadworth, Surrey, 1981; North Hollywood, Calif.: Plato Publishing, 1993). Ventriloquists also receive some notice in Hillel Schwartz's encyclopedic pastiche of twins and simulations. See Hillel Schwartz, *The Culture of the Copy: Striking Likenesses, Unreasonable Facsimiles* (New York: Zone Books, 1996), 132–137. Otherwise the scholarship is dominated by literary theorists, who, interested in the polyphony of discrepant "voices" within texts and in the varied problems of authorial voice, have taken up ventriloquism as a trope. See, for example, Annabel Patterson, "'They Say' or We Say: Protest and Ventriloquism in Early Modern England," in Janet Levarie Smarr, ed., *Historical Criticism and the Challenge of Theory* (Urbana: University of Illinois Press, 1993), 145–166; David Goldblatt, "Ventriloquism: Ecstatic Exchange and the History of Artwork," *Journal of Aesthetics and Art Criticism* 51 (1993): 389–398; Christopher Looby, *Voicing America: Language, Literary Form, and the Origins of the United States* (Chicago: University of Chicago Press, 1996), 165–174; and Elizabeth D. Harvey, *Ventriloquized Voices: Feminist Theory and English Renaissance Texts* (London: Routledge, 1992).

4. Ian Hacking, *Rewriting the Soul: Multiple Personality and the Sciences of Memory* (Princeton: Princeton University Press, 1995), esp. 142–158. See also Michael G. Kenny, *The Passion of Ansel Bourne: Multiple Personality in American Culture* (Washington, D.C.: Smithsonian Institution, 1986).

5. Reginald Scot, *The Discoverie of Witchcraft* (London, 1584; rpt. London: Rowan and Littlefield, 1973), 101. For multiple uses of the term in late antiquity and in medieval Europe, see Vox, *History and Art,* 11–39. The early modern vocabulary for soothsaying and divination was very rich; other terms used for a person given to prophetic, demonic, or ventriloquial speech included "ob," "python" or "pythonist," "engastrimyth," and "gastriloquist." Two other related terms for divination by the belly included "gastromancy" and "hariolation." See Thomas Blount, *Glossographia; Or, A Dictionary, Interpreting All Such Hard Words, Whether Hebrew, Greek, Latin, Italian, Spanish, French, Teutonick, Belgick, British or Saxon, as Are Now Used in Our Refined English Tongue* (London: Newcomb, 1656) as well as the pertinent entries in the *Oxford English Dictionary.*

6. For background on the problems the Witch of Endor created for Christian commentaries, see Valerie I. J. Flint, *The Rise of Magic in Early Medieval Europe* (Princeton: Princeton University Press, 1991), esp. 18–21, 54–56; Lynn Thorndike, *A History of Magic and Experimental Science,* 8 vols. (New York: Columbia University Press, 1923–1958), 1: 352, 448, 470–471.

7. Scot, *Discoverie,* 114, 121; Glanvill, *Saducismus,* 2: 64.

8. On possession as "sacred theater," see Clarke Garrett, *Spirit Possession and Popular Religion: From the Camisards to the Shakers* (Baltimore: Johns Hopkins University Press, 1987), esp. 4–6, 86–87.

9. For these well-known cases, see David D. Hall, ed., *Witch-Hunting in Seventeenth-Century New England: A Documentary History, 1638–1692* (Boston: Northeastern

University Press, 1991), 149, 202, 207–211, 225–229; Increase Mather, *An Essay for the Recording of Illustrious Providences* (Boston: n.p., 1684), 140. For English and European examples, see C. L'Estrange Ewen, *Witchcraft and Demonianism* (London: Heath Cranton, 1933), 148–149, 336, 452; Michael MacDonald, *Mystical Bedlam: Madness, Anxiety, and Healing in Seventeenth-Century England* (Cambridge: Cambridge University Press, 1981), 198–202; Jean Bodin, *On the Demon-Mania of Witches*, trans. Randy A. Scott (Toronto: Centre for Reformation and Renaissance Studies, 1995), 109. For a reading of these New England cases that insightfully highlights the vocality of possession, including its ventriloquial dimensions, see Jane Kamensky, *Governing the Tongue: The Politics of Speech in Early New England* (New York: Oxford University Press, 1997), 150–179.

10. Thomas Ady, *A Perfect Discovery of Witches* (London: Brome, 1661), 78.

11. Thomas Hobbes, *Leviathan; Or, The Matter, Form, and Power of a Commonwealth Ecclesiastical and Civil,* in *The English Works of Thomas Hobbes of Malmesbury,* 11 vols. (London: Bohn, 1839–1845), 3: 434; Francis Hutchinson, *An Historical Essay Concerning Witchcraft* (London: Knaplock, 1718), 8–9.

12. Blount, *Glossographia,* s.v. "ventriloquist"; John Wesley, *Letter to the Author of "The Enthusiasm of Methodists and Papists Compared"* (1749), in *The Works of the Rev. John Wesley, A.M.,* 14 vols. (London: Wesleyan Conference, 1872), 9: 7; Franklin Bowditch Dexter, ed., *The Literary Diary of Ezra Stiles, D.D., L.L.D., President of Yale College,* 3 vols. (New York: Scribner's 1901), 1: 386, 403; Frederick H. Quitman, *A Treatise on Magic; Or, On the Intercourse between Spirits and Men* (Albany: Balance, 1810), 45–48; Robert Scott, *Letters to the Rev. Frederick H. Quitman, Occasioned by His Late Treatise on Magic* (Poughkeepsie, N.Y.: Adams, 1810), 26–29. Demonic taunts, altered voices, and motionless lips remained common in accounts of exorcism in the twentieth century, so again what is at issue is not the expunging of religious frameworks, but the development of increasingly powerful alternative discourses. In one instance from Wisconsin in 1928, the officiating priest noted that there "was not the slightest sign that the lips moved" in the possessed girl, that it "was possible for these evil spirits to speak in an audible manner from somewhere within the girl." See the cases in Adam Crabtree, *Multiple Man: Explorations in Possession and Multiple Personality* (New York: Praeger, 1985), 95–106 (quotation is on p. 97). See also Michael Cuneo, "Exorcism in American Culture: Two Case Studies," paper presented 5 March 1999, Center for the Study of American Religion, Princeton University.

13. Joannes Baptista de La Chapelle, *Institutions de géométrie,* 2 vols. (Paris: Debure, 1757), 1: 10–18, 39–45; Joannes Baptista de La Chapelle, *Traité de la construction théorique et practique du scaphandre, ou du bateau de l'homme* (Paris: Debure, 1775). In the latter work (pp. 1–8) La Chapelle also uses the occasion to reassert his basic propositions about ventriloquism.

14. Joannes Baptista de La Chapelle, *Traité des sections coniques, et autres courbes anciennes* (Paris: Debure, 1765), i–ii, 113–120, 203–206; Johann Beckmann, *A History of Inventions and Discoveries,* trans. William Johnston, 4 vols. (London: Longman, Hurst, Rees, Orme, and Brown, 1817), 1: 166.

15. For the author's notation on La Chapelle in *Wieland,* see Charles Brockden

Brown, *Wieland; Or, The Transformation and Memoirs of Carwin, the Biloquist*, ed. Emory Elliott (Oxford: Oxford University Press, 1994), 181n–182n. For the 1799 pamphlet, see *Amusement-Hall; Or, A Collection of Diverting Stories, and Extraordinary Facts, with an Account of the Art of Ventriloquism, and Other Entertaining Matter* (Morristown, N.J.: n.p., 1799), 10–19. For the influence on Salverte, see Eusèbe Salverte, *The Occult Sciences: The Philosophy of Magic, Prodigies and Apparent Miracles*, trans. Anthony Todd Thomson, 2 vols. (Paris, 1829; London: Bentley, 1846), 1: 157–162, 283–284. Brewster, Stewart, and the popular guides are discussed below. Suggestive of their wide dispersion in gentlemanly circles of learning, La Chapelle's tales of Saint-Gille's exploits also caught the attention of Yale's Ezra Stiles, who extracted them at length. See "Anecdotes Relative to Ventriloquism," 23 May 1782, Ezra Stiles Papers, Beinecke Rare Book and Manuscript Library, Yale University.

16. After ventriloquism became popular on stage, various others followed up La Chapelle's treatise with their own investigations of the acoustics and physiology of the art. See, for example, John Gough, "Facts and Observations to Explain the Curious Phenomenon of Ventriloquism," *Journal of Natural Philosophy, Chemistry, and the Arts* 2 (June 1802): 122–129; F. M. S. Lespagnol, *Dissertation sur l'engastrimisme* (Paris: Didot Jeune, 1811); Anthelme Richerand, *Elements of Physiology*, trans. G. J. M. De Lys (Philadelphia: Dobson, 1813), 506–507; "Voice," *Boston Medical Intelligencer*, 39; "Ventriloquism," *Boston Medical Intelligencer*, 67; John Mason Good, *The Book of Nature* (Boston, 1826; Hartford: Belknap and Hamersley, 1845), 257–262; George Smith Sutton, *A Treatise on Ventriloquism, with Extracts from the Opinions of Several Authors Respecting that Extraordinary Gift of Human Faculty* (New Haven: n.p., 1833); Robert Tolefree, Jr., "The Voice and Its Modifications (More Particularly Ventriloquism) Briefly Considered," *American Journal of Science and Arts* 26 (1834): 76–83.

17. Joannes Baptista de La Chapelle, *Le Ventriloque, ou l'engastrimythe* (London and Paris: Duchesne, 1772), 341, 471–478.

18. Ibid., xxi, 323–360, 419–422, 438–439.

19. Dugald Stewart, *The Works of Dugald Stewart*, 7 vols. (Cambridge: Hilliard and Brown, 1829), 1: 108, 137–151, 159.

20. Ibid., 3: 166–171; David Brewster, *Letters on Natural Magic* (London: John Murray, 1842), 167, 171–172. For the point that the illusion was less about acoustics than the misdirection of the imagination, Stewart was drawing especially on an anonymous review of John Gough's "An Investigation of the Method Whereby Men Judge, by the Ear, of the Position of Sonorous Bodies, Relative to Their Own Persons." The assessment had appeared in *Edinburgh Review* 2 (April 1803): 192–196.

21. Brown, *Wieland*, 32, 69–70, 152, 165. *Wieland* is among the most widely commented upon novels of the early national era, but scholars have been imprecise in contextualizing the book's central illusionist practice of ventriloquism and the religious implications that flow from it. For a basic contextualization of this dimension of the novel, see "Historical Essay," in Charles Brockden Brown, *The Novels and Related Works of Charles Brockden Brown*, ed. Sydney J. Krause, S. W. Reid, and Alexander Cowie, vol. 1, Bicentennial edition (Kent State: Kent State University Press, 1977), 325–326. Readings that I have found especially insightful for my purposes include: Jay Fliegelman, *Prodigals and Pilgrims: The American Revolution against*

Patriarchal Authority, 1750–1800 (Cambridge: Cambridge University Press, 1982), 235–248; Jane Tompkins, *Sensational Designs: The Cultural Work of American Fiction, 1790–1860* (New York: Oxford University Press, 1985), 40–61; Steven Watts, *The Romance of Real Life: Charles Brockden Brown and the Origins of American Culture* (Baltimore: Johns Hopkins University Press, 1994), esp. 54–58, 82–89, 184–185; Bernard Rosenthal, "The Voices of *Wieland*," in *Critical Essays on Charles Brockden Brown*, ed. Bernard Rosenthal (Boston: G. K. Hall, 1981), 104–125. Watts does an especially fine job of locating the novel within Brown's wider deistic suspicions about revealed religion. For a subsequent romance featuring a rogue ventriloquist who plays on the "superstitions" of the credulous, see Henry Cockton, *Life and Adventures of Valentine Vox, the Ventriloquist* (London: R. Tyas, 1840). A more famous descendant of Carwin is L. Frank Baum's Wizard of Oz, who also used ventriloquism as a technique of mystification. See L. Frank Baum, *The Wonderful Wizard of Oz* (New York: Signet Classic, 1984), 100–103, 156–157.

22. Brown, *Wieland*, 194, 234.

23. Ibid., 163, 243; La Chapelle, *Le Ventriloque*, 341, 478.

24. Brown, *Wieland*, 243.

25. Brewster, *Letters*, 5, 176–178; Stewart, *Works*, 3: 171–173; Dugald Stewart, "Observations on Ventriloquism," *Edinburgh Journal of Science* 9 (1828): 250–252. For the original account, see George Francis Lyon, *The Private Journal of Captain G. F. Lyon of H.M.S. Hecla, during the Recent Voyage of Discovery under Captain Parry* (London: Murray, 1825), 149–150, 359–374.

26. Vladimir Bogoraz, *The Chukchee*, in *Memoirs of the American Museum of Natural History*, vol. 11 (Leiden, 1904–1909; New York: AMS, 1975), 435–439. See also Sutton, *Treatise*, 26–29; Elisha Kent Kane, *Arctic Explorations in the Years 1853, 1854, 1855*, 2 vols. (Philadelphia: Childs and Peterson, 1856), 2: 126–127; W. H. Davenport Adams, *Curiosities of Superstition, and Sketches of Some Unrevealed Religions* (London: Masters, 1882), 274–278; Daniel G. Brinton, "The Folk-Lore of Yucatan," *Folk-Lore Journal* 1 (1883): 249. On the construction of shamanism, see Gloria Flaherty, *Shamanism and the Eighteenth Century* (Princeton: Princeton University Press, 1992). On the making of fetishism, see Frank E. Manuel, *The Eighteenth Century Confronts the Gods* (Cambridge, Mass.: Harvard University Press, 1959), 184–209.

27. *Ventriloquism Explained; And Juggler's Tricks, or Legerdemain Exposed; With Remarks on Vulgar Superstitions* (Amherst: J. S. and C. Adams, 1834), unpaginated preface, x, 9, 39–40, 56, 77–78, 82–83, 114–115; "Blitz and the Darkies," *Flag of the Union*, 1 February 1851, reprinted in *Everybody a Ventriloquist: A History of Ventriloquism, with Instructions and Anecdotes Combined* (Philadelphia: Brown's, 1856), 24–25. On Potter's racial identity (he is said to have passed as "an East Indian," which would have been useful for selling his magic, and to have carefully concealed his own background), see John R. Eastman, *History of the Town of Andover, New Hampshire, 1751–1906*, 2 vols. (Concord, N.H.: Rumford, 1910), 1: 425–427; Pecor, *Magician on the American Stage*, 69–71. When one ventriloquist advertised a special show in 1802 for black Philadelphians, he was forced to cancel the performance. See Pecor, *Magician on the American Stage*, 88–89.

28. See *Everybody a Ventriloquist: Ventriloquism Made Easy, Also an Exposure of*

Magic (Philadelphia: Wyman the Wizard, 1860); Kirbye, *Origin and History*; Thomas D. Hurst, *The Practical Magician, and Ventriloquist's Guide* (New York: Hurst, 1876); Harry Kennedy, *How to Become a Ventriloquist* (New York: Tousey, 1891); Baum, *Wonderful Wizard*, 156–157.

29. Paul Garnault, *History of Ventriloquism*, trans. George Havelock Helm (Brooklyn: n.p., 1900?), 8, 32, 41–42.

30. Francis Bacon, *The Works of Francis Bacon*, ed. James Spedding, Robert Leslie Ellis, and Douglas Denon Heath, 14 vols. (London, 1857–1874; Stuttgart: Frommann, 1963), 3: 156, 162, 164.

31. See *Breslaw's Last Legacy; Or, The Magical Companion*, 5th ed. (London: Lane, 1791), viii–ix; Beckmann, *History of Inventions*, 3: 269–270; William Hooper, *Rational Recreations in Which the Principles of Numbers and Natural Philosophy Are Clearly and Copiously Elucidated*, 4 vols. (London: Davis, 1774); Philip Astley, *Natural Magic; Or, Physical Amusements Revealed* (London: n.p., 1785); Giuseppe Pinetti, *Physical Amusements and Diverting Experiments* (London: n.p., 1784); Henri Decremps, *The Conjurer Unmasked: Being a Clear and Full Explanation of all the Surprizing Performances Exhibited as Well in This Kingdom as on the Continent*, trans. Thomas Denton (London: Stalker, 1788).

32. P. T. Barnum, *The Humbugs of the World* (New York: Carleton, 1866), 294. Recent debates over magical decline versus continuity are reviewed in David D. Hall, "Introduction and Commentary," in Peter Benes, ed., *Wonders of the Invisible World, 1600–1900*, in *Annual Proceedings of the Dublin Seminar for New England Folklife*, vol. 17 (Boston: Boston University, 1995), 11–16. For the secondary work on rational recreations and illusionist demonstrations, see note 11 above, in the Introduction.

33. For the magic lantern and the ghost shows, see X. Theodore Barber, "Phantasmagorical Wonders: The Magic Lantern Ghost Show in Nineteenth-Century America," *Film History* 3 (1989): 73–86 (playbill on p. 79); Xenophon Theodore Barber, "Evenings of Wonders: A History of the Magic Lantern Show in America," 2 vols., Ph.D. diss., New York University, 1993; Pecor, *Magician on the American Stage*, 85–86, 104–112; Erik Barnouw, *The Magician and the Cinema* (New York: Oxford University Press, 1981), 19–34; Terry Castle, "Phantasmagoria: Spectral Technology and the Metaphorics of Modern Reverie," *Critical Inquiry* 15 (Autumn 1988): 26–61; Frederick Burwick, "Science and Supernaturalism: Sir David Brewster and Sir Walter Scott," *Comparative Criticism* 13 (1991): 83–114; Altick, *Shows*, 117, 217–220; Robert M. Isherwood, *Farce and Fantasy: Popular Entertainment in Eighteenth-Century Paris* (New York: Oxford University Press, 1986), 50–52, 199–201; Thomas L. Hankins and Robert J. Silverman, *Instruments and the Imagination* (Princeton: Princeton University Press, 1995), 37–71. For Robertson's own account, see Etienne Gaspard Robertson, *Mémoires récréatifs scientifiques et anecdotiques*, 2 vols. (Paris: n.p., 1831–1833), 1: 272–310. Like ventriloquism, phantasmagoria shows were also incorporated into the natural history of superstition. See Salverte, *Occult Sciences*, 1: 265–292; Brewster, *Letters*, 5–6, 57–85.

34. Thomas Paine, *The Age of Reason*, in *The Complete Writings of Thomas Paine*, ed. Philip S. Foner, 2 vols. (New York: Citadel, 1945), 1: 508.

35. Vox, *History and Art*, 41–48; Isherwood, *Farce*, 197–198; Altick, *Shows*, 36.

36. On puppets and witchcraft, see Scott Cutler Shershow, *Puppets and "Popular" Culture* (Ithaca: Cornell University Press, 1995), 34–37.

37. The best study of stage magic in North America for this period is Pecor, *Magician on the American Stage*. Also, for a very useful compilation of materials from Boston newspapers, see H. J. Moulton, *Houdini's History of Magic in Boston, 1792–1915* (Glenwood, Ill.: Meyerbooks, 1983), 1–44.

38. *Columbian Centinel*, 14 July 1804, 3. See also John Rannie, *The European Ventriloquist's Exhibition* (Portsmouth, N.H.: S. Whidden, 1808). For Rannie's shows within the wider theatrical history of the period, see David Grimsted, *Melodrama Unveiled: American Theater and Culture, 1800–1850* (Chicago: University of Chicago Press, 1968), 100–101; George C. D. Odell, *Annals of the New York Stage*, 15 vols. (New York: Columbia University Press, 1927–1949), 2: 143–144, 209–210, 344.

39. *Columbian Centinel*, 1 August 1804, 3; "Rannie's Exhibition," *Prospect; Or, View of the Moral World*, 19 May 1804, 191–192; Elihu Palmer, *Principles of Nature* (London: Carlile, 1823), 61–62, 71; *Aurora General Advertiser*, 14 April 1810, 3; *New-York Evening Post*, 7 March 1810, 3; Rannie, *European Ventriloquist's Exhibition*, 7. Rannie had been noticed as a potential ally for Palmer as early as 1802. See "On Fortune-Telling," *Temple of Reason*, 12 June 1802, 154.

40. "Love's Ignes Fatui," Scrapbook 2/108, Harry Price Library, University of London; John Ayrton Paris, *Philosophy in Sport Made Science in Earnest* (London, 1827; Philadelphia: Lea and Blanchard, 1847).

41. For Barnum's Shakers, see the handbill in Philip B. Kunhardt, Jr., Philip B. Kunhardt, III, and Peter W. Kunhardt, *P. T. Barnum: America's Greatest Showman* (New York: Knopf, 1995), 76.

42. On the "Anti-Spiritualist Illusions," see Magic Trade Catalogues, 3 vols., Harry Price Library, University of London. On the skeptical magicians, see Edward P. Hingston, *The Genial Showman, Being the Reminiscences of the Life of Artemus Ward* (New York: Harper and Brothers, 1870), 107–111; George W. Kirbye, *Origin and History of Ventriloquism, with Full and Comprehensive Instruction in the Art* (Philadelphia: Brinckloe, 1861), 4–9, 14, 35–42; Jean Robert-Houdin, "The Secrets of Stage Conjuring," 1880, Magazine Magic, Harry Price Library, University of London; John Henry Anderson, *The Fashionable Science of Parlour Magic* (London: Strand, 1855), iv–vii, 65–72, 88–95; John Nevil Maskelyne, *Modern Spiritualism* (London: Warne, 1876); James Webb, ed., *The Mediums and the Conjurors* (New York: Arno, 1976); Harry Houdini, *A Magician among the Spirits* (New York: Harper and Brothers, 1924); John Mulholland, *Beware Familiar Spirits* (New York: Scribner's, 1938); James Randi, *Conjuring: Being a Definitive Account of the Venerable Arts of Sorcery, Prestidigitation, Wizardry, Deception, and Chicanery and of the Mountebanks and Scoundrels who Have Perpetrated These Subterfuges on a Bewildered Public* (New York: St. Martin's, 1992); Joe Nickell, *Looking for a Miracle: Weeping Icons, Relics, Stigmata, Visions, and Healing Cures* (Buffalo: Prometheus, 1993).

43. *The Davenport Brothers, the World-Renowned Spiritual Mediums: Their Biography and Adventures in Europe and America* (Boston: White, 1869), 32, 95, 98–100, 114–115,

391–392; T. L. Nichols, *A Biography of the Brothers Davenport* (London: Saunders, Otley, 1864), 47–48.

44. H. P. Blavatsky, *Isis Unveiled*, 2 vols. (New York, 1877; Wheaton, Ill.: Theosophical Publishing House, 1972), 1: 105; Walford Bodie, *Stage Stories* (London: Simpkin, 1908), 14–15, 127.

45. *Everybody a Ventriloquist*, 7; Charles G. Page, *Psychomancy: Spirit-Rappings and Table-Tippings Exposed* (New York: Appleton, 1853), 42–43, 58, 61–62, 68; Kirbye, *Origin and History*, 5–6; "Ventriloquism," *National Magazine* 2 (June 1853): 529; "Voice," *Boston Medical Intelligencer*, 39.

46. *New-York Commercial Advertiser*, 20 June 1808, 3; Ibid., 15 June 1808, 3.

47. On the larger issue of Christian amusements as well as the crisscrossing of religion and theater, see R. Laurence Moore, *Selling God: American Religion in the Marketplace of Culture* (New York: Oxford University Press, 1994), esp. 40–65, 90–117.

48. "M. Alexandre," broadside, Scrapbook 2/91, Harry Price Library, University of London; "Celebrated Ventriloquists," 1880–1881, Magazine Magic, Harry Price Library; Professor Lee, "How I Became a Ventriloquist," 1879, Magazine Magic, Harry Price Library. For the mounting emphasis on entertainment alone, see also "Soirees Magiques, . . . M. Bird! The Renowned Wizard, Necromancer and Ventriloquist," broadside, 1852, Connecticut Historical Society, Hartford; "Great Attraction! . . . Signor Marenetti, the Great Ventriloquist," broadside, 1852, American Antiquarian Society, Worcester, Mass.

49. See Vox, *History and Art*, esp. 90–133; Barnouw, *Magician and the Cinema*.

50. Edward B. Tylor, *Primitive Culture: Researches into the Development of Mythology, Philosophy, Religion, Language, Art and Custom*, 2 vols. (New York: Holt, 1889), 2: 132–134, 182.

51. Hingston, *Genial Showman*, 107; Randi, *Conjuring*, xiii.

52. Robert E. Blazek, *Using Ventriloquism in Christian Education* (Littleton, Colo.: Maher, 1976), 5–6, 32. See also Bill Boley, *The Gospel Ventriloquist: Five Gospel Ventriloquist Routines* (Hopkinsville, Ky.: Boley, 1986); William H. Andersen, *111 Ways to Use Ventriloquism in Church Work* (Littleton, Colo.: Maher, 1986); Cullen Murphy, "'Hey, Let Me Outta Here!'" *Atlantic Monthly* 264 (August 1989): 62–71. That this American Christianization of magical entertainment has roots well before the 1950s is evident in two mimeographed pamphlets in the Harry Price Library at the University of London that use conjuring tricks to illustrate gospel truths: T. V. Voorhees, *Magic for Ministers* (Venetia, Penn.: n.p., 1928); and T. V. Voorhees, *The Conjurer in the Church* (Venetia, Penn.: n.p., 1928). The Fellowship of Christian Magicians, founded at a Methodist church in San Francisco in 1953, is the most visible and long-lasting organization dedicated to this confluence. For its history, see the twenty-fifth anniversary issue of *Christian Conjurer* (vol. 22, July 1978). Christian ventriloquism is presented for the first time in that group's magazine in July 1957.

53. Thomas Reid, *Essays on the Intellectual Powers of Man*, in *The Works of Thomas Reid*, 4 vols. (Charlestown, Mass.: Etheridge, 1813), 2: 83, 309, 322. See also Francis Wayland, *The Elements of Intellectual Philosophy* (Boston: Phillips, Sampson, 1855), 52–53, 85–86. Wayland's account of the effectiveness of the ventriloquist's illusion

undercuts the discriminating power that he adoringly ascribes to the ear, but he leaves this discrepancy unexplained. Stewart and Reid were both more careful.

54. Benjamin Rush, *Medical Inquiries and Observations, upon the Diseases of the Mind* (Philadelphia: Kimber and Richardson, 1812), 271–272; Eric Carlson, Jeffrey L. Wollock, and Patricia S. Noel, eds., *Benjamin Rush's Lectures on the Mind* (Philadelphia: American Philosophical Society, 1981), 351. Compare, for example, Edwards' dream of a new sensory order in heaven far exceeding that available to bodily eyes and ears. See Jonathan Edwards, *Ethical Writings*, ed. Paul Ramsey (New Haven: Yale University Press, 1989), 96–97, 378n, 380n.

55. Reid, *Works*, 2: 319–320; *Encyclopaedia Britannica; Or, A Dictionary of Arts, Sciences, and Miscellaneous Literature*, 18 vols. (Edinburgh, 1797; Philadelphia: Dobson, 1798), 18: 639–641 (emphasis added); La Chapelle, *Le Ventriloque*, 393, 400.

56. Stewart, *Works*, 3: 168–169; Carlson, Wollock, and Noel, eds., *Rush's Lectures*, 340.

57. Brown, *Wieland*, 108–109, 125.

58. Carlson, Wollock, and Noel, eds., *Rush's Lectures*, 254, 356–362, 379. Rush's epistemological eclecticism should be underlined. The Scottish psychology was a dominant source, but he was also drawing on more expressly empiricist models.

59. James McCosh, *The Senses, External and Internal* (Cambridge, Mass.: Riverside, 1882), 61–62; Thomas C. Upham, *Outlines of Imperfect and Disordered Mental Action* (New York: Harper and Brothers, 1840), 84–89, 106–108; Thomas C. Upham, *Elements of Mental Philosophy* (New York: Harper and Brothers, 1850), 93–97, 140–142.

60. Upham, *Outlines*, 85–86, 106–108; Thomas C. Upham, *Life and Religious Opinions and Experience of Madame de la Mothe Guyon*, 2 vols. (New York: Harper and Brothers, 1849), 1: 58; Thomas C. Upham, *Life of Madame Catharine Adorna* (Boston: Waite, Peirce, 1845), 146–147.

61. Key historical works on these themes include: Jean-Christophe Agnew, *Worlds Apart: The Market and the Theater in Anglo-American Thought, 1550–1750* (Cambridge: Cambridge University Press, 1986); Perez Zagorin, *Ways of Lying: Dissimulation, Persecution, and Conformity in Early Modern Europe* (Cambridge, Mass.: Harvard University Press, 1990); Karen Halttunen, *Confidence Men and Painted Women: A Study of Middle-Class Culture in America, 1830–1870* (New Haven: Yale University Press, 1982); Christopher Fox, *Locke and the Scriblerians: Identity and Consciousness in Early Eighteenth-Century Britain* (Berkeley: University of California Press, 1988); Kenny, *Passion of Ansel Bourne*; Charles Taylor, *Sources of the Self: The Making of Modern Identity* (Cambridge, Mass.: Harvard University Press, 1989); Roy Porter, ed., *Rewriting the Self: Histories from the Renaissance to the Present* (London: Routledge, 1997). The foundational discussion of personal identity and the self for the period is in John Locke, *An Essay Concerning Human Understanding*, ed. John W. Yolton, 2 vols. (London: Dent, 1961), 1: 280–293.

62. Reid, *Works*, 2: 319–320, 338–344, 357, 360. For an especially clear and concise statement of these Scottish propositions about the mind and personal identity, see John Abercrombie, *Inquiries Concerning the Intellectual Powers, and the Investigation of Truth* (New York: Harper, 1832), 68–69, 158–159.

63. Reid, *Works*, 2: 114, 319–320; "Askins, the Celebrated Ventriloquist," broadside, Harry Ransom Humanities Research Center, University of Texas, Austin. For the "inner voice" of Common-Sense moralists, see Charles Taylor, *The Ethics of Authenticity* (Cambridge: Harvard University Press, 1992), 25–26.

64. Robert Boyle, *Works*, ed. Thomas Birch, 6 vols. (Hildesheim, Germany: Olms, 1966), 6: 743; Reid, *Works*, 2: 320; Wayland, *Elements*, 51.

65. Brewster, *Letters*, 213–214.

66. Walter Scott, *The Poetical Works of Sir Walter Scott, with a Sketch of His Life* (Philadelphia: Crissy and Markley, 1848), 443; David Brewster, *A Treatise on the Kaleidoscope* (Edinburgh: Constable, 1819), 113.

67. William T. Moncrieff, *The Adventures of a Ventriloquist; Or, The Rogueries of Nicholas* (London: Duncombe, 1822), 4; J. L. Dargent, *Alexandre Vattemare: Artiste, promoteur des échanges internationaux de publications* (Brussels: n.p., 1976), 70, 85, 97. For images of Proteus in various tributes, see Dargent, *Vattemare*, 95, 100, 107. Vattemare is the only celebrity ventriloquist of the early nineteenth century to have been studied in any detail. Dargent tracks Vattemare's international itinerary through local newspaper accounts across Europe, Britain, and North America and reproduces many of these accounts. By the time Vattemare performed in the United States and Canada in 1839–1840, he had become more interested in a grand scheme for the international exchange of books than in ventriloquism—to the end, a man of the Enlightenment. On Vattemare, see also William B. Trask, "Necrology," *New England Historical and Genealogical Register* 19 (October 1865): 367–369.

68. Brewster, *Letters*, 175. For the repetition of Brewster's estimation of the effacement of personal identity, see *Black Art of Magic and Ventriloquism Combined* (New York: Benedict, n.d.), 16; *Everybody a Ventriloquist*, 6–7; Kirbye, *Origin and History*, 38. For further observations on vocal mutability, see Richerand, *Elements*, 507; "Ventriloquism, of the Celebrated Mr. Fitz James," *Omnium Gatherum* 1 (September 1810): 535–538; "Jonathan Harrington," *Gleason's Pictorial Drawing-Room Companion*, 15 May 1852, 320.

69. David Hume, *A Treatise of Human Nature*, ed. L. A. Selby-Bigge (Oxford: Clarendon, 1978), 252–253.

70. Stewart, *Works*, 3: 109, 111, 128, 134, 136, 159; Edmund Burke, *A Philosophical Enquiry into the Origins of Our Ideas of the Sublime and Beautiful*, ed. Adam Phillips (Oxford: Oxford University Press, 1990), 45. For thinking about issues of imitation, I have found especially suggestive the discussion of "mimetic desire" and "interdividual psychology" in Jean-Michel Oughourlian, *The Puppet of Desire: The Psychology of Hysteria, Possession, and Hypnosis*, trans. Eugene Webb (Stanford: Stanford University Press, 1991).

71. See "Anecdote of a Ventriloquist," *Massachusetts Magazine* 2 (June 1790): 359; "An Instance of Ventriloquism," *Weekly Magazine*, 30 June 1798, 277–278; ibid., 9 February 1799, 156; *Amusement-Hall*, 12–15; "Anecdote of a Ventriloquist," *Boston Weekly Magazine*, 20 September 1817, 199; "The Ventriloquist," *Ladies' Port Folio*, 29 January 1820, 37; "Ventriloquism," *Euterpeiad*, 7 July 1821, 59; "Anecdotes of Ventriloquism," *Albion*, 3 August 1822, 56; "The Ventriloquist; Or, A New Way of Getting

a Wife," *Ladies' Literary Cabinet,* 5 May 1821, 206; "Singular Story of a Ventriloquist, from the French," in Richard Cumberland, *The Inquisition; Or, Adventures of Nicolas Pedrosa* (Windsor, Vt.: Pomeroy and Hedge, 1816), 96–104; Margaret King Moore, *Stories of Old Daniel; Or, Tales of Wonder and Delight* (Boston: Munroe and Francis, 1830), 28–43. The 1790 article is another possible source for Charles Brockden Brown's tale. This French story was already circulating in England in the wake of La Chapelle's work. See "Anecdote of a Ventriloquist," *Universal Magazine,* 1785, in Scrapbook 21/42, Harry Houdini Collection, Library of Congress, Washington, D.C.

72. Watts especially emphasizes this theme of the fragmented or serial self in *Wieland.* See Watts, *Romance of Real Life,* 88–89.

73. On the Peales and ventriloquism, see David C. Ward and Sidney Hart, "Subversion and Illusion in the Life and Art of Raphaelle Peale," *American Art* 8 (Summer–Fall 1994): 106–107. On the issues of patriarchal authority, see Fliegelman, *Prodigals and Pilgrims,* 235–248.

74. Herman Melville, *The Confidence-Man: His Masquerade* (New York: Oxford University Press, 1989), 274, 296; A. Robert Lee, "Voices Off, On and Without: Ventriloquy in *The Confidence-Man,*" in *Herman Melville: Reassessments,* ed. A. Robert Lee (Totowa, N.J.: Vision, 1984), 157–175.

75. *Encyclopaedia Britannica,* 18: 640.

76. *Aurora General Advertiser,* 14 April 1810, 3; Rannie, *European Ventriloquist's Exhibition,* 7; William T. Moncrieff, *Memoirs and Anecdotes of Monsieur Alexandre, the Celebrated Dramatic Ventriloquist* (London: Lowndes, 1822), 7–9, 12, 27–32; *Voyages et séances anecdotiques de M. Comte* (Paris: J. G. Dentu, 1816), 2, 33–35, 103–115.

77. *Aurora General Advertiser,* 14 April 1810, 3; Rannie, *European Ventriloquist's Exhibition,* 3; George Smith, *Memoirs and Anecdotes of Mr. Love, the Polyphonist* (London: Kenneth, 1834), 7–10; "Third Week of Mr. Love," broadside, Boston 1840, American Antiquarian Society, Worcester; "Love's Ignes Fatui," and "Polyphonic Entertainments," broadsides, Scrapbook 2/108–109, Harry Price Library, University of London.

78. Antonio Blitz, *Life and Adventures of Signor Blitz* (Hartford: Belknap, 1872), 114–117.

79. Kenny, *Passion of Ansel Bourne,* 63–96 (Bourne quotation on p. 66); William James, *The Principles of Psychology,* 2 vols. (New York: Dover, 1950), 1: 294, 330, 391–393. For a good example of the shifting strands of religious and psychological frameworks, see William S. Plumer, "Mary Reynolds: A Case of Double Consciousness," *Harper's New Monthly Magazine* 20 (May 1860): 807–812. Plumer, a minister, wanted to make sense of Reynolds' "two souls" on expressly Christian grounds (as did Archibald Alexander, another investigator of her case), but the discussion was framed within the Scottish mental philosophy and the problem that divided consciousness posed to the Common-Sense verity of personal identity.

80. Upham, *Outlines,* 197. See also Abercrombie, *Inquiries,* 208–211, 256–261, 334–349.

81. Good, *Book of Nature,* 257–262; "Voice," *Boston Medical Intelligencer,* 39; "Ventriloquism," *Boston Medical Intelligencer,* 67; Lespagnol, *Dissertation.*

82. Helkiah Crooke, *Microcosmographia: A Description of the Body of Man* (London: Laggard, 1615), 573, 584, 602–604. The spread of Renaissance anatomy into the Enlightenment entails a vast literature. On the Renaissance "culture of dissection," see Jonathan Sawday, *The Body Emblazoned: Dissection and the Human Body in Renaissance Culture* (New York: Routledge, 1995). For its extension into the eighteenth century, see Barbara Maria Stafford, *Body Criticism: Imaging the Unseen in Enlightenment Art and Medicine* (Cambridge, Mass.: MIT Press, 1991). For good surveys of the ear's place in that enterprise, see Georg V. Békésy and Walter A. Rosenblith, "The Early History of Hearing: Observations and Theories," *Journal of the Acoustical Society of America* 20 (November 1948): 727–748; Alistair C. Crombie, "The Study of the Senses in Renaissance Science," *Proceedings of the International Congress of the History of Science* 1 (1964): 93–114; John W. Black, "Preface," in Joseph-Guichard Du Verney, *A Treatise of the Organ of Hearing* (New York: AMS, 1973). The most monumental medical history of the ear—its anatomy, diseases, and therapies from the ancients forward—remains Adam Politzer, *Geschichte der Ohrenheilkunde,* 2 vols. (Stuttgart, 1907–1913; Hildesheim, Germany: Georg Olms, 1967). The catalogue that Politzer includes of nineteenth-century American otologists (a specialist term of early Victorian coinage) is particularly noteworthy (2: 432–466).

83. Du Verney, *Treatise,* title page, iv, vii; Peter Kennedy, *Ophthalmographia; Or, A Treatise of the Eye, in Two Parts* (London: Lintott, 1713), 105. Kennedy included an appendix on the ear, drawing mostly on Du Verney, Schelhammer, and Antonio Valsalva.

84. Alexander Monro, *Three Treatises: On the Brain, the Eye, and the Ear* (Edinburgh: Bell and Bradfute, 1797), 221. Togno's hybrid compilation is the only American one in this list; it was published in Philadelphia by Seyfert and Phillips. But this European knowledge of the ear was widely shared by American medical men. There was, for example, a Philadelphia edition of the Saunders anatomy in 1821; there was also an American translation of Saissy's French essay by Nathan Ryno Smith, a medical professor at the University of Maryland, published in Baltimore in 1829. The latter included a supplement on the diseases of the external ear, penned by Smith himself, who was the son of one of the leading physicians and medical educators in the United States, Nathan Smith at Yale. See Oliver S. Hayward and Constance E. Putnam, *Improve, Perfect, and Perpetuate: Dr. Nathan Smith and Early American Medical Education* (Hanover, N.H.: University Press of New England, 1998), 255–257. Hence, Benjamin Rush's anatomical knowledge of the senses, including the ear, was hardly atypical. See Carlson, Wollock, and Noel, eds., *Rush's Lectures,* 315–351.

85. William Derham, *Physico-Theology; Or, A Demonstration of the Being and Attributes of God from His Works of Creation* (London: Innys, 1714), 137; William Paley, *Natural Theology; Or, Evidences of the Existence and Attributes of the Deity, Collected from the Appearances of Nature* (London, 1802; Boston: Gould, Kendall, and Lincoln, 1837), 27–31. Marveling at the excellence of God's creation through the body and its parts (including the ear) was standard in the Christian tradition, from patristic and medieval sources onward. See Elizabeth Sears, "The Iconography of

Auditory Perception in the Early Middle Ages: On Psalm Illustration and Psalm Exegesis," in Burnett, Fend, and Gouk, eds., *Second Sense*, 24–25; Elizabeth Sears,
"Sensory Perception and Its Metaphors in the Time of Richard of Fournival," in
W. F. Bynum and Roy Porter, eds., *Medicine and the Five Senses* (Cambridge: Cambridge University Press, 1993), 17–39. For a good historical overview of this
physico-theology, see John Hedley Brooke, "Science and Theology in the Enlightenment," in W. Mark Richardson and Wesley J. Wildman, eds., *Religion and Science:
History, Method, Dialogue* (New York: Routledge, 1996), 7–27.

86. John Trusler, *Twelve Sermons* (London: Legoux, 1796), sermons 1 and 2 (unpaginated).

87. Du Verney, *Treatise*, 70, 94; John Harrison Curtis, *A Treatise on the Physiology
and Diseases of the Ear* (London: Sherwood, Neely, and Jones, 1817), 60; Sawday, *Body
Emblazoned*, 128.

88. Curtis, *Treatise*, 65–66; John C. Saunders, *The Anatomy of the Human Ear*
(London: Phillips, 1806), 21–22. Curtis did pause briefly to reflect on how "the
nicety" of the ear's mechanism reflected well on the design of "a Supreme Being"
(pp. 15–16), and certainly many anatomists, including Charles Bell, still saw a theological dimension to their work. See Ludmilla Jordanova, "The Art and Science of
Seeing in Medicine: Physiognomy, 1780–1820," in Bynum and Porter, eds., *Medicine*,
130–133.

89. Du Verney, *Treatise*, 135–145.

90. David Tod, *The Anatomy and Physiology of the Organ of Hearing* (London:
Longman, 1832), 123; Joseph Williams, *Treatise on the Ear, Including Its Anatomy, Phys-
iology, and Pathology* (London: Churchill, 1840), 73–75, 205–208, 250–251. See also
Saunders, *Anatomy*, 27–28, 47–50; Curtis, *Treatise*, 56–60; J. A. Saissy, *An Essay on the
Diseases of the Internal Ear*, trans. Nathan R. Smith (Baltimore: Hatch and Dunning,
1829), 129–134; Joseph Toynbee, *The Diseases of the Ear: Their Nature, Diagnosis, and
Treatment* (London: Lewis, 1868), 363–365; Edmund Parish, *Hallucinations and Illusions: A Study of the Fallacies of Perception* (London: Scott, 1897), 122–123. Jonathan
Crary has emphasized the impact of anatomical knowledge on the subjectivizing
of vision in the early nineteenth century. Hearing parallels that story, though it
would be difficult to sustain the sort of radical disjunction in the history of perception
for which Crary is arguing. See Jonathan Crary, *Techniques of the Observer: On Vision
and Modernity in the Nineteenth Century* (Cambridge, Mass.: MIT Press, 1990), 69,
89–92.

91. John Haslam, *Observations on Insanity* (London: Rivington, 1798), 3, 5, 11,
47–49, 101. For a good sketch of Haslam's career, see Andrew Scull, Charlotte Mac-
Kenzie, and Nicholas Hervey, *Masters of Bedlam: The Transformation of the Mad-
Doctoring Trade* (Princeton: Princeton University Press, 1996), 10–47.

92. Locke, *Essay*, 2: 430–431. See MacDonald, *Mystical Bedlam*, 8–11, 168–172,
197–201, 225–226; Heyd, *"Be Sober and Reasonable,"* 6–10, 44–45, 203–205, 274–275;
Roy Porter, *Mind-Forg'd Manacles: A History of Madness in England from the Restoration to the Regency* (Cambridge, Mass.: Harvard University Press, 1987), 62–81; Hillel
Schwartz, *Knaves, Fools, Madmen, and that Subtle Effluvium: A Study of the Opposition*

to the French Prophets in England, 1706–1710 (Gainesville: University of Florida Press, 1978); Norman Dain, *Concepts of Insanity in the United States, 1789–1865* (New Brunswick, N.J.: Rutgers University Press, 1964), 183–193; Michel Foucault, *Madness and Civilization: A History of Insanity in the Age of Reason,* trans. Richard Howard (New York: Vintage, 1988), esp. 241–278.

93. Alexis de Tocqueville, *Democracy in America,* 2 vols. (New York: Vintage, 1945), 2: 142; Amariah Brigham, *Observations on the Influence of Religion upon the Health and Physical Welfare of Mankind* (Boston: Marsh, Capen, and Lyon, 1835), 182–184. See also Pliny Earle, *History, Description, and Statistics of the Bloomingdale Asylum for the Insane* (New York: Egbert, Hovey, and King, 1848), 28–29, 85, 96–97. For the American census surveys, see William Sims Bainbridge, "Religious Insanity in America: The Official Nineteenth-Century Theory," *Sociological Analysis* 45 (1984): 223–240. Brigham was much indebted to Dugald Stewart's discussion of sympathetic imitation for his views on revivals and enthusiasm.

94. William Battie, *A Treatise on Madness* (London: Whiston and White, 1758), 4–6, 58; Alexander Crichton, *An Inquiry into the Nature and Origin of Mental Derangement,* 2 vols. (London: Cadell, 1798), 1: 138, 195; 2: 55–65, 331, 342–343. See also Thomas Arnold, *Observations on the Nature, Kinds, Causes, and Prevention, of Insanity,* 2 vols. (London: Phillips, 1806), 1: 212–241.

95. Erasmus Darwin, *Zoonomia; Or, The Laws of Organic Life,* 2 vols. (London, 1794–1796; Dublin: Byrne, 1800), 2: 269–272, 278–279; Erasmus Darwin, *The Temple of Nature; Or, The Origin of Society: A Poem, with Philosophical Notes* (London, 1802; London: Jones, 1824), 98. On Darwin's views on religion, see Porter, *Mind-Forg'd Manacles,* 73–74.

96. Brown, *Wieland,* 164, 210–211, 219. Brown's novel is multilayered—a picture of the competing explanations available in the period for such religious phenomena. The authority of diagnoses like Darwin's is anything but straightforward in the text, though they do resonate with Brown's larger deistic views on revealed religion.

97. Rush, *Medical Inquiries,* 37, 45, 47, 71–72, 148, 158, 306–309, 331; Upham, *Outlines,* 84–89, 106–108. For Rush's educational and religious views, see Benjamin Rush, *The Autobiography of Benjamin Rush,* ed. George W. Corner (Princeton: Princeton University Press, 1948), 162–166, 220–221, 334–351. According to Rush, grief and love were higher sources of insanity—seven cases each—but religion surpassed onanism (three cases).

98. Alexandre Brierre de Boismont, *Hallucinations; Or, The Rational History of Apparitions, Visions, Dreams, Ecstasy, Magnetism, and Somnambulism* (Philadelphia, 1853; New York: Arno, 1976), ix–xii, 23, 407, 464. On the impact of visualist technologies on Boismont's views of hallucination, see Castle, "Phantasmagoria," 55–58.

99. Brierre de Boismont, *Hallucinations,* 77, 215, 383–386, 418.

100. Ibid., 80, 127, 172, 419–420. For subsequent use of ventriloquism in the medical discourse on female hysteria, see Janet Beizer, *Ventriloquized Bodies: Narratives of Hysteria in Nineteenth-Century France* (Ithaca: Cornell University Press, 1994), 9, 45–47.

101. Jean Etienne Dominique Esquirol, *Observations on the Illusions of the Insane, and on the Medico-Legal Question of Their Confinement*, trans. William Liddell (London: Renshaw and Rush, 1833), 2, 11–12, 71; Jean Etienne Dominique Esquirol, *Mental Maladies: A Treatise on Insanity*, trans. E. K. Hunt (Philadelphia: Lea and Blanchard, 1845), 115.

102. Esquirol, *Mental Maladies*, 97–98.

103. Parish, *Hallucinations and Illusions*, 16; Tylor, *Primitive Culture*, 2: 134, 182–183. For other examples of this late nineteenth-century literature, see James Sully, *Illusions: A Psychological Study* (New York: Appleton, 1881), 118–120; William W. Ireland, *The Blot upon the Brain: Studies in History and Psychology* (New York: G. P. Putnam's Sons, 1886), 3, 14–19; Henry Maudsley, *Natural Causes and Supernatural Seemings* (London: Kegan Paul, 1886), 162–219.

5. Voices from Spirit-Land

1. John Aubrey, *Miscellanies* (London: Castle, 1696), 1, 82–86, 90–92, 133–138; Heinrich Cornelius Agrippa, *Three Books of Occult Philosophy* (London: R.W., 1651), 412–413. The catalogue of Spiritualist sounds comes from Adin Ballou as quoted in Hiram Mattison, *Spirit-Rapping Unveiled! An Exposé of the Origin, History, Theology and Philosophy of Certain Alleged Communications from the Spirit World* (New York: Derby, 1855), 12. For the acoustic wonders of Spiritualism, see also Dellon M. Dewey, *History of the Strange Sounds or Rappings, Heard in Rochester and Western New-York, and Usually Called the Mysterious Noises!* (Rochester: Dewey, 1850). On the importance of the invocation of angels within Renaissance occultism, see Frances A. Yates, *The Occult Philosophy in the Elizabethan Age* (London: Routledge and Kegan Paul, 1979), 3–5, 20–21, 87.

2. For an analysis of the persistence of some of these Hermetic strands, see John L. Brooke, *The Refiner's Fire: The Making of Mormon Cosmology, 1644–1844* (Cambridge: Cambridge University Press, 1994). Most influential in my understanding of occultism has been the stellar work of Bradford Verter. See Bradford J. Verter, "Dark Star Rising: The Emergence of Modern Occultism, 1800–1950," Ph.D. diss., Princeton University, 1998.

3. For background on Swedenborg and the movement he spawned, see Erland J. Brock, ed., *Swedenborg and His Influence* (Bryn Athyn, Penn.: Academy of the New Church, 1988); Robin Larsen, ed., *Emanuel Swedenborg: A Continuing Vision* (New York: Swedenborg Foundation, 1988); Marguerite Beck Block, *The New Church in the New World: A Study of Swedenborgianism in America* (New York: Holt, 1932); Jane Williams-Hogan, "A New Church in a Disenchanted World: A Study of the Formation and Development of the General Conference of the New Church in Great Britain," Ph.D. diss., University of Pennsylvania, 1985; Inge Jonsson, *Emanuel Swedenborg*, trans. Catherine Djurklou (New York: Twayne, 1971); Signe Toksvig, *Emanuel Swedenborg: Scientist and Mystic* (New Haven: Yale University Press, 1948); Richard Silver, "The Spiritual Kingdom in America: The Influence of Emanuel Swedenborg on American Society and Culture, 1815–1860," Ph.D. diss., Stanford

University, 1983. For Swedenborg's Hermetic, Masonic, and kabbalistic connections, see Marsha Keith Schuchard, "Swedenborg, Jacobitism, and Freemasonry," in Brock, ed., *Swedenborg and His Influence*, 359–379; Al Gabay, "Swedenborg, Mesmer, and the 'Covert' Enlightenment," *New Philosophy* 100 (1997): 619–690; Clarke Garrett, "Swedenborg and the Mystical Enlightenment in Late Eighteenth-Century England," *Journal of the History of Ideas* 45 (1984): 67–81; E. A. Hitchcock, *Swedenborg, a Hermetic Philosopher* (New York: Miller, 1865). For one inlet into how the Swedenborgian network of publishing and reading unfolded, see Benjamin Owen Carpenter, *Adventures of a Copy of Swedenborg's Treatise, Concerning Heaven and Hell* (Chillicothe, Ohio: n.p., 1839).

4. For Swedenborg's struggle with deism, see Robert H. Kirven, "Emanuel Swedenborg and the Revolt against Deism," Ph.D. diss., Brandeis University, 1965, esp. 16–24.

5. See, for example, Warren Felt Evans, *The New Age and Its Messenger* (Boston: T. H. Carter, 1864); John Presland, *New Truths for a New Age* (London: Speirs, 1884).

6. *A Brief Account of the Life of Emanuel Swedenborg, a Servant of the Lord and the Messenger of the New-Jerusalem Dispensation* (Cincinnati: Looker and Reynolds, 1827), 15–19. For Swedenborg's devotional travails, see Emanuel Swedenborg, *Swedenborg's Journal of Dreams, 1743–1744*, commentary by Wilson Van Dusen (New York: Swedenborg Foundation, 1986), esp. 105–109, 121–122, 155–156.

7. George Bush, ed., *The Memorabilia of Swedenborg; Or, The Spiritual World Laid Open* (New York: John Allen, 1846), iii, vii–viii; George Bush, *Statement of Reasons for Embracing the Doctrines and Disclosures of Emanuel Swedenborg* (New York: Allen, 1846), 69; Enoch Pond quoted in George Bush, *Mesmer and Swedenborg; Or, The Relation of the Developments of Mesmerism to the Doctrines and Disclosures of Swedenborg* (New York: John Allen, 1847), 162–163; Benjamin Rush, *Medical Inquiries and Observations upon the Diseases of the Mind* (Philadelphia: Kimber and Richardson, 1812), 138.

8. George Field, *Memoirs, Incidents and Reminiscences of the Early History of the New Church in Michigan, Indiana, Illinois, and Adjacent States, and Canada* (Toronto: Carswell, 1879), 23.

9. William B. Hayden, *Review of the Rev. Dr. Pond on the Facts and Philosophy of Swedenborg* (Portland: n.p., 1846), 2–3; "Importance of the Knowledge Communicated Respecting the Spiritual World in Swedenborg's 'Memorable Relations,'" *Precursor* 1 (March 1837): 75–76; "Swedenborg Not a Visionary, and His Doctrines Not Congenial to a Wonder-Loving Spirit," *New Churchman* 1 (January 1842): 31–37; "Swedenborg Not a Mystic," *Medium* 2 (15 June 1850): 185. For a review of Wesley's role in medicalizing Swedenborg, see Kirven, "Swedenborg," 164–173. There was an occasional positive evaluation of Swedenborg in the asylum circles of medical psychology, but such were the exception. See Eugene Taylor, "The Appearance of Swedenborg in the History of American Psychology," in Brock, ed., *Swedenborg and His Influence*, 156–158, 171n.

10. Margaret Hiller, *Religion and Philosophy United; Or, An Attempt to Shew, that*

Philosophical Principles Form the Foundation of the New Jerusalem Church (Boston: Wells and Lilly, 1817), vii–ix.

11. Ralph Waldo Emerson, "Swedenborg; Or, The Mystic," in *The Collected Works of Ralph Waldo Emerson,* ed. Wallace E. Williams and Douglas Emory Wilson (Cambridge, Mass.: Harvard University Press, 1987), 4: 58.

12. For Swedenborg's work in natural philosophy, see, for example, Alfred Acton, ed., *The Mechanical Inventions of Emanuel Swedenborg* (Philadelphia: Swedenborg Scientific Association, 1939); Larsen, ed., *Swedenborg,* section V. For a typical defense along these lines, see Woodbury M. Fernald, *Emanuel Swedenborg as a Man of Science* (Boston, 1854; Boston: Otis Clapp, 1860).

13. John Johnson and Elizabeth Jones, *An Interesting Discussion of the Fundamental Doctrine of the Christian Religion,* 4th ed. (London: Hodson, 1818), vii, 15, 40–41; Thomas Worcester, *A Discourse, Delivered before the New Jerusalem Church, in Boston, on Christmas Day, December 25, 1818* (Boston: Cummings and Hilliard, 1819), 12.

14. Emanuel Swedenborg, *The True Christian Religion* (Boston: John Allen, 1833), no. 798. Following the common scholarly convention, references are to Swedenborg's own numbering system, not to pages, here and subsequently.

15. For an American elaboration, see William B. Hayden, *On the History of the Dogma of Infant Damnation* (Portland, Maine: Tucker, 1848).

16. "Outward Indications of a New Era," *New Jerusalem Magazine* 27 (September 1854): 142–145.

17. Hiller, *Religion and Philosophy United,* viii. See also "Except Ye See Signs and Wonders Ye Will Not Believe," *New Jerusalem Magazine* 2 (July 1829): 360–361.

18. On Swedenborg's sales, see Frank Luther Mott, *Golden Multitudes: The Story of Best Sellers in the United States* (New York: Macmillan, 1947), 305–306.

19. *An Account of a Trance or Vision of Sarah Alley* (Poughkeepsie, N.Y.: Power, 1798), 6–10. The literature on this element of popular religion in the early republic is substantial. Among the best studies is D. Michael Quinn, *Early Mormonism and the Magic World View* (Salt Lake City: Signature Books, 1987), esp. 11–15, 25, 174–175.

20. "Preface by the Translator," in Emanuel Swedenborg, *A Treatise Concerning Heaven and Hell, and of the Wonderful Things Therein, as Heard and Seen by the Honourable and Learned Emanuel Swedenborg* (Baltimore: Miltenberger, 1812), 3. This is the first American edition in what became a long run of them in the nineteenth century (seven of them between 1837 and 1854); this 1812 edition followed six British printings (the first in 1778).

21. "Preface by the Translator," ibid., 5–10.

22. Swedenborg, *Heaven and Hell,* nos. 234–236, 239; Thomas Paine, *The Age of Reason,* ed. Philip S. Foner (Secaucus, N.J.: Carol Publishing Group, 1998), 63, 68–69, 97–98. The early modern philosophical ambition for a universal language has received growing attention. For a still standard overview of the enterprise, see James Knowlson, *Universal Language Schemes in England and France, 1600–1800* (Toronto: University of Toronto Press, 1975). For specific Swedenborgian contexts, see Jonsson, *Swedenborg,* 92–104; Lynn R. Wilkinson, *The Dream of an Absolute Lan-*

guage: Emanuel Swedenborg and French Literary Culture (Albany: State University of New York Press, 1996).

23. Swedenborg, *Heaven and Hell,* nos. 259–262, 269. For a sampling of this "spiritual sense of numbers," indicative of the esoteric currents in which Swedenborg swirled, see Fernald, *Swedenborg as a Man of Science,* 433–436; Swedenborg, *Heaven and Hell,* no. 263.

24. Emanuel Swedenborg, *The Spiritual Diary,* 5 vols. (London: Swedenborg Society, 1977), nos. 1149, 4309; Swedenborg, *Heaven and Hell,* nos. 236, 245, 269.

25. Swedenborg, *Heaven and Hell,* nos. 48, 462, 463.

26. Ibid., nos. 236–238.

27. Emanuel Swedenborg, *Arcana Caelestia,* trans. John Elliott, 11 vols. (London: Swedenborg Society, 1983–1997), no. 1644. In the text, I have retained the eighteenth-century spelling *Arcana Coelestia.*

28. Swedenborg, *Heaven and Hell,* nos. 178–179, 280.

29. Richard DeCharms, *Apples of Gold in Pictures of Silver; Or, The True Rule of Scriptural Exegesis, and the Only Infallible Guide to the True Understanding of the Word of God* (Philadelphia: n.p., 1856), 8–9; Bush, ed., *Memorabilia,* 254. Swedenborg's understanding of the transparencies of angelic speech was widely reiterated and republished on the American side. In addition to the various editions of *Heaven and Hell,* see, for example, Fernald, *Swedenborg as a Man of Science,* 194–198; "World of Spirits," *New Jerusalem Magazine* 7 (December 1833): 123–124; "The Speech of Angels," *New Jerusalem Magazine* 12 (August 1839): 441–444; "Concerning the Speech of Spirits and Angels," in Bush, ed., *Memorabilia,* 241–256.

30. Emanuel Swedenborg, *The Five Senses,* trans. Enoch S. Price (Philadelphia: Swedenborg Scientific Association, 1914), no. 9; Inge Jonsson, "Swedenborg and His Influence," in Brock, ed., *Swedenborg and His Influence,* 32–33; Jonsson, *Swedenborg,* 48–49.

31. Swedenborg, *Heaven and Hell,* no. 212.

32. Swedenborg, *Five Senses,* nos. 64–65; Swedenborg, *Arcana,* nos. 68, 322; "The Spiritual Body, and the Spiritual Senses," *New Jerusalem Magazine* 44 (October 1871): 137; "The Music of Nature," *New Jerusalem Magazine* 11 (February 1838): 212. On Swedenborg's empiricism, see especially Kirven, "Swedenborg," 16–24.

33. Emanuel Swedenborg, *The Doctrine of the New Jerusalem Church Concerning Angels and Spirits Attendant on Man, and Concerning Influx, and the Commerce of the Soul with the Body* (Philadelphia: William Brown, 1829), 47; Ralph Waldo Emerson, "The Senses and the Soul," *The Dial* 2 (January 1842): 377–378. See also Swedenborg, *Five Senses,* no. 649; Massachusetts Association of the New Jerusalem Church, *The Pythonism of the Present Day* (Boston: Phinney, 1858), 10–12, 35–36.

34. Swedenborg, *Five Senses,* no. 3; Swedenborg, *Arcana,* nos. 1642, 4407; Swedenborg, *Spiritual Diary,* no. 670; Caleb Reed, "The Senses," *New Jerusalem Magazine* 11 (June 1838): 336. Much about Swedenborg's hierarchy of the bodily senses was conventionally positioned within Aristotle's long shadow—an ordering from high to low that ran sight to hearing, then with a marked drop-off for smell,

taste, and touch. See Swedenborg, *Five Senses*, nos. 56–57, 471. The more interesting mutations occurred in the spiritual senses (such as taste's loss and smell's enhancement).

35. Swedenborg, *Spiritual Diary*, no. 3567. See also Swedenborg, *Arcana*, no. 1973; "Guardian Angels," *New Jerusalem Magazine* 20 (December 1846): 148–149.

36. Reed, "Senses," 338. The antigluttony vision is from Swedenborg, *Spiritual Diary*, no. 397. It is didactically cited and applied in James John Garth Wilkinson, *Emanuel Swedenborg: A Biography* (Boston: Otis Clapp, 1849), 76–77, and in Fernald, *Swedenborg as a Man of Science*, 53, 108–109.

37. Reed, "Senses," 339; Swedenborg, *Spiritual Diary*, nos. 2386, 4093; Swedenborg, *Heaven and Hell*, nos. 181, 402, 462; Swedenborg, *Arcana*, nos. 1883, 4622; Emanuel Swedenborg, *Delights of Wisdom Concerning Conjugial Love* (Boston: Otis Clapp, 1840), no. 210. The sensuous, even material, quality of Swedenborg's heaven is explored in Colleen McDannell and Bernhard Lang, *Heaven: A History* (New York: Random House, 1988), 181–227.

38. Swedenborg, *Spiritual Diary*, nos. 323, 1150; Swedenborg, *Heaven and Hell*, no. 385; Swedenborg, *Arcana*, nos. 1514–1515, 4628–4631; Reed, "Senses," 338. The literature on the sense of smell is growing. See, for example, Susan Ashbrook Harvey, "St. Ephrem on the Scent of Salvation," *Journal of Theological Studies* 49 (1998): 109–128; Constance Classen, David Howes, and Anthony Synnott, *Aroma: The Cultural History of Smell* (London: Routledge, 1994); Alain Corbin, *The Foul and the Fragrant: Odor and the French Social Imagination*, trans. Miriam L. Kochan (Cambridge, Mass.: Harvard University Press, 1986).

39. Swedenborg, *Five Senses*, nos. 97, 101–128; Emanuel Swedenborg, *On Tremulation*, trans. C. T. Odhner (Boston: Massachusetts New-Church Union, 1899), 61, 70. Also of note is George Bush's defense of this "internal hearing," in Bush, ed., *Memorabilia*, 242–243. On Swedenborg's work on vibration, see Jonsson, *Swedenborg*, 44–46.

40. Swedenborg, *Arcana*, no. 946.

41. Emanuel Swedenborg, *The Apocalypse Explained according to the Spiritual Sense*, 5 vols. (New York: John Allen, 1847), nos. 14, 808; Swedenborg, *Heaven and Hell*, no. 96.

42. "Distinctive Qualities of Seeing and Hearing, Considered in Relation to the Reception of Truth," *New Jerusalem Magazine* 7 (May 1834): 353–355. See also Fernald, *Swedenborg as a Man of Science*, 310–315, 321; John Worcester, *Physiological Correspondences* (Boston: Massachusetts New-Church Union, 1889), 273–316.

43. "Woman and Her Sphere," *New Church Repository* 8 (October 1855): 461–465; M. M. Carll, "The Modern 'Woman's Movement,'" *New Church Repository* 6 (September 1853): 403–405.

44. Swedenborg, *Spiritual Diary*, no. 5936. Swedenborg's views on gender are most fully developed in his treatise *Delights of Wisdom Concerning Conjugial Love*. For an American linkage of the obedience of the hearkening ear to the authority of the male minister, see "Science of Correspondences: The Eye and the Ear," *New Jerusalem Magazine* 12 (January 1839): 160.

45. Swedenborg, *Heaven and Hell*, nos. 25–26, 271; Swedenborg, *Apocalypse Explained*, no. 14.

46. Swedenborg, *Spiritual Diary*, nos. 489, 491, 2108; Swedenborg, *Arcana*, nos. 687, 690, 1648–1649. These ideas are picked up in Fernald, *Swedenborg as a Man of Science*, 409; "Music in Worship," *New Jerusalem Magazine* 44 (February 1872): 421–422; "The Correspondence and Uses of Music," ibid., 33 (August 1860): 104–109; "On Music," ibid., 15 (February 1842): 214–222; ibid., 15 (April 1842): 281–290.

47. Swedenborg, *Spiritual Diary*, no. 4208; Swedenborg, *Arcana*, nos. 1646, 1764; "Science of Correspondences," 155–156. On synesthesia, see John Hollander, *Vision and Resonance: Two Senses of Poetic Form* (New York: Oxford University Press, 1975), 22–25, 42–43; David Chidester, *Word and Light: Seeing, Hearing, and Religious Discourse* (Urbana: University of Illinois Press, 1992), 14–24, 53–72; Lawrence E. Sullivan, "Sound and Senses: Toward a Hermeneutics of Performance," *History of Religions* 26 (August 1986): 1–33. Hollander is especially evocative on Romantic developments of what he calls "visionary sound."

48. John Clowes, *Letters on the Human Body* (Warwick, England: W. Rose, 1826), 85–88; "Madame Guyon and Her Mysticism," *New Church Repository* 7 (February 1854): 59.

49. Reed, "Senses," 334–335, 341. On the wider gospel of refined taste and bourgeois civility, see Richard L. Bushman, *The Refinement of America: Persons, Houses, Cities* (New York: Knopf, 1992).

50. "Preface by the Translator," in Swedenborg, *Heaven and Hell*, 10; Swedenborg, *Heaven and Hell*, nos. 87, 252–253; "On Seeing Spirits," *New Jerusalem Magazine* 1 (March 1828): 218; Benjamin F. Barrett, *Lectures on the Doctrines of the New Christian Church* (Cincinnati: Michigan and Northern Indiana Association of the New Church, 1852), 287; "Dependence of Men upon Spirits and Angels," *New Jerusalem Magazine* 8 (March 1835): 243. For arguments about the ceasing of angelic apparitions, see Henry Lawrence, *An History of Angells, being a Theological Treatise of our Communion and Warre with Them* (London: M.S., 1649), 16–19, 36; Richard Saunders, *Angelographia; Or, A Discourse of Angels* (London: Parkhurst, 1701), 192–198. Even within this framework, though, angelic powers, knowledge, and ministrations remained considerable, and Swedenborgian desires need to be seen as in keeping with much of Christian angelology.

51. W.H.B., "The Guardian Angel," *New Church Repository* 1 (May 1848): 319–320; "Correspondence," ibid., 5 (January 1852): 30–32; C. A. Tulk, "Remarkable Dream," ibid., 7 (September 1854): 402–404; James Johnston, *Last Legacy and Solemn Information Written in the Year 1826 by the Author of the Remarkable Manuscript, Entitled "Intercourse with Angels"* (n.p.: n.p., 1866), 16–17. For other examples of this supernaturalism, see J. E. Carpenter, "Guardian Angels," *New Church Repository* 6 (September 1853): 426; "To the Editor," *New Jerusalem Magazine* 5 (August 1832): 451–452; "Interesting Case of the Sickness and Death of a Young Lady in Maine," ibid., 11 (April 1838): 278–280; "Remarkable Spiritual Experience," *New Church Repository* 6 (August 1853): 366–372; "Guardian Angels," *New Jerusalem Magazine* 5 (November 1831): 112–119; "Angels," ibid., 9 (November 1835): 82–85; "Intercourse with

the Spiritual World," ibid., 10 (March 1837): 239–241; "Consociation of the Angels of Heaven, and the Spirits of Hell, with Men upon Earth," *New Churchman* 1 (July 1841): 259–268; "On the Association of Angels," *Crisis*, 1 June 1852, 28–29; "The Angel Guide," ibid., 1 July 1852, 48. The episode with Swedenborg's portrait is from James Johnston; for another instance, see Richard DeCharms, *An Introduction to Sermons against Pseudo-Spiritualism, Presenting Reasons for Their Delivery in New York* (Philadelphia: New Jerusalem Press, 1853), 41.

52. "Intercourse with Angels," *New Jerusalem Magazine* 3 (November 1829): 96; *Encyclopaedia Americana*, 13 vols. (Philadelphia: Carey and Lea, 1829–1833), 1: 244; "On Seeing Spirits," 216; "Remarks on Certain Errors Concerning the Doctrines of the New Church," *New Jerusalem Magazine* 6 (January 1833): 206–207.

53. On the wider ecclesiological crises in Swedenborgian circles that were brought to a head by Spiritualism, see Scott Trego Swank, "The Unfettered Conscience: A Study of Sectarianism, Spiritualism, and Social Reform in the New Jerusalem Church, 1840–1870," Ph.D. diss., University of Pennsylvania, 1970; Bret E. Carroll, *Spiritualism in Antebellum America* (Bloomington: Indiana University Press, 1997), 16–34.

54. John Augustus Tulk to James Glen, quoted in Block, *New Church*, 70.

55. This English episode is discussed via a letter of John Clowes in Benjamin F. Barrett, *Open Intercourse with the Spiritual World—Its Dangers and the Cautions Which They Naturally Suggest* (n.p.: n.p., 1845), 37–38.

56. John Martin, ed., *Diary of the Mission, Spiritual and Earthly, of the Late James Johnston* (n.p.: n.p., 1881), iii–v; *A Short Account of a Remarkable Manuscript, Written in the Years 1817 to 1840, Entitled "Intercourse with Angels"* (n.p.: n.p., 1866); Johnston, *Last Legacy and Solemn Information*, 13–14.

57. "Sundry Papers Regarding the Opening of the Spiritual Senses of Rev. Samuel Worcester and Members of his Family," Swedenborg Library, Bryn Athyn College of the New Church, Bryn Athyn, Penn.

58. Ibid. For the internal containment, see Swank, "Unfettered Conscience," 197–205. The group's marginalization has had its counterpart in the quick dismissals of institutionally minded historians. See Carl Theophilus Odhner, *Annals of the New Church* (Bryn Athyn, Penn.: Academy of the New Church, 1904), 500–501; Block, *New Church*, 98–99.

59. George Bush, *New Church Miscellanies* (New York: McGeorge, 1855), 248; DeCharms, *Introduction to Sermons against Pseudo-Spiritualism*, 38–42.

60. Silas Jones, *Eras of the New Jerusalem Church, Being a Few Remarks on the Present State of the Church, and Showing the Necessity of Open Intercourse with Angels for its Future Advancement* (New York: n.p., 1848), 23–27; "Sundry Papers"; Samuel H. Worcester, *A Letter to the Receivers of the Heavenly Doctrines of the New Jerusalem* (Boston: Otis Clapp, 1845), 2–3, 10.

61. Jones, *Eras of the New Jerusalem Church*, 23–27. For Jones's phrenology, see Silas Jones, *Practical Phrenology* (Boston: Russell, Shattuck, and Williams, 1836).

62. Jones, *Eras of the New Jerusalem Church*, 26–27, 31–34, 57; Worcester, *Letter*, 7–10, 19–21; Silas Jones, *Platform of the New Era of the New Church, Called New Jerusa-*

302 · Notes to Pages 228–232

lem (New York: Prall, 1848), 5, 7. These desires, widely shared across the Swedenborgian subculture, were ones that the New Era's harsh critic Benjamin Barrett well understood: "It is not strange that we should desire," he said, to hear things "from the pure and loving lips of the angels." See Barrett, *Open Intercourse*, 1–2.

63. Barrett, *Open Intercourse*, 20–21; Richard DeCharms, *Sermons Three and Four of the Series of Five Preached to the First New York Society of the New Jerusalem, against the Pseudo-Spiritualism of Modern Times* (Philadelphia: n.p., 1856), 44–51.

64. Louisa W. Ogden, *Reasons for Joining the New Jerusalem Church* (New York: Douglas, 1845), 14–17; George Bush, *Mesmer and Swedenborg*, 104–120, 138–143. For the considerable play between religious vision and animal magnetism, see Ann Taves, *Fits, Trances, and Visions: Experiencing Religion and Explaining Experience from Wesley to James* (Princeton: Princeton University Press, 1999), 128–165.

65. Andrew Jackson Davis, *Views of Our Heavenly Home* (Boston: Colby and Rich, 1878), 14–17, 104–108; Andrew Jackson Davis, *The Magic Staff* (Boston, 1858; Boston: White, 1871), 164–170, 191–192, 248, 324, 328–329, 424, 434, 441, 476.

66. DeCharms, *Sermons Three and Four*, 59; Bush, *New Church Miscellanies*, 254–256.

67. Swedenborg, *Heaven and Hell*, no. 248; "The Gift of Tongues," *New Jerusalem Magazine* 5 (January 1832): 175–186; "Pretended Miracles," *Edinburgh Review* 53 (June 1831): 277–278.

68. Conyers Middleton, *A Free Enquiry into the Miraculous Powers* (London: Manby and Cox, 1749), xxi, 91–92, 119–122, 230.

69. Ibid., 121; Benjamin Bayley, *An Essay on Inspiration* (London: J.M., 1708), 390–391, 409–413; George H. Williams and Edith Waldvogel, "A History of Speaking in Tongues and Related Gifts," in Michael P. Hamilton, ed., *The Charismatic Movement* (Grand Rapids, Mich.: Eerdmans, 1975), 61–113.

70. See Stephen J. Stein, *The Shaker Experience in America: A History of the United Society of Believers* (New Haven: Yale University Press, 1992), 105, 165–175.

71. Lee Copeland, "Speaking in Tongues in the Restoration Churches," *Dialogue: A Journal of Mormon Thought* 24 (1991): 13–33 (quotation from Young's journal is on p. 16).

72. Edward Irving, "Facts Connected with Recent Manifestations of Spiritual Gifts," *Fraser's Magazine for Town and Country* 4 (January 1832): 754–761. The *Fraser's* series continued in March and concluded in April. On the movement, see Andrew Landale Drummond, *Edward Irving and His Circle* (n.p.: Clarke, 1936); C. Gordon Strachan, *The Pentecostal Theology of Edward Irving* (London: Darton, Longman, and Todd, 1973); Margaret Oliphant, *The Life of Edward Irving* (New York: Harper and Brothers, 1862). Drummond treats Irving's embrace of tongues as a "fiasco," the derailing of an otherwise worthwhile ministry (p. 127); Oliphant is excusing; and Strachan is highly sympathetic.

73. Edward Irving, *The Day of Pentecost; Or, The Baptism with the Holy Ghost* (London: Baldwin and Cradock, 1831), 65–68; Robert Baxter, *Narrative of Facts, Characterizing the Supernatural Manifestations, in Members of Mr. Irving's Congregation, and Other Individuals in England and Scotland* (London: James Nisbet, 1833), 4, 8.

74. Edward Irving, "On Recent Manifestations of Spiritual Gifts, II," *Fraser's Magazine for Town and Country* 5 (March 1832): 200.

75. James MacDonald quoted in Strachan, *Pentecostal Theology*, 68; Irving, "Facts," 756, 760.

76. See the summary of this press coverage in Samuel J. Andrews, *William Watson Andrews: A Religious Biography with Extracts from His Letters and Other Writings* (New York: G. P. Putnam's Sons, 1900), 23–24, 112–114 (quotation is on p. 113).

77. Ibid., 5–7, 9, 23–24, 31–34.

78. Schaff quoted in Andrews, *William Watson Andrews*, 141; William Watson Andrews, *Reasons for Withdrawing from the Congregational Ministry* (Hartford: Bardwell, 1849), 3–4, 16. See also William Watson Andrews, "The Catholic Apostolic Church," *Bibliotheca Sacra* 23 (January–April 1866): 108–159, 252–256, esp. 122–125; William Watson Andrews, "Edward Irving," *New Englander* 22 (July–October 1863): 363–419, 778–836, esp. 787–802. For the group that Andrews joined, see Columba Graham Flegg, *'Gathered under Apostles': A Study of the Catholic Apostolic Church* (Oxford: Clarendon, 1992).

79. Andrews, "Edward Irving," 796, 800; Irving, "Recent Manifestations," 198–200.

80. Andrews, *William Watson Andrews*, 38.

81. Horace Bushnell, *Nature and the Supernatural, as Together Constituting the One System of God* (New York: Scribner's, 1890), 66–67, 446, 457–458. On Bushnell's views in the context of the larger debate on miracles, see Robert Bruce Mullin, *Miracles and the Modern Religious Imagination* (New Haven: Yale University Press, 1996), 66–75.

82. Bushnell, *Nature and the Supernatural*, 465–470, 478–479, 491.

83. Ibid., 457–458.

84. John Edmonds, *Speaking in Many Tongues* (New York: n.p., 1858), 3–6, 8; Nathan Francis White, *Voices from Spirit-Land* (New York: Partridge and Brittan, 1854), x–xi. See also John Edmonds, *Letters to the "New York Tribune," on Spiritualism* (New York: n.p., 1860), 45–49; Isaac Post, *Voices from the Spirit World, Being Communications from Many Spirits* (Rochester: McDonell, 1852); Frank Podmore, *Modern Spiritualism: A History and a Criticism*, 2 vols. (London: Methuen, 1902), 1: 257–263.

85. Thomas Lake Harris, *The Wisdom of Angels* (New York: New Church Publishing Association, 1857), 178, 195; Thomas Lake Harris, *Arcana of Christianity: An Unfolding of the Celestial Sense of the Divine Word*, 2 vols. (New York: New Church Publishing, 1858), 1: 180; Ralph Waldo Trine, *In Tune with the Infinite* (New York: Crowell, 1897), 117–118, 214; Thomas J. Shelton, *The Laws of Vibration* (Denver: n.p., 1896), 20.

86. Harris, *Wisdom*, 166–169; Harris, *Arcana*, 1: 319; 2: 171.

87. Wilkinson, *Swedenborg*, 82.

88. J. Everett, ed., *A Book for Skeptics: Being Communications from Angels, Written with their Own Hands; Also Oral Communications Spoken by Angels through a Trumpet, and Written Down as They Were Delivered, in the Presence of Many Witnesses* (Columbus, Ohio: Osgood and Blake, 1853), 6, 11, 14, 23–25; T. L. Nichols, *A Biography of the Brothers Davenport* (London: Saunders, Otley, 1864), 47–48; Abraham Pierce, *The*

Revelator: Being an Account of the Twenty-One Days' Entrancement of Abraham P. Pierce, Spirit-Medium, at Belfast, Maine, Together with a Sketch of His Life (Bangor, Maine: Bugbee, 1857), 9–10; "Through the Trumpet," *London Magazine*, 1915, Psychical Research Files, Harry Price Library, University of London.

89. Henry D. Thoreau, *Journal* (Princeton: Princeton University Press, 1981–), 1: 63; 2: 114.

90. Ibid., 1: 27, 277; 3: 368. On the supreme importance Thoreau accorded hearing, see Sherman Paul, "The Wise Silence: Sound as the Agency of Correspondence in Thoreau," *New England Quarterly* 22 (1949): 511–527.

91. Thoreau, *Journal*, 4: 35, 90, 383; 5: 386, 437. On Thoreau's fascination with the sounds of the telegraph wire, see Paul, "Wise Silence," 520–522; Thomas L. Hankins and Robert J. Silverman, *Instruments and the Imagination* (Princeton: Princeton University Press, 1995), 109–110.

92. George H. Lethem, "The Spirit Telephone," *London Magazine*, 1921, Psychical Research Files, Harry Price Library, University of London; B. C. Forbes, "Edison Working on How to Communicate with the Next World," *American Magazine* 90 (October 1920): 10–11, 82, 85.

93. Thomas A. Watson, *Exploring Life: The Autobiography of Thomas A. Watson* (New York: Appleton, 1926), 10–11, 37–42, 100, 114–115. On Watson's Spiritualist connections, see the dizzying work of Avital Ronell, *The Telephone Book: Technology, Schizophrenia, Electronic Speech* (Lincoln: University of Nebraska Press, 1989), 245–248.

94. The example of this use of the telephone comes from art historian David Morgan, who shared with me copies of the letters he has collected for his work on Warner Sallman, especially those letters that accented the visualized Jesus as listener. Morgan has numbered all the letters and deposited them at the Jessie C. Wilson Galleries, Anderson University, Anderson, Indiana. For this example, see letter 247. See also letters 88 and 144. For Morgan's own eye-opening use of these materials, see David Morgan, *Visual Piety: A History and Theory of Popular Religious Images* (Berkeley: University of California Press, 1998).

95. Barbara Erakko Taylor, *Silent Dwellers: Embracing the Solitary Life* (New York: Continuum, 1999), 34–35.

96. In her recent book, Susan J. Douglas has powerfully illuminated the spiritual (and specifically Spiritualist) yearnings that radio listening has long manifested. See Susan J. Douglas, *Listening In: Radio and the American Imagination, from Amos 'n' Andy and Edward R. Murrow to Wolfman Jack and Howard Stern* (New York: Random House, 1999), 40–54.

Epilogue

1. Margaret Guenther, *Holy Listening: The Art of Spiritual Direction* (Cambridge: Cowley, 1992); Lisa Summer, *Music: The New Age Elixir* (Amherst, N.Y.: Prometheus, 1996), 162, 199–205; Steven Halpern and Louis Savary, *Sound Health: The Music and Sounds That Make Us Whole* (San Francisco: Harper and Row, 1985), 161–171; Sophy Burnham, *A Book of Angels: Reflections on Angels Past and Present and True*

Stories of How They Touch Our Lives (New York: Ballantine, 1990), 84, 98, 182–188, 197, 215.

2. Annie Dillard, *Teaching a Stone to Talk: Expeditions and Encounters* (New York: Harper and Row, 1982), 72; Barbara Brown Taylor, *When God Is Silent* (Boston: Cowley, 1998), 24.

3. Dianne Skafte, *Listening to the Oracle: The Ancient Art of Finding Guidance in the Signs and Symbols All Around Us* (San Francisco: Harper, 1997), 1–2. For an excellent analysis of the contemporary pieties that surround channeling, see Michael F. Brown, *The Channeling Zone: American Spirituality in an Anxious Age* (Cambridge, Mass.: Harvard University Press, 1997).

4. Guenther, *Holy Listening*, 143; Nelle Morton, *The Journey Is Home* (Boston: Beacon, 1985), 203–205.

5. "I Like to Hear," in Carl R. Rogers, *Freedom to Learn* (Columbus, Ohio: Merrill, 1969), 222. Rogers' empathic listening is discussed in David Michael Levin, *The Listening Self: Personal Growth, Social Change and the Closure of Metaphysics* (London: Routledge, 1989), 86–88. Levin, embodying these ongoing shifts in the understanding of hearing, offers an especially eloquent description of this kind of skillful listening.

6. Morton, *Journey*, 210; John Dewey, *The Public and Its Problems* (New York: Henry Holt, 1927), 218–219.

7. Jacques Derrida, *The Ear of the Other: Otobiography, Transference, Translation*, trans. Peggy Kamuf (New York: Schocken, 1985), 35; Jacques Attali, *Noise: The Political Economy of Music*, trans. Brian Massumi (Minneapolis: University of Minnesota Press, 1985), 5–7. For an appraisal of just how much eavesdropping is going on in contemporary culture, see Vivienne Walt, "Shelves of Snooping Aids Make Privacy Hard to Buy," *New York Times*, 21 May 1998, D8.

8. Ludwig Feuerbach, *Lectures on the Essence of Religion*, trans. Ralph Manheim (New York: Harper and Row, 1967), 13–14, 27–28, 184–187. Nietzsche echoed Feuerbach's distaste for the timidity of hearing. See Friedrich Nietzsche, *Daybreak: Thoughts on the Prejudices of Morality*, trans. R. J. Hollingdale (Cambridge: Cambridge University Press, 1982), 143; Levin, *Listening Self*, 218. On Feuerbach's prominence in the formation of the hermeneutics of suspicion in the study of religion, see Van A. Harvey, *Feuerbach and the Interpretation of Religion* (Cambridge: Cambridge University Press, 1995).

9. George Steiner, *Real Presences* (Chicago: University of Chicago Press, 1989), 133–134. More affirmative sorts hail postmodernism for its openness to ontological questions and postcritical perspectives, but, in intellectual currents as shifting as these, whether such affirmations will hold up under the strain of suspicion is anything but clear.

Index